# the Unofficial Guide® to
# Microsoft® Office
# Word 2007

David J. Clark

BICENTENNIAL
1807
WILEY
2007
BICENTENNIAL

Wiley Publishing, Inc.

**The Unofficial Guide® to Microsoft® Office Word 2007**

Published by
**Wiley Publishing, Inc.**
111 River Street
Hoboken, NJ 07030-5774
www.wiley.com

For general information on our other products and services or to obtain technical support please contact our Customer Care Department within the U.S. at (800) 762-2974, outside the U.S. at (317) 572-3993 or fax (317) 572-4002.

Wiley also publishes its books in a variety of electronic formats. Some content that appears in print may not be available in electronic books. For more information about Wiley products, please visit our web site at www.wiley.com.

Library of Congress Control Number: 2006939460

ISBN: 978-0-470-04592-3

Manufactured in the United States of America

10   9   8   7   6   5   4   3   2   1

Page creation by Wiley Publishing, Inc. Composition Services

*To M. F. A.*

# Acknowledgments

In the course of my publishing career, I've been (among other things) a word processor, a copy editor, a technical editor, a project editor, an acquisitions editor, and an author. Given that experience, I would hope that I have some perspective on how much collaborative effort goes into every book published.

I would like to thank my agent, Lynn Haller, of Studio B, for putting me in contact with Wiley and seeing the contract negotiation phase of this project through painlessly. At Wiley, my thanks go to Jody Lefevre, my initial acquisitions editor, for working with me again and for giving me the opportunity to write this book. Jenny Watson took over as my acquisitions editor and has been very helpful along the way. Many thanks go to Lynn Northrup, my project editor, for her graceful encouragement and useful comments. Daniel Hodge, the technical editor, contributed many insightful comments that helped make the book better and prevented a good number of errors from making it to print. Kim Heusel, the copy editor, provided ample proof that every writer needs an editor (including writers who are also editors), clarifying my prose and figuring out what I really meant to say.

My heartfelt thanks go to my daughters, for their ability to creep about the house on tiptoe and not bother dad when he was writing, and for their patience, support, and understanding. My wife also deserves special thanks, not only for her patience, support, and understanding, but also for her valuable professional advice as a writer and editor.

Lastly, thanks go to Fletcher, my dog, who kept me company and provided me with material for some of the samples in this book.

# Credits

**Acquisitions Editors**
Jody Lefevre
Jenny Watson

**Project Editor**
Lynn Northrup

**Technical Editor**
Daniel Hodge

**Copy Editor**
Kim Heusel

**Editorial Manager**
Robyn Siesky

**Vice President & Group Executive Publisher**
Richard Swadley

**Vice President & Publisher**
Barry Pruett

**Business Manager**
Amy Knies

**Project Coordinator**
Kristie Rees

**Graphics & Production Specialists**
Jonelle Burns
Jennifer Mayberry
Melanee Prendergast
Amanda Spagnuolo

**Quality Control Technicians**
Melanie Hoffman
John Greenough

**Proofreading**
Kevin Broccoli

**Indexing**
Richard Shrout

**Book Interior Design**
Lissa Auciello-Brogan
Elizabeth Brooks

**Wiley Bicentennial Logo**
Richard J. Pacifico

# About the Author

**D**avid J. Clark has been working with Word since the days of DOS, and explaining it to users for almost as long. He has over 18 years of experience as an author, editor, translator, and technical editor of computer books, working at major computer book publishers from 1984 to 1994, and then at Microsoft from 1994 to 2002. He now runs DJC Productions, LLC and works as a freelance author and editor living in Portland, Oregon, with his wife and two daughters. His clients include John Wiley & Sons and Intel Corporation.

Contents

**T**he public beta version of Microsoft Office 2007 was downloaded by over 3 million users, making it the most popular beta of Office ever. Part of the reason for this popularity was no doubt the ability to download a fully functional and relatively stable office suite for free, albeit for a limited trial period only.

Personally, I have become rather cynical about new versions of Office over the years, and, though I'm a former Microsoft employee, I didn't always upgrade to Office on all of my PCs. In particular, Microsoft Word had not changed its user interface significantly over several versions, so as a writer and editor, I found little need to upgrade. However, I can honestly say Microsoft Office 2007 is a fundamental redesign with lots of improvements. That's good news for those of us who use a word processor all day long, as well as for those of you who only occasionally make use of Word. However, Microsoft spins every change as a benefit when some changes are frankly compromises. Some "improvements" get in the way, too. That's why in this *Unofficial Guide to Word 2007* I've tried to err on the side of practicality. I encourage the reader to learn how to use a new feature, but I also point out the downside or cumbersome aspects. If there is a new and easy way to do something but you have to go through three menus to do it, I'll tell you the two-stroke keyboard shortcut workaround if there is one.

Microsoft made fundamental changes across the board in its Office products, redesigning the user interface to address the issue of increasingly complex toolbars that had proliferated over the years. The solution, not only for Word but for other Office products, was the Ribbon: a more intuitive hybrid of a toolbar and a dialog box that uses richer graphics, preview galleries, and contextual appropriateness to better support the user's needs. The reason for this is that many tasks that tend to be time consuming, such as format and page layouts, have become more automated. I think this is good in the long run, but at first, a seasoned Word user will see the opening screen and say "Hey! Where's the File menu? Where's everything?" I spend some time in the early chapters addressing these questions.

There are more ready-made designs to work with that use an expanded feature called *themes* (akin to themes in Windows) that coordinate overarching design values (coordinating fonts, colors, and effects for graphics) across an entire document, or even across Office. You can choose a theme or create your own, and apply it not just to Word documents, but also Excel spreadsheets and PowerPoint presentations.

Quick Styles have also been added. Microsoft has taken the concept of character and paragraph styles one step further by introducing groups of preset Quick Styles that have been professionally designed for the most common types of text elements and that all complement each other within a set. For example, if you select a Heading Quick Style and a Body Quick Style, you can change the style set for the document and both the Heading and Body styles change to new but complementary Quick Styles without having to create new paragraph styles for each text element.

In keeping with this general strategy, ready-made document headers, footers, and margin page numbers have all been added, so that rather than having to create a header or footer from scratch you can simply select one from a list, and the headers and footers are compatible with the Quick Styles and themes.

Another way that Word has been noticeably improved is with Live Preview. You can now hold your mouse over a font in the font list and the selected text on the page changes to that font immediately to show you what it would look like on the fly. The change only goes into effect when you click the mouse.

While the AutoText feature still exists, Microsoft has also expanded on the idea of using existing document parts with Quick Parts and Building Blocks. Apart from the preset document parts such as headers and footers, you can also add your own boilerplate text for such applications as creating contracts from standard prewritten sections.

For business reports and academic work, the new citation and bibliography features are a lifesaver. You can create citations and a bibliography and Word takes care of getting all the formatting right: You can choose the citation style from a menu, such as MLA or CMS, and Word takes care of punctuation and so on. You just fill in the data.

The new SmartArt feature adds sophisticated diagram capabilities right into Word, allowing you to create complex organizational charts and conceptual art by choosing from a large gallery of shapes. For mathematicians, scientists, and engineers, the equation creation capability has been vastly improved from the quirky and limited Equation Editor in earlier versions of Word. You can now create a much broader range of mathematical equations and expressions quickly and easily, or even choose from a list of commonly used equations in several fields.

With this version of Word you can create PDF (Adobe Acrobat) or XPS (Microsoft) files that reliably reproduce the physical appearance of your document on different computers without relying on the document's recipient having Word. Document review and collaboration features have been expanded, and you can also inspect your document for sensitive hidden information before distributing.

Microsoft Word files are now XML-based files, and have a new file format from previous versions. You can read older Word files and still save files in the old DOC format, but this is no longer the default. The XML format is good news because it stores the structural data and the content of your document separately, making for more compact and robust document files. The XML structure also allows programmers to more readily develop applications that work directly with Word documents, so that Word can more readily be integrated into your organization's own network or Web applications.

These new features and user interface redesigns are great, but if you are a seasoned Word user, you will have to relearn where a lot of things are. The learning curve is definitely worth it, though, and this book gives you plenty of tips on the quickest or best way to do something with the new version. (Appendix C gives a summary of what has changed between Word 2003 and Word 2007.) Because pull-down menus are sparse and there is only one toolbar with a few commands on it, many things are in new (albeit generally obvious and appropriate) locations. If you are a touch-typist or you just like to use keyboard shortcuts, you will be happy to know that the tear-out card that comes in this book lists most of the common keyboard shortcuts, few of which have changed from earlier versions of Word.

## How this book is structured

This book is divided into seven parts, each grouping topics together around a general theme. The book can be read front to back, but it is intended as a reference, where you can dip in and get the information you need at the moment. If, however, you are completely unfamiliar with this version of Word, I recommend reading Part 1 if you can, which covers the basics of the user interface and navigating in Word.

Part 2 covers the formatting and appearance of your document, including the new themes and Quick Styles features.

Part 3 focuses on going public with your documents: how to print your documents; create simple Web pages; distribute documents to others; collaborate with others using revision tracking and document comparison; and how to create mass mailings, labels, and envelopes.

Part 4 is about tables. Tables can be complex and fussy things that require some extra help, but are often given short shrift in books and documentation, so I made sure to include lots of information on this topic.

Part 5 covers graphics and adding more complex document formatting to your document, such as equations and text boxes.

Part 6 covers advanced and specialized features such as protecting documents from being modified, creating reference aids such an index or table of contents, and creating macros to automate your work.

Part 7 contains the appendixes: a glossary, resource guide, and roadmap of what's new in Word 2007.

## A note on the examples

Any names used in my examples are fictitious and do not refer to any real people who might happen to have the same name by coincidence. The exception is my dog Fletcher, who exists. He really is my dog, and that is really his picture: In fact, he is whining this very minute as I write this introduction. For certain long sections of text, I have used selections from *Two Years Before the Mast* by Richard Henry Dana, a historical account of what it was like to be a sailor in the early 19th century.

## Typographical and command conventions

In this book, if you see something in **boldface** type in a sentence, or set of numbered instructions, it indicates that you are to type that text string in the location indicated. Some instructions and command line syntax use placeholder text where you should supply text of your own in italics within brackets. For instance, "click [*filename.ext*] in the File name list" would be used to indicate that you should click your document's name, such as MyLetter.docx, in the File name list.

To *click* means to click the left mouse button. To *right-click* means to click the right mouse button. If you have reversed the standard mouse buttons (because you are left-handed, for example), assume the reverse. To *double-click* means to click the left mouse button twice in rapid succession. To *triple-click* means to click the left mouse button three times in rapid succession.

When typing keyboard commands, it is often necessary to hold down one or two command keys (Ctrl, Shift, and Alt) while pressing a third key. This is indicated with a plus (+) sign. For example, *press Ctrl+Alt+V* means *press V while holding down the Ctrl and Alt keys.* Some keyboard command sequences require a key combination followed by an individual keystroke. In such situations, the second keystroke is preceded by a comma in the text to indicate that you press it after the first combination. For example, press *Ctrl+`,* " means *hold down the Ctrl key and press `, then release the Ctrl key and press ".*

## Special features

Every book in the Unofficial Guide series offers the following four special sidebars that are devised to help you get things done cheaply, efficiently, and smartly.

1. **Hack:** Tips and shortcuts that increase productivity.

2. **Watch Out!:** Cautions and warnings to help you avoid common pitfalls.

3. **Bright Idea:** Smart or innovative ways to do something; in many cases, this will be a way that you can save time or hassle.

4. **Inside Scoop:** Useful knowledge gleaned by the author that can help you become more efficient.

We also recognize your need to have quick information at your fingertips and have provided the following comprehensive sections at the back of the book:

1. **Glossary:** Definitions of complicated terminology and jargon.

2. **Resource Guide:** Lists of additional resources for learning more about Microsoft Word.

3. **Word 2003 to Word 2007 Roadmap:** A summary of what has changed from Word 2003 to Word 2007 as well as a list of Word 2003 commands and their Word 2007 equivalents.

4. **Index**

# The Basics

PART I

**GET THE SCOOP ON...**
How to start Word ▪ Finding your way around Word 2007 ▪
Opening a document ▪ Searching for a document ▪
Quitting Word

# Get In and Out

**A** t a certain point, Microsoft Word became a famous example of a product suffering from something referred to in the software industry as "feature creep." By responding to customer feedback and matching any competitor feature-for-feature, Microsoft had continued to add more and more bells and whistles to Word over the years. The initial user interface of drop-down menus and toolbars with buttons could not begin to show all the possible commands and settings that now exist without hopelessly cluttering your writing area. With Word 2007, the designers have made a concerted effort to simplify and streamline the user interface so that the user can focus on the task — writing — and not on mastering the commercial airplane cockpit that the user interface had become in previous versions.

If, like me, you spend hours of your day working with Word, the good news is that Microsoft has actually done a great job of streamlining the interface. Word 2007 is no minor incremental upgrade but a fundamental redesign that makes word processing a different experience. The bad news is that a truly significant upgrade to Word requires every user already familiar with Word to relearn many tasks. While many of them are easier than before and easy to discover without additional help, others require some orientation. If you are familiar with the previous version of Word, be sure to check out Appendix C, which gives a summary of changes as they relate to Word 2003 users.

# Starting Word

Sometimes books about Word leave out this obvious step, but you can launch Word in several different ways, and it is useful to know about them, so that you choose the one that works best for you in a given situation. This can save you time and frustration so that you can focus on writing your document.

Depending on whether you are starting a new document or revising an existing one, you have several choices about how to start Word.

## Launching Word from the Start menu

If you are starting a new document, you need to launch Word first. If you are familiar with Windows (any version from Windows 95 onward), then you know that by pressing the Start button (usually located at the bottom of your desktop in the leftmost corner of your taskbar), you bring up a menu of programs. To start Word, follow these steps:

1. Click Start.

2. Click All Programs.

3. Click Microsoft Office.

4. Click Microsoft Office Word 2007.

Once you have performed Step 4, Word opens a blank document and you are ready to begin writing.

## Pinning Word to your Start menu

You may work with Word daily so that Windows always presents Word in the short list of programs recently used when you click the Start button. To guarantee that Word shows up as an option when you click Start, you can "pin" it to the Start menu. To do so, follow these steps:

1. From the Windows desktop, click Start.

2. Click All Programs.

**Bright Idea**

If you've used Word recently, you can get started in two clicks of the mouse: click Start in Windows and then click Microsoft Office Word 2007 from the left pane of the Start menu.

3. Select and click Microsoft Office from the list of programs displayed. You may have to move to the second column of the list to do so, depending on what's installed on your computer.

4. Right-click Microsoft Office Word 2007. A popup menu appears, as shown in Figure 1.1.

**Figure 1.1.** Pinning Word 2007 to the Start menu

5. Click Pin to Start menu.

Word now appears above the line in the list of programs when you click Start, indicating that it is "pinned" to the list and will always appear. If you ever want to remove Word from the part of the list that appears every time you click Start, just click Start, right-click Microsoft Office Word 2007, and click Unpin from Start menu to remove Word (it will still appear in the list of recently used programs whenever you launch it).

## Launching Word by selecting a Word document

Because Word 2007 uses a file format different from previous versions of Word, you may have noticed after you installed Word 2007 that the icon has changed for Word documents created with older versions of Word, as shown in Figure 1.2, displaying the year as part of the icon. Any documents created from Word 97 through Word 2003 (whether on Windows or Macintosh versions) show an icon with the year 2003 displayed. If you have your current file folder set to the Details option, then you will see the file type listed as "Microsoft Office Word 1997 - 2003 Document." Documents you create or save in Word

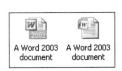

**Figure 1.2.** Word documents from older versions have a different icon.

2007 have no year displayed in the icon; they are listed simply as "Microsoft Office Word Document." Word 2007 documents are stored in XML (eXtensible Markup Language) format and have different file extensions from previous versions of Word. See Chapter 2 for more information.

If the document you want to open has been created in Word 2007 or any version of Microsoft Word, just double-click the document's icon in Windows. This launches Word and opens your document.

## Opening a document created with a different word processor or text editor

If the document was created using a different (but common) word processing application or text editor that is not installed on your computer, chances are you can open the file by just double-clicking the file's icon. You may see a dialog box first with a list of programs from which you must select Microsoft Office Word. Word 2007 then opens the file and converts it to Word 2007's file format. If the document was created using another word processing application or text editor that is currently installed on your computer, Windows assumes you want to open it with the application with which you created the file in the first place. You have two ways to get around this. You can either open the file after you have launched Word or, from Windows, follow these steps:

1. Right-click the file's icon.

2. Click Open With.

3. Click Microsoft Office Word from the list of programs, as shown in Figure 1.3.

**Figure 1.3.** Opening a non-Word document with Word using the Open With command

## Adding Word to your Windows XP Quick Launch toolbar

If you are like me, you like to have the top two or three programs you use the most available at a single click from the Windows XP Quick Launch toolbar (just to the right of the Start button on the taskbar). To add Word to the Quick Launch toolbar, first make sure that the Quick Launch toolbar is enabled. If it is not, right-click the Windows XP taskbar, click Toolbars, and click Quick Launch. To add Word to Quick Launch, follow these steps:

1. Click Start on the Windows XP desktop.

2. Click All Programs.

**3.** Click Microsoft Office.

**4.** Right-click Microsoft Office Word 2007.

**5.** Click Send To.

**6.** Click Desktop (create shortcut).

**7.** Click the Windows Desktop. A shortcut for Microsoft Office Word 2007 appears on your desktop.

**8.** Drag the shortcut to the Windows XP taskbar into the region of the Quick Launch toolbar until an I-beam cursor appears, indicating where Word's button will be inserted (to the left or right) along the Quick Launch toolbar, as shown in Figure 1.4.

**9.** Figure 1.5 shows the Word button, now present and available with a single click from the Quick Launch toolbar. (If you want to avoid a cluttered desktop, you may now drag Word's shortcut from the desktop to the recycle bin because Word is now permanently on your taskbar.)

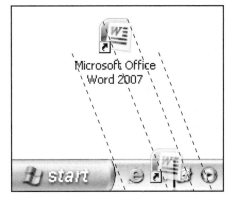

**Figure 1.4.** Adding Word to the Quick Launch toolbar

**Figure 1.5.** Word appears on the Windows taskbar, available with a single click.

## The Word environment

As I mentioned earlier, Microsoft has redesigned the interface of Word to make it easier and more intuitive to use. But what if you have been using it for many years? Don't worry! I give you a quick orientation that

**Bright Idea**

If you have more than three or four shortcuts in the Quick Launch toolbar and want them all to be visible, right-click the Windows taskbar, deselect Lock the taskbar, and drag the "grip" to the right of the Quick Launch area until all your buttons display.

works whether you are new to Word or just new to Word 2007. If you have used an earlier version of Word, some of the commands have changed or are in different places. See Appendix C for a ready reference of differences between Word 2003 and Word 2007.

After launching Word as described earlier, Word opens a window. If you launch Word by selecting a word-processing file, the document contained in the selected file appears in this window. If you launch Word without selecting a file, a blank page appears. Surrounding the selected document or blank page is the Word interface. Figure 1.6 shows some of the various elements of the Word 2007 interface.

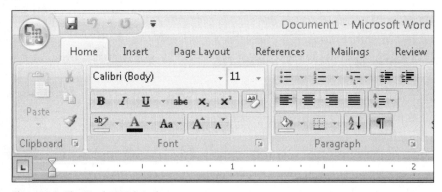

**Figure 1.6.** The Word 2007 interface

If you are familiar with previous versions of Word, you will see that the vertical ruler, the horizontal ruler (where you can adjust margins and tabs), and the scroll bars look familiar. These features are covered in detail in Chapter 4. Everything else is rearranged. Take a moment to use your mouse to move your cursor over any unknown or less than obvious elements on the screen. A pop-up description of the element appears when you hover over it with the cursor.

## Getting help

### The Word Help screen

To access help from Microsoft on using Word, click the Help button in the upper right corner of the Word screen. The Word Help screen appears, showing a toolbar with browser-style buttons for navigating the help system, as shown in Figure 1.7. Move your mouse cursor over the buttons on the toolbar to discover their functions. Below the toolbar is a window with two panes. The left pane shows a table of contents and the right pane shows the current help entry or a list of common help topics.

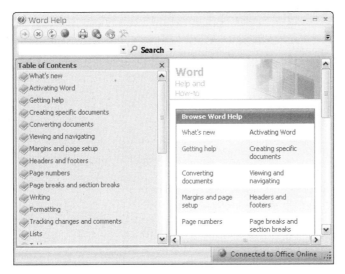

**Figure 1.7.** The Word Help screen

## *Searching Help to get an answer*

Although Microsoft is constantly updating its search engine based on how users ask questions, there really is an art to asking in such a way that you get a useful response from a computer. After all, it might take several tries to get a clear answer from a human, so what can you expect? Here are some tips to make your search for help online more efficient and less frustrating:

■ Check your spelling.

■ Use Microsoft's terminology if you know it.

■ Don't bother with capitalization or complete sentences.

■ Microsoft says two to seven words yield the best results.

**Hack**

You can also get to Help by pressing F1. Some commands offer additional contextual help when you press F1 with the mouse cursor over the command.

To search for a topic, type your text string in the box to the left of Search at the top left portion of the Word Help window just below the toolbar shown in Figure 1.8. Choose from the list of search results the topic that sounds most like an answer to your question. If you don't find what you need on the first attempt, refine your search words and try again.

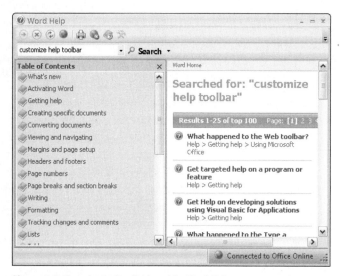

**Figure 1.8.** Search results displayed in Word Help

## The Ribbon

Microsoft Office 2007 introduces a new user interface element called the *Ribbon*. The Ribbon serves as a more friendly and flexible alternative to drop-down menus and dialog boxes. On the Ribbon are several tabs. They adapt and size themselves according to the context of your work. However, the buttons that represent various Word commands have remained essentially the same as previous versions and are also for the most part understandable to those new to Word; some additional buttons and sliders have been added that are intended to be self-explanatory or close to it. When in doubt about a button, just move your mouse cursor over it to reveal its function.

**Inside Scoop**

Once you find the help entry you need, click the Table of Contents button (it looks like an open notebook) to hide the Table of Contents and free up space to view help and your document at the same time.

**Inside Scoop**

You can free up more document working space on your screen by double-clicking a Ribbon tab. This hides the groups of commands and displays only the tabs. Double-click a tab again to redisplay the groups of commands.

### Ribbon tabs

Depending on what task you are performing in Word at a given time, these tabs will vary. When you open a document, the Home tab is on top, with the Insert, Page Layout, References, Mailings, Review, and View tabs to the right of it. You can move between Ribbon tabs by clicking the tab name.

The Home tab gives you access to the basic writing tools you will use most often in Word. The Home and other tabs are described in greater detail in subsequent chapters. For now, Table 1.1 summarizes the functions of tabs you encounter on the default Word screen.

**Table 1.1.** Tabs and their functions in Word 2007

| Tab | Function |
| --- | --- |
| Home | Cutting, copying, pasting text or format; changing font, paragraph, and style; editing commands such as find, replace, and select |
| Insert | Inserting shapes, pages, tables, illustrations, links, headers, footers, text, symbols, and equations |
| Page Layout | Selecting themes; setting up pages, page backgrounds, paragraphs, and arranging location of text and graphics on the page |
| References | Creating tables of contents, footnotes, citations, captions, indexes, and tables of authorities |
| Mailings | Creating envelopes and labels, performing mail merges, writing and inserting fields; previewing and finishing mail merges |
| Review | Proofing including spelling and grammar checking, inserting comments, tracking changes, comparing documents, and protecting documents |
| View | Selecting document views; showing/hiding ruler, gridlines, and so on; zooming to one page, two pages, or page width; arranging and working with windows |

### Groups

Under each Ribbon tab are collections of related tasks referred to as *groups*. For instance, on the Home tab you see the Clipboard, Font, Paragraph, Styles, and Editing groups. Each of the groups corresponds to a specific activity area. The most common tasks to perform within that category are listed for easy access as buttons, drop-down lists, and so on.

### Dialog Box Launcher

At the lower right corner of many groups you will see the Dialog Box Launcher button (it looks like a small box with an arrow pointing down and to the right). Click this button to expand the group into a more tra-ditional dialog box that lists all the commands in this category.

## Where's the File menu?

If you are familiar with older versions of Word, the first thing you might notice is that the File, Edit, Format, Tools, Table, Windows, and Help drop-down menus are gone, or at least appear to be. Of course, these drop-down menus all represent important functions for Word. The Ribbon and tab system replaces the drop-down menu system. In the fol-lowing sections and throughout the book I go into greater detail about the new interface. The File menu is actually still there — the Microsoft Office button in the upper left corner (the Microsoft Office logo) replaces the File menu. However, besides containing the commands you are used to seeing, some new commands appear on this menu: Prepare leads you to features that help you prepare your document for distribu-tion, and Publish leads you to features that allow you to distribute your document electronically. In addition, the Microsoft Office menu has a Word Options button at the bottom that allows you to set options and customize Word (formerly located on the Tools menu).

## Quick Access Toolbar

The Quick Access Toolbar, which looks like the top tab of an old-fashioned manila folder, appears at the top of your screen on the left. By default, it contains the Save command, the Undo command, the Repeat command, and the Customize Quick Access Toolbar command. If you prefer to have these Quick Access commands below the Ribbon, click the Customize Quick Access Toolbar button (it looks like a downward pointing triangular arrow with a line over it) and click Show Below the Ribbon. This puts the Quick Access Toolbar below the Ribbon and above the document you're working on.

## Customizing the Quick Access Toolbar

As a user, you can't modify the Ribbon tabs or choose which buttons they display. However, you can add buttons and commands to the Quick Access Toolbar (much like adding and removing buttons to the toolbar in previous versions of Word). To do so, follow these steps:

1. Click the Customize Quick Access Toolbar button.

2. To add a command from the drop-down menu, click on it. To add another command not on the short list, click More Commands.

3. Click the drop-down list of the Choose commands from: option.

4. Select the group containing the command you want to add to the toolbar, as shown in Figure 1.9.

5. Click the command you want to add to the toolbar.

6. Click Add. The command appears at the bottom of the Quick Access Toolbar list, as shown in Figure 1.10.

7. Click the up and down arrows to position the command on the toolbar list where you want it.

8. Click OK to save your changes. The new command now appears on the Quick Access Toolbar.

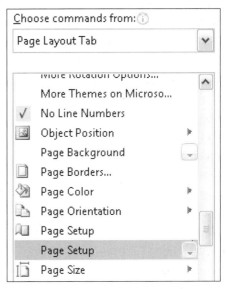

**Figure 1.9.** Selecting a command to add to the Quick Access Toolbar

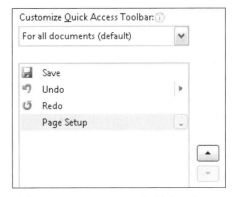

**Figure 1.10.** A new command added to the Quick Access Toolbar

> **Hack**
>
> You can also customize keyboard shortcuts from this menu. Click the Customize Quick Access Toolbar button and click the Customize button for Keyboard shortcuts. A dialog box shows you existing shortcuts and allows you to add new ones or modify existing ones.

To remove commands from the Quick Access Toolbar, select them from the Quick Access Toolbar command list and click Remove, or click Reset to return to the default list of commands, Save, Undo, and Repeat. You can customize the toolbar for all documents (the default setting) or just the one you are working on. To customize the toolbar for only the current document, select your current document's name from the Customize Quick Access Toolbar drop-down list, and then click OK. Note: This only works for Word 2007 files, not files saved in older Word formats.

## Status bar

The status bar at the bottom of the screen shows by default the current page number, the number of pages in the document, how many words are in the document, and whether Word detects any spelling or grammar errors. When you have a blank page you only see the page number and how many pages are in the document (for example, Page: 1 of 1); the other items appear as you start typing text.

### Customizing the status bar

You can customize what you want to see on the status bar by right-clicking the status bar to bring up the Status Bar Configuration options shown in Figure 1.11. Items that appear on the status

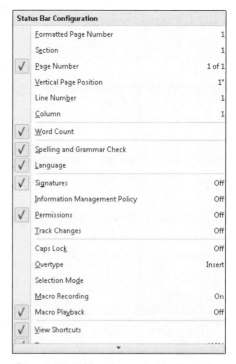

**Figure 1.11.** Making changes to the Status Bar Configuration options

**Watch Out!**

The status of the Overtype/Insert toggle command — the command that indicates whether new text inserted into existing text overwrites or pushes forward the text to the right of the cursor — no longer appears by default on the status bar. (In previous versions OVR would show to indicate that you would type over existing text.)

bar show a check mark. To make changes to what shows on the status bar, follow these steps:

1. Right-click the status bar.

2. Select the items you want to appear. (To remove items from the status bar, click the item so that the check mark disappears.)

3. When you are done making your selections, click anywhere outside the list of options to close it.

## View modes

A row of five buttons appears at the bottom of the screen, each representing a different view mode. Table 1.2 describes the different modes of viewing your document.

**Table 1.2.** Word 2007 view modes

| Button | Mode | Description |
|--------|------|-------------|
| | Print Layout | Shows the page as it will appear when printed. |
| | Full Screen Reading | Shows the page in a way that renders it easiest to read onscreen. |
| | Web Layout | Shows how the page will appear when viewed from a Web browser. |
| | Master Document Tools | Shows the page in outline form to show structure of document and master and subdocuments. |
| | Draft | Shows the page in a simplified format so that you can focus on the content rather than on the form of the document. |

# Opening documents

You can open documents in several ways in Word 2007. Although opening a document is normally a simple process, I discuss ways to save time, how to find and open documents not created in Word 2007, and how to recover documents.

## Open an existing document

If you have not yet launched Word and want to open a document, follow the steps earlier in this chapter.

If you have already launched Word and want to open an existing document, follow these steps:

1. Click the Microsoft Office button.

2. Click Open to display the Open dialog box. (You can also select from a list of Recent Documents in the right pane of this menu — type the number to the left of the file name or click the file name from the list to select it.)

3. In the Open dialog box, click the document you want to open. If you have a long list of files, you can narrow your search by typing the beginning of the filename or a wildcard character such as * (asterisk) or ? (question mark).

Table 1.3 describes the various document opening options available when you click the Open button's drop-down list.

**Table 1.3.** Document opening options in Word 2007

| Command | Use |
|---|---|
| Open | Opens and modifies existing document. |
| Open Read-Only | Opens a document without the ability to modify (useful for preventing accidental changes to important final documents; see Chapter 22 for more reliable ways to do this). |
| Open as Copy | Opens a copy of the document. Any changes you make will be made to your working copy, not the original. |
| Open in Browser | Opens a copy in your default Web browser. |
| Open with Transform | Transforms an XML document. |
| Open and Repair | Opens and repairs a document that was damaged in some way. |

**Hack**

Use the keyboard shortcut and press Ctrl+O to open the Open dialog box.

## Open a new document

By default, Word opens a new blank document when you start Word from Windows, as described earlier. To open a new blank document while in Word, or to open a new document using a template, click the Microsoft Office button and then click New. The New Document screen shown in Figure 1.12 appears. You can choose to work with a blank document, a new blog entry, or a template. Blog entries are covered in Chapter 11. Templates are a way of using prefabricated document formats to save you time. They are covered in more detail in Chapter 5. To open a Blank document, double-click Blank document and a new blank document appears. Before you save your document, Word assigns it the name Document1, Document2, and so on through the editing session. When you save a document for the first time, you are asked to assign it a name and location. Chapter 2 covers saving procedures in more detail.

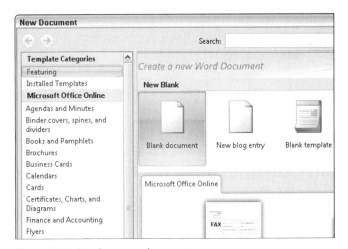

**Figure 1.12.** Creating a new document

**Inside Scoop**

If you are looking for a document that was not created in Word or if you are looking for a template, click the Files of type drop-down list and select the appropriate option.

**Watch Out!**

If you see that your document is called Document1, Document2, or the like, you have not yet saved your document and anything you have written so far could be lost. Click the Save button or press Ctrl+S to preserve your work.

## Opening a recovered document

A document needs to be recovered if Word is not closed in the normal way and the document is damaged. This can occur if you have a power outage while working on a document, lose battery power on your laptop, or some other unexpected system-level interruption. Word attempts to repair the document with the last changes that it has stored.

If you have a damaged document, Word attempts to recover any damaged files the next time you launch it. You will see a screen similar to Figure 1.13.

To view a recovered document, click the document in the Document Recovery window list to see it displayed. There may be

**Figure 1.13.** Document Recovery window

### Checking Documents for Viruses

Making sure you are working with documents free from viruses is unfortunately a fact of life in today's world. Many antivirus programs integrate with Word or your e-mail software to check for viruses prior to opening a file. If you use files you receive from others, whether via e-mail, from a server location, or from a flash drive or removable disk, make sure to perform this fundamental check. This is true whether the document you are working with is a text document or a template.

more than one version of your document; if this is the case, review them carefully to determine which ones you want to save. You can save more than one version by clicking the drop-down list to the right of the selected document, clicking Save As, and assigning a slightly different file name to each version.

## Searching for a document

For some reason known only to Microsoft, searching for a document is no longer an option from within Word. I can only surmise that it was not used often by users of Word, because the user is usually in Windows looking for the file, not Word. Another possibility, perhaps somewhat paranoid, is that Microsoft wants to encourage its customers to buy its SharePoint product to manage workgroup documents. At any rate, if you don't already know the location of the file you need, it is now necessary to use other search capabilities such as Windows to locate the file.

### Searching for a document with Windows

I won't go into great depth regarding search techniques in Windows because this is a book about Word. However, I give you the basics to get the file 90 percent of the time. To find a Word 2007 document in Windows, click Start, then Search. The Search Companion screen shown in Figure 1.14 appears. (If you don't see Search as an option on your Start menu,

**Figure 1.14.** The Search Companion in Windows XP

### Inside Scoop

For a Word 2007 document, use the extension .docx (or .docm if the document has macros). For earlier versions of Word, use .doc. For both, use .do*.

right-click the Start menu, click Properties, click Customize, click the Advanced tab, click the checkbox next to Search in the Start menu items list, and then click OK.)

### Finding a document when you know its name

From the Search Companion, follow these steps to locate your document:

1. Select Documents (word processing, spreadsheet, etc.) to answer the question, What do you want to search for?

2. If you know when you last worked on the document, click the button that best answers the "last time it was modified" question.

3. In the text field All or part of the document name: type the name of your document. If you know the extension, include that.

4. Click Search to see a set of results. If you don't see the file you need, click the Back button and click Use advanced search options to narrow your search.

### Finding a document by searching for text in the document

If you aren't sure what you named the document, you can search for text in the document. It's best to choose a short but unique word or phrase — such as Part Number 45987 or Fall 2007 Quarterly Earnings — that you know is contained in the document. To find a document by searching for text, follow Steps 1 and 2 of the previous section, and then follow these steps:

1. Click Use advanced search options.

2. Scroll down to the text box A word or phrase in the document and type your unique word or phrase.

3. Click Search to see a set of results.

# Quitting Word

Even though Word doesn't let you quit before asking whether you want to save your work, it feels a bit risky to talk about quitting Word without saving your work first. I'll just say this now, before I tell you how to quit Word: Click Save or press Ctrl+S to save your work before exiting and follow the instructions to assign a name to your file. I go into more detail about the various ways you can save your work in Chapter 2.

If you are working on just one document and you saved your last work, just click the Close button (the x). Word closes immediately.

**Watch Out!**

Even longtime PC users and geeks make this mistake. When Word asks Do you want to save the changes to [Your Document Name Here]? take two breaths and think first before answering. If you click No, all changes you made since the last save operation will be lost.

If you are working on just one document and you haven't saved your last work, you can still click the Close button, as long as you are careful to answer Yes when asked if you want to save your changes.

If you are working on multiple documents and want to close Word, click the Microsoft Office button and then click Exit Word or press X. If you have saved your work in your various documents, Word closes immediately. If you have any documents that have changes as yet unsaved, Word asks whether you want to save changes for each document where this applies, and then closes.

If Word is frozen and doesn't respond to mouse or keyboard commands, you can still exit without rebooting in most cases by pressing Ctrl+Alt+Del in Windows XP, clicking Task Manager, selecting Word from the list of applications, and clicking End Task. Warning: Any unsaved work is lost when closing Word using this method.

## Just the facts

- You can launch Word by selecting it from the Windows Start menu or by double-clicking a Word document.

- The drop-down menu system of earlier versions of Word has been replaced in Word 2007 by the Microsoft Office button (replacing the File and Tools menus) and the Ribbon, which has sets of related tasks grouped under tabs.

- The Quick Access Toolbar allows you to customize Word and add your most frequently used commands.

- Word 2007 no longer has document search capabilities; instead you must use Search from the Windows XP Start menu or some other search utility.

- After saving your work by clicking Save or pressing Ctrl+S, you can quit Word by clicking the Close button (to close just one document) or by clicking the Microsoft Office button and then clicking Exit Word.

**GET THE SCOOP ON...**
Different file types ▪ Working with older file types and
Compatibility Mode ▪ Saving and closing a document ▪
Using AutoRecover to back up your work

# Work with Documents

Microsoft has rethought how it stores data in Word document files and has come up with a new and improved way. The files are now stored in an Extensible Markup Language (XML) format. XML is a metalanguage that allows you to describe how your data is structured in an intelligent way so that the content's structure is more readily understandable. The practical benefits for Word files are that they are less easily corruptible, more compact, and more readily translated into different formats while preserving key information about the data.

This is great, but Microsoft hasn't really changed its native Word document file format since 1997, so people have been more or less happily transferring files from one computer to the other without too much concern about which version of Word the person has. Prior to Word 2007, this was really only an issue if someone was using some of Word's more ambitious layout capabilities or perhaps macros.

So with Word 2007, you need to be cognizant of what version the document is that you receive, and if you are collaborating with someone, be aware of whether that person needs to work with an earlier format. Microsoft will be releasing Word 2007 document converter or reader add-ins for earlier versions of Word, which your collaborator may not have. Fortunately, you can always work in Compatibility mode and stay safely within the confines of the capabilities of earlier versions of Word, although you will not be able to take advantage of some features, and your document will be stored in the larger DOC format. There are also many version-specific settings in the Word Options menu that allow you to "play well with others," such as the ability to specify a default format under which to save your files other than the default new Word 2007 DOCX format. You can readily convert any document from an earlier version to Word 2007, and you can change your default settings to do so always if you are confident you don't need to worry about earlier versions. I show you how to do these things in this chapter.

I also show you how to save your work, give some tips about naming files and keeping track of them, and show you how to take full advantage of the (lifesaving!) AutoRecover feature.

## Document types

The various document file types you may encounter in Word are listed in Table 2.1 along with their corresponding filename extensions. For now, I focus on document files alone. *Templates* are ready-made document formats that you create yourself or get from Microsoft or others. For more information on templates and template files, see Chapter 5.

**Table 2.1.** Document and other data file types in Word

| Icon | Extension | Word Version | File Type |
|---|---|---|---|
|  | .docx | Word 2007 | Document (no macros) |
|  | .docm | Word 2007 | Document with macros enabled |
|  | .dotx | Word 2007 | Template (no macros) |
|  | .dotm | Word 2007 | Template with macros enabled |
|  | .doc | Word 97–2003 | Document file document (with or without macros) |
|  | .dot | Word 97–2003 | Template file template (with or without macros) |

**Hack**

Although you can usually determine the file's type by its icon or Type field in the Details view in Windows, it's useful to know the filename extension as well, because you can add it in the document name field to narrow file searches.

*Macros* are small custom programs that help you automate your work. They can be either recorded or programmed, and run a command or set of commands. Macros are activated by pressing a button assigned to them or by typing an assigned key combination. Because macros can be very powerful, they can also be dangerous, either inadvertently or intentionally, when designed as malicious software, or *malware*. Word 2007 files that are macro-enabled have been given a separate file type designation, filename extension, and an exclamation point in their icons; this is to alert you to them so that you open them only if they come from a trusted source and even then only when you expect that said source sent you a document with macros. Macros from earlier versions of Word will not run in Word 2007, so when you open an older document or template that contains macros, you will not see a warning regarding macros unless you add the macros while working on the document in Word 2007. For more information on macros, see Chapter 23.

## Working with non-Word file formats

Besides various Word document file formats, you may also encounter documents created in other programs, or saved in other standard (or not-so-standard) formats, listed in Table 2.2. To open a file in Word that is not a Word document or template, follow these steps:

1. Click the Microsoft Office button.

2. Click Open.

3. Navigate to the folder containing the desired file by double-clicking the folder.

**Watch Out!**

Don't assume that you aren't susceptible to a malicious macro if you are opening a DOC file. You can add macros to such files in Word 2007. However, the default setting disables macros and displays an alert with an Enable Macros option.

4. If you know the file's name and extension, type it in the File name box; otherwise proceed to Step 5.

5. Click the Files of type drop-down list and select the file type you want to open, as shown in Figure 2.1.

6. Word displays all files of that type in the folder designated. Click the file you want to open.

7. Click Open to open the file in Word.

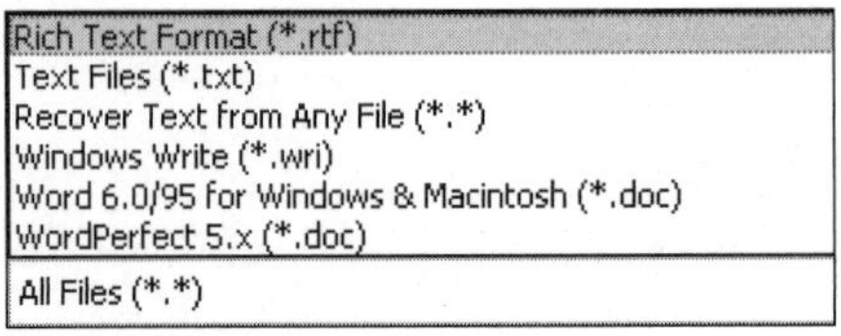

```
Rich Text Format (*.rtf)
Text Files (*.txt)
Recover Text from Any File (*.*)
Windows Write (*.wri)
Word 6.0/95 for Windows & Macintosh (*.doc)
WordPerfect 5.x (*.doc)
All Files (*.*)
```

**Figure 2.1.** Selecting a file type to open

**Table 2.2.** Some non-Word file formats accessible from Word

| Extension | Description |
| --- | --- |
| .rtf | Rich Text Format: used for transporting text while preserving most formatting; readable by numerous word processors |
| .txt | Text only file format containing only text and no formatting or graphics |
| .wri | Windows Write, ancient (Windows 3.0, 3.1) rudimentary word processing file |
| .wpd | WordPerfect document file |
| .doc or .wpd | WordPerfect 6.x document file |
| .doc | WordPerfect 5.x document file (note: same file extension as Word!) |
| .wps | Microsoft Works word processor document file |

# If you don't even know what program created the file...

Let's say you receive a file that you need to work with and the file is not a Word document, but you don't know what program was used to create the file or what file format it has been saved in. Follow these steps to open the file in Word:

1. Click the Microsoft Office button.

2. Click Open.

3. Navigate to the folder containing the desired file by double-clicking the folder.

**4.** If you know the file's name and extension, type it in the File name box; otherwise proceed to Step 5.

**5.** Click the Files of type drop-down list.

**6.** Click All Files (*.*).

**7.** Word displays all files in the folder designated. Click the file you want to open.

**8.** Click Open. If Word identifies the file as a word processing document, the file will open in Word. If it doesn't, it will open a File Conversion dialog box like the one shown in Figure 2.2.

**9.** Choose the text encoding scheme that renders the file most readable. If all encoding options render many nonsensical characters and square boxes, chances are you are dealing with an executable file or some other nondocument file that you are best off not attempting to open in Word.

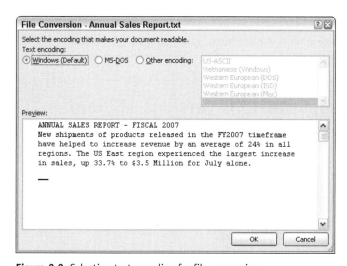

**Figure 2.2.** Selecting text encoding for file conversion

## When a template file should have been a document file

As a technical writer and editor, I often work closely with highly skilled engineers and computer scientists. However, it's surprising how often I encounter this problem. The file is not intended to be used as a template (not boilerplate or form text that will be repeatedly used), but is saved by accident as a template file (with the .dotx or .dotm file extension in

Word 2007 or .dot in earlier versions of Word). If you or someone you work with inadvertently saves a document as a template, it needs to be converted back to a document. Otherwise, odd things happen to such things as revision tracking. Fortunately, this is a simple procedure. To convert a template into a document, open the template file and then follow these steps:

1. Click the Microsoft Office button to display the screen shown in Figure 2.3.

2. Click Save As.

3. Select Word Document (*.docx) from the Save as type drop-down list, as shown in Figure 2.4.

**Figure 2.3.** The Microsoft Office menu

4. If necessary, type a new name in the File name field.

5. Click Save.

| | |
| --- | --- |
| | Word Document (*.docx) |
| | Word Macro-Enabled Document (*.docm) |
| | Word 97-2003 Document (*.doc) |
| | Word Template (*.dotx) |
| File name: | Word Macro-Enabled Template (*.dotm) |
| | Word 97-2003 Template (*.dot) |
| Save as type: | Rich Text Format (*.rtf) |

**Figure 2.4.** Saving a template file as a document

# Working with documents from previous versions of Word

If you work with others who use an earlier version of Word, or if your computer at work has an older version than your computer at home, you have several choices:

■ You can edit the document in Word 2007 Compatibility Mode, preserving the Word 97 - 2003 (*.doc) file format.

■ You can convert the document to Word 2007. This allows you to use all the features of Word 2007 and to reduce the file size. This is best if you know you won't open the document in a different version of Word.

■ You can convert the document to Word 2007 and assume the user with the earlier version of Word will upgrade or download the file converter for the previous version of Word from Microsoft.

**Watch Out!**

This last option only makes sense if you are confident that most of those who will open the document will have Word 2007 (such as in a large institution where an IT department has enforced an upgrade).

## Opening an older Word document in Compatibility Mode

When you open a Word document created with an earlier version of Word, the document opens in Compatibility Mode. You can tell that you are working in Compatibility Mode because the phrase appears in parentheses after the file's name at the top of your screen, as shown in Figure 2.5. By default, Word 2007 assumes that you want to retain the older file format. This is intended to help keep your files compatible with older versions of Word if you collaborate with someone who doesn't have Word 2007, if you use an older version at home, and so on. If you work in Compatibility Mode, you do not have Word 2007's more compact file size. In addition, the behavior of certain features of Word 2007 changes.

**Figure 2.5.** Working in Compatibility Mode

## Converting older Word documents to Word 2007 format

If you open a document created in Word 97 - 2003 (*.doc) format, you can convert the document to Word 2007 so that you have access to all of Word 2007's features and smaller and more stable file size. To do so, follow these steps:

1. Open the document.

2. Click the Microsoft Office button.

3. Click Convert. The warning dialog box displayed in Figure 2.6 appears.

4. Click OK (you may also select the Do not ask me again about converting documents check box).

**Microsoft Office Word**                                    [?][×]

This action will convert the document to the newest file format.

Converting allows you to use all the new features of Word and reduces the size of your file. This document will be replaced by the converted version.

☐ Do not ask me again about converting documents

| Tell Me More... |  | OK | Cancel |

**Figure 2.6.** Warning dialog box with information about document conversion to Word 2007 format

### How New Word 2007 Features Act in Compatibility Mode

The strategy for Compatibility Mode is to convert new features to the next best thing in earlier versions of Word. If you have a complex document to work with, review this list to see what to expect:

- Heading and body fonts are set to a fixed formatting (rather than changing with Quick Styles, as you see in Chapter 5).

- The new reference features of citations, bibliographies, and placeholder text in citations (see Chapter 22) are no longer specially tagged and become regular text.

- Content controls (such as drop-down lists) and placeholder text in content controls are no longer specially tagged and become regular text. (For more information on content controls, see Chapter 13.)

- Text boxes (see Chapter 19) and margins with relative positions lose their relative positioning and are assigned fixed positions.

- If you use Themes to change the look of your document (see Chapter 5), they are permanently converted to styles in Compatibility Mode.

- Office Art is converted to the previous version.

- Diagrams and equations are converted to images that cannot be edited.

The document is converted to Word 2007 format, and the (Compatibility Mode) notice disappears from the top of the screen, as shown in Figure 2.7. When you save the file, it is stored in Word 2007 format.

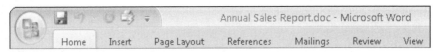

**Figure 2.7.** A document converted to Word 2007 format

## The Word 2007 compatibility packs for earlier versions of Word

If you collaborate with others or have Word 2003, 2002, or 2000 on your home PC and Word 2007 at work (or vice versa), you can also download

**Bright Idea**

In some cases, you need to have what in the software industry is referred to as *version control:* you need to keep track of various drafts and versions of a document. Word helps automate that process (see Chapters 11 and 12).

the Microsoft Office Compatibility Pack for 2007 Office Word, Excel and PowerPoint File Formats that allows you to convert and work with Word 2007 files using an earlier version of Word. To do so, first make sure you have established an Internet connection, then follow these steps:

1. Click Help.
2. In Word 2002, Click Office on the Web. In Word 2003, click Check for Updates.
3. At the Microsoft Office Web site, click the Check for Updates link.
4. Scroll through the page until you find your version of Word, and click Converters.
5. Find the Word 2007 converter, and click the Download button, following the instructions to install the converter.

## Saving and closing your new document

After you write and/or make changes to your document, you have several options for saving your work. Saving may seem simple and straightforward, but many people get into trouble by not observing some of the fine points. With the exception of occasional Word users with few documents, you need to have an organizational strategy for naming your files and determining where to store them. You also need a strategy for backing up your data as you write to preserve changes you make at regular intervals during a writing or editing session.

### Naming your document

As mentioned in Chapter 1, before you save your work Word temporarily assigns your document the filename Document1 (and Document2,

**Inside Scoop**

If you don't want to create a name, Word picks up the title (if you have one) or, failing that, the first phrase or sentence. For example, if your document begins with the line Thoughts on Immortality, Word assigns the name Thoughts on Immortality.docx to the file.

Document3, and so on throughout a session of using Word). If you start writing and see Document1 as your document name, think of it as a sign that it is time to save and name your file. Always assign the document a name if it doesn't have one already. Here are some tips on naming files:

- Use a consistent naming scheme or strategy.
- If you don't have many documents, don't be afraid to use longer filenames.
- If you have many documents to manage, don't make the filename hold all the information. Take advantage of the document's properties fields and or Windows' file folder names.

## Taking advantage of your document's properties data

Word documents all have a set of properties that you can edit and use for tracking various aspects of the document. To view and edit a subset of the current document's properties, follow these steps:

1. Click the Microsoft Office button.

2. Click Prepare or type **E** to display the screen shown in Figure 2.8.

3. Click Properties. The Properties panel appears below the Ribbon, as shown in Figure 2.9.

4. Type text in any fields shown in the Standard list of properties: Author, Title, Subject, Keywords, Category, Status, or Comments.

5. To close the Properties panel, click the Close button in the upper-right corner of the panel.

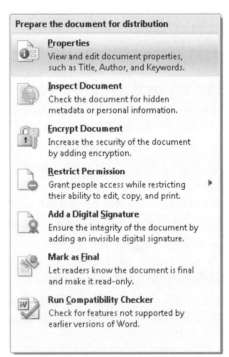

**Figure 2.8.** The Finish command showing the Properties feature

**Hack**

You can add the Properties feature to the Quick Access Toolbar (QAT): Right-click Properties from the list in the right pane of the dialog box, and then click Add to Quick Access Toolbar. You can then toggle the display of document properties on and off with the button.

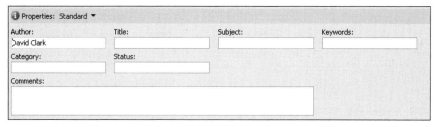

**Figure 2.9.** The document's properties are displayed below the Ribbon.

If you want to see or add more properties:

1. Click the Properties drop-down list on the Properties panel.

2. Click Advanced (rather than Standard). This displays a tabbed Properties dialog box.

3. Click the Custom tab to see the items shown in Figure 2.10.

4. Scroll through the Name list to select an existing property name, or type your own custom property name.

5. Click the Type drop-down list and choose from one of four types: Text, Date, Number, or Yes or no.

6. You may type a value in the next field (if you select Yes or no for Type, then you may select either the Yes or No radio button; the default value is Yes).

7. Click Add to add the new property to your document.

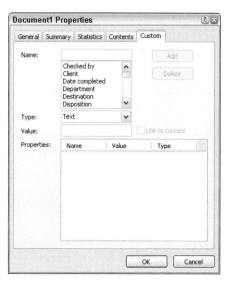

**Figure 2.10.** Adding properties in the Custom tab of the Properties dialog box

## The Save command

The easiest way to save a document is to click the Save button on the Quick Access Toolbar (which looks like a floppy disk) or press Ctrl+S. If this is the first time you have saved your document, you need to give it a name, as discussed earlier. I use the Save command constantly (meaning every few minutes) because I hate to lose my work. If I've written a paragraph, I usually click the Save button. If I get up to get a cup of coffee or answer the door, I click the Save button. If I need to switch to another application on my PC or look something up on the Internet, I click the Save button. You get the idea.

## The Save As command

The Save As command has several uses. If you have some existing business correspondence saved in a document called Customer1.docx and want to send essentially the same information to another customer, you can open Customer1.docx, make changes, use the Save As command, and type **Customer2.docx** in the File name field for the revised document. (This is mainly useful for quick one-time applications. If you want to send a form letter to a list of customers, automating the personalization process, you are better served by taking advantage of the Mail Merge features discussed in Chapter 14.) You can also use Save As to save your document to a different file format. You can save your work as a document in any one of many formats, some of which are enumerated in Tables 2.1 and 2.2. In addition, you can save your file for distribution in PDF or XPS format. To do so, click the right arrow next to the Save As command from the Microsoft Office menu and select PDF or XPS.

### Saving as PDF

PDF is an Adobe file format (PDF stands for Portable Document Format). When you save a file to this format, it prints the document into a PDF file. Anyone with Adobe Reader (available free to download from Adobe for any number of computer operating systems) can view the file. PDF files are

**Watch Out!**

While saving to PDF does deter most people from revising the document because more expensive Adobe Acrobat software is required to modify it, don't depend on PDF format alone to protect content. See Chapter 21 for more information on controlling who can modify your document.

commonly used for such things as government forms or commercial brochures downloaded over the Internet. Creating a PDF file is a way to guarantee that any copy of the file that is viewed or printed will have a uniform and predictable look, retaining all your formatting, text, and graphics.

### Saving as XPS

XPS stands for XML Paper Specification. The goal of this new file format is to create an XML-based PDF-like file format that also incorporates Microsoft Rights Management functionality. Because at this point only Microsoft uses this feature, it doesn't yet seem to make much sense unless you work in or with a large institution that uses Microsoft Rights Management.

## Customizing your document Save settings

If you take a few moments to customize your Word settings that relate to saving files, you can save yourself countless keystrokes in the future. I've selected a few common settings that can often benefit from customization.

### Changing the default file location for saving your document

If you do not specify a different location, Word saves your document in your My Documents folder on your hard drive. For example, my default file save location is as follows:

```
C:\Documents and Settings\David Clark\My Documents\
```

There are benefits to going along with the defaults because My Documents is on the Windows Start menu, and so on. However, if you routinely need to save your documents to a specific folder on your PC or a specific server location on your network, follow these steps to change the default file location:

1. Click the Microsoft Office button.

2. Click Word Options (or press I).

3. From the navigation bar on the left, click Save to see the Customize how documents are saved screen shown in Figure 2.11.

4. In the Default file location text field, type the desired file path destination on your local PC's hard drive, removable disk, or on your network. (You can also click Browse to find the location using a browser.)

5. Click OK to accept the changes.

**Inside Scoop**

You can also change settings for where you save files when working offline with files checked out from a document management server such as SharePoint Portal Server from the screen shown in Figure 2.11.

---

Customize how documents are saved.

**Save documents**

Save files in this format:     Word Document (*.docx)    ▼

☑ Save AutoRecover information every   10 ⬍   minutes

AutoRecover file location:     C:\Documents and Settings\David Clark\Application Data\Micros   Browse...

Default file location:     C:\Documents and Settings\David Clark\My Documents\   Browse...

**Offline editing options for document management server files**

Save checked-out files to: ⓘ
  ◉ The server drafts location on this computer
  ○ The web server

Server drafts location:   C:\Documents and Settings\David Clark\My Documents\SharePoint D   Browse...

**Preserve fidelity when sharing this document:**    🖼 Document1    ▼

☐ Embed fonts in the file ⓘ
  ☐ Embed only the characters used in the document (best for reducing file size)
  ☐ Do not embed common system fonts

**Figure 2.11.** Customizing the default file location

## *Making a different document format the default document type*

If you are the early adopter on Word 2007 and you know that you have to collaborate with others with earlier versions for the foreseeable future, you can change settings in Word so that your documents are saved in a different format by default. Sending your document out in different file formats to others is also discussed in Chapter 11. For now, to make Word 97 - 2003 (*.doc) the default file type for saving, follow these steps:

1. Click the Microsoft Office button.

2. Click Word Options (or press I).

3. Click Save.

4. In the section Save documents, click the drop-down list Save files in this format: to see the list of options shown in Figure 2.12.

5. Click Word 97-2003 Document (*.doc).

### *Customizing Word to maximize compatibility*

In addition to the many file format options available, Microsoft has a very long list of individual settings designed to aid users in

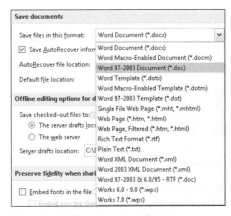

**Figure 2.12.** Changing the default document file format

maintaining layout feature behavior from older versions of Word or even WordPerfect. To review and make changes to compatibility options, follow these steps:

1. Click the Microsoft Office button.

2. Click Word Options (or press I).

3. Click Advanced to display Advanced options for working with Word.

4. Scroll down until you see Compatibility options for: as shown in Figure 2.13, and select either All New Documents or your current document from the drop-down list to specify the scope of the option changes.

5. Click the plus sign (+) next to Layout Options to view individual options.

6. Click to select or deselect any options to fix compatibility from the list.

7. Click OK to accept changes.

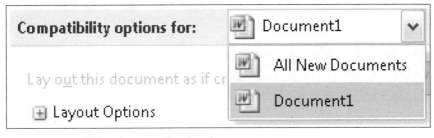

**Figure 2.13.** Specifying the scope of option changes

## Closing your document

After you save your document in one of the ways mentioned earlier in this section, you can close your document in one of several ways. If you have only one document open and you want to close the document and Word, click the Close button (the x in the upper-right corner of the window). The document closes and Word exits. If you have made changes since your last save, Word gives you one last chance to save those changes before exiting.

If you are working on multiple documents and want to close Word, click the Microsoft Office button and then click Exit Word or press X. If you have saved your work in your various documents, Word closes immediately. If you have any documents with unsaved changes, Word asks whether you want to save changes for each document where this applies, and then closes.

Finally, if you have one document open and want to close it but don't want to close Word yet, click the Microsoft Office button and click Close or press C. Word closes the document but remains available for opening other documents or changing settings.

## AutoRecover

This feature can be a lifesaver as long as you understand what it really does. Many users assume that AutoRecover in Word functions like the Save command, saving drafts every so often as you type before you saved the document. Yes and no. Yes, AutoRecover saves any open documents in their current state every so many minutes (by default ten minutes). If you have a power failure and you restart Word, it recovers the document or documents from the time of the last AutoRecover operation. However, it does not save you from such things as closing the document before saving it. If you do this, Word assumes the file is no longer valuable to you and removes it from AutoRecover status.

You can adjust the time interval for saving AutoRecover file information, and you can specify the file location for AutoRecover files (such as a

**Hack**

If Word freezes and doesn't respond to mouse or keyboard commands, you can exit without rebooting in most cases by pressing Ctrl+Alt+Del in Windows XP. Click Task Manager, select Word from the list of applications, and click End Task. Warning: Using this method results in the loss of all unsaved work.

removable drive location so that you have additional recovery options if the PC's local hard drive malfunctions). To do so, follow these steps:

1. Click the Microsoft Office button.

2. Click Word Options (or press I).

3. Click Save.

4. Make sure the check box is selected for Save AutoRecover information..., and then type a number between 1 and 120 or use the up- and down-arrow keys to select the duration of the interval between saves in minutes.

5. You can change the default location for storing AutoRecover file information by typing a new path or clicking Browse to select one using a browser.

   If you ever need to open a file that has been recovered, see Chapter 1.

## Just the facts

- Word 2007 uses an XML-based file format that is different from earlier versions of Word, so take this into account if you intend to collaborate with others or take your documents from one PC to another.

- You can work in Compatibility Mode when working with documents generated in an earlier version of Word to ensure compatibility, or you can convert the files to Word 2007 to get all the functionality of Word 2007 for your document.

- Develop a consistent naming strategy for your documents as you save them and consider taking advantage of Word's document properties fields to hold information about such things as version, author, title, client, and department.

- Word 2007 documents can be saved in many formats, such as Word 2003 or PDF, for maximum availability.

- The AutoRecover feature can help you recover your work when you experience a power failure or other unexpected interruption to your normal Word session.

GET THE SCOOP ON...
Writing and editing your work in Word ■ Copying,
pasting, and deleting text ■ Finding and replacing text ■
Checking spelling and grammar ■ Changing AutoCorrect
from a curse to a blessing

# Write and Revise

I f you have previously used an earlier version of Word
or a different word processor, the basics of writing and
editing will not seem very different to you in Word
2007. However, Word 2007 has some unique features that
can help you write and revise your work more efficiently.

I've intentionally put off showing you how to manipulate the appearance of a document until Chapter 5.
Focusing on how the document looks is one of the most
common distractions (or procrastination strategies) when
trying to write or revise the textual content of a document.
I find that many people who use word-processing software
every day make decisions that result in time-consuming,
unnecessary work because they haven't had the time to
learn some of the basic tips and tricks of working with text.
With that in mind, I cover in this chapter such apparently
obvious things as typing text, when to start a new paragraph, how to move your cursor back and forth, how to
insert text in a sentence you've already written, how to cut
and paste text within a document, and how to cut text from
one document and paste it into another.

In addition to giving you tips on the basics, I highlight
how to search for text and how to replace every instance of
one text string with another, and smart ways to take full
advantage of the AutoCorrect feature, spelling, and grammar to improve your documents. Word 2007 has made
some improvements to how it checks spelling, allowing
for spelling something correctly based on context. The

sentence "I put on a pear of pants" is composed of correctly spelled words, but *pear* should be *pair.* Word now catches this sort of thing.

I cover the essentially text-related reference topics of footnotes, citations, and so on in Chapter 22.

# Using basic editing tools

I can't tell you how many times I've watched in frustration as someone types a sentence, types a second sentence, changes his or her mind, and then repeatedly slams or holds down the Backspace key until the second sentence has been removed. Why have a powerful editing tool if you use it like a pencil and eraser? A few minutes spent learning some basic keyboard commands and tricks with your mouse can save you lots of time and enable you to think more about what you want to say and less about how to use Word to get it on the page. This book's tear-out card contains a list of keyboard shortcuts for those of you who are touch typists or fast hunt-and-peck typists. I also mention a few of them along the way.

## Typing with the keyboard

Once you open Word and have a blank document looking back at you, you see a blinking vertical line at the upper-left corner of the page. This is called the *insertion point.* As you begin typing on the keyboard, letters flow to the left of the insertion point and push the insertion point to the right. The insertion point is different from the *cursor,* which is the pointer on the screen that moves when your mouse moves. If you move the mouse in the area of the Ribbon, Quick Access Toolbar, Status bar, or Ruler, you see an arrow-shaped pointer. However, if you move it over the document working area, the cursor changes shape to an I-beam. When you type text from the keyboard, the I-beam cursor disappears so as not to distract you when you type.

## Typing new text

To type new text, avoid these common mistakes to ensure efficient and focused writing:

- Don't press the Tab key to indent paragraphs; press Enter at the end of each paragraph to separate them. (Formatting paragraphs is covered in Chapters 5 and 7.)

- Don't press Enter to end a line unless you are ending a paragraph or heading.

- Unless specifically requested to do so, don't press the Spacebar twice after periods. This is an artifact of typescripts; Word takes care of spacing sentences appropriately.

- Don't hyphenate words at the end of the line. Let Word do it. (See Chapter 8 for more details on hyphenation.)

- Don't use all capital letters for text paragraphs. If for some reason you want to make a lot of text shout from the page, there are better ways to do it, and in any case, there is a command to make everything uppercase, but it's trickier to go the other direction.

- Don't press the Backspace key to change text unless it's just a few letters. It is more efficient to highlight text or press a keyboard combination to remove unwanted text.

- Avoid working in Overtype mode. There are very few instances where this mode makes sense. It's best to leave it turned off.

When you type, you may encounter what could best be described as a red squiggle underlining a word, as shown in Figure 3.1. This is an indication that Word suspects the word is misspelled. I say *suspects* because Word's dictionary doesn't have every word in the English language, and many people work with specialized vocabulary. You can always add special words to your dictionary (I show you how later in the chapter) so that things such as your company's product names are always spelled correctly. It's been my experience that it's most efficient to correct obvious typos as I see the red squiggles appear on the screen, but then I make sure to check the entire document again later.

> Learning how to spell caln be challenging.

**Figure 3.1.** Word detects a misspelled word.

If you know you are not misspelling words but you see many words with red squiggles, it could be that you have the language setting for the wrong locality, such as English (U.S.) when it should be English (Canada). I show you how to change these settings later in the chapter.

As you type and begin to complete sentences, you may also see words, phrases, or entire sentences underlined with a green squiggle, as shown in Figure 3.2. This indicates that Word suspects a grammatical error. Fortunately, you can adjust how strict the grammar is, in case this annoys you, and I cover that later.

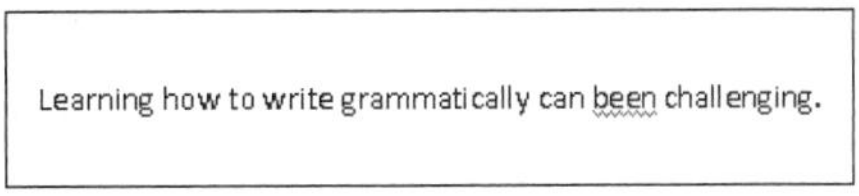

> Learning how to write grammatically can been challenging.

**Figure 3.2.** Word detects a grammatical error.

**Hack**
Word is sometimes slow in displaying the suspected grammar and spelling errors. You can force the display to speed up by selecting a block of text.

## Inserting text into a sentence

There are several ways you can insert a word or phrase into an existing sentence. In the example in Figure 3.3, I've typed the sentence "Quarterly earnings were higher due to the success of the spring product line."

Quarterly earnings were higher due to the success of the spring product line.|

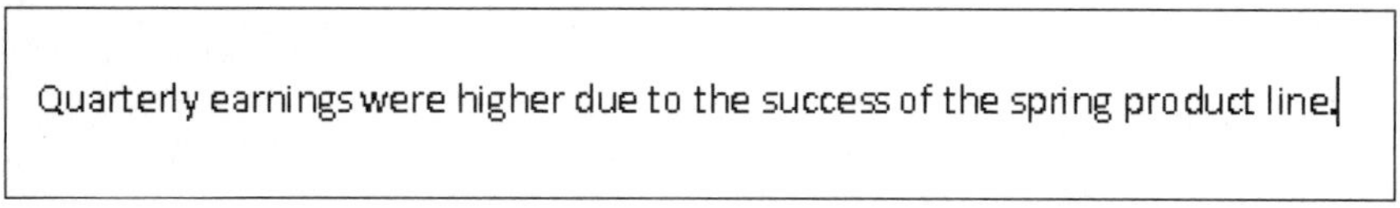

**Figure 3.3.** Typing a sentence

If I want to add the phrase "37 percent" before the word *higher,* I can move my mouse pointer to the left of the word *higher* and click, so that the insertion point appears to the left of *higher.* I can also use the arrow keys to move the insertion point from the end of the first sentence until it immediately precedes the word *higher.* After moving the insertion point where it needs to be, I type **37 percent** and insert a space. The new text is inserted into the sentence, and the text to the right of the insertion point moves to the right, as shown in Figure 3.4.

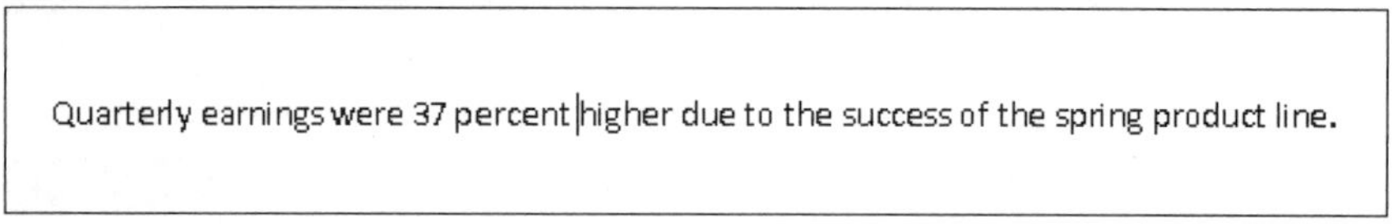

Quarterly earnings were 37 percent|higher due to the success of the spring product line.

**Figure 3.4.** Inserting text into a sentence

## Selecting text

The easiest way to select text in Word is as follows:

1. Move the mouse pointer until the I-beam cursor is at the beginning of the text you want to select.
2. Click the left mouse button and drag the mouse pointer to the right and down until the text you want is highlighted (usually the high-lighting is indicated in reversed-out type, as shown in Figure 3.5).
3. Release the left mouse button. The selected text is now highlighted.

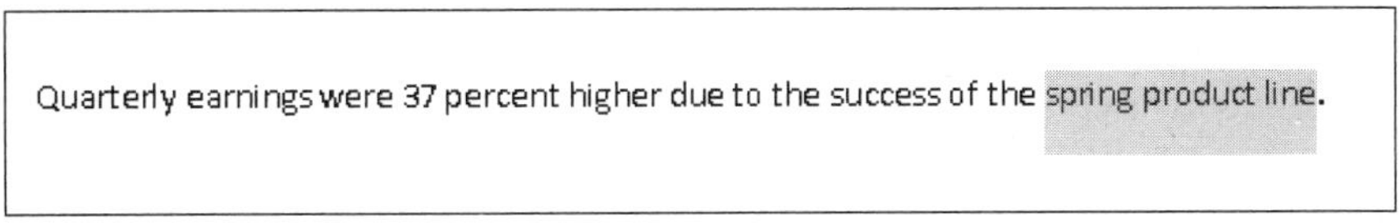

Quarterly earnings were 37 percent higher due to the success of the spring product line.

**Figure 3.5.** Selected text appears highlighted on-screen.

Here is another way to select text that is sometimes better suited when you want more precision in selecting your text:

1. Position your cursor at the beginning or end of the text you want to select.

2. Hold down the Shift key and then use the arrow keys and other cursor keypad keys (Up, Down, Left, Right, Page Down, Page Up, Home, and End) to extend the selected text.

You can perform many operations on the selected text alone, such as formatting, checking spelling, deleting, copying, cutting, and pasting. Word provides you with many ways to select text, and you can save time by learning some shortcuts for how to do so. Table 3.1 summarizes the main ways to do so with a mouse. See this book's tear-out card for keyboard shortcuts.

**Table 3.1.** Additional ways to select text

| Text to Select | How to Select It |
| --- | --- |
| Word | Double-click the word. |
| Sentence | Click the sentence while holding down the Ctrl key. |
| Line of text | Click in the margin to the left of the line (after the cursor changes from an I-beam into an arrow) |
| Paragraph | Click the paragraph three times. |
| Large block of text | Click the beginning of the text you want to select, then hold down the Shift key while clicking the end of the block of text. |
| An entire document | Press Ctrl+A. |
| A vertical block of text | Hold down the Alt key and drag the mouse pointer. |
| Text with similar formatting | Right-click an area with the type of formatting you want to find (such as a body text paragraph, italics, or a heading), and then click Select Text with Similar Formatting. |

# Copying, moving, and deleting text

Copying, moving (or cutting and pasting), and deleting text can be accomplished in several ways in Word. These operations function slightly differently with tables, graphics, and other objects, and I just focus on how these operations work for basic text paragraphs for now. See subsequent chapters that apply to tables and so on for information on how to copy, move, and delete them.

## Copying text

To copy text in Word, follow these steps:

1. Select the text you want to copy.

2. Press Ctrl+C or click Copy on the Clipboard group on the Home tab of the Ribbon, as shown in Figure 3.6. The selected text is copied to the Clipboard.

**Figure 3.6.** Using the Copy command

## Understanding the Clipboard

If you copy a selection in Word, it is stored in the Clipboard. The Clipboard is a temporary storage location for data that is being transferred from one location to another in Windows. Once you copy a selection of text to the Clipboard, you can paste it into a different location within the same Word document, into another Word document, into another Office document such as an Excel spreadsheet, a PowerPoint presentation, an Outlook e-mail message, or even into another application. The Clipboard can contain multiple bits of data from one or many different applications. It's not necessary to open the Clipboard to copy and paste the last thing you copied into a new location. However, if you have saved multiple items to the Clipboard and want to select from a list of the items currently stored, you need to view the Clipboard. To do so, follow these steps:

1. Click the dialog box launcher button in the lower-right corner of the Clipboard group on the Home tab of the Ribbon to see a window like the one in Figure 3.7. You will see a list of

**Figure 3.7.** The Clipboard window

items collected in the Clipboard. Each Clipboard item has an icon indicating the application from which it was copied, and then the first part of the text (or a thumbnail picture if it's a graphic) next to the icon as an identifier.

**2.** If the item you want is on the list, you can click it to paste it directly into your document.

By clicking the drop-down list button next to a selected item on the Clipboard, you can choose to paste or delete the item. From the Clipboard window, you can also click Paste All to paste all Clipboard items into your document, or click Clear All to delete all items from the Clipboard. The Options button provides additional options shown in Figure 3.8. To close the Clipboard, click the dialog box launcher button or click the Close button for the Clipboard window.

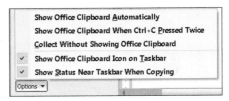

**Figure 3.8.** Clipboard options

## Pasting text

To paste text from the Clipboard into your document, position the insertion point where you want the text inserted, and then press Ctrl+V or click Paste on the Clipboard group of the Home tab on the Ribbon. The text appears at the insertion point location.

### Hiding/Showing Formatting

When you need to insert (or move or delete) text with precision, it's a good idea to make sure that you don't delete hidden codes such as spaces, tabs, and paragraph markers, because this can cause unintended effects. To show paragraph marks and other hidden formatting symbols, click the Paragraph button in the Paragraph group of the Home tab on the Ribbon, or press Ctrl+*. Among other things, you will see dots representing spaces, right arrows representing tab stops, and paragraph symbols representing the ends of paragraphs, as shown in Figure 3.9. If you find

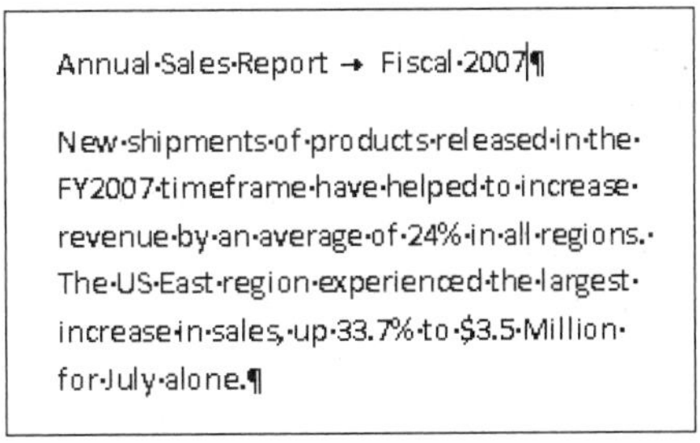

Annual·Sales·Report → Fiscal·2007¶

New·shipments·of·products·released·in·the· FY2007·timeframe·have·helped·to·increase· revenue·by·an·average·of·24%·in·all·regions.· The·US·East·region·experienced·the·largest· increase·in·sales,·up·33.7%·to·$3.5·Million· for·July·alone.¶

**Figure 3.9.** Showing paragraph marks and other formatting codes

this additional coding distracting, you can click the Paragraph button (or press Ctrl+*) again to toggle the mode back to hiding formatting codes.

## Paste Options

It's often the case that text copied from one document or part of a document has different formatting (such as a different font or font size) than the destination document. If you want to insert the text without bringing across whatever fonts and other formatting occurred in the document, you can perform the usual paste operation, as described previously, and then click the Paste Options button that appears in the document near where you insert the new text, as shown in Figure 3.10.

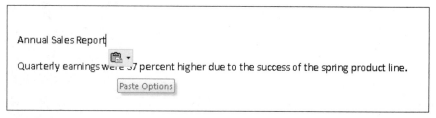

**Figure 3.10.** Paste options

Clicking the Paste Options button gives you a set of most frequently needed paste options to choose from:

- **Keep Source Formatting.**      Brings the font selection or other formatting along from the original copied text.

- **Match Destination Formatting.**  Makes the copied text match the formatting.

- **Keep Text Only.**      Pastes the text characters with no formatting.

- **Use Destination Theme.**      Makes the text match the current theme. (See Chapter 5 for more information on themes.)

In addition to the options for the current paste operation, you can click Set Default Paste to take you directly to the cut, copy, and paste settings of the Word Options window shown in Figure 3.11. This is a very useful new feature: Many Word users will be happy to know that they can finally make the paste operation insert plain text as the default.

| Cut, copy, and paste | |
|---|---|
| Pasting within the same document: | Keep Source Formatting (Default) ⌄ |
| Pasting between documents: | Keep Source Formatting (Default) ⌄ |
| Pasting between documents when style definitions conflict: | Use Destination Styles (Default) ⌄ |
| Pasting from other programs: | Keep Source Formatting (Default) ⌄ |
| Insert/paste pictures as: | In line with text ⌄ |

☑ Keep bullets and numbers when pasting text with Keep Text Only option
☐ Use the Insert key for paste
☑ Show Paste Options buttons
☑ Use smart cut and paste ⓘ   [ Settings... ]

**Figure 3.11.** Setting the default paste options

## *Paste Special*

If you want a more complete set of paste options than is provided on the Paste Options button, you can use the Paste Special command by clicking the drop-down list from the Paste button and clicking Paste Special (as shown in Figure 3.12) or by pressing Alt+Ctrl+V. This opens a dialog box similar to that shown in Figure 3.13. You can either paste the data directly into your file from the Clipboard by selecting the Paste radio button, or paste a link to the data contained in another file by selecting the Paste link radio button. The Paste As and Paste link As options vary, based on the nature of the Clipboard item you are pasting and whether you are pasting the data or pasting a link.

**Figure 3.12.** The Paste Special command

For example, although one option in Figure 3.13 is to paste the selection as a Microsoft Office Word Document Object, it could be a Microsoft Office Excel Worksheet Object or even a WordPerfect 12 Document Object. If you paste the Clipboard item as an application object, you have the option of displaying the pasted object as an icon instead of inserting it as text. When you click the object's icon while viewing the Word document, it launches whatever application is associated with the object and opens the item in a window in that application.

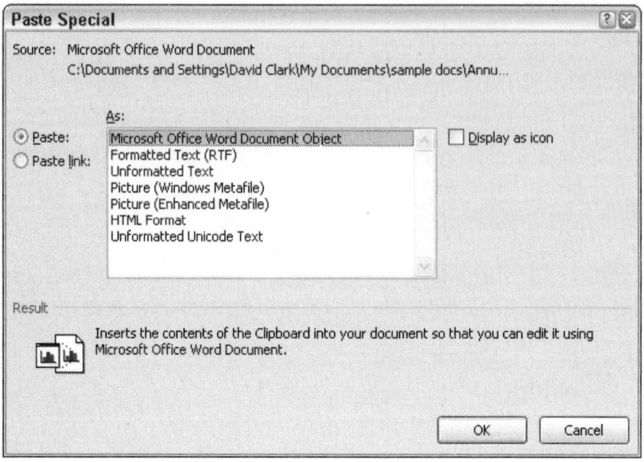

**Figure 3.13.** The Paste Special dialog box

Some additional paste options available with Paste Special are Formatted Text (RTF), HTML Format (for visibility by Web browsers), and Unformatted Unicode Text. (Unicode is an international text standard that gives each character a unique code, in effect resolving problems caused by differences between different operating systems, languages, and character sets.) You can also paste pictures or other graphic elements into your document. See Chapters 17 through 20 for more information on how to do so.

### Paste versus Paste link

If you use Paste link, a copy of the data is stored in your Word document, but the data can be updated and revised in the source file and then Word updates your Word document upon opening or printing the document. Using the Paste link option has many advantages. For example, if you paste data from different departments into a divisional report, you can paste a link with a copy of the actual data. When you open or print the report, you are asked whether Word should update the data from the source document. This feature functions slightly differently for graphics, where you have the option to paste as a link, paste a copy and a link, or paste. The reason for this is that graphics are often very large, and it makes sense to store them in a separate file and pull in the data only when needed (as for printing or displaying on the screen).

## Maintaining links

After you establish a link using the Paste link option, you can manage how the links operate by choosing Microsoft Office ⇨ Finish ⇨ Edit Links to Files to open the dialog box shown in Figure 3.14, which displays a list of links to files that are contained in your document. From this screen, you can force an update of the data by clicking Update Now, open the source document with Open Source, or click Change Source to open a browser window to select an alternate file source. You can also choose to break the link to the source document (retaining the current static version of the pasted data) by clicking Break Link.

If you don't want the link to update automatically, select the link you want to change, then select the Manual update option (the default is Automatic update). You must then select the link and click Update Now when you want to update it. You may also select the Locked option to lock the link and prevent it from being updated at all.

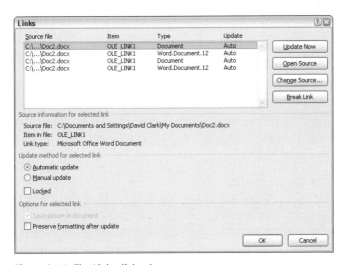

**Figure 3.14.** The Links dialog box

# Deleting text

To delete text without saving it to the Clipboard, select a section of text and press Delete. If no text block is currently selected and you press Delete, it deletes the character to the right of the insertion point. To delete the character to the left of the insertion point, press Backspace. Table 3.2 summarizes the various delete operations.

**Watch Out!**
Don't use the Delete key for cutting and pasting text. Instead, press Ctrl+X or click the Cut (scissors) button from the Clipboard group on the Home tab. If you do delete text accidentally, you can usually undo your mistake by clicking the Undo button (or by pressing Ctrl+Z).

**Table 3.2.** Delete commands

| Keystroke Sequence | Operation |
|---|---|
| Delete | Deletes selected text without moving to Clipboard. If no text selected, deletes character to right of insertion point. |
| Ctrl+Delete | Deletes word or punctuation to the right of insertion point. |
| Backspace | Deletes selected text without moving to Clipboard. If no text is selected, deletes character to left of insertion point. |
| Ctrl+Backspace | Deletes word or punctuation to the left of insertion point. |

# Moving text (cutting and pasting text)

If you want to move text from one location to another in Word, you are essentially copying the text to the Clipboard, deleting it from the original location, and then pasting it from the Clipboard to the destination. In general, the easiest way to do this is to use the mouse to drag the text to the destination. To do so, follow these steps:

1. Select the text you want to move.

2. Move your mouse cursor inside the area of the selected text.

3. Click and hold the left mouse button down while moving the cursor to the point where you want to move the text. The cursor appears as an up arrow pointing to the left with a small clear rectangle below and to the right of it.

4. Release the mouse when the cursor is where you want the text to be. The text appears and moves other text to the right and/or downward. The freshly moved text remains selected, with the Paste Options button below and to the right of it.

There are times when using the drag-and-drop method of moving text is cumbersome, such as when you move the text onto a page further along in the document. While you can still accomplish this with drag and

**Inside Scoop**

You can also copy and paste text with the drag-and-drop method: Use the same procedure as above, but hold down the Ctrl key while holding down the left mouse button. When you release the mouse button, the text is copied (rather than moved).

drop (by dragging the mouse cursor to the bottom of the document until the document scrolls to the destination page), this is awkward, especially if you scroll past the destination and have to scroll back and so on. To avoid this, use the cut-and-paste method by following these steps:

1. Select the text you want to move.

2. Click Cut (the scissors) from the Clipboard group on the Ribbon (or press Ctrl+X or Shift+Delete). This copies the selected text to the Clipboard and then deletes it from its original location.

3. Move the cursor to the point where you want to move the text.

4. Click Paste (the clipboard with a piece of paper over it) from the Clipboard group on the Ribbon (or press Ctrl+V). The text appears and moves other text to the right and/or downward. As with the drag-and-drop method, the freshly moved text remains selected with the Paste Options button below and to the right of it.

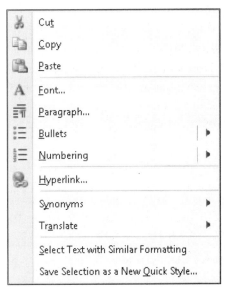

You can also get quick access to the cut, copy, and paste operations by right-clicking selected text. This gives you a menu (shown in Figure 3.15) that includes these commands.

**Figure 3.15.** Right-clicking selected text brings up Cut, Copy, Paste, and other likely commands.

## Finding and replacing text

You can find a specific text string, either to navigate or to replace that string with other text. You can also highlight all instances of a text string within the text to draw attention to each instance for reading and review purposes. To get to the commands for finding and replacing text, click Editing (the binoculars) on the Ribbon to bring up the full Editing group of the Home tab, as shown in Figure 3.16. Although it appears together with Find and Replace in Word, the Go To command is covered in Chapter 4 because it is more of a navigational tool.

## Finding text

There are several ways to refine an operation to find text in a document. I start with a simple find operation to locate the next example of a text string and then show you how to find all instances of a text string, both in a selected block of text or in an entire document.

**Figure 3.16.** Find and Replace commands in the Editing group on the Home tab

### *Finding the next instance of a text string*

To find a text string in a document (*occupants* in this example), follow these steps:

1. Press Ctrl+F or choose Home ⇨ Editing ⇨ Find. This brings up the Find tab of the Find and Replace dialog box shown in Figure 3.17.

**Figure 3.17.** Typing text for a simple Find operation

2. Type **occupants** in the Find what text box. Once you find the text string, you can click in the found text to edit it. The Find and Replace dialog box remains open in the foreground. You can drag it by its title bar to move it out of the way if necessary.

3. Click Find Next to move to the next occurrence of the word *occupants* in the document, as shown in Figure 3.18.

Figure 3.18. Word finds the next instance of the text.

**4.** When you have searched to the end of the document and dealt with all instances of the search string, the message box shown in Figure 3.19 appears. Click OK.

Figure 3.19. Reaching the end of a text search

**5.** Click the Close box, click Cancel, or press Esc to close the Find and Replace dialog box.

To find text within a selected block of text, select the block of text first, and then follow the previous steps. The only difference is that upon completing the search of the section, the dialog box offers you the option of searching the remainder of the document instead of continuing the search at the beginning of the document.

### Finding and selecting all instances of a text string

If you need to find and select all occurrences of a text string, follow Steps 1 and 2 in the previous instructions, but then click Find All. If you currently have no text selected, you just see one option, Main Document. If you have a block of text currently selected, you can choose between finding all instances of the text string in the selected block of text by clicking Current Selection, or by clicking Main Document to search the entire document, as shown in Figure 3.20.

**Inside Scoop**

To cancel a Find operation, press Esc or click Cancel on the Find tab of the Find and Replace dialog box.

**Bright Idea**

Word stores all the search strings in a session. If you need to find a text string again that you've already looked for recently, click the drop-down list button in the Find what text box to select from a list of strings you've already searched for.

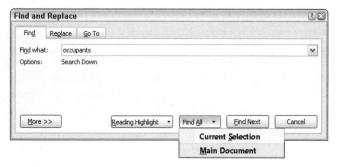

**Figure 3.20.** Finding all instances of a text string

## Finding and highlighting all Instances of a text string

You can search for a text string throughout the document and highlight every instance of the text string (so that you can review each occurrence quickly). To find and highlight all instances of a text string, follow these steps:

**1.** Press Ctrl+F or choose Home ➪ Editing ➪ Find.

**2.** Type the text string you want to find in the Find what text box.

**3.** Click Reading Highlight (or press Alt+R).

**4.** Click Highlight All. All instances of the text string are highlighted, as shown in Figure 3.21.

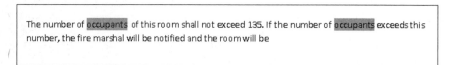

**Figure 3.21.** Highlighting all instances of a text string

To clear highlighting, click Reading Highlight again and then click Clear Highlighting to remove all highlighting created with this command. Don't confuse the Reading Highlight feature with the other highlighting

**Watch Out!**

Note that this is an all-or-nothing feature. If you have separately highlighted several terms in separate searches, clicking Clear Highlighting removes them all no matter what you have as a text string in the Find what text box.

feature that is akin to manually highlighting selections of text. Clicking Clear Highlighting does not remove the other form of highlighting.

## Replacing text

Replacing text is actually two operations: finding a text string and replacing it with another. You can also use this feature to find and delete by replacing the found string with nothing.

Because finding and replacing text can cause unanticipated mischief, there are some things you should bear in mind about Word's default settings and behavior when preparing to do a Replace operation:

- Capitalization is based on the text string you are searching for, not the replacement text string.

- Replacing short words can introduce errors because they may form parts of other words.

- Try to use a long enough (and therefore specific) text string to ensure accurate find operations by Word.

- Check your spelling for your text string. (If you misspell your text, Word doesn't second-guess your work like Google or other Web search engines.)

### Replacing text one instance at a time

In most cases, it is best to replace every instance of a text string one at a time. This way, you have a chance to review each instance for context. For example, if you want to search for every occurrence of *lock* and replace it with *combination lock*, you might come across the phrase *It's nearly nine o'clock*. You wouldn't want to replace that particular instance, because you would end up with *It's nearly nine o'ccombination lock*. To find and replace text of a selected block of text, follow these steps:

1. Press Ctrl+H or choose Home ⇨ Editing ⇨ Replace.

2. Type the text string you want to find in the Find what text box, as shown in Figure 3.22. As you type text, the grayed-out buttons become available at the bottom of the box.

**Figure 3.22.** Typing text to find and replace

**3.** Type the replacement text string in the Replace with text box, or click the drop-down list button to select from the list of previous replacement text strings you've used in the current session, or leave the Replace with text box blank by clicking the text box.

**4.** Click Find Next or press F to locate the first instance of your search string. Word searches your document and selects the text string (the Find and Replace dialog box may move out of the way to show you the selected text), as shown in Figure 3.23.

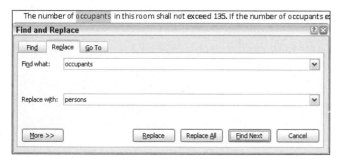

**Figure 3.23.** Word finds and selects the search string to replace.

**5.** If you want to replace the text in this instance, click Replace or press R and the replacement text is entered in the selected area. Word moves to the next instance that it finds of the search string. If you want to skip a particular instance of the text string and not replace it, click Find Next (or press F) instead.

**Watch Out!**
You can't undo just one replacement you notice you made two replacements back; you have to undo all back to that point, so be careful when you review each instance of replacing text.

**6.** When you have searched to the end of the selection and found and dealt with all instances of the search string, the dialog box shown in Figure 3.24 appears. Click Yes to go to the beginning of the document and continue the search, or No to end the search.

**7.** Click the Close box, click Cancel, or press Esc to close the Find and Replace dialog box.

**Figure 3.24.** Reaching the end of a Find and Replace operation

To find and replace text within a selected block of text, select the block of text first, and then follow the previous steps. The only difference is that upon completing the search of the section, the dialog box offers you the option of searching the remainder of the document instead of going to the top of the document.

### Using Replace All (pushing the big red button)

The Replace All button is not really red, but it should be treated that way. When you click Replace All (or press A) during a Find and Replace operation, Word goes through the document and replaces every instance of your search string without showing you each instance. At the end of the operation, you see a dialog box like the one in Figure 3.25, listing the number of instances replaced.

**Figure 3.25.** A dialog box summarizing replacements in a Replace All operation

**Bright Idea**

To reduce the danger of making unintended replacements with a Replace All operation, you can select a block of text smaller than the entire document upon which to perform the Replace All operation. Just make sure to say No when asked to search the remainder of the document.

## Refining your text search

You've seen the basic Find and Replace operations, but there are many ways to refine your search and you can also search for and replace things other than simple text strings. To do so, click More in the Find and Replace dialog box or press M to see the Search Options shown in Figure 3.26. (Once opened, you can click Less or press L to hide the Search Options list once more.) The Replace tab is used in this example, but the options are identical for Find and for Replace.

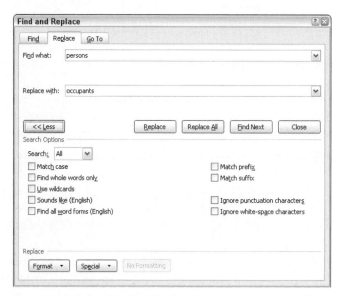

**Figure 3.26.** Find and Replace Search Options

### *Search Options*

The Search drop-down list in the Search Options area pertains to direction of the search. The default setting is All, meaning the search operation starts at the insertion point and works down (toward the end) and then goes to the beginning until it gets to the insertion point where it started. With the Down setting, the Find or Find and Replace operation starts from the current insertion point location and moves toward the end of the document (or selected text). With Up, the Find or Find and Replace operation begins at the insertion point and then works backward toward the beginning of the document (or selected text). Table 3.3 summarizes the behavior of the additional search options, and the following section discusses one of these, wildcards, in more detail.

**Table 3.3.** Search options

| Search Option | Description |
|---|---|
| Search All | Searches entire document or selected text, from insertion point to end of document or selection, then from beginning of document or selection to insertion point. |
| Search Down | Searches document or selected text, starting at insertion point and moving toward end of document. |
| Search Up | Searches document or selected text, starting at insertion point and moving back toward beginning of document. |
| Match case | Matches exact case (uppercase or lowercase) of letters in text string of Find what text box. When selected, uses case of replacement text (does not necessarily match case of found text). |
| Find whole words only | Skips text strings embedded within other words during search. |
| Use wildcards | Allows wildcards in text strings (see section below). |
| Sounds like (English) | Allows searches for homonyms (example: using *sails* to find *sales*). |
| Find all word forms (English) | Searches for related word forms (example: searching for *surface* yields *surface, surfaces, surfaced,* and *surfacing*). |
| Match prefix | Used to find instances of a particular prefix (such as *quasi-*). |
| Match suffix | Used to find instances of a particular suffix (such as *-ing*). |
| Ignore punctuation characters | Used to search for a text string without regard to internal punctuation variations. |
| Ignore white-space characters | Used to search for a text string without regard to internal variations in white-space characters (such as spaces or tabs). |

As you select search options, they appear listed under the Find what text box. Note that some search options are mutually exclusive. For example, you can't select both Use wildcards and Sounds like (English) — you must choose one.

## Using wildcards

If you have a large document and you want to refine your search at the individual character level, you can take advantage of the Use wildcards option. *Wildcards* are characters or sets of characters used in a search string to represent a type or set of characters rather than a literal one. They operate to a certain extent like a wildcard such as a joker in a deck of cards, representing whatever the player needs it to represent. This can be useful when you have a specific text string pattern you want to search for. Table 3.4 shows a list of available wildcards in Word, some of which are admittedly fairly esoteric. The following sections give some more typical examples.

**Table 3.4.** Wildcards in find and replace operations

| Wildcard | Description | Usage |
|----------|-------------|-------|
| ? | Finds a single character | *b?t* finds *bat*, *bet*, *bit*, and *but* |
| * | Finds a string of characters | *b\*t* finds *bat*, *bought*, and *burnt* |
| <(text) | Finds string that starts with *text* | *<(per)* finds *person* and *peril*, but not *interloper* |
| (text)> | Finds string that ends with *text* | *(per)>* finds *interloper* and *caliper*, but not *person* or *vipers* |
| [aei] | Finds any one of specified characters *aei* | *s[aei]t* finds *sat*, *set*, and *sit* |
| [m-z] | Finds characters in range *m-z* | *[a-f]awn* finds *dawn* and *fawn* but not *yawn* (must be in ascending order) |
| [!m-z] | Finds any characters except those in range *m-z* | *[!a-f]awn* finds *lawn* and *yawn*, but not *dawn* or *fawn* |
| {n} | Finds *n* instances of the last character | *sho{2}t* finds *shoot* but not *shot* |
| {n,} | Finds at least *n* instances of the last character | *sho{1,}* finds *shot* and *shoot* |
| {n,m} | Finds *n* to *m* instances of the last character | *3{1,4}* finds *3*, *33*, *333*, and *3333* |
| @ | Finds any number of instances of the last character | *x@* finds *x*, *xxxx*, and so on |

### Searching for a string with one unspecified character

This can be useful when searching for a phrase with some slight varia-tion. For example, if you want to search for all instances of numbered chapters in a book with eight chapters, you could search for them using the *?* wildcard. To do so, follow these steps:

1. Open the Find and Replace dialog box and perform a Find or Replace operation as described earlier.

2. Select the Use wildcards option.

3. Type **Chapter ?** in the Find what text box.

4. Click Find Next. This finds Chapter 1, Chapter 2, and so on.

### Searching for a string of characters

Use the * wildcard to look for a text string with a string of unspecified characters in it. For example, if you are looking for a product name that sometimes begins with *Quikstart* and other times with *Quickstart,* you can find both variations by following these steps:

1. Open the Find and Replace dialog box and perform a Find or Replace operation as described earlier.

2. Select the Use wildcards option.

3. Type **Qui*start** in the Find what text box.

4. Click Find Next. This finds both the *Quikstart* and *Quickstart* variations.

### Searching for a specific list of characters

You can also use wildcards to search for *run* and *ran* in the same search operation. To do so, follow these steps:

1. Open the Find and Replace dialog box for a Find or Replace opera-tion as described earlier.

2. Select the Use wildcards option.

3. Type **r[au]n** in the Find what text box.

4. Click Find Next. This finds instances of either *ran* or *run.*

### Inside Scoop

If you need to search for a character that Word uses as a wildcard while wild-cards are enabled, type a \ before the character (example: use \? to look for ?).

## Finding formatting

Word 2007 has simplified and streamlined the way formatting can be changed to suit your needs. Be sure to read Chapter 5 to see how to make changes quickly and easily. There are times, however, when you need to find a specific example of formatting or find and make a change to that formatting. If you want to find formatting regardless of the text, such as any boldface, follow these steps:

1. Open the Find and Replace dialog box for a Find operation (Ctrl+F).

2. If the Find and Replace dialog box is not expanded to show additional options, click More.

3. Click Format to see the types of formatting that you can search for, as shown in Figure 3.27.

4. Click Font for this example to open the dialog box shown in Figure 3.28. As you can see, you can select from many attributes that relate to fonts. You can select more than one attribute to search for.

5. Click Bold from the Font style drop-down list.

6. Click OK.

7. Click Find Next to find and select the next instance of bold text in your document, or click Find All to find and select every instance of bold text.

To find specific text with formatting, type the text in the Find what text box and then follow the previous procedure to apply formatting.

**Figure 3.27.** Types of formatting for which you can search

**Figure 3.28.** Selecting font attributes for which to search

## Finding and replacing formatting

You can also include formatting in your replacement text, or just change the formatting. To do so, follow these steps:

1. Open the Find and Replace dialog box for a Replace operation (Ctrl+H).

2. If the Find and Replace dialog box is not expanded to show additional options, click More.

3. Click in the Find what text box to select formatting for the text to be found.

4. Click Format to see the types of formatting that you can search for.

5. Click Font for this example. As with a Find operation, you can select from many attributes that relate to fonts. You can select more than one attribute to search for.

6. Click Bold from the Font style drop-down list.

7. Click OK.

8. Click in the Replace with text box to switch to replacement text. Notice that the label above the Format button changes to Replace and the format search options are listed for the Find what text box, as shown in Figure 3.29.

9. Click Format.

10. Click Font.

11. Click Regular in this example from the Font style drop-down list. This removes all the bold from the text.

12. Click Find Next to find and replace individual instances of bold text in your document and replace them with regular text, or click Replace All to remove every occurrence of bold from the text.

As with a Find operation, you can apply formatting to specified find and replacement text. To do so, type the text in the Find what text box and then follow the previous procedure to apply formatting. Next, type text in the Replace with text box and click Format to apply formatting to the replacement text.

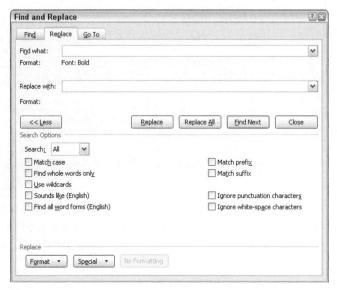

**Figure 3.29.** Adding formatting to the Replace with text string

# Finding special characters

You can search for things besides formatting and text strings in Word. To do so, click Special in the Find and Replace dialog box to see a list of options.

To find a special character, follow these steps:

**1.** Press Ctrl+F.

**2.** Click Special.

**3.** For this example, click Paragraph Mark (or press P). The special character appears as a letter, number, or symbol preceded by a caret symbol (^): in this case, ^p.

**4.** Perform the rest of the Find operation.

**Hack**

There are also codes that you can insert yourself like wildcards, but they are somewhat tricky. I recommend just using the Special menu, since it has a complete list. For the codes, see "Use codes to find letters, formatting, fields, or special characters" in Word's Help system.

You can combine special character searches with text strings and formatting.

## Replacing with special characters

You can also replace with special characters and other items, although it is a subset of what you can search for. To do so, click Special in the Find and Replace dialog box after clicking in the Replace with text box and you see a list of options.

To replace with a special character, follow these steps:

1. Press Ctrl+H.

2. Type what you want to search for in the Find what text box. (For this example, click Special and select Manual Line Break, which will show ^l in the text box.)

3. Click in the Replace with text box.

4. Click Special.

5. For this example, click Paragraph Mark (or press P). The special character appears as a letter, number, or symbol preceded by a caret symbol (^): in this case, ^p.

6. Perform the rest of the Replace operation.

As with Find operations, you can combine special character replacements with text strings and formatting.

## Checking spelling and grammar

As a professional writer and editor, I take full advantage of Word's spelling and grammar checking all the time. This allows me to focus on the fine points of meaning and the clarity and organization of my writing. I tend to check my spelling and grammar as I write whenever a red (for spelling) or green (for grammar) squiggle appears and correct things as I go. However, I also make sure to do a final spelling and grammar check at the end of my document to make sure I catch things that I may have missed along the way. In addition to alerting you as Word perceives potential problems, it takes it upon itself to correct a short list of common typos without your consent as you type along. This feature is called AutoCorrect. (I describe AutoCorrect in more detail shortly.)

**Watch Out!**

Word doesn't check the spelling and grammar of text in Charts, SmartArt, WordArt, Equations, and so on. You need to review or modify these items separately.

If you don't want to have spelling checked as you type, choose Microsoft Office ⇨ Word Options ⇨ Proofing and click Check spelling as you type and Use contextual spelling in the section When correcting spelling in Word so that neither box has a check mark.

# Checking your spelling

To check spelling for your document, choose Review ⇨ Proofing ⇨ Spelling & Grammar from the Ribbon, or just press F7. To check a block of text only, select the block of text and then press F7.

If you have no spelling or grammar errors, you will just hear an alert and see the dialog box shown in Figure 3.30. If, however, there are some potential misspellings or grammatical errors in your document, the dialog box shown in Figure 3.31 appears. This example shows a spelling error.

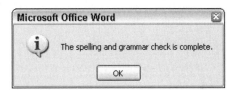

**Figure 3.30.** A spelling and grammar check is complete.

## *Accepting Word's suggested correction*

To accept one of Word's suggested corrections, click the appropriate correction from the list of suggestions and click Change. If you want to change every instance of this misspelling in the document (such as when converting British English *colour* to U.S. English *color*), click Change All. Word moves to the next misspelled word or grammar error in your document.

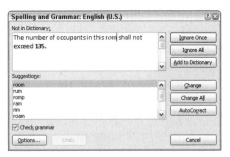

**Figure 3.31.** The Spelling and Grammar dialog box

**Hack**
If you want to turn off grammar correction, when the Spelling and Grammar dialog box first appears, deselect the Check grammar option so that no check mark appears.

### When Word doesn't offer the right correction
If Word identifies an error but doesn't offer a suggested correction or the suggestions in the list are incorrect, you can type the correction your-self by editing the word in question in the Not in Dictionary text box. If satisfied with your correction, click Change to accept your edit or click Undo Edit to try again.

### Adding the correction to AutoCorrect
If you identify an error that you make all the time and want Word to cor-rect it automatically as you type, click AutoCorrect. This corrects all instances of the error in the current document and adds the correction to the AutoCorrect list.

### Ignoring the correction
If Word identifies something that is not in its dictionary but that you know is correct, you have several options. You can ignore the current instance by clicking Ignore, or ignore all instances of the error by click-ing Ignore All.

### Adding a term to your custom dictionary
If Word identifies something that is not in its dictionary but that you know is correct, you can also add it to your custom dictionary. This is par-ticularly useful if you use technical vocabulary or foreign words in your writing. To add a term, make sure you are really spelling it correctly and then click Add to Dictionary.

### Editing your custom dictionary
You can also edit your custom dictionary in Word, either to add a list of specialized vocabulary words that you know you are going to use or to fix inadvertent misspelled words you have added to your custom dictionary.

To add a word or phrase, follow these steps:

1. Choose Microsoft Office ⇨ Word Options ⇨ Proofing.

2. In the When correcting spelling in Office programs section, click Custom Dictionaries. A dialog box like that shown in Figure 3.32 appears.

3. Select the appropriate dictionary from the list (the default custom dictionary is CUSTOM.DIC).

4. Click Edit Word List. A dialog box like the one in Figure 3.33 appears.

5. Type the term you want to add in the Word(s) box. It can be a phrase (such as *sub rosa*) rather than a single word, if need be.

6. Click Add. The new word or phrase appears in alphabetical order in the Dictionary list.

7. When done, click OK three times to confirm your edits and return to the main Word editing screen.

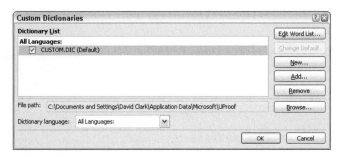

**Figure 3.32.** The Custom Dictionaries dialog box

To delete words from your custom dictionary, follow Steps 1 to 4 in the previous section and then click the word you want to delete from your custom dictionary. Click Delete or Delete All to remove all terms from your custom dictionary. This does not delete the actual file CUSTOM.DIC; it will just be an

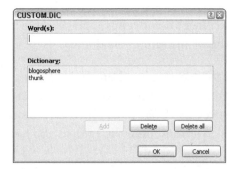

**Figure 3.33.** Editing your custom dictionary

**Watch Out!**
Clicking Add in the Custom Dictionaries dialog box doesn't add a word to your dictionary; it gets you started down the road of adding a new dictionary. Use Edit Word List to add words to your dictionary.

empty file, and will still be available for you to start anew with more terms.

## Contextual spelling

One of the problems with computerized spell checking is that the computer usually can't tell when you type a word that is unlikely in the context but nevertheless not misspelled. For example, if you type "I chopped down an oaf tree" and checked it with a previous version of Word, this mistake would slip right through because *oaf* is definitely a word, although it is not a type of tree. Word 2007 often identifies such mistakes and puts a blue squiggle under the word as you type to indicate that it suspects a mistake. As I mention earlier in this chapter, it also catches mistakes made by using homonyms (words that sound like other words but are spelled differently and have different meanings) such as *pear* and *pair*. By default, this feature is turned on, although you can turn it off.

## Other customized settings

You can change settings for how Word catches spelling errors by choosing Microsoft Office ⇨ Word Options ⇨ Proofing and making changes to the selections in the section When correcting spelling in Office programs shown in Figure 3.34.

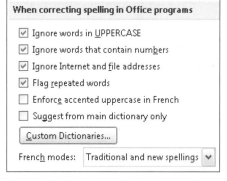

**Figure 3.34.** Changing settings for correcting spelling

## Using exclusion dictionaries

While you cannot edit the main Word dictionary, you can add an exclusion dictionary. This is particularly useful if you flag obscenities or offensive terms (Microsoft gives the example of *public* being misspelled without its *l*, which yields an embarrassing but correctly spelled word). This feature is also useful if

**Inside Scoop**

To suppress the display of the squiggly lines for a particular document or all documents, choose Microsoft Office ⇨ Word Options ⇨ Proofing, and then select the appropriate check box in the Exceptions for section. Note that this does not turn off AutoCorrect.

you have specific spellings that you want to enforce for use within your own organization when more than one are technically correct (such as *grey* and *gray*, or *appendixes* and *appendices*). To add words to an exclusion list, follow these steps:

1. In Microsoft Windows Explorer in Windows XP, go to C:\Documents and Settings\your name\Application Data\Microsoft\Uproof. (If you can't see Application Data in Documents and Settings folder for your user name, choose Tools ⇨ Folder Options ⇨ View, and click Show hidden files and folders in the Advanced Settings section and click OK.)

2. You will see several files. Right-click the file ExcludeDictionaryEN0409.lex.

3. Click Open With.

4. Click Select the program from a list and click OK.

5. Click Notepad or WordPad (*not* Microsoft Office Word) from the list of programs and click OK.

6. Type each word you want to consider to be flagged as misspelled in the exclusion dictionary, using all lowercase letters and separating each word with a line by pressing Enter (including the last word in the list).

7. Choose File ⇨ Save and then File ⇨ Exit to save your changes and exit Notepad or WordPad. When you next open Word, the words listed in your exclusion dictionary appear as misspelled when you check spelling or if you enter them as new text.

You can also use this method to edit your custom dictionary, adding words that will be *accepted* by Word as correctly spelled, the opposite function of the exclusion dictionary. The custom dictionary is normally found in the same location on your computer with the file name CUSTOM.DIC. Use the previous steps to add or delete words to your custom dictionary.

# Checking your grammar and writing style

Grammar and writing style checking in Word are richly implemented and well done. I can't stress enough how useful a tool this is. As a writer, I would buy Word just for this feature alone. In fact, I just reworded the last sentence due to something that caught Word's attention as I was typing. One of the keys to making the grammar and style checking work for you is to adjust the settings to fit your writing style or writing context. By default, Word checks only grammar. Each type of grammatical error category can be turned on or off. If you elect to turn on the style checker, you can also browse through the types of style mistakes that Word catches and decide which ones you want Word to flag.

## Working with grammar and style suggestions

By default, style is not selected. To turn on style checking, choose Microsoft Office ⇨ Word Options ⇨ Proofing, and then click Grammar & Style from the Writing Style drop-down list in the section When correcting grammar in Word. Click OK to accept the changes.

To review your document or selection for grammar and make or ignore suggested changes, follow these steps:

1. To check your document or selection, press F7 or choose Review ⇨ Proofing ⇨ Spelling & Grammar.

2. When your first grammar or style error occurs, the dialog box shown in Figure 3.35 appears. If you are working on your PC, you notice that the text in question appears in green (not red or blue as for spelling).

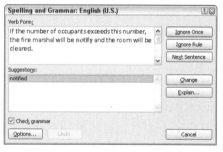

**Figure 3.35.** Reviewing suggestions for correcting grammar and style

At this point, you have several options:

■ If Word provides an appropriate change in the Suggestions list, click Change to accept the suggestion and Word makes the change and goes to the next spelling, grammar, or style error.

■ If you want to make the change by editing the text, you may do so by making the changes in the text box that includes the error.

- If you don't understand why Word thinks this sentence has a grammar or style error, click Explain to get a more thorough explanation of the class of error (such as verb agreement or passive voice).

- If you want to ignore this instance of the error or style suggestion, click Ignore Once.

- If you want to ignore all occurrences of the grammar or style rule (such as Sentences beginning with And, But, and Hopefully), click Ignore Rule.

- To move to the next sentence, click Next Sentence (without resolving the problem).

You can cancel a spelling and grammar checking session at any time by pressing Escape or clicking Cancel.

### Making changes to grammar and style settings

You may find that the nature of your subject matter necessitates long sentences, and so you always get flagged for having sentences more than 60 words long. Alternatively, perhaps you are working in a field that requires you to use more passive voice than is typical. You can turn off individual grammar and style rules by choosing Microsoft Office ⇨ Word Options ⇨ Proofing. In the section When correcting spelling and grammar in Word, click Settings to see the dialog box shown in Figure 3.36. The first three items listed under Require have drop-down lists because they are not universal rules but have preferences. The default is don't check for any of them. For example, the first setting, Comma required before last list item, has to do with what are referred to in the publishing industry as serial commas or Oxford commas. In U.S. book publishing, such commas are usually expected, as in the example: "cars, boats, and trains." In magazine and newspaper publishing, the final comma is often omitted: "cars, boats and trains." To enforce

**Figure 3.36.** Changing grammar and style settings

serial commas, click always in the drop-down list. To mark serial commas as an error, click never. To allow both, leave as don't check.

**Inside Scoop**

To remove all style checking, click Grammar Only in the Writing style drop-down list.

In the Grammar or Style sections, you can turn any of the individual rules on or off by selecting or deselecting the appropriate check box. To change all settings back to their defaults, click Reset All. (The Style section is not shown in Figure 3.36. Scroll down past the Grammar section to see it.)

### What is readability?

If you need to make sure that your writing meets a certain grade-level standard, or if you just want to assess a document with objective, quantifiable metrics, you can use Word's readability statistics. The things measured include number of words per sentence, percentage of passive voice, average number of syllables per word, and so on. Readability statistics are turned off by default. To turn readability statistics on, choose Microsoft Office ⇨ Word Options ⇨ Proofing, and select the Show readability statistics check box in the section When correcting grammar in Word. Upon the completion of a spelling and grammar check, a dialog box like the one in Figure 3.37 appears, dividing the statistics into three categories: Counts, Averages, and Readability. The counts and averages are self-evident. The readability category requires some explanation.

The Passive Sentences statistic lists the percentage of sentences that are written in the passive voice. As an example, the following sentence is in the passive voice: "The ball was picked up."

| Readability Statistics | |
|---|---|
| **Counts** | |
| Words | 222 |
| Characters | 1077 |
| Paragraphs | 21 |
| Sentences | 10 |
| **Averages** | |
| Sentences per Paragraph | 2.0 |
| Words per Sentence | 14.0 |
| Characters per Word | 4.4 |
| **Readability** | |
| Passive Sentences | 0% |
| Flesch Reading Ease | 57.8 |
| Flesch-Kincaid Grade Level | 8.6 |

**Figure 3.37.** Viewing your document's readability statistics

This sentence is in the active voice: "She picked up the ball." Active voice is considered less abstract, therefore more engaging, and more readable.

The Flesch Reading Ease statistic is derived from a formula based on the average length of sentences and the average number of syllables per word, with 100 being the most readable and 0 being the least. Your optimal level is likely in the 60 to 70 range.

The Flesch-Kincaid Grade Level test uses U.S. school grade levels as a measurement, also using a formula based on the average length of sentences and average number of syllables to derive a statistic. Therefore, a score of 9.0 indicates that the text sample is at a reading level suitable for U.S. ninth grade (nine years of school after kindergarten). A level of 13.0 or higher would indicate a university-level writing sample.

# Tweaking AutoCorrect so it doesn't annoy you

Most of the time I am grateful to have Word's AutoCorrect feature. However, one of the most frequently asked questions I get about Word is "How do I turn off that *&#$ AutoCorrect feature?" Usually, just one or two items occasionally get in the way with this feature. I know that many users aren't actually aware of how many times Word has changed *hte* to *the* for them. However, if you spell something differently intentionally as I just did with hte, it's easily corrected: Just delete the corrected word, and type it again in the way you typed it originally. This alerts Word that you intended to type it that way, and it won't correct you a second time. You can turn off specific corrections or entire classes of error if they annoy you, as you soon learn.

## Adding terms to AutoCorrect list

As I mention in the section on checking your spelling, you can add frequently made corrections to your AutoCorrect list to be corrected as you type simply by clicking AutoCorrect when you make that correction during a checking session. You can also review, add, and delete terms from your AutoCorrect list. To do so, choose Microsoft Office ⇨ Word Options ⇨ Proofing ⇨ AutoCorrect Options to see the AutoCorrect dialog box shown in Figure 3.38. The first section has to do with capitalization rules. You can elect to turn on or off any of these rules or modify their exceptions.

**Inside Scoop**

Here's how to turn off AutoCorrect: Choose Microsoft Office ⇨ Word Options ⇨ Proofing ⇨ AutoCorrect Options. Click all the check boxes to remove the check marks. The same applies for Math AutoCorrect and the other tabs in this dialog box.

**AutoCorrect: English (U.S.)**

| AutoCorrect | Math AutoCorrect | AutoFormat As You Type | AutoFormat | Smart Tags |

☑ Show AutoCorrect Options buttons

☑ Correct TWo INitial CApitals

Exceptions...

☑ Capitalize first letter of sentences
☑ Capitalize first letter of table cells
☑ Capitalize names of days
☑ Correct accidental usage of cAPS LOCK key

☑ Replace text as you type

Replace:          With: ◉ Plain text   ○ Formatted text

| (c) | © |
| (r) | ® |
| (tm) | ™ |
| ... | ... |
| :( | ⊗ |
| :-( | ⊗ |
| :) | ☺ |

Add          Delete

☑ Automatically use suggestions from the spelling checker

OK          Cancel

**Figure 3.38.** Making changes to AutoCorrect settings

The second section, Replace text as you type, gives commonly misspelled words and their replacements. You can scroll through the list and add new items. If you add new items, make sure to check that you've spelled them correctly. You can also delete items. Note that deleting an item from AutoCorrect does not affect the regular spelling checker; it just prevents Word from correcting the item as you type.

## Making use of exceptions

You can make changes to the exceptions Word stores for its AutoCorrect rules by adding or deleting words. To do so, click Exceptions in the AutoCorrect dialog box and add or delete text entries as needed.

**Bright Idea**

Take five to ten minutes to review the AutoCorrect list, removing things you think would be annoying and adding any common mistakes you know you make that aren't on the list (making sure to double-check the spelling for your corrections, of course).

## Just the facts

- Learning some keyboard shortcuts and mouse tricks can save you lots of time with basic typing in Word.

- Copying, moving, and deleting text can be accomplished in many ways, some better suited for small changes, other ways better suited for large changes and for precision.

- You can use Word to find and replace text, formatting, and special characters, and there are many ways to fine-tune the search.

- Checking spelling is easy and there are ways to customize the process to suit your needs.

- You can check for style and readability of your documents to improve your writing.

GET THE SCOOP ON...

Choosing the best view ▪ Organizing your thoughts with outlining ▪ Zooming around ▪ Going to the right spot ▪ Splitting your windows ▪ Comparing two documents

# View and Navigate

If you have used earlier versions of Word, you may be confused at first by names of the document views offered. They don't all correspond to earlier versions. First, Word no longer has a View pull-down menu. The View tab on the Ribbon includes most of the same commands, however, including the various document views. The document view buttons have moved from the horizontal scrollbar to the Status bar, and as a result, the horizontal scrollbar disappears if you have your view set to see the page's entire width, thereby saving some screen space for your document. The document view known as Draft corresponds to Normal view in older versions, and Full Screen Reading corresponds to Reading Layout in Word 2003.

In this chapter, I show you each document view and its intended uses. Because I've talked with many writers who like to have the bare minimum of commands visible to reduce distraction while writing, I include a sidebar on how to show the fewest commands possible and still be able to edit the text. (You can make it even simpler if you just want to read the document, and I show you how to do that, too.)

Word's viewing and navigation commands are easy to access, so you can size your view quickly using the Zoom button and Zoom slider on the Status bar. Scrolling through your document is another apparently obvious task where many users never bother to take the two minutes to learn to take advantage of Word's Go To commands, the mouse wheel, and so on. I show you how to use a feature that has been in Word for several versions now and is very convenient and powerful, but few people seem to know about it: the Select Browse Object button on the vertical slider bar. Lastly, I describe how to compare different sections of a document and how to compare different versions of the same document.

## Selecting your document view

Because the process of creating and working with a document involves different activities with different priorities, Word provides you with several ways to view the document that are suited to different phases of its creation. If you think of a document as having a lifecycle, you could start with the Outline view to create a thematic structure for the textual content of the document; use Draft view to write and revise the text; use the Print Layout or Web Layout view for adding formatting, layout, and graphics; and finally Full Screen Reading view for reading a completed document on-screen. You may not need to switch views and go through all these steps, and you may switch often between views during the document-creation process, but this gives you the basic idea of how the views are designed. I use this lifecycle order to describe each of the views.

## Using Outline view to plan what you want to say

If you are planning a document of more than a few paragraphs, it is always a good idea to start with an outline. In fact, sometimes an outline is good for even a few paragraphs. If you start developing your ideas in Outline document view, it is much easier to move sections around and reorder your thoughts. By default, Word opens a new blank document in Print Layout document view. To change to Outline document view, click Outline on the Status bar, or click the View tab on the Ribbon, and then click Outline in the Document Views group shown in Figure 4.1. This brings up Outline document view, as shown in Figure 4.2. Notice that a new Outlining tab appears to the left of the Home tab on the Ribbon, containing groups of commands for outlining,

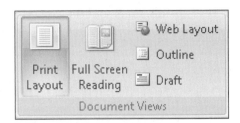

**Figure 4.1.** Document view options

working with a master document, and to close Outline document view.

Don't confuse outlines with tables of contents or multilevel lists. A table of contents is a guide that is added as a summary while the Outline view shows the actual

**Figure 4.2.** The Outline document view showing the Outlining tab on the Ribbon

document. Multilevel lists are lists that occur in the document but are related to the topic at hand and are not topic headings that represent the document's entire hierarchical structure. See Chapter 7 for multilevel lists and Chapter 22 for tables of contents.

### Creating a document outline in Outline view

To create an outline, follow these steps (I provide sample text for illustrative purposes that I use throughout this section):

1. Click Outline or choose View ⇨ Outline from the Ribbon. Notice that to the left of the insertion point is a gray circle containing a minus sign (as shown in Figure 4.2). This indicates that the current outline level contains no sublevels. Note also that the drop-down lists both display Level 1, indicating that the current item is at the first level of your outline, assuming that the title of the document is not part of the outline.

2. Type **Introduction** at the insertion point and press Enter. The insertion point moves to the next line and adds another gray circle with a minus sign, as shown in Figure 4.3.

3. Type **Pre-European Settlement of the Pacific Northwest** and press Enter.

4. Press Tab, and type **European Archeological Research** and press Enter. Notice that the insertion point moves to the right so that the item is indented, and the gray circle of the

**Figure 4.3.** Adding an item to an outline

previous line now contains a
plus, indicating that the previous item now contains a
second-level item, as shown
in Figure 4.4.

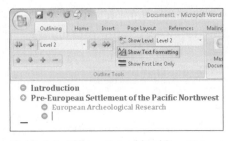

## Promoting and demoting text

To *promote* or *demote* an item (raise
or lower the level of the item in
the outline's hierarchy), you can

**Figure 4.4.** Adding a second-level item to an
outline

use the green left and right arrows, respectively, that surround the current level drop-down list. Clicking the green double arrows either pro-
motes the heading to the highest level in the outline (left double arrows)
or demotes the heading to body text (right double arrows).

To promote an item one level using the same example, follow these
steps:

1. Type **Native Oral Traditions** and press Enter. Now type **Early
   European Settlements.** This last item's topic isn't really subordinate
   to the item Pre-European Settlement of the Pacific Northwest. Early
   European Settlements ought to be Level 1.

2. To promote the Early
   European Settlements item
   to Level 1, click the green
   left arrow in the Outline
   Tools group or press
   Alt+Shift+Left arrow. Early
   European Settlements is now
   promoted to Level 1, as
   shown in Figure 4.5.

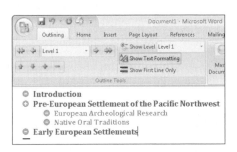

**Figure 4.5.** Promoting an item in the outline

## How much detail do you want to see?

You can type paragraphs or summaries of material that you want to
include as body text in Outline view as well. Don't worry about seeing too

**Hack**
You can use the keyboard shortcut Alt+Shift+Left arrow to promote a heading or
Alt+Shift+Right arrow to demote a heading.

much detail. You can also choose how many levels are visible at a time. To add body text with the same sample, follow these steps:

1. Click to the right of the last letter in the item Native Oral Traditions and press Enter. This adds a new Level 2 item.

2. To change this new blank Level 2 item to Body text, click the Level drop-down list and click Body text.

3. Now create some sample text: Type **A rich oral tradition exists regarding human habitation in the Pacific Northwest, and the Columbia River and surrounding volcanoes play key roles.** Note that if the Level is Body text, there is no plus or minus sign but a smaller gray dot, as shown in Figure 4.6. Because this is the lowest level, no sublevels can exist.

**Figure 4.6.** Typing body text in the outline

### How many levels?

With the running sample, there are now three item levels — two levels of heading and the body text itself. What if you only want to see the Level 1 items? Just click the Show Level drop-down list and select Level 1. Doing so with the sample gives you the view shown in Figure 4.7.

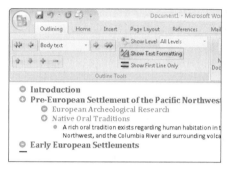

**Figure 4.7.** Showing only Level 1 items

### Collapsing and expanding items

You can fine-tune your Outline view by collapsing or expanding individual parts of your outline, so that you can focus on one section at a time. To expand an item using the sample, follow these steps:

---

**Inside Scoop**

Note that the second item in Figure 4.7 has a plus sign, indicating more items at lower levels. There are nine possible levels, and you can elect to display 1 through 9 to see heading items. You must select All Levels to see body text.

1. Click in the item Pre-European Settlement of the Pacific Northwest to select the item.

2. To expand the section, you have several choices. Double-click the plus sign next to the item to fully expand all subitems, as shown in Figure 4.8. To expand to see one subitem level, click the plus sign (+) in the Outline Tools group of the Outlining tab or press Alt+Shift++ (that is, hold down Alt and Shift while pressing the + key). Repeat the procedure to further expand the subitems.

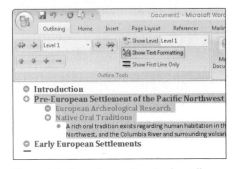

**Figure 4.8.** Expanding an item to show all subitems

To collapse an expanded item using the sample, follow these steps:

1. If not already selected, click the item to be collapsed by clicking to the left of it (it's only necessary to select the first line of the item).

2. To fully collapse an item, double-click the plus sign to the left of the item. To collapse the item one level at a time (starting with body text and working up toward Level 1), click the minus sign (–) in the Outline Tools group of the Outlining tab or press Alt+Shift+– (that is, hold down Alt and Shift while pressing the – key), as shown in Figure 4.9. Repeat the procedure to further collapse the subitems.

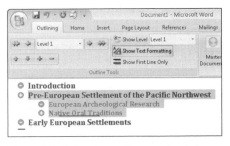

**Figure 4.9.** Collapsing an item one level at a time

### Showing the first line only

If you have many multiline items, or if you want to show just the first line of body text items, click Show First Line Only or press Alt+Shift+L. All multiline items display their first line only, followed by an ellipsis (...) to indicate that there is more text to view, as shown in Figure 4.10. To show the additional lines again, click Show First Line Only or press Alt+Shift+L again to turn the feature off.

**Showing or hiding text formatting**

By default, Word displays Level 1 items with their formatting intact, with a corresponding large font, Level 2 items in smaller font, and so on. If you find this distracting or impractical (it is especially impractical after more than a few levels) you can click Show Text Formatting to turn this feature off, giving you a plain text view for all items in the outline, as shown in Figure 4.11. Click Show Text Formatting again to turn the feature back on.

**Figure 4.10.** Showing the first line of text only

**Figure 4.11.** Hiding text formatting

## Moving items up and down in the outline

One of the main reasons to use the Outline view is that you can move large sections of your document around while still keeping an eye on the big picture. Using cutting and pasting commands or dragging blocks of text around is more cumbersome and more prone to error. To move a section using your sample, follow these steps:

1. Select the collapsed item (and all its subitems) that you want to move. For the example, double-click the gray circle to the left of Native Oral Traditions to collapse the item.

2. Click the up arrow in the Outline Tools group of the Outlining tab (or press Alt+Shift+Up arrow) to move the selection up one item in the outline, as shown in Figure 4.12.

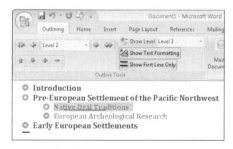

To move an item down in the outline, use the same procedure but click the down arrow in the Outline Tools group of the Outlining tab (or press Alt+Shift+ Down arrow).

**Figure 4.12.** Moving an item up one level

**Watch Out!**

If you have an item expanded and you select just the top level, the sublevels will not move along with the top-level item. To move subitems along with the top-level item, fully collapse the item before performing the move operation.

## Using the Master Document feature

In previous versions of Word, it sometimes made sense on large documents, such as book-length projects, to work with a master document and subdocuments. I give a summary of these features only, because, with the increased speed and capacity of modern PCs, working with master and subdocuments is no longer necessary, although the feature remains intact in Word 2007 for backward compatibility's sake. You create a master

### Making the Simplest Screen Possible

Some writers prefer to have as few bells and whistles in front of them as possible so that they can devote their concentration to their words. While Word 2007's Ribbon is an improvement for finding commands and previewing the effects of formatting on your document, it uses quite a bit of screen space and can be distracting. If you are a writer who needs a screen that looks as much like a white sheet of paper as possible, follow these tips to streamline the screen so that there is a minimum of distraction:

■ Use Draft view.

■ Press Ctrl+F1 to hide the Ribbon.

■ If the Ruler is visible, click the View Ruler button to hide it.

■ Click Customize Quick Access Toolbar, and remove any unwanted commands.

■ Right-click the Status bar and deselect any displayed items.

■ Right-click the Windows taskbar and click Properties, then select the Auto-hide the taskbar option.

When you complete these changes, you will have as close to a plain sheet of paper as you can get in Word, but you are still able to use editing commands. Remember, you can always use the Full Screen Reading document view if you just want to read the document without editing.

document by adding a subdocument to your current document. To do so, choose View ⇨ Outline ⇨ Show Document ⇨ Master Document ⇨ Create (to create a new subdocument) or View ⇨ Outline ⇨ Show Document ⇨ Master Document ⇨ Insert (to insert an existing document). Each subdocument is stored as a separate file in Windows (thus when you create a new subdocument using the Create command, you are asked to supply a name and folder location). When viewing the master document, you can show all subdocuments as part of the master document or choose Master Document ⇨ Collapse Subdocuments to collapse the subdocuments. Collapsing a subdocument shows a link to the subdocument file, as shown in Figure 4.13. Right-clicking the lock icon brings up commands related to the link. Commands available by clicking Master Document are summarized in Table 4.1.

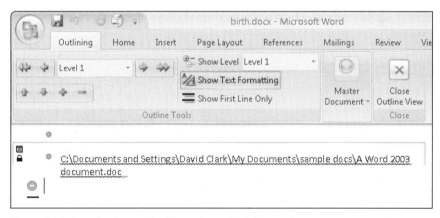

**Figure 4.13.** A master document with a collapsed subdocument

| Table 4.1. Master document commands | |
|---|---|
| **Command** | **Use** |
| Show Document | Toggle command that displays or hides the controls for the links to subdocuments |
| Collapse Subdocuments | Collapses contents of subdocuments and displays only a hyperlink to subdocument file location |
| Expand Subdocuments | Expands subdocuments to display contents within master document |
| Create | Creates subdocument (in a separate file) |

*continued*

**Table 4.1.** *continued*

| Command | Use |
|---|---|
| Insert | Inserts a subdocument into current master document from an existing file |
| Unlink | Deletes the link to a subdocument and makes subdocument contents permanently part of master document |
| Merge | Merges multiple subdocuments into one subdocument |
| Split | Splits document; all content past the insertion point becomes part of a new subdocument |
| Lock Document | Prevents any changes made in master document from being transferred back to subdocuments |

## Using Draft view to focus on writing

By default, Word 2007 opens in Print Layout mode, which shows all parts of the document that print on the page. However, if you want to maximize the writing area, or if you want to focus on writing and revising content and not be distracted by page headers, page footers, or gaps between printed pages, then select Draft document view. To do so, click Draft from the Status bar or choose View ⇨ Draft from the Ribbon. To give a sense of the differences, compare Figure 4.14, which shows a document with two-column text and a page header crossing from one page to the next in Page Layout document view, with Figure 4.15, which shows the same section of text in Draft document view.

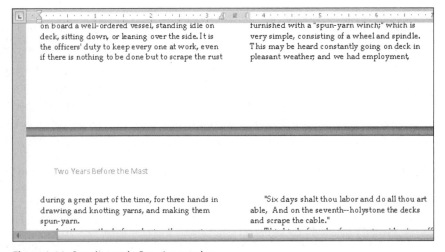

**Figure 4.14.** Sample text in Page Layout view

Note that in Page Layout view, both columns are shown as they will appear on the page, while in Draft view they appear as one long column. No page header containing the title is seen in Draft view, and page breaks are marked only with a dotted line. Draft mode is particularly useful when working with multicolumn text.

ship--such as spun-yarn, marline, seizing-stuff, etc.--are made on board. The owners of a vessel buy up incredible quantities of "old junk," which the sailors unlay, after drawing out the yarns, knot them together, and roll them up in balls. These "rope-yarns" are constantly used for various purposes, but the greater part is manufactured into spun-yarn. For this purpose every vessel is furnished with a "spun-yarn winch;" which is very simple, consisting of a wheel and spindle. This may be heard constantly going on deck in pleasant weather; and we had employment, during a great part of the time, for three hands in drawing and knotting yarns, and making them spun-yarn.

    Another method of employing the crew is, "setting up" rigging. Whenever any of the standing rigging becomes slack, (which is continually happening), the seizings and

**Figure 4.15.** Sample text in Draft view

# Using Print Layout view to see how things will look when printed

Print Layout document view is the default view when working in Word. (To return to Print Layout from Draft, Web Layout, or Outline document view, choose View ⇨ Print Layout from the Ribbon; to return to Print Layout view from Full Screen Reading view, click Print Layout.) Print Layout view shows you essentially what the document will look like when printed. It is particularly useful when you work with page layout, text formatting, and inserting nontext elements such as pictures or charts into your document.

# Using Web Layout view to see your document as a Web page

Web Layout document view is for use when working with documents that will ultimately become Web pages. To access Web Layout view, click Web Layout on the Status bar, or choose View ⇨ Web Layout on the Ribbon. Because Web pages are not divided into finite rectangular paper pages, but are scrollable pages of indeterminate length, no page numbers or page breaks appear when viewing a document in Web Layout view (unless you have at some point inserted page breaks manually). For more information on creating Web pages using Word, see Chapter 10.

**Bright Idea**

For reviewing how things will actually look in print, use the Print Preview feature. Print Preview more directly corresponds to print on the page than Page Layout. For example, Print Preview suppresses nonprinting characters such as paragraph marks. To learn more about Print Preview, see Chapter 9.

## Using Full Screen Reading view to read a document

Full Screen Reading document view is designed for reading a document. Although you can set this mode to allow typing and editing, it's more suited to reading. This is essentially an e-book reader format. To read a document in Full Screen Reading document view, click Full Screen Reading on the Status bar or choose View ⇨ Full Screen Reading from the Ribbon. When you do so, a screen like the one in Figure 4.16 appears. As you can see, the user interface is greatly simplified. It is reduced to a taskbar at the top and two arrows on the page used as page turners — when you mouse over them they turn into hands for turning the page. The Tools command brings up common tasks associated with reading a document on-screen, as shown in Figure 4.17. Clicking View Options gives you access to commands related to viewing the document, such as increasing or decreasing text size, and viewing one or two pages at a time. Some of these options are shown in Figure 4.18.

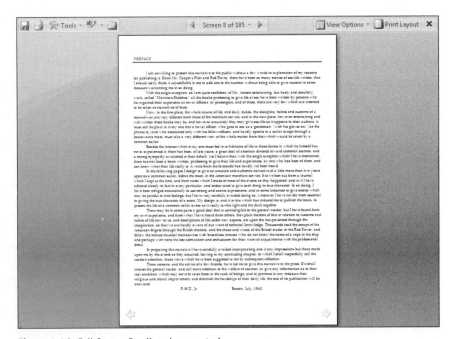

**Figure 4.16.** Full Screen Reading document view

## Using Zoom to size your document view

Word 2007 has made it easy to zoom in or out and view your document at a different size: Just click and drag the Zoom slider shown in Figure 4.19. Drag the slider bar to the left to zoom out and make the text smaller (down to 10 percent) or to the right to zoom in and make the text bigger (up to 500 percent). The size in percentage is shown to the left, where the middle of the slider is 100 percent. Alternatively, you can click Zoom Out (the minus button at the left of the slider) or click Zoom In (the plus button at the right of the slider). Using the slider changes the Zoom percentage in increments of 1 percent. Clicking the Zoom In and Zoom Out buttons changes the Zoom percentage in increments of 10 percent.

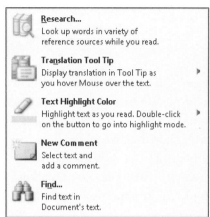

**Figure 4.17.** Tools for Full Screen Reading document view

Clicking the Zoom percentage window opens the Zoom dialog box shown in Figure 4.20. This dialog box includes a preview showing the size of the monitor relative to the page, as well as a sample of text size. Select radio buttons to zoom to 200, 100, or 75 percent size. You can also zoom to Page width, Text width, Whole page, or Many pages. If you click the Many pages radio button (available only in Print Layout view), you can select how

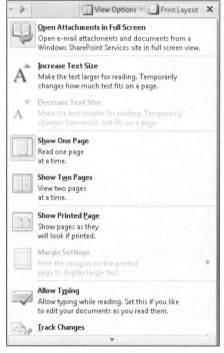

**Figure 4.18.** View Options for Full Screen Reading document view

**Watch Out!**

If you take a ruler and put it up to the monitor, you see that the inch mark at 100 percent bears no relation to the actual linear measurement. You can rely on the ruler being accurate when the document is printed, however.

many pages you want to see at a time by clicking the button immediately below the Many pages radio button. (There is a practical limit, however; you can't show pages smaller than 10 percent of their original size.) You can also type in a percent or change the scrolling value with up and down arrows.

**Figure 4.19.** The Zoom slider and button controls on the Status bar

## Scrolling through your document

There are many ways to scroll through your document. Drag the vertical scroll bar slider to the right of the page to scroll up or down through your document without moving the insertion point. All other scrolling meth-

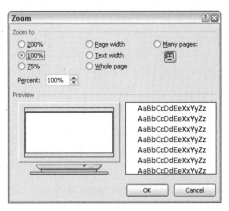

**Figure 4.20.** The Zoom dialog box

ods (except using the mouse wheel) move your insertion point so that it displays in the area of the document that is currently visible. Using the vertical scroll bar to move to another area of text also leaves any selected block of text intact. Using other navigation methods to move through the document automatically removes selection when moving the insertion point to the new area. If you are viewing a page at a size where the left and right edges are not visible, you also see a horizontal scroll bar. Drag the slider to shift the view to the left or right.

**Hack**

If you have a mouse with a wheel, you can use the wheel to zoom in and out by holding down the Ctrl key and rolling the wheel forward to enlarge (zoom in) and backward to reduce (zoom out).

**Hack**

You can right-click the vertical slider to Scroll Here (takes you to the point of the mouse click), Top, Bottom, Page Up, Page Down, Scroll Up (moves up one line), or Scroll Down (moves down one line). Clicking the horizontal slider allows you to Scroll Here, to the Left Edge, Right Edge, Page Left, Page Right, Scroll Left, and Scroll Right.

## Browsing by objects

The Select Browse Object button (Alt+Ctrl+Home) on the vertical scroll bar is a very useful tool that few people seem to be aware of. Figure 4.21 shows the windows you see when you click the Select Browse Object button. Mouse over the individual icons to see what type of object each icon represents. Table 4.2 shows a list of objects you can select with this

**Figure 4.21.** The Select Browse Object button

button. Once selected, you can click the double arrows to go to the next instance of the selected object. The default object selected is a page, so clicking the double downward-pointing arrow takes you to the next page.

**Table 4.2.** Browsing by objects

| Button | Object | Description |
|---|---|---|
| {a} | Field | Goes to next or previous merge field |
| | Endnote | Goes to next or previous endnote |
| | Footnote | Goes to next or previous footnote |
| | Comment | Goes to next or previous comment |
| | Section | Goes to next or previous section |
| | Page | Goes to next or previous page |
| → | Go To | Brings up the Go To tab of the Find and Replace dialog box |

*continued*

| Button | Object | Description |
|--------|--------|-------------|
| **Table 4.2.** *continued* | | |
| 🔍 | Find | Brings up the Find tab of the Find and Replace dialog box |
| ✏️ | Edits | Goes to next or previous edit |
| ☰ | Heading | Goes to next or previous heading |
| 🖼️ | Graphic | Goes to next or previous graphic |
| ▦ | Table | Goes to next or previous table |

## Using the mouse wheel

If you have a mouse wheel, you can use it much like a vertical scroll bar. Roll the wheel forward to move up in the document and backward to move down. If you click the mouse wheel, an indicator with an up arrow, a dot, and a down arrow appears on the screen. Moving your mouse up on the screen scrolls the screen up, and the indicator changes to an up arrow. The farther you move the mouse up the screen, the faster the screen scrolls upward. If you move the pointer down past the center of the screen, the indicator changes to a down arrow. The more you move the mouse down, the faster it scrolls downward. To stop using the mouse wheel to scroll, click the left mouse button or the mouse wheel.

## Using the cursor keys

You can use the cursor keys to scroll through the document. As mentioned earlier, doing so moves the insertion point (and therefore removes selection from any block of text currently selected). The tear-out card for this book lists cursor key combinations and shortcuts for moving through the text.

**Hack**

Once you choose an object with the Select Browse Object button, you can press Ctrl+PageUp or Ctrl+PageDown to go to the previous or the next object, respectively.

# Using Go To

Use Word's Go To command to jump to many types of specific locations in your text. To use Go To, press Ctrl+G or choose Home ⇨ Editing ⇨ Go To on the Ribbon. This brings up the Go To tab of the Find and Replace dialog box, as shown in Figure 4.22. The Go to what list box allows you to select the type of location to which you want to go. Table 4.3 describes the various types of jump locations available as well as additional options or behavior. The default type of jump location for the Go To command is Page. To go to a specific page, type the page number in the Enter page number text box and click Go To. This brings you to the specified page and moves the insertion point to that page. Unless you click Close, the dialog box remains open. You can also use + and – and a number to move a specified number of pages. For example, to move eight pages forward, type **+8** in the Enter page number text box. Many of the other types of jump locations function exactly the same way: Section, Line, Footnote, Endnote, Graphic, Equation, and Heading. The other types have some unique behaviors described in Table 4.3.

**Figure 4.22.** The Go To tab of the Find and Replace dialog box

**Table 4.3.** Jump location types for the Go To command

| Type | Description |
| --- | --- |
| Page | Type *n* to go to page *n*, type **+n** to go forward *n* pages, or type **-n** to go back *n* pages. |
| Section | Type *n* to go to section *n*, type **+n** to go forward *n* sections, or type **-n** to go back *n* sections. |
| Line | Type *n* to go to line *n*, type **+n** to go down *n* lines, or type **-n** to go up *n* lines. |

*continued*

## Table 4.3. *continued*

| Type | Description |
|------|-------------|
| Bookmark | Type **bookmark name** or select from drop-down list. |
| Comment | Type **reviewer's name** or select from drop-down list; type **+n** to go forward n comments or type **-n** to go back n comments. |
| Footnote | Type **n** to go to footnote n, type **+n** to go forward n footnotes, or type **-n** to go back n footnotes. |
| Endnote | Type **n** to go to endnote n, type **+n** to go forward n endnotes, or type **-n** to go back n endnotes. |
| Field | Type **field name** or select from drop-down list; type **+n** to go forward n fields or type **-n** to go back n fields. |
| Table | Type **n** to go to table n, type **+n** to go forward n tables, or type **-n** to go back n tables. |
| Graphic | Type **n** to go to graphic n, type **+n** to go forward n graphics, or type **-n** to go back n graphics. |
| Equation | Type **n** to go to equation n, type **+n** to go forward n equations, or type **-n** to go back n equations. |
| Object* | Type **object name** or select from drop-down list; type **+n** to go forward n instances of the selected object type or type **-n** to go back n instances of the selected object type. |
| Heading | Type **n** to go to heading n, type **+n** to go forward n headings, or type **-n** to go back n headings. |

*Objects in this case refer to things such as embedded Microsoft Office Excel Worksheets or an Adobe Acrobat Document.

You can insert bookmarks into your document. These are invisible when printed but can serve as navigation aids while reading or revising a longer document. To add a bookmark, move the insertion point to where you want the bookmark, and then choose Insert ⇨ Links ⇨ Bookmark. This opens the Bookmark dialog box shown in Figure 4.23. To add a new bookmark, type a name (it can be no longer than 40 characters and can only contain letters or numbers and no punctuation). From this dialog box you can also delete any bookmarks, sort them by name or location, hide them, or go to a selected bookmark.

# Working with windows

**Figure 4.23.** Working with bookmarks

If you work with a larger document, you may find it necessary to open more than one window for the same document so that you can compare two sections of text, or perhaps perform cut and paste operations. You may also want to open and work with two documents. You can access commands related to windows (small w) in the Window group of the View tab of the Ribbon.

## New Window

To open a new window in the current document, choose View ⇨ New Window. This opens a new window in the foreground that takes up the entire screen and is a duplicate of the original single document window. With one window open, the top line of the screen appears with the filename and application (*Filename*.docx - Microsoft Word). When you have more than one window open for the file, each window is numbered (*Filename*.docx:1 - Microsoft Word, Filename.docx:2 - Microsoft Word, and so on).

## Switch Windows

Once you open a second window, you can switch between them (having one in front of the other) by choosing View ⇨ Switch Windows on the Ribbon and selecting the window you want to be in the foreground from the list like the one shown in Figure 4.24. To close a second window for a single document, click the window's Close button. If you are prompted to save changes, that means you are closing the last window and therefore closing the file itself, so take care

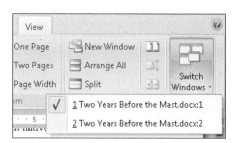

**Figure 4.24.** Switching between two window views of the same document

to save changes before closing. You can switch between two separate open documents in the same way using the Switch Windows command.

You can also switch windows by clicking the button on the Microsoft Windows taskbar for the window that you want in the foreground. Because the Windows taskbar button often only has room to display the first part of the filename, you might have to mouse over the window's button on the taskbar to see the window's full name and number, as shown in Figure 4.25.

**Figure 4.25.** Switching between two windows using the Microsoft Windows taskbar

## Split

You can also split a window into two views by choosing View ⇨ Split on the Ribbon. This displays a gray horizontal bar across the screen, as shown in Figure 4.26. Use the mouse or cursor keys to place it between the lines where you want to split the window into two views, and then click the mouse or press Enter to split the document. The document is now split into two views, as shown in Figure 4.27. Moving the cursor to the place between the two views changes the cursor to a Resize tool that you can drag with your mouse to make one view larger. To remove a split, choose View ⇨ Remove Split on the Ribbon.

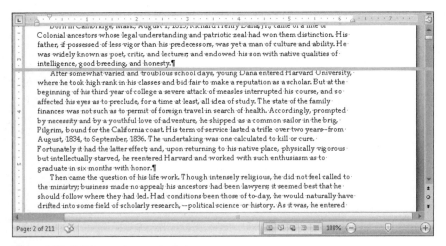

**Figure 4.26.** Splitting a document window

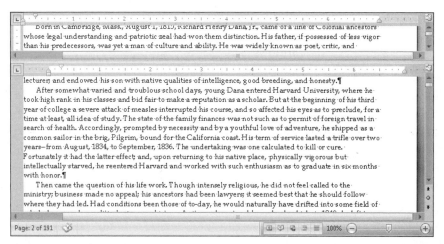

**Figure 4.27.** A split window view

## Arrange All

Choose View ⇨ Arrange All on the Ribbon to have all open windows showing at the same time, as shown in Figure 4.28. You can use this mode to compare documents or cut and paste text between documents. To view one window at a time, click the window and then click the Maximize button.

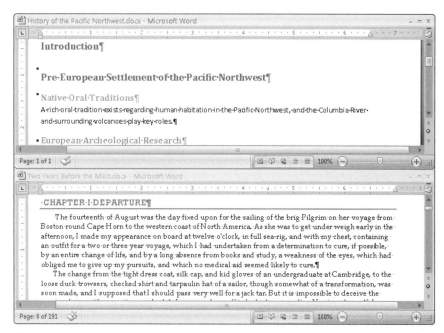

**Figure 4.28.** Using Arrange All to bring all windows to the foreground

**Hack**

Depending on your screen resolution and number of open windows, Arrange All sometimes hides the Ribbon to show more of the document. If this happens and you need access to the Ribbon, drag the active window's corner and stretch it until you see the Ribbon again.

## Viewing two documents side by side

Sometimes it is easier to compare two documents side by side, particularly if you compare two files that are in fact two versions of the same document. To do this, open each file and choose View ➪ View Side by Side. This displays two windows side by side as shown in Figure 4.29. Once arranged side by side, you can have each document scroll at the same time by choosing View ➪ Synchronous Scrolling in either document's window. To turn off synchronous scrolling, choose the command a second time. To swap the documents from left to right, choose View ➪ Reset Window Position in the right window.

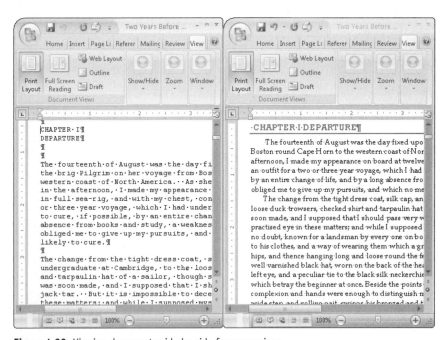

**Figure 4.29.** Viewing documents side by side for comparison

## Just the facts

- Choosing the right document view saves time and effort.

- Using Outline view can help in organizing your document and moving around sections of text efficiently.

- Word has lots of quick and easy ways to enlarge or reduce the size of text for ease of reading or stepping back to look at page layout.

- You can view more than one part of a single document or several documents at a time to compare and cut and paste efficiently.

- You can compare two versions of the same document side by side and have them scroll in a synchronized manner.

# Get the Look Just Right

**GET THE SCOOP ON...**
Using a template ■ Adding content controls ■ Making the
most of Quick Styles ■ Working with styles

# PART II

# Get the Look Faster with Templates and Styles

I f you already have a rich inventory of customized templates, you can import templates and styles you have toiled over in previous Word versions. However, it really is worth the effort to make sure to take advantage of Quick Styles and Themes. If you work with these features, you have sweeping control over your documents. As one might expect, the Quick Styles and Themes provided by Microsoft "out of the box" are serviceable enough. If you want your organization or personal work to stand out from the rest, though, it's best to learn how to add your own Quick Styles and Themes. If you work in an organization with specific fonts, color palettes, and/or enforced design specs, Quick Styles and Themes are a perfect way to streamline the process of rendering new documents in the corporate format. Quick Styles and Themes also make it easier for a smaller organization to have a consistent look. Quick Styles are covered in this chapter. Themes are covered in Chapter 8.

One of the reasons I stress learning to use Quick Styles and Themes is what you can do with them in combination with templates. Microsoft provides a small starter set of basic templates along with Office 2007, but the number and variety of ready-made documents available online is much larger. When templates first appeared, they were really only a basic starter set of the most general business forms: great if you needed to come up with a letterhead in a hurry, but not particularly helpful if you needed to create a more complex or specific document. Now many of the templates are very specific to individual industries or tasks, such as a collection letter, power of attorney, or direct deposit authorization. If you have added your own styles to the style gallery and have created customized themes, you can apply them to Word 2007 templates and literally change them in an instant to your personal style or that of your organization.

# Creating your document using a template

In Chapter 1, I describe how to open a blank document, and it might leave you with the impression that you can elect to use a template or not. In reality, every document you create uses a template. If you don't specify a template, or you start Word from the Start menu rather than by opening an existing document, then by default you open a blank document that uses the Normal.dotm template.

## What you need to know about Normal.dotm

The file Normal.dotm works much as Normal.dot worked in earlier versions of Word. This file stores your default style settings. Some of the default settings are different in Word 2007. For example, if you open a blank document (thereby using the Normal.dotm template), your font is set to Calibri in 11 points. In earlier versions, this would have been 12-point Times New Roman. (Fonts and font sizes are covered in more detail in Chapter 6.) As with earlier versions, your initial paragraph style is aligned left (with a ragged-right margin), and the style name for the default paragraph style is Normal. However, there are also a set of default styles for headings, numbered lists, and so on. One new aspect if you are familiar with earlier versions is that in Word 2007 there is also a default theme.

### Making changes to Normal.dotm

You can edit and make changes to Normal.dotm just as you can with any other template file, which I cover later in this chapter. Because it is the template used for every new blank document, it's best to confine yourself to setting such things as paper size, page margins, default theme, default style set, and so on, and not to add any text or graphics. Normal.dotm is not the file to use to create a corporate letterhead or other such form. It holds the settings you want to keep track of when you want to start with a blank piece of paper. For example, if you want to use Garamond as your default font at all times, or if you always use A4 or legal (8.5-x-14-inch) paper instead of U.S. letter size (8.5 x 11), you can make these changes to the Normal.dotm file. Every blank document you begin starts with these settings as defaults.

To open and edit Normal.dotm, follows these steps:

**1.** Open Word and choose Microsoft Office ⇨ Open.

**2.** Click Trusted Templates in the Look in navigation bar.

**3.** Select Normal.dotm, and click Open.

Alternatively, you can use Windows Explorer to find and double-click Normal.dotm, which is by default in the following location: `C:\\Documents and Settings\[Your user name]\Application Data\Microsoft\Templates`.

Note that you may need to choose Tools ⇨ Folder Options ⇨ View, and select Show Hidden Files and Folders if Application Data doesn't appear in your user name's folder.

Customized Quick Access Toolbar settings, customized keyboard shortcuts, and macros can also be stored in Normal.dotm (hence the file extension .dotm, meaning a Word 2007 template file containing macros). I tend to accumulate a certain number of customized commands and a preferred set of QAT buttons that I use in a broad range of documents, so it makes sense to store them in Normal.dotm rather than in a more specialized document or template file. If you do spend any amount of time storing settings to Normal.dotm, make sure to back up a copy of the file.

### What happens if Normal.dotm is deleted?

If for some reason Normal.dotm is deleted or corrupted, Word creates a new one using Word's default settings when you next open Word. However, if you spend a good deal of time customizing your Normal.dotm template, it makes sense to back up the file so that you can restore it if it is deleted.

## Choosing a template

Now that we've dispensed with what amounts to the default template, let's investigate customized templates. Templates are ready-made document

**Watch Out!**

Make sure you use templates from a trusted source. Because templates often contain macros, they can also be used to cause mischief. By default, Word does not enable macros when opening templates. Only enable macros if you trust the source of the template.

formats that you create yourself or get from Microsoft or others. Some examples are letterhead stationery, business cards, invoices, and resumes. Word 2007 comes with a starter set of basic templates, and, assuming you have Internet access as you work with Word, you have access to many more templates. You can also create your own templates or work with those provided to you in your organization. Templates can be stored locally on your hard drive, on a network server, or can be downloaded from the Internet.

### *Starting a new document using an installed template*

To start a new document using a template that is already installed on your PC, follow these steps:

1. Start Word and choose Microsoft Office ⇨ New to see a window like that shown in Figure 5.1.

2. The left pane of the window is a list of template categories. Click Installed Templates to see a window like Figure 5.2.

3. Scroll down through the Installed Templates list, and click Median Letter and then Create. A new business letter opens, with fields for you to type common information such as sender company name, sender company address, and so on, a portion of which is shown in Figure 5.3.

4. To add text to one of the text fields, click anywhere in the field. In this example, click the words TYPE THE SENDER COMPANY NAME at the top of the page. A blue tab appears to the left of the field, as shown in Figure 5.4.

5. Type the company name in the sender company name field. In this example, type **John Wiley & Sons, Inc.**

6. To save the file generated using a template, click Save. You need to assign it a name. In this example, type **Sample Letter** in the File name text box and click Save. Note that the document is saved in Word Document (*.docx) format.

**Figure 5.1.** The New Document window

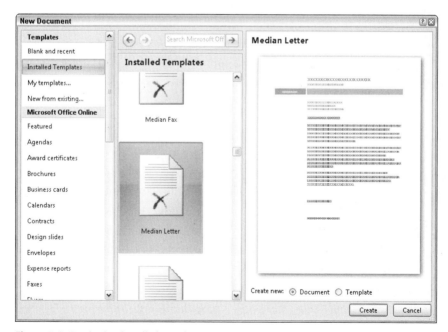

**Figure 5.2.** Previewing installed templates

**Figure 5.3.** A Business Letter template with text fields

**Figure 5.4.** Selecting a field in which to type text

### Starting a new document using a template from Microsoft Office Online

If your PC is connected to the Internet, you can take advantage of the large and frequently updated gallery of templates available through Microsoft Office Online. To access online templates, make sure your PC is connected to the Internet and then choose Microsoft Office ⇨ New. From the left pane of the New Document window, you can select a category of template from the Microsoft Office Online list (using this method automatically narrows the search to Word templates only). Alternatively, you can take your Web browser to office.microsoft.com and click Templates from the left navigation bar to view a list of templates. This method differs only slightly from the one described here.

Microsoft creates many of its own templates, but some are provided by other companies or individuals. In fact, you can create and submit a template yourself or suggest one that needs to be done. Many templates are provided at no charge, but there are also commercial template bundles available. You can browse templates by category. Some sample categories are agendas, business cards, contracts, forms, and invitations. Some categories are sufficiently large that they have subcategories. You can also perform a text search to find a template, and you can filter your search by trust level (electing to hide or show templates provided by other users in the community). You can also filter by Office application.

**Hack**

If you look for a Word template with your Web browser, be sure to filter your search to look only for Word templates (as opposed to Outlook, Excel, or InfoPath templates). This greatly simplifies your search.

Paper product and business forms companies such as Avery also offer free galleries of templates that work with their paper products that you can download at no cost from their Web sites.

Once you review a category or search results, you can scroll through the templates, as shown in Figure 5.5. Each template has a name, an image, the provider, the Office application, a date, and a star rating and the number of votes in the star rating. Click the template's name or image once, and a larger preview image appears to the right as well as the download size and estimated download time, like the one shown in Figure 5.6. The category window allows you to sort the templates by rating, date, or name. The View drop-down list lets you choose between Details or Thumbnails view. You can also show or hide community templates (those contributed by other users). If the template appears to be something that might work for you, click the Download button in the lower-right corner. This opens a new document using the freshly downloaded template. If you want to store the template locally on your PC to use again, choose Microsoft Office ⇨ Save As, save in Trusted Templates, save as type Word Template (*.dotx), type a filename, and click Save. If you save your templates in this folder, they are readily accessible as My Templates when you open a new document.

### Working with templates from earlier versions of Word

You can work with templates from earlier versions of Word. If you don't need to modify the template in any way, you can use it in its earlier form (*.dot format) in Compatibility mode, as described in Chapter 2. If the template contains a custom toolbar, macros, or pull-down menu commands, they are grouped together and added as the Add-Ins tab at the far right of the Ribbon. When you click Add-Ins, a Ribbon area is displayed. Depending on the template, the Ribbon area may have several rows of commands or drop-down lists, and may or may not scroll to the left and right. A richly featured template example is shown in Figure 5.7.

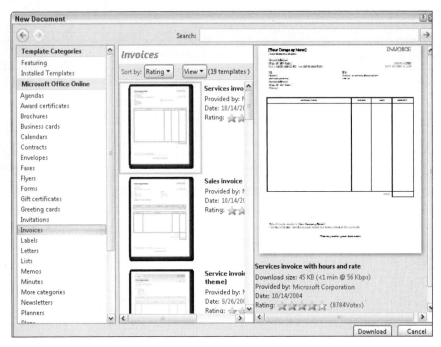

**Figure 5.5.** Browsing online templates

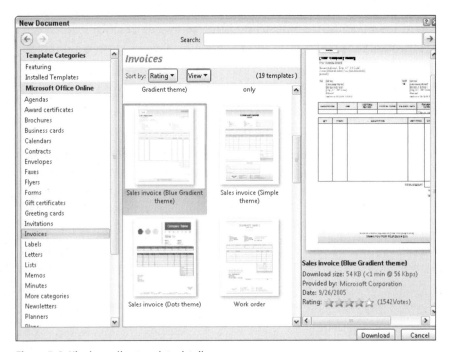

**Figure 5.6.** Viewing online template details

**Figure 5.7.** A template from an earlier Word version uses the Add-Ins tab on the Ribbon.

## Converting templates from earlier versions to Word 2007

If you want to take full advantage of Word 2007 features with a template from an earlier version of Word, first convert the template to Word 2007 format. To do so, follow these steps:

1. Open the template file you want to convert by pressing Ctrl+O or choose Microsoft Office ⇨ Open. (Don't use the New command — this opens a new document file using the template. You want to open and modify the template file itself.)

2. Choose Microsoft Office ⇨ Convert.

3. An explanatory dialog box appears. Click OK.

4. Press F12 or choose Microsoft Office ⇨ Save As.

5. To save the template in the default templates folder, click Trusted Templates.

6. Type the template name, such as **book draft** in this example, in the File name text box, as shown in Figure 5.8.

7. If the file contains macros and you are comfortable with the source of your template, click Word Macro-Enabled Template (*.dotm) in the Save as type drop-down list. Note that the file extension in the File name field will change to .dotm. If you do not know whether the template has macros, or if you do not want them enabled, click Word Template (*.dotx) instead.

8. Click Save.

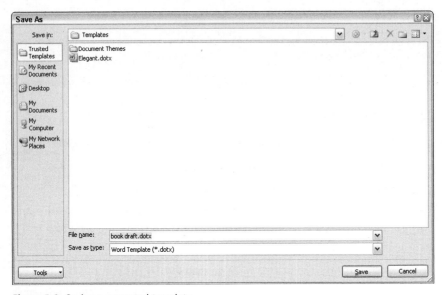

**Figure 5.8.** Saving a converted template

9. If you elect to save the template as a Word template (*.dotx) and
   there are macros contained in the template, you may see a dialog
   box like the one shown in Figure 5.9. This indicates that macros
   (in this case in the form of a VBA project) are contained within the
   template. To strip out the macros from the template, click Yes. To
   keep and convert the macros to Word 2007, click No, and go
   back to Step 7, clicking Word Macro-Enabled Template (*.dotm)
   this time.

**Figure 5.9.** When you convert a template with macros
to a macro-free template, you encounter this dialog box.

You now have a Word 2007 template, to which you can apply Quick
Styles, Themes, and other Word 2007 features.

# Creating your own custom template

If you plan on working with a type of document more than once, consider creating a template. Spending a few minutes upfront creating templates can save you lots of formatting time so that you can concentrate on the content of your document. You can create a template by starting with a blank template or by modifying an existing one.

### Creating a template from scratch

To create a new template, follow these steps:

1. Choose Microsoft Office ⇨ New.

2. Click Blank template from the New Blank section of the New Document window, as shown in Figure 5.10.

3. Click Create.

At this point, you have opened a blank template that has the default name Template1. You can now add text, graphics, styles, and so on until your template is complete. To save the template, click Save and assign it a name. If you have created macros, be sure to save as type Word Macro-Enabled Template (*.dotm).

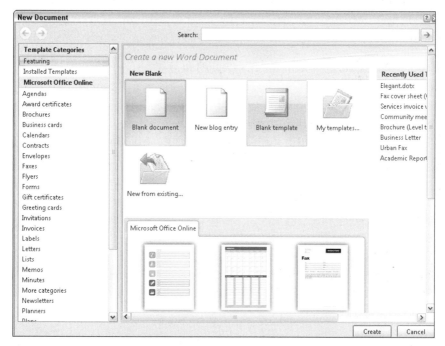

**Figure 5.10.** Starting with a blank template

## New from existing

To modify an existing template, choose Microsoft Office ⇨ Open. Select Trusted Templates, click the template you want to modify, such as FormLetter1.dotx, and click Open as Copy from the Open drop-down list. This way, you won't inadvertently modify the original template. When you finish making modifications to the template, press F12 or choose Microsoft Office ⇨ Save As to assign the modified template a new name. (If you use the Save command instead, the file will be referred to as a copy, such as Copy of FormLetter1.dotx.)

## Adding content controls to templates with the Developer tab

If your template serves the function of a form, you can save time and effort by adding content controls such as text controls or drop-down list controls to the template to speed up and simplify data entry. You can also add macros to templates or use Visual Basic to program macros, but these topics are covered in Chapter 24. For now, I show you how to add a text control, a drop-down list control, and a date picker control to a blank template to make it easier to fill out a form.

You can add content controls and macros to document files as well. However, it usually makes most sense to add content controls and macros to templates that can then be used repeatedly to create individual documents.

### Displaying and working with the Developer tab

To add content controls or macros to your template, you need to display the Developer tab. To do so, choose Microsoft Office ⇨ Word Options ⇨ Personalize. In Top options for working with Word, select the checkbox Show Developer tab in the Ribbon and click OK. Clicking the Developer tab on the Ribbon brings up the commands shown in Figure 5.11.

**Figure 5.11.** The Developer tab on the Ribbon

**Inside Scoop**

If you develop a form to collect and distribute information throughout an organization, consider using Microsoft Office InfoPath 2007 instead of Word to do the job. If the focus is on text and presentation, Word is more suitable.

The Controls group on the Developer tab has several types of control available to you. The different types are listed in Table 5.1. You can insert a control into your document by clicking the corresponding button. Once you insert the control, you can make changes to that control's property settings by selecting the control and clicking Properties. Design mode allows you to make changes to certain property settings more readily. Click Design Mode to turn this mode on or off. You cannot insert one control inside of another control — if you have a control selected, you cannot insert another one into the file. However, you can use the Group command to group the controls together. You can also name groups and lock them so that they cannot be deleted. The best way to see how these commands work together is to illustrate with a few examples, as I have provided in the following sections.

**Table 5.1.** Content controls in Word 2007

| Button | Name | Description |
| --- | --- | --- |
| Aa | Rich Text | Inserts a formatted text control |
| Aa | Text | Inserts a plain text control |
| 🖼 | Picture | Inserts a picture control |
| ▦ | Combo Box | Inserts a combo box — a drop-down list that allows other user text input |
| ▦ | Dropdown List | Inserts a drop-down list that allows user to select from a list |
| 📅 | Date Picker | Inserts a date field — user can type a date or click the pop-up calendar to select one |

*continued*

**Table 5.1.** *continued*

| Button | Name | Description |
|---|---|---|
| 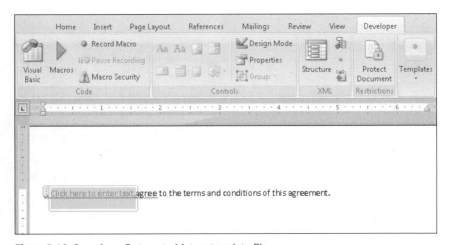 | Building Block Gallery | Inserts a building block control — allows user to choose from a list of document building blocks (see Chapter 21) |
| | Legacy Tools | Brings up a menu of legacy controls — user can choose from a list of form fields and ActiveX controls |

### Inserting a text control into your template

You can insert text controls in your document. These are commonly used when you have a block of text but a portion requires the user to "fill in the blank." The text field can be this blank. You can use the placeholder text to give the user data entry instructions. Text content controls come in two types: Text and Rich Text. For this example, I use the plain text control. To insert a text control into a template, follow these steps:

1. Follow the previous steps for creating a blank template and displaying the Developer tab on the Ribbon.

2. Type **I agree to the terms and conditions of this agreement.** (This is sample text; feel free to supply your own here.)

3. Move the insertion point so that it is between the space and the first letter of *agree.*

4. Click Text from the Controls group on the Developer tab. Your screen should look like Figure 5.12.

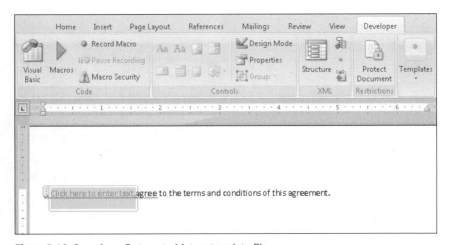

**Figure 5.12.** Inserting a Text control into a template file

**5.** Click Design Mode. The appearance of the control changes, so that it looks like the control shown in Figure 5.13. In this mode, you can edit the placeholder text shown in the control.

**Figure 5.13.** The Text control in Design mode

**6.** Use your mouse or cursor keys to highlight the placeholder text Click here to enter text.

**7.** Press Delete.

**8.** Type **Insert your full name here.**

**9.** Click Properties to see the dialog box in Figure 5.14.

**10.** Type **Customer Name** in the Title field.

**11.** Select the Content control cannot be deleted checkbox in the Locking section.

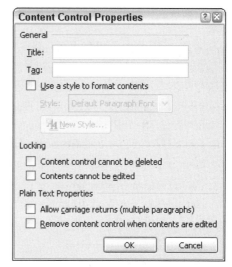

**Figure 5.14.** Setting control properties

**12.** Click OK.

**13.** Click Design Mode to turn off that mode. Your named control should now look like the one shown in Figure 5.15.

**Figure 5.15.** A named Text control

**Hack**

Another way to access a control's properties is to right-click the control and then click Properties in the pop-up box.

**Inserting a Dropdown List control into your template**

A drop-down list is commonly used when you have a set of choices from which the user can select one. You can use the placeholder text to give the user data entry instructions. Once you insert the Dropdown List control, you can add, delete, modify, or change the order of individual list entries from the control's properties box. To insert a Dropdown List control into a template, follow these steps:

1. Follow the previous steps for creating a blank template and displaying the Developer tab on the Ribbon.

2. Type **This equipment lease is renewable on a  basis.** Be sure to enter two spaces between *a* and *basis*. (This is sample text; feel free to supply your own here.)

3. Move the insertion point so that it is between the two blank spaces after *on a* and before *basis*.

4. Click Dropdown List from the Controls group on the Developer tab. Your screen should look like Figure 5.16.

5. Click Design Mode. Your control should look like the one shown in Figure 5.17.

**Figure 5.16.** Inserting a Dropdown List control into a template file

6. Use your mouse or cursor keys to highlight the placeholder text Choose an item.

7. Press Delete.

**Figure 5.17.** The Dropdown List control in Design mode

8. Type **Select a lease duration here.**

9. Click Properties to see the dialog box in Figure 5.18.

10. Type **Lease Duration** in the Title field.

11. Select the Use a different style for text in this control check box, and select Emphasis from the Style drop-down list.

12. Select the Content control cannot be deleted check box in the Locking section.

13. Now you can add items from which the user can choose. Click Add in the Drop-Down List Properties section of the dialog box.

14. Type **daily** in the Display Name field of the Add Choice dialog box. Notice that the Value field automatically fills in the same text string as shown in Figure 5.19. If for some reason you need these values to be different, just type a different string in the Value field.

15. Click OK to accept the entry.

16. Repeat Steps 13 to 15 twice, typing **weekly** in the Display Name field the first time and **monthly** in that field the second time. When finished, the dialog box should look like Figure 5.20.

**Figure 5.18.** Setting Dropdown List control properties

17. Click OK to close the dialog box.

**Figure 5.19.** Adding choices to a Dropdown List control

18. Click Design Mode to turn that mode off.

19. To select an item from the list, click the down arrow and then click an item, such as "weekly," as shown in Figure 5.21.

20. Click somewhere in the document outside the Dropdown List control to see the selected item appear in the Emphasis style (italics) within the text, as shown in Figure 5.22.

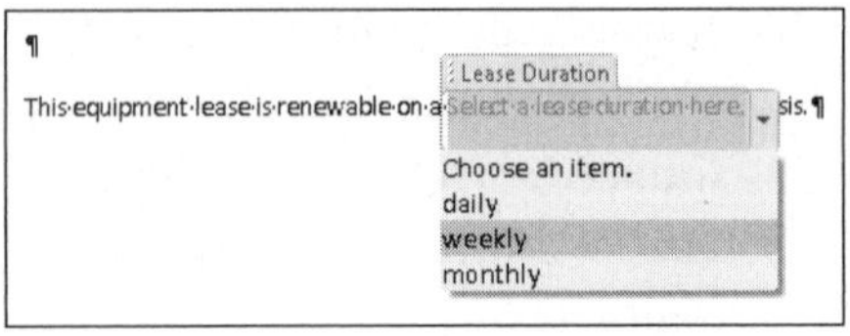

**Figure 5.21.** Selecting an item from the Dropdown List control

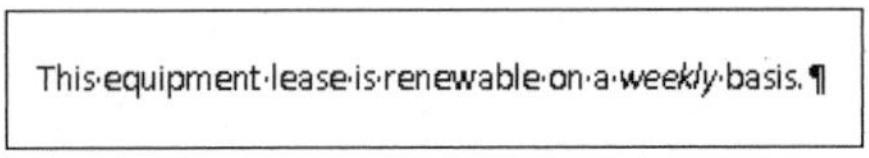

**Figure 5.22.** Selected text appears in the document

**Figure 5.20.** A Dropdown List control with several user list choices added

### Inserting a Date Picker control into your template

The Date Picker control is used to make it easier to enter a calendar date into a form. You can use the placeholder text to give the user data entry instructions. Once you insert the Date Picker control, you can determine the date format and other details from the control's properties box. To insert a Date Picker control into a template, follow these steps:

1. Follow the previous steps for creating a blank template and displaying the Developer tab on the Ribbon.

2. Click Date Picker List from the Controls group on the Developer tab. Your screen should look like Figure 5.23.

3. Click Properties to see the Content Control Properties dialog box, as shown in Figure 5.24.

**Figure 5.23.** Inserting a Date Picker control into a template file

4. Type **Start Date** in the Title field.

5. In the Date Picker Properties area, click the format that looks like October 17, 2006 (with your current date) to choose M/d/yyyy format.

6. Click OK to accept the entry. The Date Picker control appears in the document.

7. Click the control's down arrow to bring up a calendar shown in Figure 5.25 from which you can select the day, month, and year, or you can click Today to get the current date.

### Removing a content control

To completely remove a content control from your template or document, select the control and press Delete. Sometimes you may want to retain the data that has been entered using the control but remove the control itself. To do this, follow these steps:

1. Making sure the Developer tab is visible, select the content control you want to remove.

2. Click Design Mode.

3. If you have locked the control by checking Content control cannot be deleted, you must first unlock the control by clicking Properties and clearing the check box and clicking OK.

**Figure 5.24.** Setting Date Picker control properties

**Figure 5.25.** Using the Date Picker control

**4.** Right-click the control to bring up a pop-up box.

**5.** Click Remove Content Control.

If there was any data entered using the control, it remains in your document, but the content control itself is deleted. If you have not yet entered any data using the control, you can also use this method to completely remove the control from the template or document.

# Using Quick Styles

If you want to take advantage of a set of ready-made styles that will work for you in most situations without doing a lot of custom formatting, consider using Quick Styles. In combination with Style Sets and Themes, of which you learn more later on in this chapter, you can use a powerful grouping of preconfigured styles that are designed to work well with each other from a graphic design perspective. The best way to see how Quick Styles work is to walk through a simple example.

## Choosing a Quick Style

Choosing a Quick Style is easy. In fact, to do so, just start typing in a blank new Word 2007 document. This is the Normal style in Quick Styles using the Default style set and Office theme. Style sets and themes are covered later. For now, I show you how to sample and select different styles for your text. To change a Quick Style, follow these steps:

**1.** Start a blank new document in Word.

**2.** Type **The artist is the creator of beautiful things.**

**3.** Highlight the sentence you just typed.

**4.** Click Quick Styles from the Home tab to see the Quick Styles gallery shown in Figure 5.26.

**5.** Without clicking, move your mouse cursor over various Quick Styles. Notice how the text changes as you move over each new Quick Style; this is the Live Preview feature. (The Live Preview feature works in Print Layout view. If you are in Print Layout view and you still don't see this happen, click Microsoft Office ⇨ Word Options ⇨ Popular and check the option Enable Live Preview.)

**6.** Click the Quick Style called Intense Quote, because this sentence is a quote. The sentence is now in blue text, in boldface italicized type, with a horizontal rule beneath it, as shown in Figure 5.27. This example continues in the next section.

**Watch Out!**

Applying a Quick Style to a selected block of text that contains character formatting such as italics applied to a specific word may strip out the character formatting. Check in Live Preview to make sure the selected Quick Style preserves what you need before clicking to apply the style.

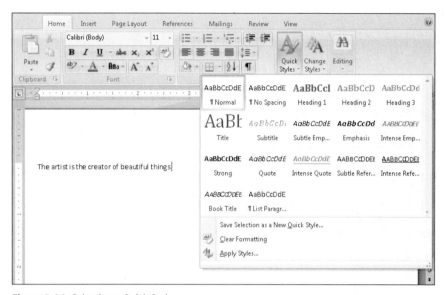

**Figure 5.26.** Selecting a Quick Style

*The artist is the creator of beautiful things.*

**Figure 5.27.** The new Quick Style is selected.

## Creating your own Quick Styles

If the subset of possible styles that Quick Styles provides doesn't meet your needs, you can always add Quick Styles to the Styles Gallery. To do so, follow these steps:

1. Starting after Step 6 of the previous section, press Enter to start a new line.

2. Type **Oscar Wilde**. Because the quote is from Oscar Wilde, develop a Quick Style for attribution.

3. Select Oscar Wilde and choose Home ⇨ Shrink Font or press Ctrl+<.

4. With Oscar Wilde still selected, press Ctrl+R (or choose Home ⇨ Align Right). Your screen should look something like Figure 5.28.

*The artist is the creator of beautiful things.*

Oscar Wilde

**Figure 5.28.** Adding text to be formatted

5. With Oscar Wilde still selected, choose Home ⇨ Quick Styles ⇨ Save Selection as a New Quick Style. The Create New Style from Formatting dialog box shown in Figure 5.29 appears.

**Figure 5.29.** Adding a new Quick Style

6. Type **Attribution** in the Name field and click OK.

7. Choose Home ⇨ Quick Styles to see the new Attribution Quick Style displayed in the Style Gallery shown in Figure 5.30.

## Clearing formatting

In a sense, you can't really clear formatting, because you always need to have some settings. What

**Figure 5.30.** The new Quick Style now appears in the Style Gallery.

clearing formatting is really doing is setting all the format changes back to the default Normal paragraph style, with no character formatting

### Inside Scoop
When you add your own styles to Quick Styles, stay with the selected fonts and colors for that Quick Style. You defeat the purpose of Quick Styles if you add a visually incongruous element to a matched set.

> **Hack**
>
> If you have trouble with formatting a section of text, such as the text not appearing as it should after you select a style, try clearing the formatting for that section and reapplying the style or formatting. See the section on Style Inspector for more fine-tuning.

turned on (no italics, underline, and so on), the default Word font (11-point Calibri), and no color changes. If you have modified your Normal.dotm file to change the Normal paragraph style, clearing formatting resets the selected section to whatever your Normal.dotm file has.

Use the Clear Formatting command with care. Don't use Clear Formatting after you use the Select All command to select an entire document if you want to retain such things as italics on words for emphasis. If you have headings and body text marked differently, all essentially change to body text. In other words, Clear Formatting is not a tool for fine work. Use the Style Inspector described later in the chapter for clearing a specific type of formatting from a specific style. (Headers and footers are not affected by the Select All command and will therefore not become body text. See Chapter 8 for more details on these page components.)

To clear formatting, select the text for which you want the formatting cleared and choose Home ⇨ Quick Styles ⇨ Clear Formatting. If you select a partial paragraph, the paragraph formatting in the entire paragraph is cleared (set back to Normal paragraph style). Any character formatting that you apply in the unselected part of the paragraph is retained. For more information on character formatting, see Chapter 6. For more information on paragraph formatting, see Chapter 7.

## Applying styles

If you want to apply a style quickly from your current template to the section of text you are working on, select the text and then choose Home ⇨ Quick Styles ⇨ Apply Styles. This opens the Apply Styles dialog box shown in Figure 5.31. As you start typing the style's name in the Style Name

**Figure 5.31.** Selecting a style with the Apply Styles command

field, Word uses the AutoComplete feature to finish the name as you type. For example, if you start typing **in,** Word completes it with Intense Quote. This feature is very useful if you have a lot of styles to choose from. You can also reapply or modify the style or launch the expanded Styles window from this dialog box.

## Choosing a style set

You have seen how Quick Styles provides you with a simple and prefabricated set of basic styles that go well together. But what if you don't like blue? Or Calibri font? Not to worry, besides the default style used up to this point, there are ten more sets of Quick Styles to choose from: Classic, Default (Black and White), Distinctive, Elegant, Fancy, Formal, Manuscript, Modern, Simple, and Traditional. You can also create your own style sets. To select a style set, choose Home ⇨ Change Styles ⇨ Style Set. If you have text in your document or template, you can get a live preview of what the style set looks like by mousing over its name from the Style Sets window to view the changes to the text in your document. To change the Style Set, click the new Style Set. Note that this feature only works with Word 2007 documents and templates (there is no live preview in Compatibility mode).

## Working with styles

From the Styles window, you can create, select, inspect, or manage styles. You can also set options for the Style Gallery. To access the Styles window, choose   Home ⇨ Styles   (click   the   dialog   box launcher for the Styles group on the Home tab of the Ribbon). This opens a window like the one shown in Figure 5.32. Note that your custom Quick Style Attribution is listed. Because Show Preview is selected, each style is displayed in its appropriate font, size, color, and so on. Note that Attribute is aligned right in the list (as you designated in the example earlier in the chapter). To the right of each style is a paragraph mark (for paragraph style, the letter *a* for character style, or a paragraph mark

**Figure 5.32.** The Styles window

**Inside Scoop**

To view more of the Styles list without scrolling, deselect the Show Preview check box so that the style names all appear in one smaller font. This usually makes all styles in the Style Gallery visible at the same time.

and an *a* for linked style). If you mouse over a style, a window pops up to show that style's attributes. Clicking the down arrow to the right of the style brings up a list of operations that you can perform on that style. If you select a built-in style or protected style, you are not able to delete the style.

At the bottom of the Styles window are several additional buttons and settings. Show Preview allows you to choose between plain and formatted versions of each style in the display window. Disable Linked Styles, when selected, disables styles that are linked (combinations of paragraph and character styles). The three buttons are summarized in Table 5.2. In addition to the buttons, the Options command brings up options related specifically to what displays in the Styles window.

**Table 5.2.** Style command buttons in the Styles window

| Button | Name | Function |
|--------|------|----------|
| | New Style | Creates a new Quick Style based on currently selected style and opens a dialog box where you can name and make changes to the new style. |
| | Style Inspector | Opens a dialog box that displays all paragraph and text-level formatting applied to a selected block of text. From the Style Inspector you can also clear or modify formatting of the selected text or open the Reveal Formatting pane. |
| | Manage Styles | Opens a dialog box that allows you to manage all styles in the current document or template. From the Manage Styles dialog box you can delete, rename, restrict, import, export, and make changes to any of these styles. |

## Using the Style Inspector

The Style Inspector is useful when you have lots of styles and formatting, or when you have received a document from someone else and need to work with it but are unfamiliar with just how that person went about formatting the text. Clicking Style Inspector in the Styles window opens the dialog box shown in Figure 5.33. A preview of the selected paragraph or Quick Style is shown in the Paragraph formatting section. By clicking the preview window, you get a drop-down list with the same commands as when you click on a style in the Styles window. Clicking the button to the right of the Paragraph formatting preview windows resets the paragraph formatting of the current selection to Normal style. The lower window in the Paragraph formatting

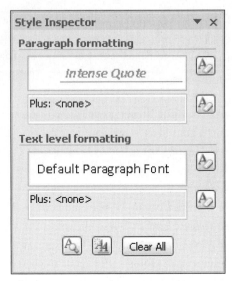

**Figure 5.33.** Using the Style Inspector

section (containing Plus: <none> in Figure 5.33) shows any additional paragraph formatting you have applied to the selection but have not incorporated as part of a style. For example, perhaps you have selected Intense Quote as the Quick Style but have also centered it vertically on the page rather than aligning it left. This modification appears in the Plus section. The button to the right of this section clears any of this additional paragraph formatting. Analogously, the Text level formatting section has to do with character styles applied or individual text-level changes made. For example, the Emphasis Quick Style is an example of a character style because it takes the default paragraph font and adds bold and italic attributes to it. In the Plus section, an example would be changing the font to Times New Roman or adding underlining without adding these changes to the style.

The buttons across the bottom of the Style Inspector provide additional detail. The leftmost button with the A and magnifying glass opens the Reveal Formatting pane to the right of your document. This is useful if you want to examine formatting as you review your document. The middle button is the New Style button, which is explained earlier. The Clear All button has the affect of clearing all formatting for the selected text, so use it with care.

## Managing styles

Click Manage Styles to open a large dialog box with multiple tabs designed to be your control center for managing styles in Word. The changes you make here affect all instances of a given style, either in the current document or for new documents based on the current template. This dialog box is not for making changes to an individual paragraph. I will not discuss every permutation of the commands and options available in this dialog box because very few readers will make use of all these features. Instead, I touch on the most relevant. When you first click Manage Styles from the Styles window, the Edit tab appears as shown in Figure 5.34.

From the Edit tab you can select any style in the current or available templates to view or modify. You can choose a Sort order in which the styles appear (here and in the Styles Gallery). The sort orders available are Alphabetical, As Recommended, Font, Based on, and By type. As Recommended refers to the feature in the Recommend tab that allows you to recommend certain styles first. Many of these sort

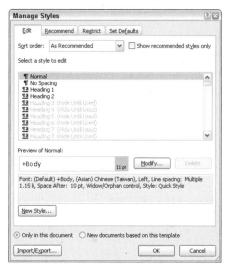

**Figure 5.34.** The Edit tab of the Manage Styles dialog box

options are obvious. The Recommend tab allows you to set recommendations for styles to any level or degree you could wish for. The Based on sort order groups all the styles based on another style together (in alphabetical order by base style). By type groups all styles by type of style, in the following order: character styles, linked styles, paragraph styles, table styles, and list styles. Once you select a file, you can modify it, either just for this document or for all new documents based on this template, depending on which radio button you select. You can also import or export styles between the current document and the template by clicking Import/Export.

The Restrict tab is shown in Figure 5.35. It may seem a bit like Big Brother to have such a tab, but it's actually a wonderful way to protect your hard formatting and design efforts during the later stages of a collaborative writing and revision effort. By reducing the number of visible styles for a given document or template, you can reduce the number of formatting mistakes when you try to stay within some design specifications. You can even lock in the Theme or Quick Style Set.

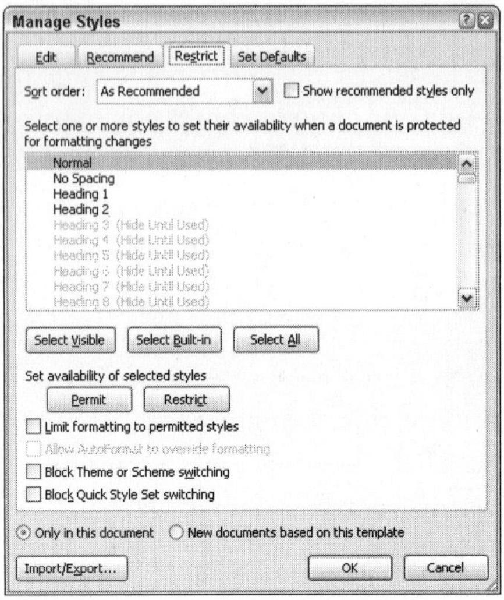

**Figure 5.35.** The Restrict tab of the Manage Styles dialog box

The Set Defaults tab allows you to change the default paragraph and character settings for your document or template.

# Just the facts

- You can save a lot of repetitive work by using templates or creating your own.

- The Normal.dotm template is the standard template that stores all the custom settings that you want to apply when you open a blank document in Word.

- Adding content controls can enhance form templates.

- Quick Styles provide ready-made sets of complimentary styles for different parts of your document.

- Word provides many tools for managing the various types of styles that automate your document formatting.

GET THE SCOOP ON...
Choosing the right font ▪ Using boldface, italics, and
special effects ▪ How to select font sizes ▪ Using color
to enliven your documents ▪ Changing the character
spacing ▪ How to save design time with character styles

# Format Your Characters

**Chapter 6**

I f you want to change the look of your document, one of the most effective ways is to select a font that best reflects the message or information you wish to convey. Using a clear, unobtrusive, readable font for business documents and an eye-catching, artistic font for advertisements are just two examples of how this can work for you. Although selecting a font is easy, there are some important things you need to know to get the most out of your documents and avoid frustrations.

Changing font sizes is also simple, but you may from time to time need to make some custom adjustments. Learning how to fine-tune your character size helps when you need to make a document fit on a fixed number of pages, or you have a headline or large message that needs to fit in a fixed amount of space.

Character styles can help you automate and simplify your work, particularly if you have a standard personal or corporate style that you want to convey in all of your documents.

Lastly, the proliferation of inexpensive color printers and output for the screen or the Web has made the use of color in documents a common practice, and I show you how to use color quickly and effectively.

## Selecting fonts

You can always use the default font selected by Microsoft if you are writing for practical reasons and can't be bothered with trying out numerous fonts on your documents to make them appear stylish. With style sets and themes, Microsoft even attempts to give you a bit more selection. However, you may want to make a unique impression; perhaps you want to catch the attention of a new potential client. Choose whichever font you like, but take a moment to read these suggestions, because they may help you when you need to give your document just the right look.

One of the truly useful new features in Word's user interface is the ability to see a quick preview of how your document will appear simply by placing the mouse cursor over the desired font, as shown in Figure 6.1. This allows you to get a sense of how the document will look in several different fonts without going through the effort of selecting text, changing the font, and then changing again by trial and error until you get the right one. (Note: This feature does not work in Draft view.)

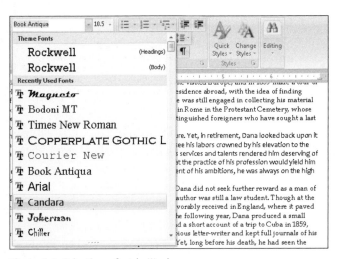

**Figure 6.1.** Selecting a font in Word

To change your font, follow these steps:

1. Click the Home tab.

2. Select the text for which you want to change the font. (If you haven't typed any text yet and therefore have nothing to select, the font you select will apply to all text from the cursor forward until you change the font again.)

**Inside Scoop**

The icons to the left of the font name indicate the type of font; TT indicates a TrueType font; a printer icon indicates a font resident in your printer's memory. More details on TrueType and Printer Fonts are covered later in this chapter.

3. Click the drop-down list in the Font box of the Home tab containing font names. The first fonts in the list are those that you have most recently worked with followed by a bar, and then all the fonts available to you in alphabetical order. The name of each font is displayed in the character style of that font. For example, the name of the font Magneto in Figure 6.1 appears in Magneto font itself.

4. Click a font from the drop-down list to select it. The selected text now appears in the new font, as shown in Figure 6.2.

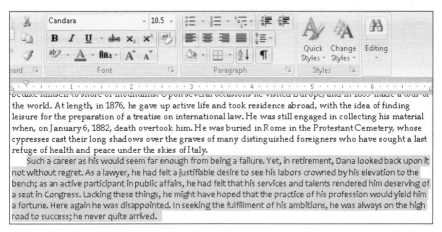

**Figure 6.2.** The selected text appears in the new font.

## Choosing the right font for the job

If you are interested in page layout and typography, there are many great books on the subject (see Appendix D). In this section, I provide you with the basics to help you make intelligent choices about fonts in your day-to-day work.

You may notice that this book uses different fonts for headings than it does for the text of individual paragraphs. If you leaf through books on your bookshelf, you see, for the most part, that the font used for the individual text paragraphs — what's often called the *body* of the text — is of a type with little feet at the end of many of the letters. This kind of font is called a *serif* font. Those with no feet are called *sans serif* fonts. You can compare the difference in Figure 6.3. Books and other printed materials of greater length usually use a serif font for the body text for ease of reading. If you are writing longer documents that you expect to be printed, it's best to choose standard serif fonts for the body

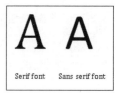

Serif font     Sans serif font

**Figure 6.3.** Serif and sans serif fonts

text. Some examples of standard fonts you see when reading large amounts of text are Times, Garamond, and Bodoni. If you are producing a shorter document, there's no need to be so conservative, but make sure that the body font is clear and legible (avoid using fancy, decorative, or novelty fonts unless they are headings or labels).

### Choosing a font for screens

Just as most printed materials use serif fonts, most Web sites and text-intensive software programs use sans serif fonts. If you are writing documents that will be seen on-screen only, the conventional wisdom is to use sans serif fonts such as Calibri or Verdana for easy reading. Screen resolution (the sharpness of the picture) is usually in the range of 72 dots per inch (dpi) to 120 dpi. Compare this to printers, which typically produce 300 to 1200 dpi. Because the tiny serifs tend to blur on-screen, sans serif fonts make more sense in this context.

### Choosing a font for headings

Because headings are usually in larger type than body text, you have fewer practical limitations. You can use a larger size of the same font or a different font entirely.

## Fonts, font families, font styles, and effects

In the modern world of digital type, a font is a set of characters all created in one unifying style. The font is stored in a file that contains all the information required to draw each character on the screen, in whichever

**Watch Out!**

With all the fonts now available to choose from, remember the dictum *less is more*. If you put more than a few fonts in a single document, the design will appear busy and you'll lose the reader's attention. Try to avoid the "ransom note" look by choosing one to three complementary fonts for your document.

**Watch Out!**
Some display fonts have only a reduced set of characters (sometimes only uppercase). Make sure to check when using such fonts if you want to use lowercase letters or special (nonalphanumeric) characters.

size required. Most fonts have been designed to make the minor adjustments required so that they continue to work whether in smaller or larger sizes. More details on font sizes are found later in the chapter. Fonts often come in font families. For example, Arial, Arial Black, and Arial Narrow are all fonts in the Arial font family. Arial is the base font, Arial Black is a wider and heavier version, and Arial Narrow is a vertically condensed version of the font. In addition to fonts and font families, fonts also have bold and italic versions. In Microsoft Word, a font's style is Regular, Italic, Bold, or Bold Italic. In addition to the variations to fonts discussed so far, Word provides ways to further render special effects for each character: superscript (as for a footnote number or trademark), subscript (common in formulae), underlining, strikethrough (used to show deletions in revised documents), and various design effects such as Shadow and Emboss.

# How to change a font style or special effect

It's easy to change your text from regular to italic or bold, add a special effect, or choose a combination of font styles and effects. I show you how to italicize existing text. Other font styles can be turned on in essentially the same way by clicking the appropriate button. Table 6.1 lists the buttons and keyboard shortcuts for font styles (and there's an abbreviated list on the tear-out card in the inside front cover of the book as well).

## How to italicize text

The easiest way to italicize text is to follow these steps:

1. Select the text you want to italicize.
2. Click the *I* button on the Home tab or press Ctrl+I. (If you haven't typed any text yet and therefore have nothing to select, the italics will apply to all text from the cursor forward until you change it again.) To remove italics, just select the text and click the button again.

**Table 6.1.** Font styles

| Style | Sample | Button | Keyboard Shortcut |
|---|---|---|---|
| Bold | **Sample** | **B** | Ctrl+B |
| Italic | *Sample* | *I* | Ctrl+I |
| Underline* | <u>Sample</u> | <u>U</u> ▾ | Ctrl+U |
| Strikethrough | ~~Sample~~ | ~~abc~~ | none |
| Subscript | Sample$_x$ | $x_2$ | Ctrl+= |
| Superscript | Sample$^x$ | $x^2$ | Ctrl++ |

* Click the Underline drop-down list button to select an underline style or color.

## There's bold and then there's bold

While Word can convert regular fonts to italic or bold programmatically, you may encounter italic or bold versions of fonts in a family that are listed separately in your font list. These font versions have been specially designed to be italic or bold (or extra bold) and are treated as separate fonts by Word. For example, if you have text in Futura and you select bold, you will not be selecting the font Futura Bold (or Futura Extra Bold). To do that, you need to select the special bold font by choosing the font as described earlier.

## How to select special effects

It's great that you can make a word bold by clicking an icon, but there are far too many font effects to fit across the top of the screen as icons. To take advantage of less common special effects for fonts, follow these steps:

1. Select the text to which you want to apply the special font effect.

2. Click the dialog box launcher in the lower-right corner of the Font group on the Home tab to open the Font dialog box. The Font tab of the Font dialog box appears, as shown in Figure 6.4.

**Inside Scoop**

If you are working with themes, you may see a style preceded by a plus sign (such as +Body in Figure 6.4), which indicates the theme font for the selected text style (such as body, header, and so on).

3. Under Effects, click the check box for the effect you want to use (Small caps is selected in Figure 6.4) and the Preview window displays the effect on the currently selected text. To turn off the effect, click the text and then click the box to deselect it.

**Figure 6.4.** The Font tab of the Font dialog box

The Hidden effect requires some explanation. You can use this effect when you want to have something visible on-screen (such as instructions on a form) that won't print in the final copy. In addition to these effects, you can select from among 16 underlining styles by clicking the Underline style drop-down list in the Font dialog box. You can select an underline color (separate from the font color) using the Underline color drop-down list.

## TrueType Versus Printer Fonts

If you are just working on documents that will be printed on your reasonably modern local printer, you won't need to worry about this distinction. Any TrueType or printer font should work fine. However, if you intend to work on the document on one computer and print it from another, or intend to use a printer that you don't have currently installed, you need to know this distinction. Many printers come with a set of custom fonts resident in their memory. These fonts become visible to any Windows application when you install the printer.

# Selecting font sizes

Changing the size of characters in Word is as simple as clicking an icon. However, there are times when more precision is required. In this section, I first show you the easy way to change font size, then give some practical tips on what sizes are appropriate for different uses, and lastly give some tips on character placement and making things fit.

## How to quickly increase or decrease font size

To increase or decrease font size:

1. Select the text whose font you want to increase or decrease.

 2. Click the Increase Size button (to increase the font size by a standard increment) or the Decrease Size button (to decrease the font size by a standard increment). The selected text changes size accordingly.

## How to select a specific font size

If the previous method doesn't allow you enough precision, or if you know you want a really huge or tiny size and don't want to keep clicking the button until you get there, there is a better method to select a specific font size. To change the font's point size, follow these steps:

1. Select the text whose size you want to change.

2. Click the drop-down list to the right of the font name in the Font box of the Home tab.

3. Click the desired size from the list. The selected text appears in the new size.

## A point size primer

Fonts are measured in points. Without getting into a long discussion about technical typographical definitions, suffice it to say that there are approximately 72 points to an inch. Thus, if you want letters that are

**Inside Scoop**

If you are distributing your finished document to others who may not have all the fonts you have, you can embed fonts in the document itself. Choose Microsoft Office ⇨ Word Options ⇨ Save and select the Embed fonts in the file option.

**Inside Scoop**

The drop-down list displays only a list of common sizes, but you can select other sizes (numbers between those in the list, or smaller or larger than those on the list) by typing the number in the list box. For example, to select 9.5, click inside the font size box so that the current number is highlighted and type **9.5**.

approximately half an inch high, select 36-point font size. This works as a rule of thumb, but it's important to note that all fonts are not alike (some are shorter, wider, taller, and narrower than others) so this can only be a rough estimate.

Common point sizes for body text are in the 10- to 12-point range. Reserve point sizes smaller than 10 points for things like obligatory legal notices and the like. Point sizes larger than 12 points tend to be for headings, labels, signage, and so on.

# Applying color to text

You can add color to your fonts in Word. If you have used previous versions of Word, applying colors works essentially the same way, except that you are offered the selected color palette for the current theme as a first set of options for colors, so that you can keep things looking consistent if you use a theme.

## How to use colors

You can do all kinds of strange things with colors if you want to grab someone's attention, but remember to choose color that's appropriate for the intended reading medium and the content of the document. If your document will be read online and not printed, you can be freer in your color choices. If you know that the document will be printed on a color printer, you will still have a good deal of freedom with color choices, although there are some limitations: brighter reds and greens can become washed out on home color printers when using plain (non-photo) cartridges. If you want something bright red for emphasis and it ends up washed-out pink, it might defeat your intended purpose. Of course, many printed documents end up printed in black ink only. If you know that at least sometimes your document with color fonts will be printed in black and white, you can test by printing in black and white or grayscale, to make sure that the black-and-white or grayscale version is acceptable.

The medium or printer is not the only factor that makes a difference with color choices, of course. The type of message you want to convey is also important and the role that particular section of text plays in the document. For example, use black or very dark colors for body text against a white or very light background. (I describe how to use color backgrounds in Chapter 8.) Using reversed-out text, with light font color on a dark background, is a great way to add emphasis, as it is used in this book for the chapter number and table titles, but should be avoided for body text (whether on-screen or printed).

## Changing font colors

To change a font color in Word, select the text to which you want to apply the color, and click Font color to open the Font color dialog box, as shown in Figure 6.5. Table 6.2 describes the different color settings. If you want to change something to black and keep it that way, don't choose Automatic (even though this is often black). Instead, select Black from the font colors. Automatic accepts the default font color for a given style or theme.

If you want more colors to choose from, click More Colors to see the dialog box shown in Figure 6.6. The Standard tab shown in Figure 6.6 gives over 140 colors, grays, black, and white to choose

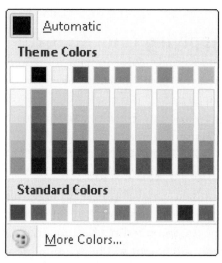

**Figure 6.5.** Choosing a font color

from. Clicking the Custom tab opens the custom color tool shown in Figure 6.7. You can create a color by selecting the amount of red, green, or blue on a scale of 0 to 255 using the RGB color model. Clicking the Color model

**Inside Scoop**

If you have a document with color fonts but the printer only prints black and white, there's no need to change the font colors. Use your printer settings to deal with this issue. (Printing is described in Chapter 9.)

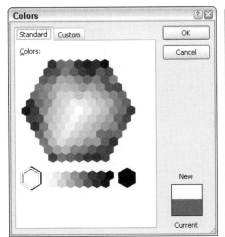

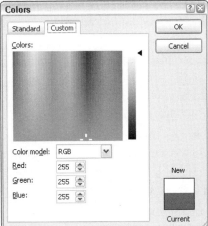

**Figure 6.6.** Choosing a font color from a larger palette

**Figure 6.7.** Creating a custom font color

drop-down list allows you to switch to the other color model, HSL (Hue, Saturation, Luminance). Hue is the actual color. Saturation determines the color's intensity, 0 being least intense and 255 being most intense. Luminance determines the color's brightness, 0 being the darkest and 255 the brightest.

**Table 6.2.** Font color settings

| Setting | Usage |
| --- | --- |
| Automatic | Use default font color selections for styles and themes. |
| Theme Colors | Provides color palette from current selected theme. |
| Standard Colors | Provides basic color palette to choose from. |
| More Colors | Opens a dialog box with an expanded standard color tab and a Custom Colors tab for selecting very specific custom colors. |

# Character spacing

Occasionally you may find the need to adjust the spacing of individual words or characters. The Character Spacing tab of the Fonts dialog box allows you to make these sorts of changes. For those familiar with recent previous versions of Word, this has not changed at all. You can condense or expand characters horizontally using percentage, condense or expand the distance between characters horizontally by a specific amount, raise or lower the characters on the line, or turn font kerning on or off. To make these changes to selected text, choose Home ⇨ Font ⇨ Character Spacing to display the Character Spacing tab shown in Figure 6.8.

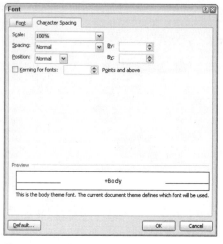

**Figure 6.8.** Making changes to character spacing

## Changing character scale in percentage

Occasionally you may need to squeeze or stretch characters to make them fit in a specific area of your document, or you may want to make characters appear squeezed or stretched for effect. You can use the Scale setting to accomplish this. The preset selections range from 33 percent to 200 percent, but you can type your own percentage number into the Scale text box. Note that the characters and the spaces between them are condensed or expanded from left to right but the height and point size remain the same, so that at 50 percent reduction characters appear narrow and at 200 percent enlargement characters appear wide, as illustrated in Figure 6.9.

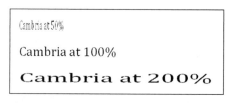

**Figure 6.9.** Results of changing character scale

## Condensing and expanding character spacing

Occasionally you will need to fit a large amount of text into a finite space. This happens most often to me when I have a heading with very large letters (such as a 72-point font size) that I try to fit across a single page on one line. This can happen when you have many words in a smaller font and you can't edit them down any further. Conversely, you may have a page where you want the word or phrase to spread evenly across the page and want it to take up more space. This setting affects the spacing

**Hack**

Condensing and expanding character spacing does not work with script (or cursive) fonts where the characters are intended to link. Use the Scale option to preserve the visual linking of cursive characters instead.

between characters, not the physical appearance of the characters themselves. Consequently, if you try to condense the characters too much they "step on each other's toes", as shown in Figure 6.10.

To condense or expand character spacing, click Spacing on the Character Spacing tab and choose Condensed or Expanded. In the By box, you can use the up and down arrows to increase or decrease the space by tenths of the default unit of measurement, which is points (pt.), you can type a point measurement, or you can type a different unit of measurement such as inches (") or centimeters (cm). To return everything back to normal, click Normal in the Spacing list.

character spacing

Cambria 24 pt. normal

character spacing

Cambria 24 pt. condensed by 1 pt.

characterspacing

Cambria 24 pt. condensed by 3 pt.

c h a r a c t e r   s p a c i n g

Cambria 24 pt. expanded by 4 pt.

**Figure 6.10.** Examples of condensed and expanded character spacing

## Raising and lowering characters on the line

You may need to raise or lower characters from the baseline. Superscript, Subscript, Footnote, and Equation features are most often used to accomplish this task. However, occasionally you will need to fine-tune the elevation of characters, and you can choose to raise or lower the position of characters. Click Raised or Lowered in the Position list. In the By box, you can use the up and down arrows to increase or decrease the amount to raise or lower the characters by the default unit of measurement, which is points (pt.), you can type a point measurement, or you can type a measurement with a different unit of measurement such as inches (") or centimeters (cm). To return everything back to normal, click Normal in the Position list.

## Taking advantage of font kerning

In typography, kerning is the technique of allowing characters to nest more closely together and avoid extra white space. This is really fine work and isn't noticeable in most circumstances. It becomes a concern at large point sizes with certain awkward letter combinations. To turn this feature on, click Kerning for fonts. The size of the currently selected font appear in the Points and above list, but you can override this and type a point size or use the up and down arrows to scroll to a point size.

# Working with character styles

In Chapter 5, I discuss styles in some detail. Character styles in particular are styles that you create and use that apply to individual characters and words as opposed to paragraphs or documents.

## Creating a new character style

For example, if you have a brand name that you want to always appear in 11.5-point Magneto font in dark blue, you can create a character style to do just that. To do so, follow these steps:

1. From a blank new document, press Alt+Ctrl+Shift+S or choose Home ⇨ Styles to open the Styles window.

2. Click New Style. The Create New Style from Formatting dialog box appears, as shown in Figure 6.11.

3. In the Name field, type **logo**.

4. Click Character in the Style type drop-down list.

5. In the Formatting section, click the font drop-down list and select Magneto.

6. In the point size list, type **11.5** and press Enter.

7. In the Font Color list, mouse over the fourth color at the top of the Theme Colors palette, and a label pops up with the text Dark Blue, Text 2. Click to select it. Your screen should look like Figure 6.12.

8. Note that you now have the option of saving this new style just for this document or for all new documents based on the current template. For this example, leave the option set to Only in this document and click OK.

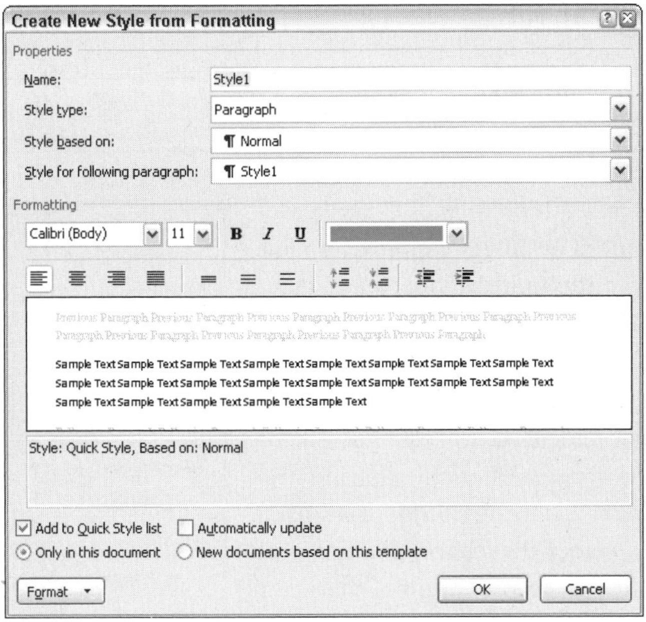

**Figure 6.11.** Creating a new character style

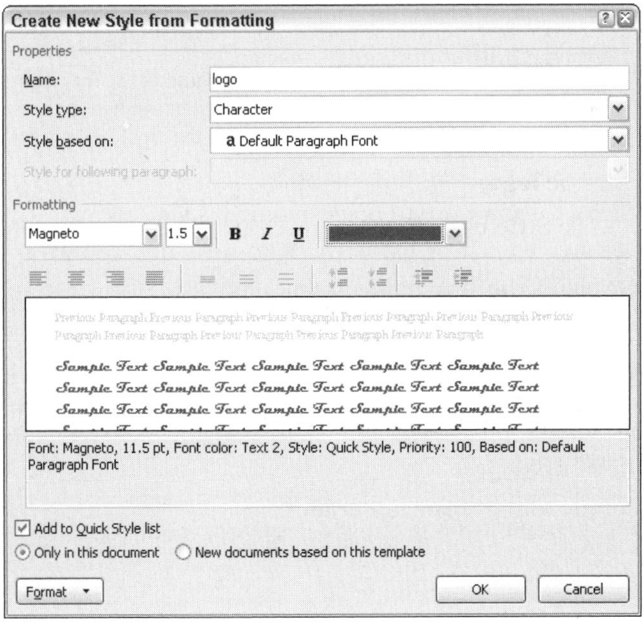

**Figure 6.12.** The new character style's settings

**Bright Idea**

You can select all text with similar formatting by right-clicking the selected text. Click Select Text with Similar Formatting from the pop-up menu and by doing so make modifications to all the selections at once.

The logo style is now added to your Quick Styles list for this document. The Styles window remains open, and you can see the new style listed as a character style (with an "a"), as shown in Figure 6.13.

## Applying a character style

You can apply a character style to selected text by first highlighting the text and then applying the character style. To start a new section of text with a new character style, select the character style and start typing. Follow these steps to apply a character style to existing text:

1. Select the text to which you want to apply the style.

2. Choose Home ⇨ Quick Styles.

3. Click the desired Quick Style, such as logo in this example. The selected text appears as soon as you mouse over it. (Note that you can also click the Apply Styles button here to begin typing a style's name. This works well if you have a long list of styles because the Apply Styles feature completes the style name as you type.)

**Figure 6.13.** The new character style appears in the list of Quick Styles.

## Just the facts

■ Use the right font for the job. Fonts suited for headings are not always suited for body text.

■ Avoid using too many fonts in one document.

■ You can preview the look of a font in Word by looking at a selected
section while mousing over the various fonts available in your list.

■ Word offers a wide variety of effects and colors that you can apply to
characters.

■ You can streamline your formatting and give your document a more
unified look by taking advantage of character styles.

**GET THE SCOOP ON...**
Setting paragraph alignment and indentation ▪ Using
paragraph styles ▪ Formatting bulleted and numbered
lists ▪ Creating multilevel lists

# Format Your Paragraphs

**M**uch of what I cover in this chapter has to do with what is commonly thought of as paragraph formatting. You have paragraphs of text, and you want to indent them, align them at the right margin, or perhaps make them hanging paragraphs. However, some things that you might not think of as paragraphs at all use paragraph formatting. In Word, as in most other word processors and page layout programs, a paragraph conceptually constitutes a text string (or other type of data) between two paragraph marks. That means that paragraph formatting applies to other things, such as headings, titles, lists, captions, or graphics.

I focus first on typical paragraph formatting such as indents, tabs, and alignment. After showing you how to make such changes one at a time, I show you how to use paragraph styles. Analogous to character styles, paragraph styles in Word serve the function of allowing you to store a group of settings that relate to paragraph formatting and assign the settings a name, so that you can readily make a group of formatting changes all at once. Next, I discuss bulleted, numbered, and multilevel lists, and how to change settings for lists such as bullet style, numbering style, and indentation.

# Selecting paragraph format settings

When you make changes to paragraph formatting, it is a good idea to show formatting codes on-screen as you work. If dots appear between each word, and each paragraph you type concludes with a paragraph symbol, then you already have these codes turned on. If you see no such codes, press Ctrl+* (that is, press Ctrl+Shift+* because you have to press Shift to access *), or click Show/Hide Paragraph in the Paragraph group of the Home tab to display codes. Figure 7.1 shows an example of text with paragraph marks displayed at the end of every paragraph. When a new paragraph starts, Word displays text continuing until it reaches a margin, and then it wraps the text to the next line without starting a new paragraph. New lines that start between paragraphs are called soft returns (as opposed to the hard return of pressing Return or Enter). If you don't like how Word decides to break the line, you can insert a manual line break by pressing Shift+Enter. An example of how this appears on-screen is shown in Figure 7.2. When you use manual line breaks, all paragraph formatting of the current paragraph is retained.

those·of·a·common·sailor,·and·he·eats·and·sleeps·in·the·cabin;·but·he·is·obliged·to·be·on·deck·nearly·all·the·time,·and·eats·at·the·second·table,·that·is,·makes·a·meal·out·of·what·the·captain·and·chief·mate·leave.¶

The·steward·is·the·captain's·servant,·and·has·charge·of·the·pantry,·from·which·every·one,·even·the·mate·himself,·is·excluded.·These·distinctions·usually·find·him·an·enemy·in·the·mate,·who·does·not·like·to·have·any·one·on·board·who·is·not·entirely·under·his·control;·the·crew·do·not·consider·him·as·one·of·their·number,·so·he·is·left·to·the·mercy·of·the·captain.¶

The·cook·is·the·patron·of·the·crew,·and·those·who·are·in·his·favor·can·get·their·wet·mittens·and·stockings·dried,·or·light·their·pipes·at·the·galley·on·the·night·watch.·These·two·worthies,·together·with·the·carpenter·and·sailmaker,·if·there·be·one,·stand·no·watch,·but,·being·employed·all·day,·are·allowed·to·"sleep·in"·at·night,·unless·all·hands·are·called.·This·state·of·things·continued·for·two·days.¶

**Figure 7.1.** Showing paragraph marks

The·cook·is·the·patron·of·the·crew,·and·those·who·are·in·his·favor·can·get·their·wet·mittens·and·stockings·dried,·or·light·their·pipes·at·the·galley·on·the·night·watch.·These·two·worthies,·together·with·the·carpenter·and·sailmaker,·if·there·be·one,·stand·no·watch,·but,·being·employed·all·day,·are·↵
allowed·to·"sleep·in"·at·night,·unless·all·hands·are·called.·This·state·of·things·continued·for·two·days.¶

**Figure 7.2.** A manual line break appears above a paragraph mark.

To make changes to a paragraph's formatting, click somewhere in the paragraph (it is not necessary to select the entire paragraph), and then click the appropriate button in the Paragraph group of the Home tab of the Ribbon, as summarized in Table 7.1. If you want the changes to apply to more than one paragraph, select the group of paragraphs you want to change. Some additional paragraph format settings are accessible by clicking the Paragraph dialog box launcher on the Home tab, which opens the Paragraph dialog box shown in Figure 7.3. The Indents and

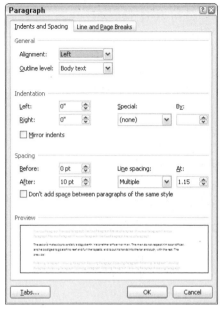

**Figure 7.3.** The Paragraph dialog box

Spacing tab has some general settings in addition to indenting and spacing. The Line and Page Breaks tab covers options that determine when a new page or line starts.

**Table 7.1.** Paragraph formatting commands

| Button | Name | Function |
|---|---|---|
| | Bullets | Click to create a list with a bullet (a dot or some other symbol) to the left of each paragraph. Click again to turn off bullets. |
| | Numbering | Click to create a numbered list, with each paragraph being a numbered item. Click again to turn off numbering. |
| | Multilevel List | Click to create a multilevel list, with each paragraph being a numbered item. Click again to turn off the multilevel list feature. |
| | Decrease Indent | Click to decrease the indentation of the paragraph from the left page margin by one default tab stop (0.5 inches by default). |

*continued*

## Table 7.1. *continued*

| Button | Name | Function |
|---|---|---|
| | Increase Indent | Click to increase the indentation of the paragraph from the left page margin by one default tab stop (0.5 inches by default). |
| | Align Left (Ctrl+L) | Click to align paragraph to left page margin with ragged-right paragraph margin. |
| | Center (Ctrl+E) | Click to center paragraph between left and right page margins. |
| | Align Right (Ctrl+R) | Click to align paragraph to right page margin with a ragged-left paragraph margin. |
| | Justify (Ctrl+J) | Click to align text to left and right page margins, inserting extra space between words to even out the edges. |
| | Line spacing | Click to select line spacing. |
| | Shading | Click to select background shading for a selected paragraph or block of text. |
| | Border | Click to create a border of currently selected border style for the current paragraph. Click again to turn off border style. |
| | Sort | Click to sort selected paragraphs in alphabetical or numeric order, ascending or descending. |
| | Show/Hide Paragraph (Ctrl+*) | Click to show/hide paragraph and other formatting marks. |

## Aligning paragraphs

You can align paragraphs in one of four ways in Word: Align Left, Center, Align Right, or Justify, as described in Table 7.1. For larger amounts of body text, I suggest limiting yourself to the Align Left or Justify settings for readability's sake.

Aligning the paragraph to the left gives you a paragraph that is flush with the left edge of the page margin and ragged on the right, getting as close to the right margin as possible without crossing it. When the right margin approaches, the paragraph starts a new line with the next word (if no hyphenation is being used) or with the next part of a hyphenated word (if hyphenation is used).

If you select the Center option, paragraphs are centered within the left and right page margins. This option is often used for headings and titles. If the paragraph is more than one line in length, it has ragged-left and right margins.

Use Align Right to have a right margin that is flush with the right page margin. This gives you a ragged-left margin. Align Right is used for such things as headers and footers (see Chapter 8), or return addresses and dates in correspondence. I recommend avoiding right-aligned paragraphs for large amounts of body text, because in English and other Western left-to-right reading cultures, ragged-left margins make it difficult to keep your place in the paragraph when you move to the next line.

In typography, to *justify* is to align the text with the left and right margins, as we have with this paragraph. This is done by adding extra spacing between words. The wider the line, the better this technique works. Conversely, if you have a very narrow line, such as text that is presented in several columns on a page, justifying the paragraph may appear awkward. You can mitigate this by turning on hyphenation for justified paragraphs.

## Indenting paragraphs

There are several ways you can indent paragraphs in Word. Choose your method by determining whether you want to indent the paragraphs using visual cues or by specifying units of measurement. You can slide the controls on the ruler to use visual cues to decide how you want things to look, or you can specify indentation by clicking buttons or typing measurements in a box. I show you how to do both.

The word *indent* is used by Microsoft to refer to the left and right margins of all lines of the paragraph, even if the formatting involved by the indent setting creates no indentation at all. Two examples of this are a

**Bright Idea**

If you want to have a centered paragraph offset from the rest of the text but don't want ragged-left and right margins, use Justify as an alignment setting and then reduce the left and right margins by equal amounts using left and right indents.

hanging paragraph whose first line hangs out to the left of the margin for the rest of the paragraph, as shown in Figure 7.4, or an outdented paragraph that extends outside the page margin, as shown in Figure 7.5. It's useful to note here that indenting a paragraph is not the same as creating a page margin. Paragraph indentations are made *relative* to the left and right page or column margins.

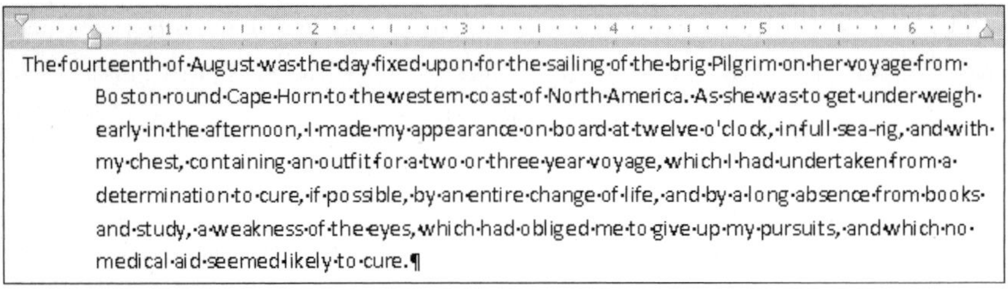
The·fourteenth·of·August·was·the·day·fixed·upon·for·the·sailing·of·the·brig·Pilgrim·on·her·voyage·from·Boston·round·Cape·Horn·to·the·western·coast·of·North·America.·As·she·was·to·get·under·weigh·early·in·the·afternoon,·I·made·my·appearance·on·board·at·twelve·o'clock,·in·full·sea-rig,·and·with·my·chest,·containing·an·outfit·for·a·two·or·three·year·voyage,·which·I·had·undertaken·from·a·determination·to·cure,·if·possible,·by·an·entire·change·of·life,·and·by·a·long·absence·from·books·and·study,·a·weakness·of·the·eyes,·which·had·obliged·me·to·give·up·my·pursuits,·and·which·no·medical·aid·seemed·likely·to·cure.¶

**Figure 7.4.** A hanging paragraph

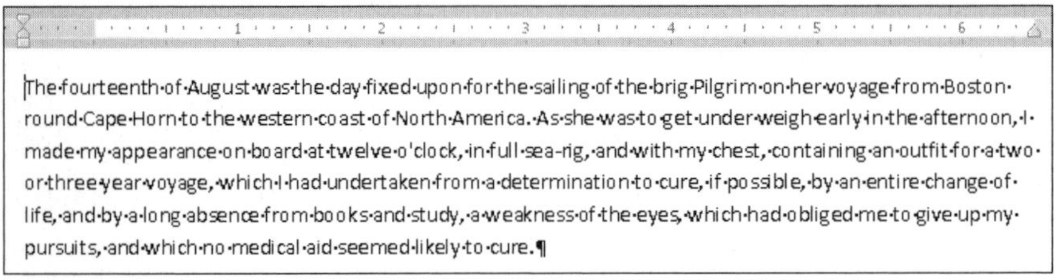
The·fourteenth·of·August·was·the·day·fixed·upon·for·the·sailing·of·the·brig·Pilgrim·on·her·voyage·from·Boston·round·Cape·Horn·to·the·western·coast·of·North·America.·As·she·was·to·get·under·weigh·early·in·the·afternoon,·I·made·my·appearance·on·board·at·twelve·o'clock,·in·full·sea-rig,·and·with·my·chest,·containing·an·outfit·for·a·two·or·three·year·voyage,·which·I·had·undertaken·from·a·determination·to·cure,·if·possible,·by·an·entire·change·of·life,·and·by·a·long·absence·from·books·and·study,·a·weakness·of·the·eyes,·which·had·obliged·me·to·give·up·my·pursuits,·and·which·no·medical·aid·seemed·likely·to·cure.¶

**Figure 7.5.** A paragraph margin extending outside that of the page margin creates an outdented paragraph.

## *Indenting using the Ruler*

There are many ways to distinguish between two paragraphs of body text, including indenting the first line or adding extra space after the last line of every paragraph, which is covered in the next section.

### Indenting the first line of a paragraph

The most common way to signify the start of a new paragraph is to begin the first line indented slightly from the left margin. To do this using the Ruler, follow these steps:

1. Click somewhere within the paragraph you want to indent, or highlight the group of paragraphs if there are several to indent.
2. Click the downward-pointing arrow at the top left side of the Ruler. (If your Ruler is not visible, click the View Ruler button at the top of

the vertical scroll bar to display it.) This is the First Line Indent pointer. A vertical rule appears, which makes it easier to see what you are doing, as shown in Figure 7.6.

**3.** Drag the pointer to the right (one-half inch for this example). The paragraph shifts and Word indents the first line, as shown in Figure 7.7.

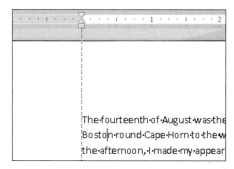

**Figure 7.6.** Word displays a vertical rule when you click the First Line Indent pointer.

### Creating a hanging paragraph

You can also leave the first line flush left and indent the remaining lines of a paragraph. This is called a hanging paragraph. To create a hanging paragraph using the Ruler, follow these steps:

**1.** Click somewhere within the paragraph you want to indent, or highlight the group of paragraphs if there are several to indent.

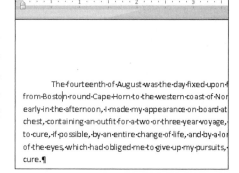

**Figure 7.7.** A paragraph with the first line indented

**2.** Click the upward-pointing arrow at the top left side of the Ruler. (If your Ruler is not visible, click the View Ruler button at the top of the vertical scroll bar to display it.) This is the Hanging Indent pointer. A vertical rule appears, which makes it easier to see what you are doing, as with indenting a paragraph.

**3.** Drag the pointer to the right (one-half inch for this example). The first-line point stays in place at the left margin, and the rest of the lines of the paragraph shift, as shown earlier in Figure 7.4.

**Hack**

To quickly create a hanging paragraph with the first line flush left and the subsequent lines indented by one default tab stop (usually one half inch), just press Ctrl+T.

### Indenting the right and left paragraph margins

You can change the left and right paragraph margins on the ruler, too. You can indent the left margin for an excerpt or other special block of text, or you can indent the left and right margins. To do so, follow these steps:

1. Click somewhere within the paragraph you want to indent, or highlight the group of paragraphs if there are several to indent.

2. Click the rectangle at the base of the downward- and upward-pointing arrow at the top-left side of the Ruler. (If your Ruler is not visible, click the View Ruler button at the top of the vertical scroll bar to display it.) This is the Left Indent pointer. A vertical rule appears, which makes it easier to see what you are doing, as with indenting a paragraph.

3. Drag the pointer to the right (one-half inch for this example). The entire paragraph shifts to the right. (Note that if the paragraph has a first-line indent or a hanging indent, the first line still moves to the right the same amount as the rest of the text, preserving the indented or hanging aspect of the paragraph.)

4. Drag the upward-pointing arrow at the far right of the Ruler (this is the Right Indent pointer) to the left (again one-half inch in this example), and the right margin of the paragraph shifts to the left, giving you the inset paragraph like the one shown in Figure 7.8.

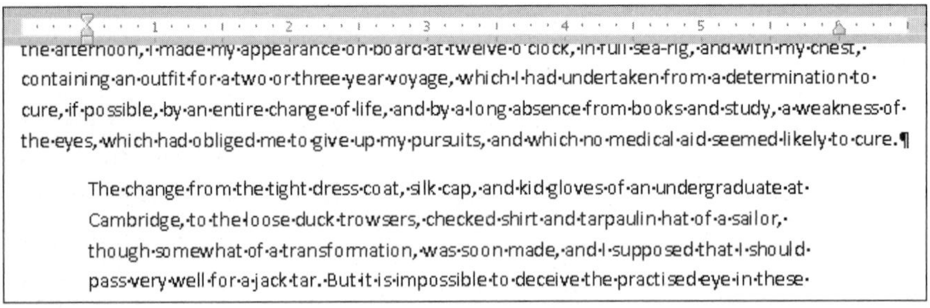

**Figure 7.8.** A paragraph with reduced left and right margins

You can also use the Ruler pointers to extend your paragraph outside the page margins (indicated by the blue bars on the left and right edges of the Ruler), but only out to the edge of the paper.

**Watch Out!**
Most printers can't print closer than one-quarter to one-half inch from the edge, though Word allows you to set paragraph margins to the paper edge. Words drop off the page if you try this. To see what will actually print on the page, use Print Preview (see Chapter 9).

## Indenting using other controls

Using the Ruler for setting paragraph indents is particularly convenient for simple documents like letters or notices where creating a balanced visual appearance is more intuitive. If, however, you are working with a more advanced page layout or a larger and more complex document, need more precision, or are working with paragraph styles (which I discuss later in the chapter), you can use the controls found on the Ribbon and in the Paragraph dialog box.

You can increase or decrease a paragraph's indentation by the default tab stop distance (usually one-half inch) just by clicking the Increase Indent or Decrease Indent buttons in the Paragraph group of the Home tab on the Ribbon. For a little more precision, you can click the Page Layout tab and click the up and down arrows in the Indent Left or Indent Right scroll boxes, or type a value.

For more settings and details, click the dialog box launcher for the Paragraph group (on either the Home or Page Layout tabs). This displays the Indents and Spacing tab of the Paragraph dialog box, as shown earlier in Figure 7.3.

In addition to allowing you to indent paragraph margins, create paragraphs with an indented first line, and set hanging paragraphs, you can also indent paragraphs for mirror page designs using Mirror indents. If you have a multipage document with margins that are different for recto (right) and verso (left) pages, you can select the Mirror indents option. The Left and Right paragraph margins switch to Inside and Outside margins, so that you can set paragraph margins for a two-page spread.

Note that from this dialog box you can also change the paragraph alignment and change its outline level (body text, Level 1, Level 2, and so on). Spacing and tabs are also accessible from here, but I cover spacing later in this chapter and tabs in Chapter 8.

To make changes to the paragraph indentation settings in Word, click in the paragraph or select the paragraphs to which you want the changes to apply, change the settings, and then click OK. Unlike with the Ruler, the changes only go into effect and are visible when you click OK.

## Line and paragraph spacing

In Word, you can select line spacing for individual lines within a paragraph or for the space that separates paragraphs. You can use relative measurements, such as 1 line and 1.5 lines, or you can use precise linear measurements in points.

In professional page layout and design, specifications for font size often specify the height of the entire line including the space between lines, or *leading* (an artifact from the days of lead type when the typesetter literally added lead). For example, if the design calls for 11-point Garamond type, it might have 12-point leading. This would be referred to as "11 over 12." Because most of us don't work in professional print design shops, Word does this work for us by default. When you select a font and font size, Word automatically determines the appropriate number of points that should constitute a single line. Word also makes some assumptions about spacing before and after paragraphs. However, if you work with precision design specifications, Word has the ability to make such professional settings as well, and I show you how in this section.

You have several choices for how you adjust line spacing for paragraphs in Word. If you just want to double-space your paragraph or add a bit of space before or after until it looks right, use the Line Spacing button shown in Table 7.1. When you click this button, you get a subset of available line spacing options, as shown in Figure 7.9. Clicking a number from the list spaces the lines in your paragraph using a line as a unit of measurement. In other words, choosing 2.0 double-spaces your paragraph, 1.0 single-spaces it, and so on. Clicking More opens the Paragraph dialog box shown

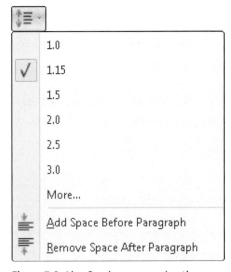

**Figure 7.9.** Line Spacing command options

in Figure 7.3. Clicking Add Space Before Paragraph or Remove Space After Paragraph adds approximately one line of space before a paragraph or removes a line of space after a paragraph, respectively. These last commands are not always the same; they depend on your selected paragraph's current settings. If you have no spacing before a paragraph, it gives you the option to add some. If you have some spacing before the paragraph, it gives you the option to remove it. The same holds true for the setting for after a paragraph.

For a complete set of line spacing options, click the Paragraph dialog launcher from either the Home or Page Layout tabs to see the Indents and Spacing tab shown in Figure 7.3. I recommend using this dialog box for adjusting spacing settings for precision work and for creating and modifying paragraph styles, discussed later in this chapter. The Spacing section allows you to set line spacing within the paragraph and spacing before and after a paragraph. You can also select the option Don't add space between paragraphs of the same style, which has some practical applications when you want to prevent excessive space when two paragraphs of a given format that normally don't occur one after the other end up stacked together, such as two headings.

### Setting spacing before and after paragraphs

You can add space before or after a paragraph or paragraph style. First, give some thought to the context, particularly when you are determining this for a paragraph style rather than for a single paragraph. Does it make the most sense to have extra space after this type of paragraph or before another type of paragraph? Once you determine the answer, you have several ways to add space. If you have no need to make special spacing, you can accept the current settings or select Auto by clicking the down arrow past 0 pt in the Before or After list box. This uses Word's default settings and rules of thumb and accepts the settings of any preset styles. To add space before a paragraph, follow these steps:

**Inside Scoop**

Not comfortable with points? You can type in inches (in or ") or centimeters (cm) in the Before and After list box or in the At box if Line spacing is set to At least or Exactly. Word converts your value to points automatically.

1. Click somewhere within the paragraph before which you want to add space, or highlight the group of paragraphs if there are several.

2. Click the Paragraph dialog box launcher from the Home or Page Layout tab of the Ribbon.

3. Click the up arrow in the Before list box several times to get to 24 pt (or type **24 pt** in the box). The Preview box shows the effect the setting change has, as shown in Figure 7.10.

4. Click OK to accept the change, like the one shown in Figure 7.11.

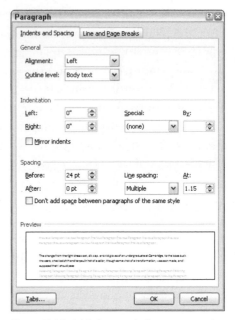

**Figure 7.10.** Adding space before a paragraph

You can follow the same procedure to add space after a paragraph by using the After list box.

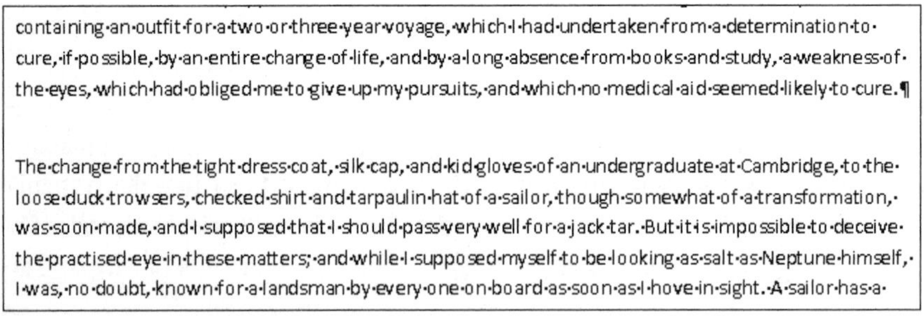

containing·an·outfit·for·a·two·or·three·year·voyage,·which·I·had·undertaken·from·a·determination·to·
cure,·if·possible,·by·an·entire·change·of·life,·and·by·a·long·absence·from·books·and·study,·a·weakness·of·
the·eyes,·which·had·obliged·me·to·give·up·my·pursuits,·and·which·no·medical·aid·seemed·likely·to·cure.¶

The·change·from·the·tight·dress·coat,·silk·cap,·and·kid·gloves·of·an·undergraduate·at·Cambridge,·to·the·
loose·duck·trowsers,·checked·shirt·and·tarpaulin·hat·of·a·sailor,·though·somewhat·of·a·transformation,·
was·soon·made,·and·I·supposed·that·I·should·pass·very·well·for·a·jack·tar.·But·it·is·impossible·to·deceive·
the·practised·eye·in·these·matters;·and·while·I·supposed·myself·to·be·looking·as·salt·as·Neptune·himself,·
I·was,·no·doubt,·known·for·a·landsman·by·every·one·on·board·as·soon·as·I·hove·in·sight.·A·sailor·has·a·

**Figure 7.11.** The paragraph preceded by 24 points of space

### Setting line spacing

Line spacing settings can be the ones available back in the days of typewriters (single-, double-, and triple-spaced), they can be smaller fractions of a line, or they can be set with unit measurements. To access the settings for fine-tuning line spacing, click the Paragraph dialog box launcher from the Home or Page Layout tab of the Ribbon. To set line spacing by multiples of a single line, select Single, 1.5 lines, Double, or Multiple in the Line spacing list box. If you select Multiple, you need to specify a number between 0 and 132. If you use the up and down arrows with Multiple, it goes in 0.5 line increments. You can specify a line increment with the precision of two decimal places (such as 3.25 lines).

You can also set line spacing by points. To do so, select At least or Exactly in the Line spacing list box and then specify the height of the line in points. To set line spacing to an exact number of points, follow these steps:

1. Click somewhere within the paragraph before which you want to add space, or highlight the group of paragraphs if there are several.

2. Click the Paragraph dialog box launcher from the Home or Page Layout tab of the Ribbon.

3. Click Exactly in the Line spacing list box.

4. Click the up or down arrow in the At list box to get to 18 pt (or type **18 pt** in the box). The Preview box shows the effect the setting change has, as shown in Figure 7.12.

5. Click OK to accept the change, as shown in Figure 7.13.

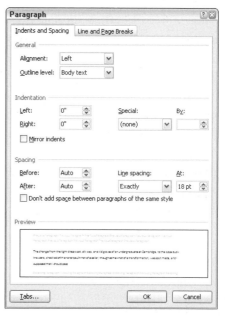

**Figure 7.12.** Adding 18-point line spacing to a paragraph

---

### Watch Out!
The Exactly and At least settings for line spacing refer to the height of the entire line (or the distance between the baseline of each line of text), not the space between the letters.

The·change·from·the·tight·dress·coat,·silk·cap,·and·kid·gloves·of·an·undergraduate·at·Cambridge,·to·the·
loose·duck·trowsers,·checked·shirt·and·tarpaulin·hat·of·a·sailor,·though·somewhat·of·a·transformation,·
was·soon·made,·and·I·supposed·that·I·should·pass·very·well·for·a·jack·tar.·But·it·is·impossible·to·deceive·
the·practised·eye·in·these·matters;·and·while·I·supposed·myself·to·be·looking·as·salt·as·Neptune·himself,·
I·was,·no·doubt,·known·for·a·landsman·by·every·one·on·board·as·soon·as·I·hove·in·sight.·A·sailor·has·a·
peculiar·cut·to·his·clothes,·and·a·way·of·wearing·them·which·a·green·hand·can·never·get.·The·trowsers,·
tight·round·the·hips,·and·thence·hanging·long·and·loose·round·the·feet,·a·superabundance·of·checked·
shirt,·a·low-crowned,·well·varnished·black·hat,·worn·on·the·back·of·the·head,·with·half·a·fathom·of·black·

**Figure 7.13.** A paragraph with 18-point line spacing

## Line and page breaks

When you work with multipage documents, you can use Word's line and page break settings to prevent awkward page breaks automatically. This can prevent such things as the first line of a new paragraph being the last on a page (an *orphan*), the last line of a paragraph starting on a new page (a *widow*), or a heading at the bottom of the page with the text that is meant to go beneath it starting the next page. To access these settings, select a paragraph or paragraph style, then click the Paragraph dialog box launcher from the Home or Page Layout tabs on the Ribbon. Click the Line and Page Breaks tab to see the screen shown in Figure 7.14. Table 7.2 summarizes the Pagination section features related to line and page breaks.

**Figure 7.14.** The Line and Page Breaks tab of the Paragraph dialog box

## Adding shading and borders to paragraphs

You can add background shading or borders to your paragraph by selecting the entire paragraph and then clicking the Shading or Border button in the Paragraph group on the Home tab, as summarized in Table 7.1.

**Table 7.2.** Pagination options for paragraphs

| Option | Description |
| --- | --- |
| Widow/Orphan control | Prevents first line of paragraph only at end of page or last line only of paragraph at top of page |
| Keep with next | Used with headings, illustrations with captions, and other paired elements to prevent them from being separated across a page break |
| Keep lines together | Prevents the breaking of a paragraph across a page |
| Page break before | Keeps paragraph at top of page (example: chapter titles) |

### Adding background shading to paragraphs

You can add a background color to a selected paragraph or group of paragraphs. Click the down arrow on the Shading button to see a list of colors options shown in Figure 7.15. The selected paragraph changes as you mouse over different colors so that you can preview what things will look like before you commit to a color with a mouse click (in Print and Web Layout view). You can choose from a range of colors or no color. When a color is selected, a rectangle appears shaded behind your paragraph, as shown in

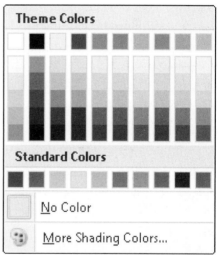

**Figure 7.15.** Choosing a background shading color for a paragraph

Figure 7.16. If your font is in black or a dark color and you choose a sufficiently dark color, gray, or black, your font converts to white so that the paragraph remains legible.

**Bright Idea**

Using the Shading button doesn't allow you to make any adjustments to how far the background color extends outside the paragraph. If you want more control over the size and shape of the background, use the Options button of Borders and Shading discussed in the next section.

The·fourteenth·of·August·was·the·day·fixed·upon·for·the·sailing·of·the·brig·Pilgrim·on·her·voyage·from· Boston·round·Cape·Horn·to·the·western·coast·of·North·America.·As·she·was·to·get·under·weigh·early·in· the·afternoon,·I·made·my·appearance·on·board·at·twelve·o'clock,·in·full·sea-rig,·and·with·my·chest,· containing·an·outfit·for·a·two·or·three·year·voyage,·which·I·had·undertaken·from·a·determination·to· cure,·if·possible,·by·an·entire·change·of·life,·and·by·a·long·absence·from·books·and·study,·a·weakness·of· the·eyes,·which·had·obliged·me·to·give·up·my·pursuits,·and·which·no·medical·aid·seemed·likely·to·cure.¶

**Figure 7.16.** A paragraph with background shading

If you want to turn off paragraph shading, choose No Color (not white) if your page background is a color other than white.

## Adding borders to paragraphs

You can add border lines to a selected paragraph or group of paragraphs. Click the down arrow on the Border button to see a list of options shown in Figure 7.17. To add a border that surrounds a selected paragraph, follow these steps:

1. Select the paragraph to which you want to add a border.

2. Click the down arrow on the Borders button to see the list of options displayed in Figure 7.17.

3. Click Outside Borders. The selected paragraph now has a border surrounding it.

Note that Outside Borders is now set as the Border button option. If you click the button (and not the down arrow) with a new paragraph selected, outside borders are added to it. If you click the button while a paragraph is selected that has outside borders, the button removes the outside borders. In other words, it functions like an on/off switch for whichever border setting you have selected.

**Figure 7.17.** Choosing a paragraph border option

The Border button gives you what amounts to a starter set of the amazing number of combinations you can choose from. To access these additional settings, click Borders and Shading to see the dialog box shown in Figure 7.18. From the Borders tab of this dialog box you can select from several styles of border, choose the width, color, and shape of the lines forming the border, and so on. In the Preview window, you can click a side of the preview paragraph to add or remove a border, or use the top, bottom, left, or right border buttons.

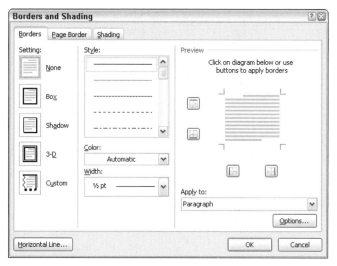

**Figure 7.18.** The Borders and Shading dialog box

### Adding a horizontal line

You may have occasion to use a horizontal line as a section separator or part of the design for a heading. To add a simple horizontal line between paragraphs, place your insertion point at the end of the paragraph where you want to add a horizontal line, click the down arrow list button on the Borders button, and select Horizontal Line. This inserts a plain horizontal line across the page as its own paragraph. If you want to see more choices (and there are many varieties available besides a black line), click Borders and then click Horizontal Line.

## Sorting text

If you have a list of items, you can use Word's sort feature to sort them alphabetically, numerically, or by date, in either ascending or descending

**Watch Out!**

The Horizontal Line feature adds a line as a paragraph, so if you insert it in the middle of a paragraph you will split your text paragraph in two.

order. To sort a simple list of words each on its own line as shown in Figure 7.19 into ascending alphabetical order, follow these steps:

1. Select the text (paragraphs) to be sorted.

2. Click Sort from the Paragraph Group of the Home tab to open the dialog box shown in Figure 7.20.

3. Verify that in the Sort by field, Paragraphs is selected, and that in the Type field, Text is selected. Click Ascending.

4. Verify that the No header row option in the My list has section is selected, and click OK.

**Figure 7.19.** A simple list to be sorted

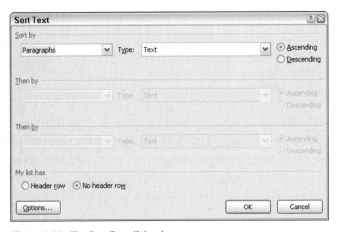

**Figure 7.20.** The Sort Text dialog box

To better illustrate the Sort feature's abilities, assume you have a shipping manifest with a produce order such as the one shown in Figure 7.21. The list is comprised of three columns separated by tabs, and it has a header row. Say you want to sort the list first by invoice in ascending numerical order, and then by

| Invoice | → | Case-Quantity | → | Item-Description¶ |
|---------|---|---------------|---|-------------------|
| 89709 | → | 2 | → | Kumquats¶ |
| 89709 | → | 12 | → | Apples¶ |
| 89712 | → | 8 | → | Apples¶ |
| 89712 | → | 6 | → | Mangoes¶ |
| 89655 | → | 5 | → | Oranges¶ |
| 89655 | → | 6 | → | Apples¶ |
| 89655 | → | 7 | → | Mangoes¶ |

**Figure 7.21.** A sample list to be sorted

**Inside Scoop**

The Case sensitive sort option is not obvious. If it is selected, lowercase *a* precedes uppercase *A*, followed by lowercase *b*. If not selected, the letter *a* terms are grouped together irrespective of their case.

Item Description in ascending alphabetical order. To do this, follow these steps:

1. Select the entire list including the header row.

2. Click Sort.

3. For My list has, click Header row. This identifies each column by the text string (separated by tabs) of the header row above each column.

4. In the Sort by field, click Invoice. Note that Word correctly identifies this as a number type sort.

5. In the first Then by field, click Item Description. This is identified correctly as a text type sort.

6. Click Options to open the Sort Options dialog box shown in Figure 7.22. Verify that the Tabs option in the Separate fields at section is selected (if it is not, select Tabs).

7. Click OK twice to perform the sort. The results appear in Figure 7.23.

**Figure 7.22.** The Sort Options dialog box

| Invoice | → | Case·Quantity | → | Item·Description¶ |
|---------|---|---------------|---|-------------------|
| 89655 | → | 6 | → | Apples¶ |
| 89655 | → | 7 | → | Mangoes¶ |
| 89655 | → | 5 | → | Oranges¶ |
| 89709 | → | 12 | → | Apples¶ |
| 89709 | → | 2 | → | Kumquats¶ |
| 89712 | → | 8 | → | Apples¶ |
| 89712 | → | 6 | → | Mangoes¶ |

**Figure 7.23.** A multilevel sort has been performed to the list.

# Working with paragraph styles

Now that I've described what you can do to a paragraph's format, it makes sense to show you how to make those changes in a smart and efficient way. I describe in Chapter 5 how to use the Quick Styles that come ready for you to use. This section shows you how to build your own paragraph styles.

## Some tips on storing your styles

When you create or modify a paragraph style, it needs to be stored somewhere. You can store paragraph styles either within your document or in your template. If you intend to use the paragraph styles all the time in your daily work, you can store them in your default (Normal.dotm) template. This technique works fine as long as you bear in mind a few things.

Everyone using Word has a Normal.dotm or Normal.dot file. If you give a custom paragraph style a common name and another person receives your document, your paragraph style might be overridden by that person's Normal.dotm settings if the Automatically update document styles option in the Templates and Add-Ins dialog box is selected. (This can also occur with any other template if one copy of the template has been modified in some way.) As an example, say you send a document to someone and you have modified the Normal paragraph style, changing Word 2007's default font Calibri to Arial and changing the paragraph alignment to Justified. If this other person opens your document in Word with the Automatically update document styles option selected, all your Normal paragraphs are converted back to left-aligned Calibri font (or whatever that person happens to have changed his or her Normal style to).

Three ways are available to avoid this problem. First, make sure that the Automatically update document styles option is not selected. In Word 2007, choose Microsoft Office ⇨ Word Options ⇨ Add-Ins. Select Templates in the Manage list and click Go. This brings you to the Templates and Add-Ins dialog box where you can deselect the checkbox for the Automatically update document styles option and click OK. In Word 2003 or Word 2002, choose Tools ⇨ Templates and Add-Ins, deselect the checkbox, and click OK. Second, make sure to avoid modifying existing common styles. Assign any of your own styles or modified styles a distinctly new name. Third, consider creating a new template and using it instead of Normal.dotm if you are creating several new paragraph styles.

## Creating a new paragraph style

You can create a new paragraph style by selecting format settings for a paragraph and then saving those changes as a paragraph style, or you can create a new style by making changes in a dialog box. Each method has its uses, so I'll show you how to do both.

### Saving the current paragraph's settings as a paragraph style

The quickest and easiest way to save the current paragraph's style is to follow these steps:

1. Right-click while the insertion point is in the paragraph whose style you want to save as a paragraph style. (In this example, I start with a paragraph in Normal Quick Style, and change the font to Bodoni MT, the font size to 12 points, and the paragraph alignment to Justified.) A pop-up menu like the one shown in Figure 7.24 appears.

2. Click Save Selection as a New Quick Style from the pop-up menu to create a Quick Style.

3. In the Name field of the Create New Style from Formatting dialog box, type **Book Para No Indent,** as shown in Figure 7.25. At this point you could click Modify to view more settings. I discuss those in the next section.

4. Click OK.

### Creating a new paragraph style using the New Style command

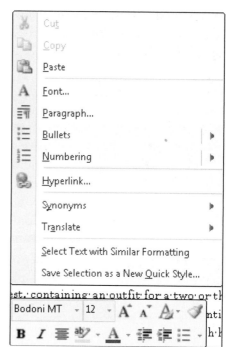

**Figure 7.24.** Right-clicking the mouse opens the pop-up menu.

**Figure 7.25.** Creating a new Quick Style

You can also create a new style from the Styles window. To do so, follow these steps:

1. Click in the paragraph upon which you want to base the new paragraph style. (In this example, as with the previous one, I start with a

**Bright Idea**

If you want the character formatting of your style to be usable on blocks of text smaller than a paragraph, use the quick right-clicking method shown previously, which creates a linked style by default, or choose Linked (paragraph and character) in the Style type list.

paragraph in Normal Quick Style, change the font to Bodoni MT, the font size to 12 points, and the paragraph alignment to Justified.)

**2.** Click the Styles dialog box launcher (or press Alt+Ctrl+Shift+S).

**3.** Click the New Style button to see the larger Create New Style from Formatting dialog box shown in Figure 7.26.

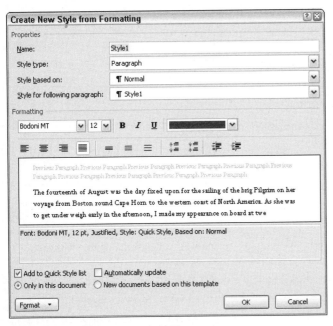

**Figure 7.26.** Modifying new style settings

**4.** In the Name field of the Create New Style from Formatting dialog box, type **Book Para No Indent**.

**5.** At this point, you can click OK and you have a Quick Style named Book Para No Indent. However, to make an additional modification in the Style for following paragraph list box, select Book Para No Indent. With this option selected, you can press Enter to end a paragraph, and the next one is in the same Book Para No Indent style. (This does not convert the next already existing paragraph to this style.)

6. Click OK to create the new style.

7. In the Styles window (which should still be open), click the Style Inspector button. The newly named style is now displayed for the selected paragraph, as shown in Figure 7.27.

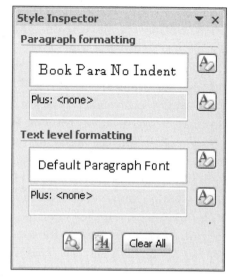

**Figure 7.27.** The new style is revealed in the Style Inspector.

## Just What Is a Linked Style?

A linked style can be thought of as a combination of a paragraph style and a character style. A paragraph style may contain not only paragraph format settings (such as alignment and line spacing), but may also contain character style information (such as font and font size). If you apply a paragraph style to a block of text within a paragraph, all the settings of the entire paragraph containing the selected text change: font, font size, alignment, and so on. If you apply a linked style to just a selection of text within the paragraph, then only the character formatting changes. The best way to describe how a linked style works is to give an example. Let's say you have a style called Corp Logo that includes the corporation name and logo in blue 14-point Arial font, centered on the page, with 24 points of space following the paragraph. If Corp Logo is a linked style you can apply it to your corporation name within a paragraph of text, and the corporate logo appears in blue 14-point Arial font, but it would not center the entire paragraph and add 24 points of space afterward.

You can click Disable Linked Styles on the Styles window (Alt+Ctrl+Shift+S) to disable this feature.

There are a few extra details you should know about the settings in the Create New Style from Formatting dialog box shown in Figure 7.26. If you don't name a style, it is assigned the name Style1, Style2, and so on. You cannot overwrite an existing style name. If you apply formatting to the current paragraph, make sure you know what the current paragraph's style is, because any new style is based on the current one. (The default is Normal.) If you delete a style that another style is based upon, the base style reverts to Normal, but the new style would still contain all the formatting modifications of the deleted style. The Formatting section allows you to perform additional formatting changes to the style, and clicking the Format button gives you access to additional formatting settings.

In most cases, it makes sense to take advantage of the Quick Style list, so leave this checked unless for some reason you don't want the style to appear in the style gallery. The Automatically update option can be selected if you are confident that updates to the base style or this style coming from a new template won't cause problems. In my experience, it's best to leave this alone unless you have specific cause to update the styles.

Finally, you can choose to save your style changes only for the current document or for new documents based on this template. The default setting is only to save the style for the current document. If you save for New documents based on this template, remember that if you have started a new document with the Normal.dotm template, this can cause you problems if you send the file to others (or open the document on a different PC).

## Modifying an existing paragraph style

You can modify an existing style in Word. If you are working with styles that come with Word, I recommend creating a new style based on the existing style instead. If you are working with your own custom style and you want to modify it, follow these steps:

1. Click the Styles dialog box launcher (or press Alt+Ctrl+Shift+S).

2. Click the Manage Styles button to open the dialog box shown in Figure 7.28.

3. Click Modify to see the Modify dialog box. This is essentially identical to the Create New Style from Formatting dialog box except that you cannot change a style's type. If it's a paragraph style, for example, you cannot convert it to a linked style.

4. Make any changes and then click OK.

## Updating a style to match a selected block of text

To update an existing style to match a current selection, click the style's drop-down list arrow in the Styles window to see the options shown in Figure 7.29. Click Update [*style name*] to Match Selection to have the style formatting match your current selection.

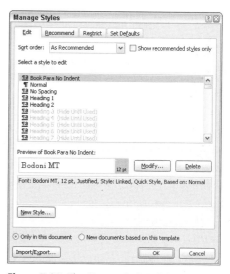

**Figure 7.28.** The Manage Styles dialog box

## Removing a paragraph style

If you want to remove a style, there are several methods available to you, depending on your needs. You can remove all the formatting and reset the style to Normal, you can remove all instances of a style from text within a document, you can remove a style from the Quick Style gallery, or you can delete a style entirely.

### Removing a style from text

If you just want to clear all formatting and reset the style to Normal, select the text and then click the Clear Formatting button in the Font group of the Home tab on the Ribbon.

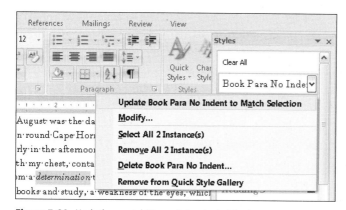

**Figure 7.29.** Updating a style to match selected text

> **Inside Scoop**
>
> If you just want to remove some additional formatting added to the block of text but want to keep the style intact, use Style Inspector from the Styles window and click the Clear Paragraph Formatting or Clear Character Formatting buttons next to the Plus windows.

To remove all instances of the style in the current document, click the drop-down list button next to the style in question and then click Remove All [*x*] Instance(s) to remove all instances of that style and reset those paragraphs to Normal (*x* being the number of instances of the style found in the document).

### Removing a style from the Quick Style gallery

To remove a style from the Quick Style gallery, click the drop-down list button next to the style in question and then click Remove from Quick Style Gallery. (This does not delete the style, but it does remove it from the gallery. To add it back to the gallery, click Manage Styles in the Styles window, click Modify, and select the Add to Quick Style list option.)

### Deleting a style

To delete a style, click the drop-down list button next to the style in question and then click Delete [*style name*]. You cannot delete Normal or built-in Heading styles. Curiously, if you attempt to delete other built-in Quick Styles, they will not be deleted, but any instances of the deleted built-in style will be reset to Normal.

## Working with lists

Word 2007 provides you with three basic types of lists: bulleted lists, numbered lists, and multilevel lists. They are summarized in Table 7.1, earlier in this chapter. You may have occasion to use other Word features to create lists, such as lists in the form of tables (see Chapters 15 and 16) or lists created as reference aids (see Chapter 22). For now, I focus on these three basic types.

One thing that applies to all these types of lists is that items within the lists are separated by a paragraph mark (by pressing Enter). Also, you can either type your list first, select it, and then apply a list style, or you can start by clicking the list's button and creating the list as you go. Clicking the list's button again while the list is selected removes the list feature.

**Inside Scoop**

Use the ruler if you need to adjust the distance between bullets or numbers and their corresponding text items. It works just as it would for a hanging paragraph.

## Creating a bulleted list

To create a bulleted list from an existing list, follow these steps:

1. Create a new blank document and type the following text, ending each line by pressing Enter:

    **Drink plenty of water**

    **Take vitamins**

    **Exercise regularly**

2. Select the text.

3. Click the Bullets button in the Paragraph group of the Home tab on the Ribbon. This gives you a bulleted list using the default bullet style, as shown in Figure 7.30.

> •→ Drink·plenty·of·water¶
> •→ Take·vitamins¶
> •→ Exercise·regularly¶

**Figure 7.30.** Creating a bulleted list

### Choosing a bullet

To choose a different bullet (other than the default), follow these steps:

1. Using the previous example, select the bulleted list.

2. Click the Bullets list button to see the bullet gallery shown in Figure 7.31. Note that hovering over a bullet previews the bullet in the list in your document in Print and Web Layout views.

3. Click the new bullet to accept the change. The new bullet is now the default bullet for your document until you change it again.

### Defining a new bullet

If you don't like the short list of bullets in the bullet gallery, you can choose a special symbol from a font or choose a picture for your bullet. To choose a symbol from a font, follow these steps:

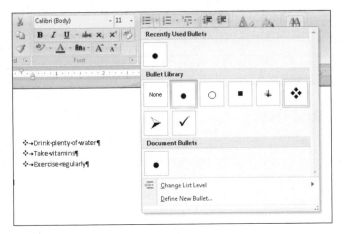

**Figure 7.31.** Changing the bullet style

1. Using the previous example, select the bulleted list.

2. Click the Bullets list button.

3. Click Define New Bullet. The Define New Bullet dialog box appears, as shown in Figure 7.32.

4. Click Symbol to open the dialog box shown in Figure 7.33. By default, the special Symbol font is selected, but you can choose any font installed in Windows.

5. Click the symbol you want to use as a bullet. In this example, the spade is selected. The Define New Bullet preview shows the new symbol.

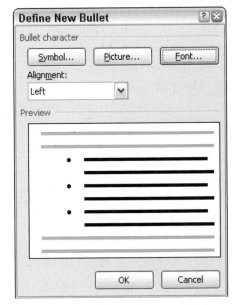

**Figure 7.32.** Defining a new bullet

6. Click OK. The bulleted list now displays the new bullet.

**Watch Out!**

If you choose a symbol for your bullet from a font that is not likely to be available on another computer, choose Microsoft Office ➪ Word Options ➪ Save, and then select the Embed fonts in the file option. This ensures that the bullets appear as you intended if your document is opened on another PC.

You can also choose a picture instead of a symbol from a font. Clicking Picture opens a gallery of ready-made bullet graphics from Microsoft. You can also search online via text or import your own bullet from any number of graphics file formats by clicking the Import button.

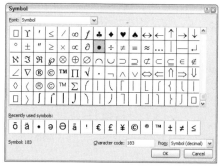

**Figure 7.33.** Choosing a symbol for the new bullet

# Creating numbered lists

Numbered lists are particularly handy because they keep track of the numbering for you. If you delete an item, the list is renumbered. If you add an item, the list also is updated. To create a numbered list from an existing list, follow these steps:

1. Create a new blank document and type the following text, ending each line by pressing Enter:

   **Drink plenty of water**

   **Take vitamins**

   **Exercise regularly**

2. Select the text.

3. Click the Numbering button in the Paragraph group of the Home tab on the Ribbon. This gives you a numbered list using the default number format.

### Choosing a number format

To choose a different numbering (or lettering) format, follow these steps:

1. Using the previous example, select the numbered list.

2. Click the Numbering list button to see the Numbering Library shown in Figure 7.34. Note that hovering over a number format previews the format in the list in your document.

3. Click the new number format to accept the change. The new number format is now the default for your document until you change it again.

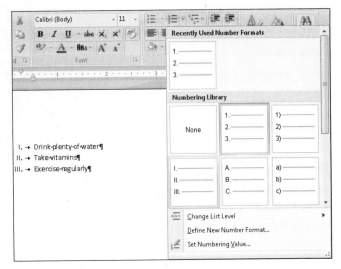

**Figure 7.34.** Changing the number format

## *Defining a new number format*

If you don't like the short list of number formats in the Numbering Library, a larger list available that you can use to add elements to create a custom number format. To do so, follow these steps:

1. Using the previous example, select the numbered list.

2. Click the Numbering list button.

3. Click Define New Number Format. The dialog box displayed in Figure 7.35 appears.

4. Click the Number style drop-down list and choose from one of the available styles. For this example, select 1st,

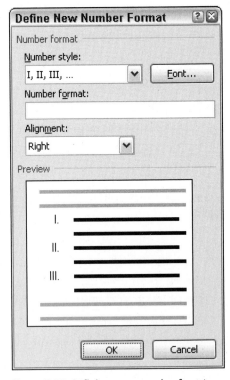

**Figure 7.35.** Defining a new number format

2nd, 3rd. (You can also choose a different font for the number by clicking Font, or change the alignment by choosing Left, Right, or Center from the drop-down list.)

5. By default, the number is followed by a period. You can remove the period or replace it with another character or string of characters by editing the Number format. For this example, select the period and type a colon (:). The preview shows the new number format with a colon.

6. Click OK. The numbered list now displays the new number format, as shown in Figure 7.36.

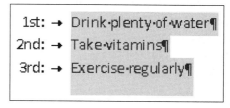

**Figure 7.36.** The new number format appears in the numbered list.

### Setting the number value

In some situations you may start a numbered list, add some paragraphs, and continue with the numbering where you left off or even start numbering from an entirely different number. For these situations, click the Numbering list button, and then click Set Numbering Value, which displays the options shown in Figure 7.37. If you use the Start new list option and select a new starting value (the Set value to list box), your list starts with the new number. If you are continuing from the previous list in the document, select the Continue from previous list option. That way, if you edit the list and remove one of the numbered items, the entire list (both the first list and the later continuation) is renumbered consecutively. When you finish changing settings, click OK to make them go into effect.

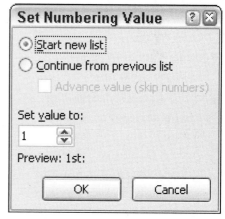

**Figure 7.37.** The Set Numbering Value dialog box

# Creating a multilevel list

A multilevel list can be either a bulleted or a numbered list. Most multi-level lists are outlines (that appear as such in the document, as opposed to Outline view), step-by-step instructions for procedures with subproce-dures, organizational bylaws, and so on. With multilevel lists, it is most practical to apply the multilevel list feature at the beginning of the process. That way, you can create subordinate items as you go with less chance of making mistakes in assigning level. Alternatively, you can cre-ate a list and indicate subordinate levels between entries by pressing Tab (or by clicking Increase Indent) once for every sublevel. If you then select the list and click Multilevel list, Word converts each indented item to its corresponding sublevel.

To create a multilevel list from scratch, follow these steps:

1. For this example, create a new blank document.

2. Click the Multilevel List button in the Paragraph group of the Home tab on the Ribbon. This gives you a multilevel list library to choose from. Notice that when you mouse over a list style, it expands to give you a more detailed preview, as shown in Figure 7.38.

3. Click the list style that begins with 1), a), and i). If you have not used this feature before, this is the Current List style by default. You will see the initial 1) followed by a tab.

**Figure 7.38.** Previewing a multilevel list style

**Inside Scoop**
Other Word features are better suited for creating certain types of multilevel lists: to organize your document with headings, use the Outline view (Chapter 4); to create a table of contents, use the Table of Contents feature (see Chapter 22).

4. Type **Fauna** and press Enter.

5. Press Tab to indent to level 2, then type **Arthropoda**, and press Enter.

6. Note that the level is the same as the previous. Type **Chordata** and press Enter.

7. This time, you want to create an additional level (in this example, a subphylum of Chordata). Press Tab again to indent to level 3, then type **Vertabrata**, and press Enter.

8. For the next item, you want to enter a level-1 entry. Press Shift+Tab twice to promote the entry to level 1 from level 3.

9. Now type **Flora**. Your list should now look like Figure 7.39.

To change the multilevel list style, select the list, click Multilevel List, and click the new list type from the list library to change the selected list.

```
1}→Fauna¶
    a}→Arthropoda¶
    b}→Chordata¶
        i}→ Vertabrata¶
2}→Flora¶
```

**Figure 7.39.** A multilevel list

### Defining a new multilevel list

If you don't find the list you like in the multilevel list library, you can create almost any conceivable multilevel list style in Word. To access numerous settings for customizing lists, choose Multilevel List ⇨ Define Multilevel List. To view the entire list of settings, click More, which opens the full dialog box shown in Figure 7.40. It's beyond the scope of this book to discuss all of these options, but you can see from examining the dialog box that just about any known numbering system is possible.

### Defining a new list style

If you spend much time customizing a multilevel list, you quickly come to the conclusion that you can save time by storing all the setting information as a style. To do this, choose Home ⇨ Multilevel List ⇨ Define New List Style to open the dialog box shown in Figure 7.41. You can then name

**Inside Scoop**

If you want a visual cue when selecting levels for entries, choose Home ⇨ Multilevel List ⇨ Change List Level, and then select a previewed level.

your list style and make any formatting changes. You can gain access to the many numbering options in the New Multilevel list dialog box by choosing Format ⇨ Numbering. When you finish choosing settings, click OK to save the new list style.

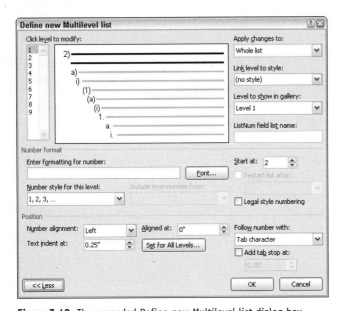

**Figure 7.40.** The expanded Define new Multilevel list dialog box

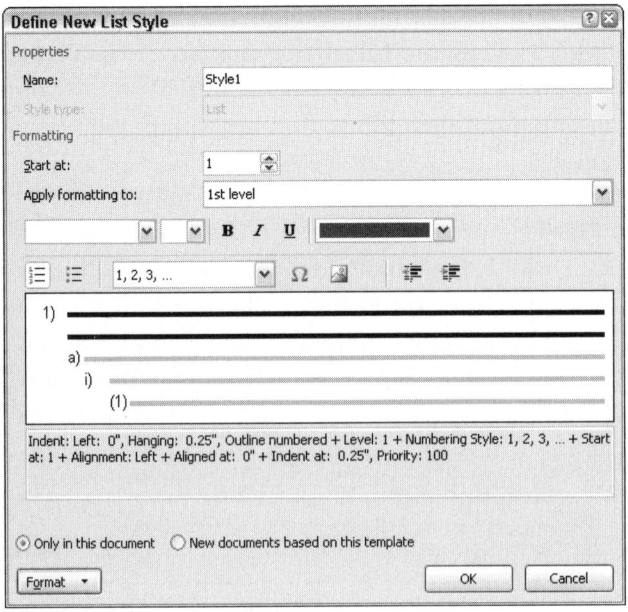

**Figure 7.41.** Defining a new list style

## Just the facts

- Most paragraph format settings can be made from the buttons in the Paragraph group of the Home tab of the Ribbon.

- You can fine-tune your paragraph formatting adjustments by clicking the Paragraph dialog box launcher on the Home tab.

- Use paragraph styles to save time and give your documents a consistent look.

- A wide variety of lists are available using the Bullets, Numbering, and Multilevel List commands.

**GET THE SCOOP ON...**
Giving your documents a professional look with
Document Themes ■ Setting up your page ■ Adding head-
ers, footers, page numbers, and more ■ Inserting a page

# Format Your Pages

**T**his chapter describes the features of Word that help you change the look of your page or your entire document, as opposed to your character or paragraph. However, these divisions are not always clear. When in doubt, I try to defer to how Microsoft chooses to divide the commands.

First, I discuss Document Themes, an expanded feature in Word 2007 that is a bit like Windows Themes, allowing you to change many different types of formatting all at once with a unified design theme. After themes, I discuss how to set up your page: This is a big topic, and it includes setting margins and tabs, selecting paper size, working with multicolumn text, how to insert page and section breaks in your document, using line numbering, and working with hyphenation. I then move on to adding headers, footers, page numbers, borders, background colors, and water-marks. Last, I show you how to insert cover pages and blank pages: a handy new feature for larger documents.

## Working with Document Themes

You can choose from built-in themes or create your own theme based on an existing one. This is great if you want to maintain a consistent corporate or organizational identity across many documents. Themes also work with Excel and PowerPoint so that your spreadsheets, slide presentations, and documents can have a unified look. Themes do this by using a set of two fonts (one for headings and one for body text), a small color palette of compatible colors, and a consistent way to treat graphical effects like SmartArt. The document theme, theme font, theme colors, and theme effects can be customized. The customized settings are stored in your Templates\Document Themes folder. That way, custom themes are not bound to one template or application. If you create a custom theme but close the current document without saving, the custom theme will still exist.

## Changing Document Themes

If you open a blank document in Word 2007, a theme is already selected by default (the Office theme). To change a document's theme, choose Page Layout ⇨ Themes, and then select a theme from the themes gallery shown in Figure 8.1 by clicking it. Note that as you mouse over a new theme, colors, fonts, and effects in your document change enabling you to preview the new theme on the fly. If you decide you want the document to revert back to its original theme, choose Page Layout ⇨ Themes ⇨ Reset to Theme from Template. If you are using Normal.dotm and have not modified it, this will be the Office theme. If you have changed and saved the theme for Normal.dotm or are using another template for the document, it reverts to whichever theme you assigned to that template.

The built-in themes are typical Microsoft default designs: They are certainly professional looking, but they are by necessity fairly bland and predictable because they are designed to appeal to just about everybody. In the rest of this section, you learn how to make changes to individual aspects of themes (fonts, colors, and effects) and how to create your own customized themes.

## Fonts

As mentioned in Chapter 6, it's best to limit the number of fonts you use in a document. With Document Themes, you have two fonts to choose from: one for headings and one for body text. (Of course, it's perfectly

**Hack**

To get a better view when previewing themes, you can resize the theme gallery using the grip (three dots) in the lower-right corner of the theme gallery window.

acceptable to have just one font for both headings and body text also; some of the built-in themes use only one font for both.) The theme fonts work in conjunction with Quick Styles to coordinate a wide range of styles in a compatible way. This is accomplished by using the two base fonts (or if you so choose, one base font) and varying the size and font treatment, adding bold, a different color, and so on.

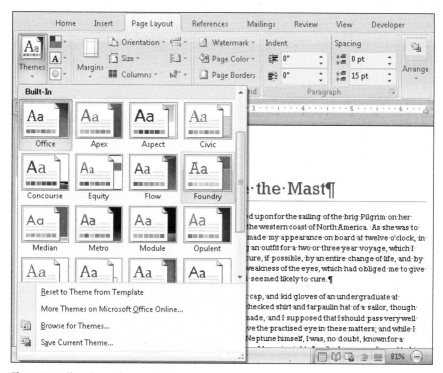

**Figure 8.1.** Changing a document's theme

## Choosing theme fonts

To choose a set of existing theme fonts, choose Page Layout ⇨ Themes and click the Font button to show the list of theme fonts. As with themes, if you hold your mouse over a new theme font set, you can see a live preview of what the new theme font set would look like, as shown in Figure 8.2. In the figure, I moved the title over to the right so that I could see its preview. If you leave your mouse over a new theme font set long enough, the live preview goes away and the document displays your current font

**Bright Idea**

If you want all your documents to have that pre-Office 2007 look, open Normal.dotm and select the Office Classic theme font, which gives you Arial headings and Times New Roman body text. Save the Normal.dotm template to make this your default theme.

settings. To see the preview again, simply move the mouse to another theme font set and then back again. (One limitation to this feature is that you tend to have headings blocked so that you can't get a good idea what the new font looks like unless the heading is long, centered, or aligned right.) When you decide on a new theme font set, click the font to implement the change.

To have your document's fonts revert to the default fonts for the current theme, just reselect the current theme (Page Layout ⇨ Themes, and then click the theme).

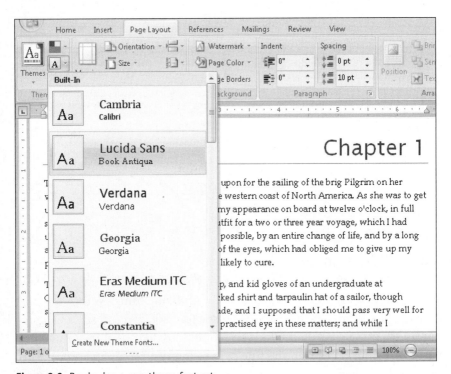

**Figure 8.2.** Previewing a new theme font set

## *Creating new theme fonts*

You can't actually create new fonts with Word, but you can make any installed fonts into theme fonts. This is particularly useful if you have chosen a particular font or set of fonts to use for all corporate communications to the outside world. To create a custom theme font set, follow these steps:

1. Click the Theme Fonts button from the Page Layout tab of the Ribbon.

2. Click Create New Theme Fonts to display the dialog box shown in Figure 8.3.

**Figure 8.3.** The Create New Theme Fonts dialog box

3. If you know the name of the font you want to select as your heading font, you can click the Heading font box and begin typing the font's name (**Gill Sans MT** in the example shown in Figure 8.4) until the font's name appears in the box. Alternatively, you could select the font from the drop-down list. Once selected, it appears in the Sample window.

**Figure 8.4.** Entering data for the new custom theme font

4. Follow the same procedure for the body font (**Times New Roman** in the example shown in Figure 8.4).

5. In the Name field, type **Corporate**, so that your dialog box looks like Figure 8.4.

6. Click Save to save your changes. The new fonts are selected for the current theme.

---

**Hack**

If you are comfortable editing XML files, you can change fonts for a custom theme font set by editing its XML file: Custom theme fonts are stored in …\Templates\Document Themes\Theme Fonts\[*Custom Theme Font Name*].xml. Just change the font name to exactly match the new font name you want to use.

When next you view the Theme Fonts, your new custom font appears at the top of the list, as shown in Figure 8.5. If you mouse over your custom theme font set, the assigned name, Corporate in this example, pops up for identification purposes.

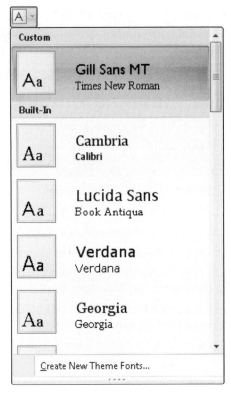

**Figure 8.5.** The new custom theme font set appears at the top of the list.

## Colors

You can select individual colors that Word uses with the current theme. It's useful to understand an important distinction about how colors are used with themes as opposed to choosing a fixed color from a color palette. Each theme has a set of colors with designations such as "Text/Background 1 - Dark" and "Accent 1." If you are using themes, or if you choose theme colors when choosing font or background colors when formatting or creating styles, these designations are used to determine the color rather than a fixed RGB or HSL color.

### Choosing theme colors

The easiest way to change the theme's colors is to choose a different built-in color set from one of the other themes and assign it to the current theme. To do this, click the Theme Colors button from the Themes group on the Page Layout tab to see the menu shown in Figure 8.6. As with theme fonts, you can see a live preview of theme color changes by

**Bright Idea**

If your document will be printed in black ink only, you can choose the Grayscale theme color set to display only black, white, and shades of gray.

moving your mouse over a theme color set. Click the Theme Colors set that you want to implement the new setting.

### Creating a new custom color set

Besides the built-in color schemes that are assigned to each built-in document theme, you can create your own custom theme color set. In the following example, we start with the Office theme and modify it so that we have a theme color set called Corporate Red. The example will be most effective if you already have some text and headings to look at. To change the colors for the current theme, follow these steps:

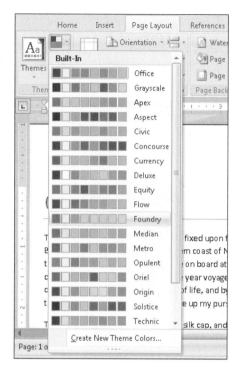

**Figure 8.6.** Choosing theme colors

1. Click the Theme Colors button from the Page Layout tab on the Ribbon.

2. Click Create New Theme Colors to display the dialog box shown in Figure 8.7.

3. Click Text/Background - Dark 2.

4. Click the leftmost standard color (Dark Red). Notice that the background color in the left side of the sample changes to dark red.

5. Click Accent 1.

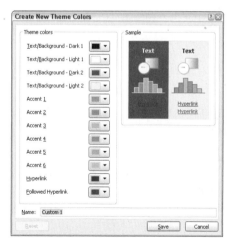

**Figure 8.7.** Creating new theme colors

6. Click Light Blue in the Standard Colors row (fourth from the right). Notice that the shaded object in the sample changes to light blue.

**7.** Highlight the default name in the Name field "Custom 1" and type
**Corporate Red.**

**8.** Click Save to save the new custom Theme Colors set (or Reset to
revert to the current Theme Colors).

You can create custom colors in much the same way you would font
colors, either by choosing from a palette or by specifying RGB or HSL
values.

## Effects

In addition to fonts and colors, you can also change certain line and fill
effects with Document Themes. This is particularly useful for such things
as graphical elements such as shapes and SmartArt (see Chapter 17).

While you cannot create your
own custom effects, you can select
from a list of predefined effect
styles. To do so, click the Theme
Effects button in the Themes
group of the Page Layout tab on
the Ribbon, which displays the
dialog box shown in Figure 8.8.
As with document themes, theme
fonts, and theme colors, if you
mouse over a theme effects set,
the effects are previewed live in
your document. Click the theme
effects set to implement the new
setting.

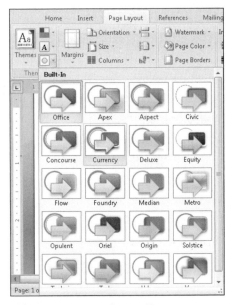

**Figure 8.8.** Selecting theme effects

## Saving a custom theme

Once you customize your selec-
tions of theme fonts, theme colors, and theme effects to your satisfaction,
you can save all of them together as a new custom theme. To do so,
choose Page Layout ⇨ Themes ⇨ Save Current Theme. A dialog box
like the one shown in Figure 8.9 appears. Type a name for the theme in
the File name field. The new theme with the file name extension .thmx is
added to the Document Themes folder within your Templates folder.
When you next click Themes, your custom theme appears at the top of
the list, as shown in Figure 8.10.

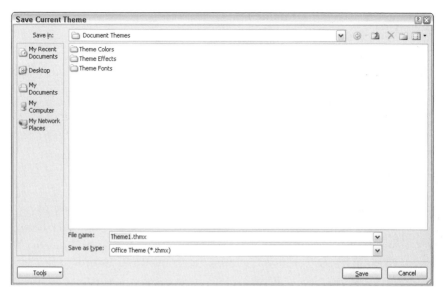

**Figure 8.9.** Saving the current settings as a custom theme

## Other document themes commands

If you want your theme to revert to the original theme for your current template, choose Page Layout ⇨ Themes ⇨ Reset to Theme from Template. To look for new themes that may become available via Office Online, make sure you have established an Internet connection and choose Page Layout ⇨ Themes ⇨ More Themes on Microsoft Office Online. If you need to find a theme that is not listed (because it is not in the default theme location), choose Page Layout ⇨ Themes ⇨ Browse for Themes.

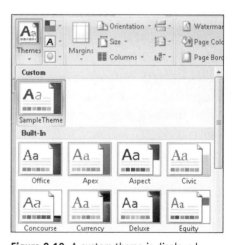

**Figure 8.10.** A custom theme is displayed.

## Setting up your page

In this section, various adjustments you can make to the page are covered, although some of the settings, such as margins, tabs, and hyphenation, can apply to individual paragraphs as well. Most of the commands discussed are accessible from the Page Layout tab on the Ribbon.

Before discussing margins and tabs, it's important to mention that tabs and paragraph margin settings are made relative to the page margins, not the edge of the page. Thus, if you have a paragraph left margin that is set to 0, it is really set to the left page margin. If your left page margin is 1 inch, then a paragraph with a left margin of 0 will start 1 inch from the left edge of the paper. The same holds true for tabs.

## Setting page margins

You can set page margins in Word with the ruler by selecting from preset sets of typical page margins on the Ribbon, or by typing values in a dialog box. You can also set the page margins using the vertical and horizontal rulers. (If your Ruler is not visible, click the View Ruler button at the top of the vertical scroll bar to display it.) You can also choose Page Layout ⇨ Margins and select one of the margin settings, or click the Page Setup dialog box launcher from the Page Layout tab of the Ribbon to type page margin values in the dialog box.

### Setting the left and right page margins with the ruler

To set the left and right page margins with the ruler, you first need to understand the difference between page margins and what most of us would think of as paragraph margins, which are called *indents* in Word's user interface. The page margins on the horizontal ruler are indicated by the colored bar (usually blue) to the left and right of the paragraph indent pointers and sliders.

The left indent, first-line indent, and hanging indent pointers are usually lined up at the left page margin, forming a sort of hourglass on top of a box at the edge of the color bar on the left side of the ruler. To change the left margin, you need to move your mouse pointer between the upward-pointing hanging indent point and the downward-pointing first-line indent pointer. It is a bit tricky to do, but when you succeed,

**Hack**

If it's too hard to point to the left margin, you can drag the left, first line, and hanging indents out of the way first by dragging the left indent pointer (the rectangle below the hourglass), and then dragging it back into place after adjusting the left page margin.

---

### A Word About Sections

In Word, the term *section* has a very specific meaning. It is used to indicate a new area of the document that may have different page formatting, page headers, numbering, columns, and so on. You can have a new section start with a new page or in the middle of a page (as when the top half of the page has two columns of text and the bottom half has one column only). Section breaks come in various types, and they are discussed in detail later in this chapter.

---

your mouse cursor changes from a single arrow pointing to the upper left into a double arrow pointing left and right, and the pop-up label will say Left Margin. Once you see the double arrow, click and drag the left page margin to the left or right to the new desired location. The paragraph indents all move as you change the left margin.

To change the right page margin, click the edge of the color bar at the right side of the horizontal ruler when you see the double arrow described previously and the pop-up label that says Right Margin. This is easier to do than the left margin because usually only the right indent pointer is aligned with the right margin. Drag the right margin to where you want it to go. Only the right indent moves along with the right margin; the left margin and other paragraph indents stay where they are.

After you set the left and right page margins, you can still move paragraph indents outside the page margins either with the pointers on the ruler or by using paragraph formatting.

### *Setting the top and bottom margins with the ruler*

To change the top and bottom margins using the vertical ruler, click the edge of the color bar at the top or bottom of the vertical ruler: The mouse pointer changes to a double upward- and downward-pointing arrow. While holding the left mouse button, drag the color bar to where you want the margin to be.

### *Using preset margins*

Word 2007 has added a page margin gallery of preset margins. To select a set of left, right, top, and bottom margins from the list, choose Page Layout ⇨ Margins. You can select from the gallery of available preset

**Bright Idea**

If you want to use Word 2003 margin defaults, which are different from Word 2007, select the Office 2003 Default setting.

margins, some of which are shown in Figure 8.11. This gallery does not feature a live preview: You have to click the new page margin setting and put it into effect to see what it looks like.

### Setting custom margins

To specify your own custom page margins, choose Page Layout ⇨ Margins ⇨ Custom Margins. (You can also set custom margins by choosing Page Layout ⇨ Page Setup.) This displays the dialog box shown in Figure 8.12. You can set the left, right, top, and bottom margins. (The default measurement is inches.) You could also type **cm** or **mm** after the number value and Word converts the metric value to inches to two decimal places.

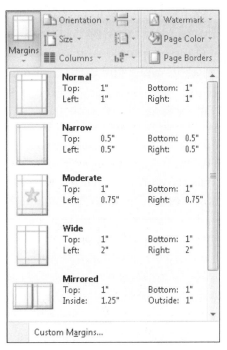

**Figure 8.11.** Selecting margins from a preset margin gallery

In addition to these margins, you can set a gutter width and gutter position. The *gutter* is an additional outside margin that you can set when you intend to print and bind your document. If your pages are bound, you need a certain amount of extra margin to take into account the part of the page that does not lie flat. The Gutter setting allows you to adjust this. The Gutter position setting allows you to set the position of the gutter if the Multiple pages setting is Normal: The document can be bound at the left edge (Left) or at the top edge (Top). If you have the Multiple pages set to another setting, such as Book fold or Mirror margins, the gutter position is automatic.

**Inside Scoop**

Word 2007 stores your last custom page settings in the margin gallery at the top of the list with the name Last Custom Setting.

Once you change the margins, you can decide whether you want them to apply to the current section, this point forward, or the whole document. If you selected text when you created the custom margin settings, your options are selected sections, selected text, or the whole document. When you make all necessary changes, click OK to put them into effect.

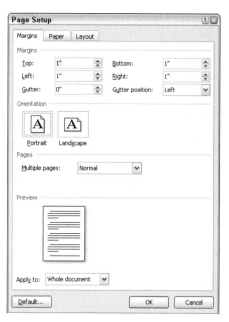

**Figure 8.12.** Margins can be set in the Margins tab of the Page Setup dialog box.

## Working with tabs

Tabs (or tab stops) are a way to make text line up vertically. Tabs are a vestigial element of typewriter technology that can still be used for simple columns of information. If you intend to create sophisticated tabular material, use Word's table features (see Chapters 14, 15, and 16), which eliminate the need to set tabs manually.

### Working with tabs using the ruler

You can set, move, or clear tabs using the horizontal ruler. To add a tab using the ruler, click the Tab Type button in the upper-left corner at the intersection between the vertical and horizontal rulers until you see the icon that represents the appropriate tab type described in Table 8.1. Then move your mouse pointer to the horizontal ruler and click at the location where you want to insert the tab. Figure 8.13 shows an example of tabular material

**Figure 8.13.** Using tabs to format columns of text and numbers

with a left tab, two bar tabs, a center tab, and a decimal tab. Once you set the tabs, press Tab to move your cursor to the first (leftmost) tab. After typing the text for the first tab, press Tab again to move to the next tab. Note that bar tabs insert a bar when you set them and require no typing of text. To change a tab on the ruler, first select all lines (paragraphs) that you want to have affected by the change, and then drag the tab to a new location along the ruler, or click the tab type to change its type, as the case may be. To clear a tab using the ruler, drag the tab off the ruler. One feature, having a leading character, such as dots or dashes preceding a tab, is only available from the Tabs dialog box (see the following section).

**Table 8.1.** Tab types

| Symbol | Type | Description |
|--------|------|-------------|
| ⌞ | Left | Aligns text to the right of the tab |
| ⊥ | Center | Centers text at the tab |
| ⌟ | Right | Aligns text to the left of the tab |
| ⊥ | Decimal | Aligns numbers (or text) at the period (decimal point) typed at the tab |
| ⏐ | Bar | Inserts a vertical bar at the tab |

### Working with tabs from the Tabs dialog box

You can add new tabs, change their settings, or clear tabs from the Tabs dialog box. To launch the Tabs dialog box, choose Home ⇨ Paragraph ⇨ Tabs. The dialog box shown in Figure 8.14 appears. To set tabs, follow these steps:

**Hack**

If you have existing tabs, you can display the Tabs dialog box by double-clicking one the tabs. (Double-clicking the ruler with no tabs works, too, but it also inserts a tab wherever you double-click.)

1. In the Tab stop position field, type **1"** for this example. (You can just type **1** here, because the default measurement is inches. You can also type **cm** or **mm** after the number value and Word converts the metric value to inches to two decimal places.)

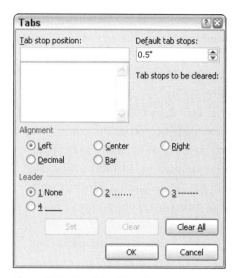

2. For this example, select Left in the Alignment section and None in the Leader section.

3. Click Set. The first tab of 1" is displayed in the list, but it has not yet been added to the document.

**Figure 8.14.** The Tabs dialog box

4. To add another tab, type **3** in the Tab stop position field.

5. Select Right in the Alignment section and 2........ in the Leader section.

6. Click Set.

7. Click OK. The tabs are now set on the ruler.

8. Press Tab and type **Chapter 23**.

9. Press Tab and type **347**. You now have a left-aligned tab with text followed by a row of dots that leads to the right-aligned page number.

To clear an individual tab, select all paragraphs for which you want the action to apply, and then double-click on an existing tab to open the Tabs dialog box, select the tab you want to clear from the list under Tab stop position, and click Clear. If you want to clear all tabs, click Clear All. Again, you must select all paragraphs for which you want the action to apply; otherwise, it only applies to the current paragraph.

## Selecting paper size and page orientation

You can select from a list of common U.S., European, and Asian paper sizes by choosing Page Layout ⇨ Size. Select your paper size from the list or choose Page Layout ⇨ Size ⇨ More Paper Sizes to display the dialog box in Figure 8.15. From the dialog box you can select one of the sizes in the list or specify the width (between 0.1 and 22 inches) and height (also between 0.1 and 22 inches) for a custom size. As with other linear measurements, you may substitute metric units by typing **mm** or **cm** after the numeric value and Word converts the value to inches to two decimal places.

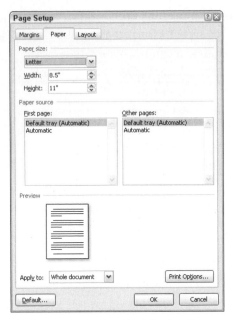

The term page orientation refers to whether the longest paper dimension is vertical (portrait) or horizontal (landscape). The default is portrait. To change the page orientation, choose Page Layout ⇨ Orientation and then click Portrait or Landscape.

**Figure 8.15.** The Paper tab of the Page Setup dialog box

## Working with multiple columns of text

To create multiple columns of wrapped text on a single page, choose Page Layout ⇨ Columns and choose from one of the options shown in Figure 8.16. (This is primarily designed for simple running columns of text and graphics, where adjoining columns require no vertical alignment with each other. If you want to create columns in a table where entries align vertically, the table feature described in Chapters 15 and 16 is better suited.) The Columns feature applies to either an entire document or an entire section of text.

If you want to change a single column of text to two evenly spaced columns, choose Page Layout ⇨ Columns ⇨ Two. In Word 2007, you have

**Hack**

You can adjust the left and right column margins by dragging them along the horizontal ruler as you would the page margins.

five preset options: One, Two, Three, Left, and Right. The first three are evenly spaced columns of the number specified. The Left option gives you a narrow left column and a wider right column. The Right option gives you the reverse. If you want to create more columns, adjust their widths, or do other custom settings, choose Page Layout ⇨ Columns ⇨ More Columns to see the dialog box shown in Figure 8.17. From here you can choose a preset column setting or select a number of columns from 1 to 19. Practically speaking, more than three or four are rarely used. The maximum number varies depending on the size and orientation of your paper. You can elect to have a thin vertical rule separate each column by selecting the Line between option. You can type values into the Width and spacing fields for each column. (Only three rows of columns show at a time, but if you have more, these fields become a scrolling list.) Select the Equal column width option to keep all columns of equal width and spacing.

In the event you want to have a page with more than one column format, such as one column

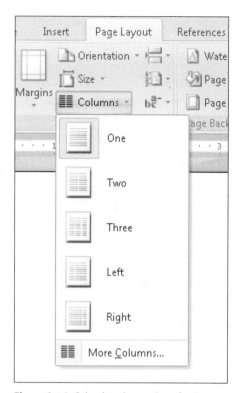

**Figure 8.16.** Selecting the number of columns of text

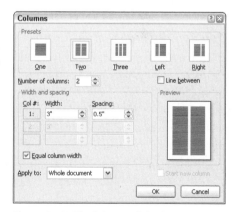

**Figure 8.17.** The Columns dialog box

at the top followed by two columns below, use a continuous section break to accomplish the task. An example is given in the following section.

## Page and section breaks

You can use section and page breaks to start new pages or begin new sections of page formatting on the same page, including page numbering, headers and footers, columns, and margin settings. Table 8.2 gives a summary of the various types of breaks. To add a page or section break, position the insertion point where you want the break to occur, and then choose Page Layout ⇨ Insert Page and Section Breaks. From the list, choose the appropriate break type, based on the descriptions available.

**Table 8.2.** Page and section break types

| Name | Break Type | Description |
| --- | --- | --- |
| Page | Page | Starts a new page |
| Column | Page | Starts a new column |
| Text Wrapping | Page | Starts a new text element on a Web page |
| Next Page | Section | Starts a new section on a new page |
| Continuous | Section | Starts a new section without starting a new page |
| Even Page | Section | Starts a new section on the next even page |
| Odd Page | Section | Starts a new section on the next odd page |

### Creating different page formats on the same page

To illustrate the use of section breaks, I show you how to combine single- and two-column formats on the same page. To do so, follow these steps:

1. If they are not currently visible, press Ctrl+* to make paragraph and other formatting marks visible.

2. Position your cursor immediately following the paragraph mark for the last line of text that you want to be single column (this should put it on the first line of the next paragraph).

**Watch Out!**

Any page formatting is stored at the section break. If you delete a section break, you delete any formatting specific to the section that precedes it. The page formatting for the following section is used.

**3.** Choose Page Layout ⇨ Insert Page and Section Breaks ⇨ Continuous. You will see a section break mark as shown in Figure 8.18.

**4.** Choose Page Layout ⇨ Columns ⇨ Two. The page now has a single column of text at the top followed by two columns below the section break, as shown in Figure 8.19.

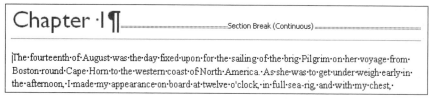

**Figure 8.18.** A continuous section break inserted in the document

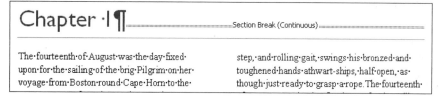

**Figure 8.19.** Two different column formats appear on the same page.

### Using a page break to start a new page

To start a new page (with the same page formatting as the previous page), position your cursor immediately following the paragraph mark for the last line of text that you want to be on the first page. To add a page break, you have three options. You can press Ctrl+Enter, choose Insert ⇨ Pages ⇨ Page Break, or choose Page Layout ⇨ Insert Page and Section Breaks ⇨ Page. Because a page break does not change formatting from the previous page, you don't risk losing formatting by deleting it, either.

## Line Numbers

You may find occasion to add line numbers along the side of the text of your document. Some such uses are numbered legal documents, transcripts, and academic texts. To add line numbering for the current page or section, choose Page Layout ⇨ Line Numbers to see the menu shown in Figure 8.20. As you can see from Figure 8.20, you have several self-explanatory choices regarding how you start line numbering and when you restart it.

By default, Word numbers every line consecutively starting with 1. If you want to choose a different numbering pattern or change how far the numbers appear from the text, choose Page Layout ⇨ Line Numbers ⇨ More Line Numbering (which takes you to the Layout tab of the Page Setup dialog box), then click Line Numbers to see the dialog box shown in Figure 8.21. Select the

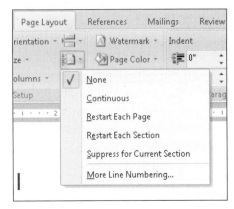

**Figure 8.20.** The Line Numbers menu

Add line numbering option to turn the feature on. You can start at any number between 1 and 32767 (although I don't recommend line numbering over three digits if you can avoid it; it's better to break up things into sections). You can set the spacing from text also. If you want to allow Word to determine the appropriate spacing, leave Auto (or type **Auto**) as the setting. You can also specify spacing from 0.1 to 22 inches (in theory). Clicking the up arrow increases the distance in 0.1-inch increments starting with 0.1 inches. You can also type a value. If

**Figure 8.21.** The Line Numbers dialog box

you don't want to see the number on every line, but on, for example, every tenth line, type the increment (it must be an integer from 1 to 100) and the current line number will appear every *x* lines, *x* being the increment you specify in the Count by field. Figure 8.22 shows an example with line numbering every fifth line.

## Chapter 1

The fourteenth of August was the day fixed upon for the sailing of the brig Pilgrim on her voyage from Boston round Cape Horn to the western coast of North America. As she was to
5   get under weigh early in the afternoon, I made my appearance on board at twelve o'clock, in full sea-rig, and with my chest, containing an outfit for a two or three year voyage, which I had undertaken from a determination to cure, if
10   possible, by an entire change of life, and by a

**Figure 8.22.** Line numbers every fifth line

**Bright Idea**

If you have a section or type of text that you don't want numbered, you can suppress at the paragraph level (or for the style) by checking the Suppress line numbers option on the Line and Page Breaks tab of the Paragraph dialog box.

# Hyphenation

By default, Word does not use hyphenation to break words at the right margin. Instead, it adds small amounts of incremental spacing between the words across the line so that they line up (if justified) or appear nearly lined up (if centered or left aligned). There are situations in which hyphenation makes sense, however. Some examples are text lines with very long words and lines with narrow margins, such as multicolumn or tabular text. Word has a hyphenation feature that makes word break decisions based on entries in its dictionary. You can either review each hyphenation decision (Manual) or allow Word to make the decision (Automatic). You can also use special characters to help control where or if a word is hyphenated or where a line should break. To turn hyphenation on for your document, choose Page Layout ⇨ Hyphenation. The menu shown in Figure 8.23 appears.

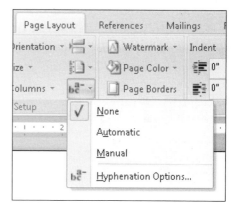

**Figure 8.23.** Hyphenation options

## *Manual hyphenation*

Manual hyphenation, as defined by Microsoft, is not typing a hyphen when you think you are near the end of a line. In fact, please don't do that unless you are using a typewriter. Instead, Word scans the document, querying you at each potential hyphenated word at the end of a line, suggesting a break and location for the hyphen. To begin manual hyphenation, choose Page Layout ⇨ Hyphenation ⇨ Manual Hyphenation. When Word encounters its first candidate for hyphenation, a dialog box like that seen in Figure 8.24 appears. You can either except Word's suggestion by clicking Yes, use the mouse or cursor keys to move the location of

---

**Bright Idea**

If you have a section of type of text that you don't want hyphenated, you can suppress hyphenation at the paragraph level (or for the style) by selecting the Don't hyphenate option on the Line and Page Breaks tab of the Paragraph dialog box.

**Watch Out!**

If you use manual hyphenation, you can't turn it off and remove hyphens at the click of a button. You must delete each one manually. However, if you later edit the text, causing the lines to break at different words, the manually hyphenated words will close back up as needed.

the hyphen and then click Yes, or reject hyphenating the word entirely by clicking No. If you want to abort the hyphenation session, click Cancel. If you don't abort the hyphenation session, Word queries you for each potential hyphenated word break (usually only once a paragraph or so) until the end of the document, at which time you see a notification that hyphenation is complete. At this point, click OK to exit hyphenation.

**Figure 8.24.** Reviewing hyphenation with the Manual Hyphenation feature

### Automatic hyphenation

You can also elect to have Word hyphenate your document automatically. Word scans the document, hyphenating words at the end of a line based on its own internal rules. (These rules can be adjusted; see the section on hyphenation options to see how.) To begin automatic hyphenation, choose Page Layout ⇨ Hyphenation ⇨ Automatic Hyphenation. When Word completes the operation, a notification that hyphenation is complete appears. At this point, click OK to exit hyphenation. If, after hyphenating the document this way, you decide you don't want to have the document hyphenated, choose Page Layout ⇨ Hyphenation ⇨ None to revert back to no hyphenation, and the hyphens are automatically removed.

### Hyphenation options

If you want finer control over hyphenation, choose Page Layout ⇨ Hyphenation ⇨ Hyphenation Options. The dialog box shown in

Figure 8.25 appears. Select the Automatically hyphenate document option to have Word begin hyphenating the document as soon as you click OK. If you want to change settings and then hyphenate manually, leave this option unchecked and click Manual instead of OK after making any setting changes.

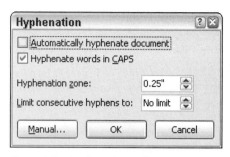

**Figure 8.25.** Hyphenation options

To avoid hyphenating acronyms (or anything else in all uppercase letters), deselect the check box for the Hyphenate words in CAPS. To extend or reduce the zone within which Word determines whether to hyphenate a word, use the arrow keys for the Hyphenation zone option. Adjusting the hyphenation zone is only useful when you are working with extreme sizes (very large text, very small text, or very narrow columns). Otherwise, it's best to let Word use the 0.25-inch zone for which Word is optimized. Finally, you can limit the number of consecutive hyphens. The default is No limit, but many compositors and proofreaders suggest limiting the number to 1, because consecutive broken words make it hard for the reader to find the next line correctly.

### Adding special characters to control hyphenation

Although you wouldn't want to do this for large amounts of text, it is sometimes useful to take advantage of special characters to force hyphenation to go a certain way. You may want a term or text phrase never to be hyphenated, such as a trademark or Internet address. You may always want a word to break at a certain place. Table 8.3 shows the various special characters available by choosing Insert ⇨ Symbol ⇨ More Symbols ⇨ Special Characters. Select the special character and then click Insert to insert it into your document. Table 8.3 also shows shortcut keys where applicable. Of course, you can also just type a hyphen sometimes. Use this method only when you are typing a term that already contains a hyphen, such as *Pre-Raphaelite* or *half-baked*.

**Table 8.3.** Special characters for controlling hyphenation

| Appears as* | Character | Keyboard shortcut | Description |
|---|---|---|---|
| – | nonbreaking hyphen | Ctrl+Shift+_ | Use in string with hyphen that you don't want to break a line, such as a phone number. |
| ¬ | optional hyphen | Ctrl+- | Use to control where a word breaks, inserting at the desired break point. |
| ° | nonbreaking space | Ctrl+Shift+Space | Use to prevent Word from breaking a line at a space (as in a heading). |
| ⬚ | no-width optional break | | Use to suggest a break with no hyphen (usually used for nontext characters). |
| ⬚ | no-width non break | | Use to prevent hyphenation (as with a trademark). |

*When formatting codes are displayed

# Laying out the page

This section covers page layout features such as page headers, footers, numbers, borders, backgrounds, watermarks, and so on. If you are thinking of creating a page with a complex design and atypical form, I suggest using the features described in Chapter 20.

## Adding headers, footers, and page numbers

You can add headers (a repeating heading that runs across the top of each page) or footers (a repeated treatment across the foot of the page) to your document. You can either start by adding a header and/or footer, or add them later. If you have complex formatting, you should add them at the beginning so that you take them into account when designing the page. You can have different headers or footers for different sections of text, have different headers or footers for odd and even pages, and you can elect to have a different header for the first page.

In Word 2007, you can choose from some preset headers and footers to make things a bit easier. I show you how to use the presets or create your own. Another new feature in Word 2007 is the ability to add page numbers in the outside margin of a page. This means Microsoft had to break out the page number feature from headers and footers, where it traditionally resided in previous versions of Word. Of course, you can still place the page number in the header or footer as before. You can access all these features from the Header & Footer group on the Insert tab of the Ribbon.

### Inserting preset headers and footers

You can save yourself time by choosing from the gallery of preset headers and footers available in Word 2007. To access these preset headers, choose Insert ⇨ Header; to access these preset footers, choose Insert ⇨ Footer. Most of the headers and footers are designed in pairs. Mousing over individual headers and footers in the gallery gives you a descriptive summary for each of the preset designs. For example, for the first preset header, Accent Triangle (title/date), the description is "Left-aligned title and right-aligned date with subtle accent line." Once you decide on a header or footer type, you can insert it into your document by clicking it.

To insert a preset matching header and footer from the gallery, follow these steps:

1. In a new blank document, choose Insert ⇨ Header.
2. Click Annual. The header is inserted onto the page, and a new design tab for headers and footers appears on the Ribbon, as shown in Figure 8.26.
3. Type **Annual Report** (in the Type the document title box).
4. Click Year.
5. Click the arrow to the right of the year to display a calendar. Select the year by clicking on a day within the desired year or click Today for the current year.
6. Click Footer (located in the Header & Footer Tools group of the Design tab).
7. Click Annual to insert the footer into the document. Note that this footer incorporates a page number into the design.
8. Click Close Header and Footer to finish the procedure.

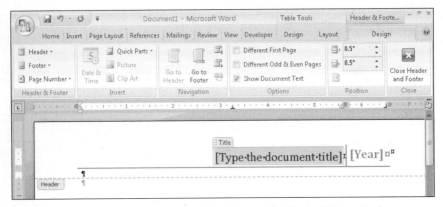

**Figure 8.26.** A new preset header showing the Design tab for Header & Footer Tools

## Working with headers and footers

Once you add a header and/or footer and close the Header and Footer design view, you can edit the main area of your document as needed. To make changes to the header or footer, double-click the header or footer to return to the design view.

### Header and footer options

Many multipage documents call for a different header and/or footer for the first page, or use different information on even and odd pages. You can check these options in the Options group of the Design tab. This automatically creates different first-page headers, or odd and even page headers. These two options can also be combined. You can also use the section break feature described earlier to create different headers or footers for new sections, such as new chapters. Don't use the Continuous type of section break if you want to change the header for the new section; choose Next Page, Even Page, or Odd Page instead. Otherwise, your header or footer will continue from the previous section. In the Options group you can also deselect the check box for Show Document Text if you find the main document text distracting and want to view the header or footer content only.

### Header and footer navigation

To navigate between headers and footers, you can click Go To Header or Go To Footer in the Navigation group of the Design tab. This lets you switch between the header and footer of the current section easily. If you have a different first-page header or footer, if you have different odd and

**Inside Scoop**

You can easily modify the character formatting of any text in the header or footer by selecting the text and then right-clicking it. Make any changes necessary from the pop-up menu.

even headers and footers, or if you use section breaks to create more than one header or footer type, you can click the Next Section or Previous Section buttons to go to the next or previous header or footer. Clicking Link to Previous uses the content from the previous section for the current section. (This option is useful for situations such as different odd and even headers but identical footers.)

### Positioning headers and footers

You can adjust the space between the top of the page and the header with the Header from Top list box in the Position group of the Design tab. Use the up- and down-arrow keys to make adjustments in 0.1-inch increments or type your own value. You can likewise adjust the space between the bottom of the page and the footer with the Footer from Bottom list box.

As with earlier versions of Word with a blank header or footer, the ruler is set so that the first text you type is left aligned, followed by a center tab at the center of the page and a right tab at the right margin. This means you can add an element for the left margin, then press Tab and add an element to be centered, press Tab again, and add an element to be right aligned. You can make changes to the tabs and margins on the ruler as you would with the main part of the document, or you can click Insert Alignment Tab in the Position group on the Design tab to display the dialog box shown in Figure 8.27. The difference between this and the standard Tabs dialog box is that you have a choice to make the alignment tab relative to the margin (that is, the page margin) or the indent.

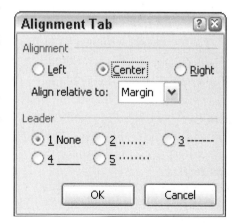

**Figure 8.27.** The Alignment Tab dialog box for headers and footers

### Adding a new blank header or footer

You may want to create your own header or footer and eschew the preset designs. You might think there would be a "blank" or "new" option, but there is not. To create a new blank header, choose Insert ⇨ Header ⇨ Edit Header instead of selecting a header. If you have chosen a preset header and you want to remove it and start with a blank one, choose Insert ⇨ Header ⇨ Remove Header instead. It gets you to the same place. To create a new blank footer, choose Insert ⇨ Footer ⇨ Edit Footer instead of selecting a footer. As with headers, if you have chosen a preset footer and you want to remove it and start with a blank one, choose Insert ⇨ Footer ⇨ Remove Footer.

### Adding date, time, or page number

To add a date or time to a header or footer, click Date & Time from the Insert group of the Design tab. You can choose from a large list of date, time, and combination date/time formats in the Date and Time dialog box. Select the Update automatically option to create an updateable field. Press F9 to update the field (there's a limit to how automated this feature is).

To add a page number to an existing header or footer, choose Quick Parts ⇨ Field and begin to type **Page** or select it from the list in the Field names list of the Field dialog box. Choose a format for your page number and then click OK to insert the field into your header or footer. You can modify the numbering format or the starting number by right-clicking the page number button and selecting Edit Field in the popup menu that appears, as shown in Figure 8.28. This displays a dialog box where you can change such settings.

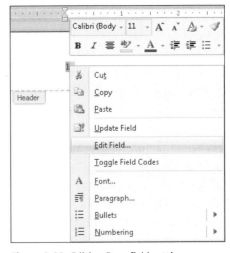

**Figure 8.28.** Editing Page field settings

### Adding other items to headers and footers

You can add many elements to headers and footers. It is beyond the scope of this book to include all possible permutations. Following are two examples that represent some ways you can better automate the

**Watch Out!**

Using the gallery of formatting page numbers to insert a page number into a header or footer becomes awkward. Try using the simple page field type for headers and footers and the Page Number feature for stand-alone page numbering.

process of adding header and footer material to larger or more complex documents without retyping text or cutting and pasting.

In the first example, I have a style I call Chapter Title (simply the Title style in the default Quick Styles saved with the name Chapter Title). I want to have the chapter title appear on each header after the first page of the chapter, but not on the first page, because that already has the chapter title in the main document, formatted in the style Chapter Title. To do this, follow these steps:

1. In preparation, create a document of at least two pages with a chapter title. Select the chapter title, apply the Title quick style, right-click the chapter title paragraph, click Save Selection as a New Quick Style, name it Chapter Title, and click OK.

2. Choose Insert ⇨ Header ⇨ Edit Header.

3. In the Options group of the Design tab now visible on the Ribbon, select Different First Page. Note the Header label changes to First Page Header, as shown in the sample document shown in Figure 8.29.

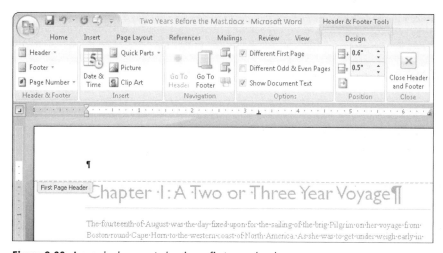

**Figure 8.29.** A sample document showing a first-page header

4. Click Next Section in the Navigation group of the Design tab. This brings you to a new header, labeled simply Header (as opposed to First Page Header) on the second page of your document.

5. Choose Quick Parts ⇨ Field from the Insert group of the Design tab.

6. In the Field names section of the Field dialog box, start typing **StyleRef** (or scroll through the list until you find this field type). Your screen should look something like Figure 8.30.

7. Click Chapter Title and then click OK.

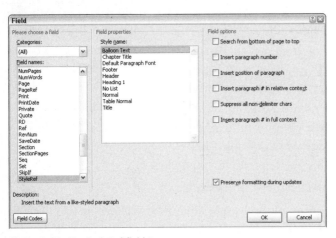

**Figure 8.30.** The StyleRef field type

Your second page has now pulled the text of the Chapter Title paragraph into the header, as shown in Figure 8.31, and will use the current Chapter Title content for subsequent pages until a new Chapter Title paragraph occurs.

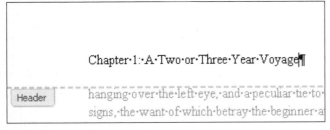

**Figure 8.31.** Using a StyleRef field to insert the content of a paragraph style into a header

In the second example, I show you how to take advantage of an automatically populated document property field (see Chapter 2) to add information into a document. If you make full use of document properties, you can create headers that routinely display important tracking data. For now, I just show you how to add the document's author by pulling the author name from the Author property for the document and putting it in the document's footer. To do this, follow these steps:

1. In a new blank document, choose Insert ⇨ Footer ⇨ Edit Footer.

2. Choose Quick Parts ⇨ Document Property ⇨ Author.

3. The author's name appears in the footer. At this point, you can type your name or any name, and it updates not only the footer, but also the Author document property.

### Adding page numbers to your document

To add page numbers to your document, choose Insert ⇨ Page Number and select one of the options displayed in Figure 8.32. The Top of Page, Bottom of Page, Page Margins, and Current Position menu items display galleries of possible page number formats. The Page Margins item refers to page numbers displayed at the left and right edge of the page, as opposed to at the top or bottom.

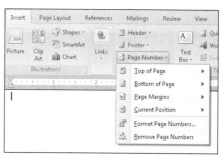

**Figure 8.32.** Page number options

You can select a number format, include a chapter number, and control when numbering starts. To do so, choose Insert ⇨ Page Number ⇨ Format Page Numbers to see the dialog box shown in Figure 8.33. If you have already inserted a page number, you can change format and numbering by selecting the page

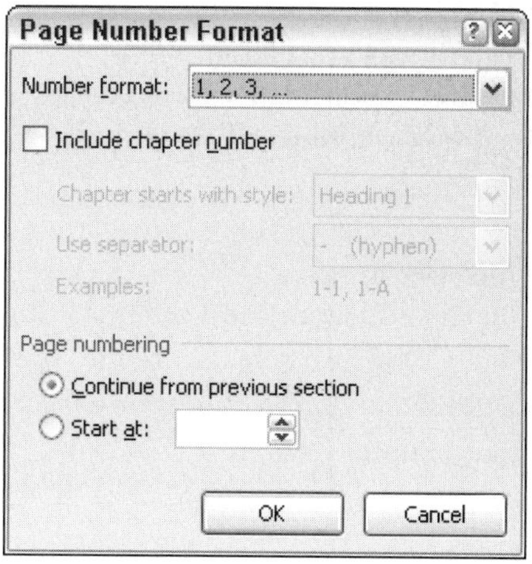

**Figure 8.33.** The Page Number Format dialog box

number and clicking the Format Page Numbers button. If you elect to include chapter information, you can choose the style to use and the separator to use between chapter and page number. Page numbering can be continuous (Continue from previous section) or can start at any number from 1 to 99999999. I suspect the practical upper limit is somewhat lower.

## Adding page backgrounds

You can add watermarks, colors, and borders to pages in Word. Commands to create page backgrounds of various types are located in the Page Background group of the Page Layout tab.

### Watermark

A watermark in physical stationery was historically a stationer's mark, visible when held up to the light. In Word, a watermark is a text or graphic design that is printed as a page background. It is usually a text message such as *Draft* or *Confidential* displayed in lighter text and printeddiago-

nally across the page. To add a watermark, choose Page Layout ⇨ Watermark and choose from the standard gallery of watermarks, or choose Page Layout ⇨ Watermark ⇨ More Watermarks to see the options shown in the Printer Watermark dialog box shown in Figure 8.34. To remove a watermark, choose Page Layout ⇨ Watermark ⇨ Remove Watermark.

**Figure 8.34.** Printed watermark options

### Page color

You can add colors and other shading effects by choosing Page Layout ⇨ Page Color. You select a theme, standard, or custom color much as you would select one for a font or paragraph background as described in previous chapters.

You can also choose from a number of background shading effects by choosing Page Layout ⇨ Page Color ⇨ Fill Effects to display the dialog box shown in Figure 8.35. The Gradient tab is shown in Figure 8.35, and the effects are evident. The Texture tab allows you to choose from color texture images of such textures as burlap, linen, crumpled brown paper, and so on. The Pattern tab allows you to choose a two-color dot pattern (by default black and white). You can choose a foreground and a background

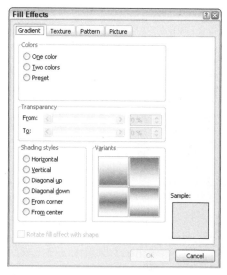

**Figure 8.35.** The Fill Effects dialog box

color for the pattern options. The pattern effects look like those in the very earliest Mac and Windows 1.0 graphics applications. The Picture tab uses a picture from a file as a page background. The difference between this and the watermark picture option is that the watermark option appears lighter and is automatically reduced to fit the page size. To remove any background color or fill effects, choose Page Layout ⇨ Page Color ⇨ No Color.

### Page borders

You can choose from any number of border types for your page. Choose Page Layout ⇨ Page Borders to display the dialog box shown in Figure 8.36. Once you get to the dialog box, the options are essentially unchanged from earlier versions of Word. You can choose from one of the common box types in the Setting list or create your own border by selecting Custom as the setting and then choosing each line's style, color, or width. You can also add art borders; some of the basic ones are fine, but they tend to be the lowest common denominator of clip art.

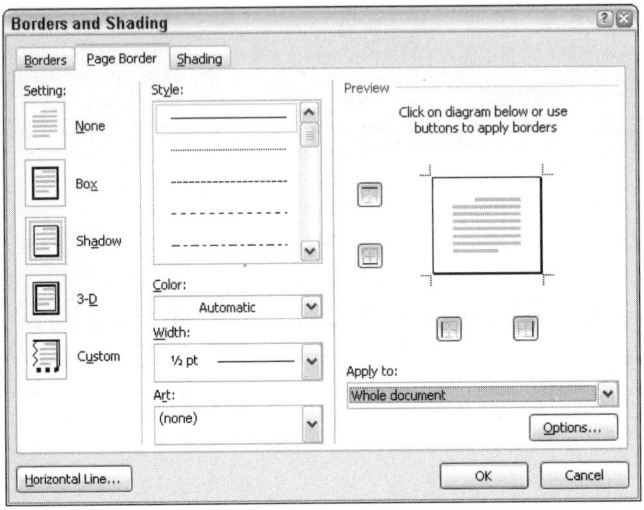

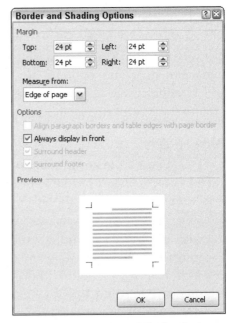

**Figure 8.36.** Page border settings

If you want to fine-tune the arrangement of page borders and, perhaps more importantly, how well they behave with tables, paragraphs, headers, and footers, choose Page Layout ⇨ Page Borders ⇨ Options to see the dialog box shown in Figure 8.37.

## Vertical alignment

I'm often surprised at the number of people who use Word daily but don't know about this feature. I use it any time I need to create a printed business letter. You can align your text vertically on the page, either from the top (the default we are all familiar with), the center (very useful for

**Figure 8.37.** The Border and Shading Options dialog box

**Bright Idea**

You can also create a custom cover page. To do so, create the page, select it, then choose Insert ⇨ Pages ⇨ Cover Page ⇨ Save Selection to Cover Page Gallery. In the Create New Building Block dialog box, assign the cover page a name. By default, all custom cover pages are stored in Building Blocks.dotx.

letters and notices), justified, or bottom. To access this feature, choose Page Layout, click the Page Setup dialog box launcher, click the Layout tab, and then select one of the four options from the Vertical alignment list.

# Inserting pages

If you need to attach a cover page to your document, add a blank page, or insert a page break, you can use the commands in the Pages group of the Insert tab on the Ribbon.

## Cover pages

To add a cover page to your document, choose Insert ⇨ Pages ⇨ Cover Page and choose from the gallery of preset cover pages. Once you decide on a cover page, click it to insert it into your document.

## Blank pages and page breaks

When I first saw the Blank Page option I asked myself why is this different from inserting two page breaks in a row? The answer is that the page is, in fact, really blank. If you create a multipage document, you may need to insert a blank page that is truly blank (with no headers or footers). Inserting two page breaks in a row creates a page with no text, but page background, header, footer, watermark, or page number information is still printed. To have a truly blank page, choose Insert ⇨ Pages ⇨ Blank Page.

You can also insert a more typical page break by choosing Insert ⇨ Pages ⇨ Page Break. However, it's easier just to press Ctrl+Enter to accomplish this.

## Just the facts

- Use Word's Themes feature to make document-wide design changes easily and consistently.

- Most page layout commands are available from the Page Layout tab of the Ribbon.

- Selecting from a common set of predefined margins and paper sizes can be accomplished from the Page Layout tab of the Ribbon.

- Ready-made headers, footers, page numbers, and cover sheets are available to save you time and effort.

# Go Public with Your Documents

GET THE SCOOP ON...
One-click printing ▪ Setting your printing options ▪
Previewing your document before you print it ▪ Choosing
a printer ▪ Printing to a fax

# PART III

# Print Your Document

A lthough printing to physical paper is less common than it once was, it is still one of the main reasons to use Word. Printing is also used as a metaphor for such things as printing to a fax machine or printing to Microsoft Office Image Writer (a program, not an actual physical printer) to create an MDI image for annotation or TIFF image for faxing. The add-in for creating a PDF (an Adobe Acrobat file) also worked as a printer driver in earlier versions of Word. Creating a PDF is now accomplished with Save As (see Chapter 2). This chapter covers quick printing, setting common printing options, working with Print Preview, and printing your document to local printers, network printers, and fax machines. Merge printing (mass mailings, form letters, and so on), envelope, and label printing are covered in Chapter 14.

Because of the wide variety of printers and printing environments, I can't cover every permutation here. I describe common tasks and useful things to know or watch out for. However, each printer driver is different, and so certain aspects of the printer's setup will be unique to your printer. I can't promise to cover some baffling situation you may encounter if it's specific to your printer. One key concept to bear in mind is that your printer is installed to work with Windows, not with Word. If you have printing questions or problems only with Word, they may well be

**Inside Scoop**

If you are having a problem with your printer, click Start, Printers and Faxes in Windows, and then click Troubleshoot printing or Get help with printing in the See Also section of the Printers and Faxes window.

addressed in this chapter. Questions or problems between your printer, your network, or Windows, aren't addressed here.

## Printing with Quick Print

If you have already set up a printer as a default printer, it's a good idea to add the Quick Print command to your Quick Access Toolbar. To do so, click the Customize Quick Access Toolbar button and click Quick Print. This adds a Quick Print button (a printer with a check mark indicating that it is the default printer) to the Quick Access Toolbar. Once the Quick Print button is displayed, you can print a copy of a document just by clicking the Quick Print button. Word prints the entire current document with whatever your current settings are for printer preferences for that printer. If your default printer is set to print two copies collated, clicking Quick Print will do just that. Bear in mind that you can set your default printer's preferences from Windows or from within another application, so it may not be set to how you last used it in Word if you changed say, from color printing to black and white only for some other application the last time you used the printer.

## Setting printing options

Microsoft has chosen to sprinkle its printing commands throughout Windows and Word. I have chosen to divide the various settings for printers into categories based on where you find them in the Windows or Word user interface, although in many cases a setting can appear in more than one place. Broadly speaking, settings related to printing can be divided into four categories: printing preferences in Windows, printer properties in Windows, Print dialog box settings in Word, and Word

**Watch Out!**

When you click Quick Print, it really does start printing immediately — not after clicking OK. Make sure you are ready to print before using this command.

**Inside Scoop**

If you don't see Printers and Faxes on your Windows Start menu, click Start, Control Panel, and then Printers and Faxes (if your Control Panel is in Classic view), or Start, Control Panel, Printers and Other Hardware, and then View installed printers or fax printers (if your Control Panel is in Category view).

printing options. The first two categories of settings are accessed by clicking Start and then Printers and Faxes in Windows. If you have at least one printer or fax machine installed, you see the list of printer tasks shown in Figure 9.1, including selecting printing preferences and setting printer properties. (If you have no printing devices installed in Windows, your only options in Printer Tasks will be Add a printer and Install a local fax printer.) The printer selected in Figure 9.1 has an icon with a check mark next to it, which indicates that the selected printer is the default printer. When you send a document to be printed, this is the printer that is used unless you expressly choose another one for a print job.

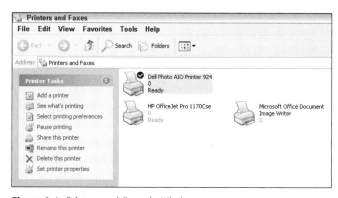

**Figure 9.1.** Printers and Faxes in Windows

## Printer preferences in Windows

To access printer preferences for a printer, click Start and then Printers and Faxes. Next, either click to select one of the displayed printers and then click Select printing preferences, or right-click a printer and click Printing Preferences. (Perhaps just to make things interesting, clicking the Properties button in the Print dialog box in Word displays these same printer preferences in Windows for whichever printer you have selected in the Print dialog box in Word. This is different from the printer properties in Windows, which are discussed in the next section.)

Once you launch printing preferences for a particular printer, you see a variety of options created by that printer's manufacturer with its print driver. Some printer drivers are very simple and have correspondingly simple preferences settings. Most recent ones are quite ambitious. Figure 9.2 shows just one of several tabs in a large dialog box with many options that came with my most recent home office inkjet printer. Figure 9.3 shows you the advanced options from a different manufacturer for an older office laser printer to give you a sense of the range of settings available.

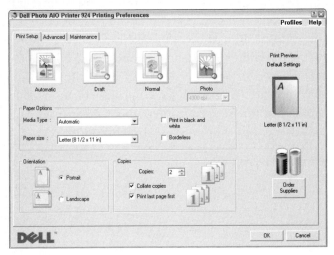

**Figure 9.2.** Dell Photo AIO Printer 924 printing preferences

This list won't be exhaustive, but in general, the printing preferences determine the following:

- The quality of the printing (how fine the resolution, how slowly the paper goes through the printer, and so on)
- The type of paper (size, thickness, surface)
- How the paper is fed into the printer
- The orientation (portrait versus landscape)

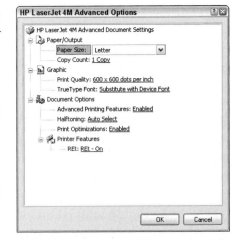

**Figure 9.3.** Hewlett-Packard LaserJet 4M advanced options

- The number of copies to print
- Whether to print one-sided or two-sided copies
- Layout options such as printing multiple pages per sheet, banners, posters, booklets
- Which ink to use (black, color, photo)
- Whether to collate copies (1, 2, 3, 1, 2, 3) or not (1, 1, 2, 2, 3, 3)

From the printing preferences dialog box, you can often print a test page and determine ink levels. Mine even allows me to buy more supplies (direct from the original manufacturer, of course!) at the click of a button. Unfortunately, the technical terminology each printer manufacturer uses for features varies. As an actual example, one manufacturer calls the feature that allows you to print reduced versions of more than one page on a single sheet of paper Multiple pages per sheet, and another manufacturer calls it N-Up. Refer to your printer's online help and printed manuals if you are not sure about a given setting.

## Printer properties in Windows

The printer's Properties dialog box in Windows is more standardized than the preferences. A sample Properties dialog box is shown in Figure 9.4. You may see an additional tab, such as an About tab. If your printer has only a black ink cartridge, the Color Management tab will be absent, of course. Fax machines have a different dialog box.

On the General tab, you get basic information about the printer, such as its name, location, a comment field, and capabilities. These fields are most

**Figure 9.4.** A sample printer's Properties dialog box

useful when you work with a local area network and you share a printer with others. If you have a stand-alone local printer sitting near your computer, you can change the name of the printer and add location and

## Overlapping Features

Some printers have special format or layout features that Word also creates on its own. Occasionally, these features step on each other's toes. For example, when printing multiple pages on a single sheet of paper, if I select Word's Zoom feature in the Print dialog box and select 2 pages in the Pages per sheet field, I should not choose N-Up and 2 pages on my printer's preferences setting. If I do, I get four tiny pages printed on one sheet because the two features multiply the effect. If you see what you suspect is a duplicate feature, try using one or the other and then use the one that works the best for you.

comments. If it is a network printer, you cannot change or add to this information unless you are a network administrator with the appropriate privileges.

The General tab also has a Printing Preferences button that gives you access to the dialog box mentioned in the previous section, as well as a Print Test Page button that prints a page. The page content for this test page is generated by Windows. Printing a test page from this dialog box is a good way to test connectivity between Windows and your printer and to see a list of what driver files, version, and port are being used. It's not designed to test the mechanical abilities of your printer, though, because it just prints the Windows logo and some plain text. If you know your printer is communicating correctly with Windows and you want to see a more complete test or check your printer's print resolution, color adjustment, and the like, use the printer manufacturer's own test page feature. Sometimes this printer test page feature is located within a maintenance tab or advanced tab in the Printer Preferences dialog box, and other times it is created by pressing buttons on the printer's physical control panel.

The subsequent tabs apply to features usually administered by a network administrator or printer administrator, such as printer access, time availability, job spooling, and so on, and they are beyond the scope of this book.

## The Print dialog box in Word

You can accomplish most typical print operations just by using the settings in the Print dialog box. The Print dialog box is what appears when you press Ctrl+P or choose Microsoft Office ⇨ Print, as shown in Figure 9.5.

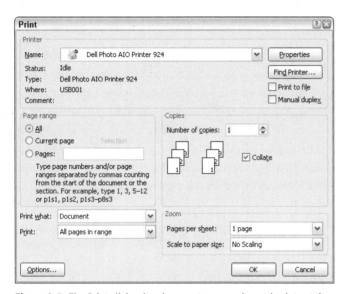

**Figure 9.5.** The Print dialog box has most commonly used print settings.

### *Selecting a printer*

To select a printer in the Print dialog box, click the Name list and select your printer. If you are working with a new document that you want to print from your default printer in Windows, you don't need to do anything extra here. If you want to choose a different printer, just choose it from the Name list of all currently available printers.

If you don't see the printer and your PC is connected to a local area network that uses network printers, you can click Find Printer to begin searching for the appropriate printer using the Find Printers dialog box. If you are not connected to a network, you will see the error message "The Directory Service is currently unavailable." This is a generic message that applies whether you have problems accessing your directory service or you don't have a directory service to access in the first place.

If you can't see a printer that you know should be on your list as a local printer, you have a problem with your printer and Windows, and you need to either install the printer drivers in Windows (add a printer in the Printers and Faxes window) or you have a different connectivity issue, such as a port conflict. See the Troubleshoot printing feature in Windows described earlier in the chapter for assistance in solving the problem.

### Printing on both sides of a sheet of paper with Manual duplex

If your printer doesn't have an automatic two-sided printing feature, you can select the Manual duplex option so that Word stops after printing the first page and allows you to take it out of the printer and reinsert it after turning it over to print the second side. This works for multipage documents as well (printing all of one side, then turning the sheets over and putting them back in to print the second side). When you finish printing the first side, a message appears telling you to flip the paper and put it back in the printer.

### Printing to a file versus printing to an offline printer

Print to file is a sparsely documented feature of Word that is an artifact of plain-text printing in DOS. It allows you to generate the binary that is sent to your printer and save it in a file. If you need to print a file when you are using your laptop and you are not connected to a printer, there is an easier solution. In Windows, click Start, then Printers and Faxes. Right-click the printer you want to use eventually to print the file. In the pop-up menu, select Use Printer Offline, then print your document. A warning appears that Word is not able to print the document. Click OK. You have stored your document in that printer's print queue. The next time your PC is connected to the printer, click Start, then Printers and Faxes in Windows, and right-click the printer again. This time in the pop-up menu, click Use Printer Online. This reactivates the print queue for that printer and it starts printing immediately.

If, for some reason, you need to send the printer binary to another person, you can't use the print queue technique. Select the Print to file option in the Print dialog box. When you print your document, Word displays a dialog box in which you are asked to name the file (it will be saved with the file extension .prn) and select a location for the file. Once you print the document to a file, you must use command line syntax to send it to the printer. Note that this only works if you send it to the same printer you selected in Word; otherwise, you are sending binary garbage to your printer. If your printer is connected to a parallel or serial port, to send the binary PRN file to the printer in Windows, click Start, and then Run, type **cmd.exe**, and click OK. Type COPY C:\\[pathname]\[filename].PRN /B [port] where C: is the drive containing the PRN file, and press Enter. Windows sends the binary data from the PRN file directly to the port. If your printer is connected to a USB port, you can only use this method if your printer is shared. Once it is shared and has an assigned name, click Start and then Run. Type **cmd.exe**, and click OK. Type COPY C:\\ [pathname]\[filename].PRN /B \\[computer name]\[printer name] where C: is the drive containing the PRN file, and press Enter.

### Selecting a page range to print

You can print an entire document, the current page, the current selection (the current block of selected text), or a range of pages. If you select the Pages radio button in the Page range section of the Print dialog box, you can print any combination of pages and sections. Use a dash to indication a range, such as 1-3 to print pages 1 through 3. Use a comma to separate individual page numbers or ranges. As an example, type **1, 5, 7-10** to print pages 1, 5, and 7 through 10. You can be even more specific in Word 2007 and specify sections as well. When you do this, you need type a *p* before the number of the page and an *s* before the number of the section. Thus, if you type **p1s3**, Word prints page 1 of section 3. Below the Page range section, in the Print field, you can choose to print All pages in range, Odd pages, or Even pages.

The Print what field allows you to print the document, the document properties, the document showing markup, a list of just the markup, the styles, the building block entries, or the key assignments.

---

 **Hack**

If you want to print to the end of the document from a specific page (for example, page 5) and you don't know the number for the final page, just specify 5-99 or some other number for the final number that is comfortably longer than the document.

### Selecting the number of copies and collating

If you are printing more than one copy, you can use the up- and down-arrow keys in the Number of copies field or type a number between 1 and 32767. By default, the pages of multipage documents are collated; that is, all pages of the first copy are printed first, followed by the second copy, and so on. If you want all copies of page 1 printed first, followed by all copies of page 2, and so on, deselect the Collate check box.

### Printing multiple pages per sheet

The Pages per sheet feature in the Zoom section of the Print dialog box allows you to print more than one page per sheet by reducing the pages to fit more to a sheet. I find this useful when I have a long document that I want to review that is not in a particularly small font. I can print two pages per sheet and they are still legible.

### Scaling to paper size

Use the Scale to paper size option to scale your document to fit a different paper size. For example, if you have a contract formatted for US Legal 8.5 x 14-inch paper, you can select Letter to reduce the scale of the document so that it fits on 8.5-x–11-inch paper.

## Word's print options

You can change settings that relate to printing by clicking Options in the Print dialog box, or by choosing Microsoft Office ⇨ Word Options ⇨ Display. The options shown in Figure 9.6 appear.

**Figure 9.6.** Word's printing options

By default, Word prints any drawings. However, if you are working with a document destined to be professionally printed with high-resolution illustrations, you may want to print only text for proofing purposes. For such situations, deselect the check box. Clearing this check box also suppresses the printing of floating text boxes.

Background images and colors in Word documents are suppressed when printing by default. If you want to print them, select the Print background colors and images option. You can print a separate sheet containing a plain text page listing your document's properties with each print job by selecting the Print document properties option. Any text selected as hidden can be printed by selecting the Print hidden text option.

**Watch Out!**
If you have the magnifier selected (as it is by default) you can use the cursor to magnify a section of text, but you cannot edit text or make changes to fonts or paragraphs.

Selecting the remaining two options updates fields or linked data with the most recent information before sending the document to the printer.

## Working with Print Preview

The idea of having a print preview feature originated in the days before WYSIWYG (what you see is what you get) word processors. It was necessary for text-based word processors to have a separate graphics application that presented an approximation of what documents would look like when printed. Using Word 2007, you can accomplish most of your work in Print Layout view, where you have a built-in print preview as you work. However, the Print Preview feature is still very useful for such things as seeing the effect of changing margins or watching for awkward page breaks. To access Print Preview, press Ctrl+F2 or Alt+Ctrl+I. You can also click Microsoft Office, click the arrow next to Print, and click Print Preview. You can make changes to page setup commands, such as margins, orientation, and page size. You can also access the Print dialog box and printing options in Word. You have several ways to zoom in and out to review the document. You don't have access to themes or styles from within Print Preview. To return to Page Layout or Draft view, click Close Print Preview.

## Printing your documents

This section walks you through two ways to print documents and covers additional information that is important or useful for printing documents that have not been covered by describing Microsoft's various ways of interfacing with printers with Windows or Word.

**Inside Scoop**
You can monitor the progress of the printing by clicking the printer icon on the Windows taskbar to view the print queue. This is also the place to cancel printing if necessary.

## Printing the current document

To print the current document in Word, first save it, and then follow these steps:

1. Press Ctrl+P or choose Microsoft Office ⇨ Print to display the Print dialog box.

2. In the Printer section, check that the correct printer is listed in the Name field; if not, select it.

3. If you want to change printer-specific settings, such as color or print quality, click Properties and make changes accordingly.

4. In the page range, select All to print the entire document, Current page to print the page where the insertion point is currently located, or Pages and type a page number or range of pages.

5. Select the number of copies or accept 1.

6. Click OK. Your printer should print your document.

If the document is long, you may experience a delay between clicking OK and seeing your document print.

## Printing from Windows

If you want to print a document by selecting it in Windows, follow these steps:

1. Navigate to the folder containing the document you want to print.

2. Click the Word document file you want to print, as shown in Figure 9.7, and click Print this file. (The Print this file option only appears if you select a single file.)

3. Word opens, prints a copy of the file using the default printer and settings, and then closes.

You can also simply right-click a Word document in Windows and click Print to print the document. If you want to print several documents, you can select the documents you want to print, right-click, and then

**Bright Idea**

If you find it useful to drag documents to the printer to print them, you can make this more efficient by creating a shortcut for each printer and putting the printer shortcuts on the Desktop. You can then drag documents to the printer shortcuts to print them.

click Print to print all of them. Each document opens in Word, prints, and then closes Word.

If you want to print to a different installed printer from Windows, open the Printers and Faxes window, and then open the folder containing the document or documents you want to print to a printer other than the default printer. Drag the documents onto the desired printer's icon to print them.

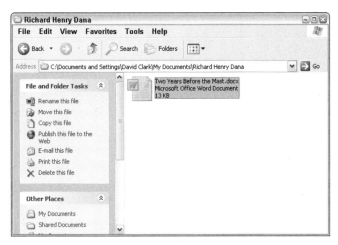

**Figure 9.7.** Selecting a Word document to print in Windows

## Selecting a printer

As mentioned earlier, you can choose a printer in Windows as your default printer in the Printers and Faxes window, or you can select a printer in Word in the Print dialog box. You may have certain documents that you always print on one printer and other documents that you always print on another printer. However, you can only have one default printer. You can either choose a printer at print time to make sure that you print to the correct printer, or drag the file in Windows onto the correct printer's icon as described earlier.

If you prepare a document on a PC that doesn't list the printer you will be using on a different PC to print, you may find that the page numbering is slightly different due to differences in the size of the printable page on different printers. A workaround is to install the printer driver for the eventual printer and select it as the default printer when working on your document to fix this.

## Printing to fax

If you have a fax machine attached to your computer and installed in Windows, you can send documents directly to fax. To do so, follow these steps:

1. Open the document you intend to fax in Word.

2. Press Ctrl+P or choose Microsoft Office ⇨ Print to display the Print dialog box.

3. In the Printer section, select the correct fax machine from the list of printers and faxes in the Name field.

4. Click OK. This opens the Send Fax Wizard.

5. Click Next to display the Recipient Information screen of the Send Fax Wizard, as shown in Figure 9.8.

6. Select or type the recipient name and fill in relevant information. When finished, click Next to display the cover page screen shown in Figure 9.9.

7. To add a cover page, select the option Select a cover page template with the following information. Fill in any necessary information, choose a template, and click Next.

8. In the Schedule screen, choose a time to send the fax (immediately, when discounts apply, or at a specific time in the next 24 hours). In this screen you can also assign the fax a priority (high, medium, low). Click Next.

9. At this point, you can click Finish to send or Preview Fax to preview the appearance of the fax in the Microsoft Office Document Imaging application.

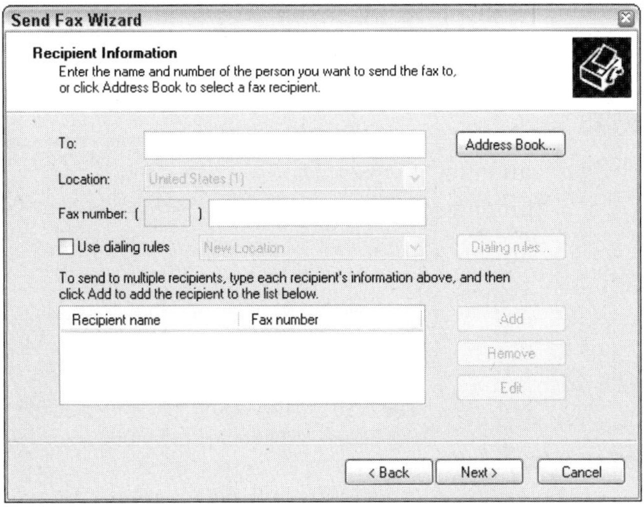

**Figure 9.8.** Adding recipient information in the Send Fax Wizard

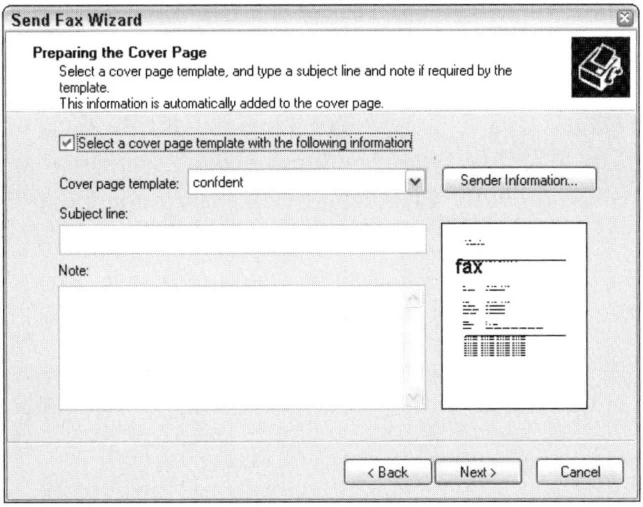

**Figure 9.9.** Adding a cover page in the Send Fax Wizard

# Printing to Microsoft Office Document Image Writer

Microsoft Office 2007 comes with a set of tools that include Microsoft Office Document Imaging and Microsoft Office Document Scanning. These tools use a print driver called Microsoft Office Document Image Writer (not to be confused with the old Apple ImageWriter printer). The

Microsoft Office Document Imaging and Scanning tools are used to scan and manipulate scanned images and to perform OCR (Optical Character Recognition) operations on scanned documents so that they can be translated from graphic files into text documents.

**Figure 9.10.** Setting output format for Microsoft Office Document Image Writer printing

However, if you want to generate a graphic image of a document, such as a TIFF (Tagged Image File Format) to be sent as a fax, for example, you can do so by selecting Microsoft Office Document Image Writer. The default format for saving is a Microsoft format called MDI that compresses the information. If you want to save as TIFF, as for a monochrome fax, click Properties in the Print dialog box before printing and click the Advanced tab shown in Figure 9.10. Select the TIFF radio button under Output format. By default, the output TIFF file is placed in your My Documents folder, but you can change the destination folder by clicking the Default folder's Browse button. When you finish making changes, click OK, and then click OK again in the Print dialog box to print the file to a TIFF file.

## Just the facts

- To print a single copy of the current document with default settings at the click of a button, display the Quick Print button on the Quick Access Toolbar.

- Some settings for your printer are accessible in Word while others are accessible in Windows.

- Because each printer's capabilities are different, Printer Preferences dialog boxes vary greatly from printer to printer.

- To change settings or select a printer before printing, use the Print command (Ctrl+P).

- You can use Print Preview to fine-tune the layout of your document's pages before printing.

**GET THE SCOOP ON...**
Working with Web Layout view ▪ Adding links to your
document ▪ Making your document into a Web page ▪
Setting Web options

# Create Documents
# for the Web

This chapter focuses on creating documents for viewing by a Web browser, either on the Internet, on a corporate or organizational intranet, or on the desktop. I will not give a lesson in HTML here. Instead, I show you how to use Word as a layout and design tool for very basic Web pages. First, I introduce the Web Layout view, which is more useful when working with documents viewed in a browser. I then start simple with showing you how to include links within your document that work whether you are viewing the document in Word or with a browser. Next, I describe the different ways you can save your document for the Web. Finally, I describe various Web option settings in Word.

## Working in Web Layout view

If you want to create Web pages in Word, it's a good idea to switch from Page Layout or Draft view to Web Layout view by clicking View ⇨ Web Layout. The chief difference between Page Layout and Web Layout view is that Web Layout view has no fixed left or bottom margin. You can also tell that you are in Web Layout view by checking the document view selection buttons on the status bar. As you can see in Figure 10.1, you won't see any page edge. If you resize your editing window, the text changes how it wraps accordingly.

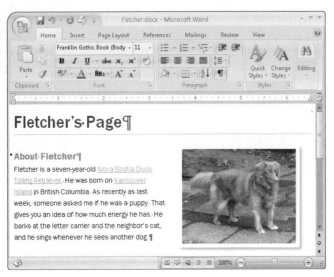

**Figure 10.1.** Working in Web Layout view

Web Layout view does a good job of approximating what your Web page will look like when viewed from a browser. However, once you create a Web page, it is a good idea to view it with a browser to make sure it looks as you expect it to. If the page is going to be posted to the Internet, it is a good idea to view it with more than one browser (such as Internet Explorer 6.0 and Mozilla Firefox 1.5). Later in this chapter, I describe how to create a Web page that doesn't rely on Microsoft-only features if you plan to have the page viewed in a multiple-browser environment such as the Internet.

# Working with hyperlinks

You can take advantage of the hyperlink feature to include links when designing a Web page in Word. You can also use hyperlinks to jump from one spot to another within a Word document. This can be useful in a longer or complex document with a table of contents or reference materials at the back. You can insert hyperlinks that jump to other parts of the same document while you view the document in Word, such as headings or bookmarks. You can also insert hyperlinks that jump to other addresses (local file addresses, Internet addresses, or intranet addresses).

If you want to create a Word document with hyperlinks to other parts of the same document using bookmarks, follow these steps:

**Bright Idea**

If you are reading a document with internal hyperlinks, you may find it annoying to press Ctrl when you click. Viewing the document in Full Screen Reading view allows you to use a single click to jump to a hyperlink.

1. Open a document in Word with a few paragraphs of text, or create one.

2. Find a location to which a hyperlink should take the reader other than a heading, such as a definition, data table, or copyright information. Click the location so that the insertion point is where you want the reader to be taken by the hyperlink. At this point, if the place you want to take the reader with a hyperlink is not a heading, you must add a bookmark at that location in the document so the hyperlink has something to link to.

3. Choose Insert ⇨ Links ⇨ Bookmark.

4. In the Bookmark name field of the Bookmark dialog box, type a descriptive name (**Fletcher** in the example) and click Add.

5. Now select the text you want the reader to click to bring you to the bookmark's location.

6. Next, move your cursor to the place where you want to insert the hyperlink in your document. Choose Insert ⇨ Links ⇨ Hyperlink. This displays the Insert Hyperlink dialog box. By default, the Existing File or Web Page option in the Link to field is selected.

7. Click Place in This Document in the Link to field to see a view like the example shown in Figure 10.2.

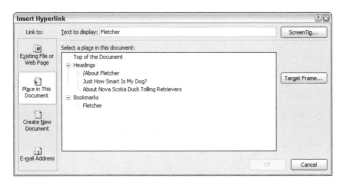

**Figure 10.2.** The Place in This Document option in the Link to field allows you to choose a heading or bookmark within the document.

**Inside Scoop**

You can delete a bookmark from the list by choosing Insert ⇨ Links ⇨ Bookmark, selecting the bookmark you want to delete, and clicking Delete.

8. Click ScreenTip to add a pop-up screen tip when the reader mouses over the hyperlink (this is optional). Type the text (**How Fletcher got his name.** in this example) in the ScreenTip text field of the Set Hyperlink ScreenTip dialog box, as shown in Figure 10.3.

**Figure 10.3.** Adding ScreenTip text for a hyperlink

9. In the hierarchical display of your document shown in the Select a place in this document field, you will notice that you can assign a hyperlink to a heading or bookmark location. In this example, click Fletcher in the Bookmarks section, and click OK.

10. The hyperlink is inserted, and the text changes color and is underlined, indicating to the reader that it is a hyperlink. Hover the mouse over the hyperlink to see the ScreenTip pop-up as shown in Figure 10.4. If you did not add ScreenTip text, it still shows the reader the message "Ctrl+Click to follow link" when the reader mouses over the hyperlink.

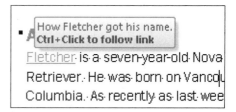

**Figure 10.4.** Hovering over the hyperlink with your mouse displays a ScreenTip.

In Word documents, you can also add links to headings within the document, links to an e-mail address, links to other files, or links to Internet addresses. The next example shows you how to add a link for a heading within the document and how to add a link to an Internet address. Your PC should be connected to the Internet to follow this example. To learn how, follow these steps:

1. Open a document in Word with headings and text that refers to a heading, or create a sample document that meets these criteria.

2. Select the text you want the reader to click to bring you to the heading's location. (In the example shown in Figure 10.1, this is the phrase *Nova Scotia Duck Tolling Retriever* in the first paragraph.)

3. Choose Insert ⇨ Links ⇨ Hyperlink to display the Insert Hyperlink dialog box.

4. In the Link to field, click Place in This Document.

5. In this example, we skip adding a ScreenTip. In the hierarchical display of your document shown in the Select a place in this document field, click the heading to which you want to link. In the example, the heading is About Nova Scotia Duck Tolling Retrievers, as shown in Figure 10.5.

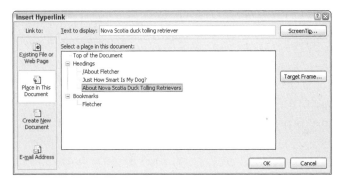

**Figure 10.5.** Selecting a heading as a hyperlink

6. Click OK to create the hyperlink. If you hover over the now-underlined phrase *Nova Scotia Duck Tolling Retrievers* in the example, you see the message "Current Document" prior to "Ctrl+Click to follow link."

7. Test the link by holding down the Ctrl key. As you move your cursor over the hyperlink, it should convert to a pointing hand (as if in a Web browser). While still holding down the Ctrl key, click the hyperlink. It should take you to the heading you selected. Note that the original link color has changed, indicating that you have been to this link before.

8. Next, add a hyperlink to an Internet address. To do so, highlight a word or phrase that should take you to an Internet address. In this example, shown in Figure 10.6, this is *Vancouver Island.*

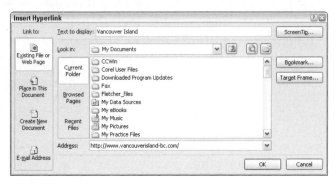

**Figure 10.6.** Adding a link to an Internet address

9. Choose Insert ➪ Links ➪ Hyperlink to display the Insert Hyperlink dialog box. In the Link to field, click the Existing File or Web Page option.

10. Type the Internet address in the Address field, as shown in Figure 10.6. Be sure to type **http://** (or **https://**, **ftp://**, or whatever other protocol is required) prior to the address. The drop-down list also has a list of recently visited Web pages from your browser to choose from. When you have checked and are satisfied that you have typed the address correctly, click OK.

11. Test the link by holding down the Ctrl key. As you move your cursor over the hyperlink, it should again convert to a pointing hand (as if in a Web browser). If you hover over the now-underlined phrase Vancouver Island in this example, you see the Internet address (the URL) prior to "Ctrl+Click to follow link." While still holding down the Ctrl key, click the hyperlink. It should launch your default browser and take you to the Internet address you selected.

You can follow the same procedures just covered to have a link take you to an e-mail address. When the reader Ctrl+Clicks such a hyperlink, it launches the reader's default e-mail program and opens a new e-mail message addressed to the e-mail address in the link. Likewise, you can have the hyperlink take the reader to another file. The file can be any type of file; it is not limited to Word documents. If you type a recognizable URL

**Hack**

If you get a Page Not Found error, close your browser and right-click the hyperlink in Word. Click Edit Hyperlink in the pop-up window and double-check that you typed the Internet address correctly.

or e-mail address in your document, Word automatically creates a hyperlink for you.

To remove a hyperlink, right-click the hyperlink and select Remove Hyperlink.

## Creating Web pages

You have essentially three choices when you create a Web page using Word:

- Single File Web Page (*.mht; *.mhtml)
- Web Page (*.htm; *.html)
- Web Page, Filtered (*.htm; *.html)

The Single File Web Page option can be used for archiving material and for saving a Web page as a single file. The Web Page option is for creating Web pages for broader distribution. The Filtered version of this option filters out tags only relevant in Microsoft Office.

You can design your page using the formatting commands available in Word, including text boxes, graphics, and fonts. I recommend working in Web Layout view, which approximates how the page will look in your browser. If you use themes, you can change themes (even after you have saved the document as a Web page). When you are satisfied with your Web page and have added any hyperlinks, graphics, and so on, you can save the file as a Web page. To do so, press F12 (or choose Microsoft Office ⇨ Save As), and select one of the file types described in more detail below.

While you are working in the Save As dialog box, you can elect to change the title displayed in the title bar of the browser. To do so, click Change Title and type a new page title in the Page title field of the Set Page Title dialog box, as shown in Figure 10.7, and then click OK.

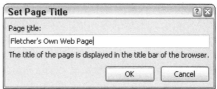

**Figure 10.7.** Setting the page title

## Creating a single-file Web page (MHTML)

You can save a Web page with all of the page's content (text, graphics, and so on) all contained in one file, as an MHTML file. MHTML is an acronym for MIME HTML. To further explain the acronyms, MIME stands for Multipurpose Internet Mail Extensions. MIME is an Internet Standard that supports media other than text such as graphics, video, and sound. HTML stands for HyperText Markup Language, which is the Internet standard for tagging text content so that computers can inter-pret contextual significance and that allows you to jump from link to link and so on. With MHTML, nontext files such as graphics and audio clips are embedded in the actual HTML files, rather than stored in a separate folder on the Web server. MHTML makes it easier to archive, copy, or send Web pages in e-mail. In earlier versions of Word, this file type was referred to as Web Archive, but is now called Single File Web Page. The file extension remains the same: .mht or .mhtml.

To save a Word document as MHTML, select Single File Web Page (*.mht; *.mhtml) in the Save As dialog box. You can then click Save to save the page in MHTML format. When viewing different file types in a Windows directory all based on the same document, as shown in Figure 10.8, you can see that the MHTML file has a different icon with a framed picture indicating it contains other media. It is also substantially larger in size than the Word document (which compressed the other media) and the standard HTML file (which stores the media in a supporting folder).

**Figure 10.8.** One document saved as Word, MHTML, and HTML files

## Creating a Web page or filtered Web page

In addition to the MHTML single-file solution, you can save a document as a standard Web page, with support content such as graphic images,

**Watch Out!**
MHTML is an Internet standard that is not implemented identically across dif-ferent browsers. If you create MHTML in Word, you will have the most reliable results using Internet Explorer or Word to view the files. Don't use this format to put together public Web pages.

**Watch Out!**

If you add effects to your picture, it will be converted to PNG format when saved, whatever format you choose. PNG format is supported by most modern browsers, but not by older browsers.

audio, and video files stored in a folder. This is the preferred method if you are editing files that are eventually going to appear on the Internet or on a corporate or organizational intranet.

If you plan on editing and modifying your Web pages and taking advantage of some bells and whistles like themes, picture effects, and chart effects, you should first save your working Web page in the Web Page format. If you intend to post your Web page to the Internet, save that copy in the format Web Page, Filtered. The filtered version simplifies picture effects and converts modifiable SmartArt and charts into static graphics that you can no longer manipulate to the same degree, so it is a good idea to have one version for editing and a simplified final version for broader Web consumption.

You can use Web Options settings described in the next section to control the complexity of your Web pages design, simplifying it for maximum predictable appearance on the widest number of browsers, or allowing complexity if you are confident your viewing audience will have the latest version of Internet Explorer running on their systems.

Once you save your Web page in HTML format, the file will have an associated folder containing related files. If, for example, your Web page's filename is Fletcher.htm, then the associated folder will be named Fletcher_files. If you delete the Web page file, the associated folder is also deleted. If you move or copy the Web page file, the associated folder is also moved or copied to the same location. You cannot rename the associated folder without causing the Web page to malfunction; you must rename the Web page file instead.

If you decide to replace a graphic or audio file contained in the associated folder with a new version, you can do so, provided you give it exactly the same name.

You can change the name and location of an image, provided you edit the HTML source code, changing the data contained within the brackets in the section:

```
imagedata src="[folder]/[graphic filename.ext]"
```
to the new values.

**Watch Out!**

The one place where this handy pairing doesn't work is when you want to restore a Web page from the Recycle Bin in Windows. You must select both the Web page HTM file as well as the associated folder in order for the Web page to be fully restored.

# Setting Web Options

To make changes to Web Options in Word, choose Microsoft Office ⇨ Word Options ⇨ Advanced ⇨ Web Options. The dialog box shown in Figure 10.9 appears. The Browsers tab allows you to make adjustments to settings that affect how reliably your Web page's appearance reproduces in a given browser. The first option allows you to adjust these settings by selecting from a list. Disappointingly (but perhaps quite

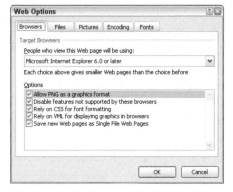

**Figure 10.9.** The Browsers tab of the Web Options dialog box

predictably), Microsoft has not bothered to address browsers produced by others with the exception of ancient versions of Netscape Navigator. Your options are Internet Explorer/Netscape Navigator 3.0, Internet Explorer/ Netscape Navigator 4.0, and then Internet Explorer 4.0 or later, 5.0 or later, and 6.0 or later. There is no mention of Mozilla Firefox, Opera, or Safari. If you want to fine-tune your Web page's compatibility for a wider range of viewers, you will need to make individual setting adjustments. I've summarized the distinctions in Table 10.1.

## Table 10.1. Web options settings for target browsers

| Option | Explanation |
| --- | --- |
| Allow PNG as a graphics format | Most current browsers support this graphics format that allows for transparency to some degree. For Internet Explorer 6.0 or later. |
| Disable features not supported by these browsers | This option refers to the Target Browsers section's drop-down list.* |

| Option | Explanation |
|---|---|
| Rely on CSS for font formatting | CSS (Cascading Style Sheets) were implemented in version 4.0 of both Internet Explorer and Netscape Navigator. CSS governs formatting and layout in HTML documents. |
| Rely on VML for displaying graphics in browsers | VML (Vector Markup Language) is an XML-based language for displaying vector graphics. Supported only by Internet Explorer 5.0 and later. Avoid using unless you are confident your Web page viewers will be using a recent version of Internet Explorer. |
| Save new Web pages as Single File Web Pages | Option available only for browsers Internet Explorer 5.0 and later. Avoid using with other browsers. |

* Thus, if you select Internet Explorer 5.0 or later, the "Allow PNG..." option check box will be cleared.

The Files tab of the Web Options dialog box shown in Figure 10.10 allows you to enable or disable the feature that creates an associated folder for files used by your Web page with the Organize supporting files in a folder option. If you deselect this option, the supporting files appear by default in the same folder as the Web page's HTM file. You can also disable long file-

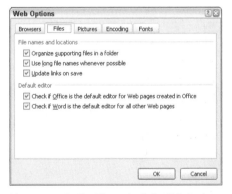

**Figure 10.10.** The Files tab of the Web Options dialog box

names if need be, disable the automatic update of links on save, or disable default editor checking.

The Pictures tab allows you to set the target monitor screen size. The default size is 800 x 600 pixels, with 96 pixels per inch. The Encoding tab allows you to set the character encoding (useful if you work with multi-language Web pages). The Fonts tab allows you to determine the character set (Arabic, Cyrillic, English/Western European/Other Latin script, Greek, and so on). You can also set a proportional font (where letters take up more or less space depending on their width) or fixed-width font (where each letter is allotted the same amount of horizontal space regardless of character width), and font size.

After making any changes to the Web Options, click OK to save the setting changes and close the Word Options dialog box.

## Just the facts

- Use Web Layout view to see your document in Word as it would appear in a browser window.

- Whether saved as a Word document or as a Web page, you can insert hyperlinks into your document that direct the reader to a bookmarked location within the same document, to a heading, to another document, to an Internet address, or to an e-mail address.

- You can save a Web page as a single MHTML file that embeds non-text information into the HTML, which is good for archiving and for browsing with Internet Explorer only, version 5.0 onward.

- You can save your Word document as a standard Web page, preserving most of the formatting and layout.

**GET THE SCOOP ON...**
Posting a blog entry with Word ■ Sending your document
in e-mail or as a fax ■ Keeping fonts the same when
sending documents to others ■ File compatibility issues

# Send Your Documents to Others

**Y**ou can send a document you create in Word in many ways, from posting it as a blog entry to sending it as a file attachment. This chapter shows you how to send your document to others and gives you some useful hints to ensure that the recipient receives your document in the form that you intended. Some related topics are covered in other chapters. This chapter focuses on the successful transmission of your information. Chapter 12 focuses on features that have to do with collaborating with others such as comments, revision tracking, and document comparison. Chapter 21 deals with such security issues as protecting your document from further editing, stripping out hidden personal data, and so on.

One handy new feature of Word is creating a blog entry. If you maintain one or more blogs, you can now register your blog with Word so that you can create a new post from within Word and send it to your blog to publish with the click of a button. Sending your document using e-mail has changed somewhat; you can no longer choose Word as your editor in Microsoft Outlook, although the Outlook Editor is essentially a specialized and slightly simplified version of Word. I tell you how to use Word to create your document or send a Word file as an attachment. I also tell you how to send your document using an Internet fax service.

Chapter 11

Finally, there are some things you should know to guarantee that your document arrives in a form that the recipient can work with. I show you how to embed fonts so that your document uses the same ones when opened by someone on a different PC, give you some tips on working with Compatibility Mode, and offer some suggestions on saving in older file formats for recipients who don't have Word 2007.

## Creating a blog entry

If you have a blog (short for Web log), you may want to take advantage of some of Word's editing, formatting, and proofing capabilities for your posts to your blog (also known as blog entries). Prior to Word 2007, you could only accomplish this by creating a post in Word, copying it to the Clipboard, logging in to your blog's Web interface, creating a post, and then pasting in your blog entry.

With Word 2007, you can post an entry to your blog without ever leaving Word. You must have already set up a blog with a blog Web site. In the example, I use a sample blog I created using Blogger, a blog hosting service that is a subsidiary of Google. At the time of this writing, Word supports major blog interfaces but support for categories and image upload is limited and depends on the particular blog host you are working with. You can publish posts directly from Word to the blog, post draft blog entries to the blog to be reviewed and published later, and you can open and manage existing blog posts. Depending on your blog host, you can also insert tables, links, charts, photos, SmartArt, equations, and symbols into your blog entry.

You can select some font formatting, such as font selection, a subset of font effects such as bold, italic, and strikethrough (things such as emboss and shadow aren't available), and font color. You can indent text, align paragraphs, and create numbered or bulleted lists. Quick Styles are available, also. You can use Word's proofing tools (spelling, grammar, research, thesaurus, translation, language setting, and word count).

**Watch Out!**
When posting content to a blog, make sure you understand the copyright implications. For example, don't post a copyright image on your blog. Instead, provide a link to the image on the copyright holder's Web site.

To set up Word to create blog posts and post a blog entry, follow these steps:

1. In Word, choose Microsoft Office ⇨ New.

2. Double-click New blog post from the list of templates.

3. The Register a Blog Account dialog box appears. We will set up the blog account later, so click the Register Later button.

4. You will see a blank blog entry with a different set of commands on the Ribbon, as shown in Figure 11.1.

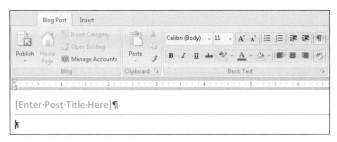

**Figure 11.1.** A blank blog entry in Word

5. Click Enter Post Title Here and type **A Sample Post**. This gives the individual post a title on your blog.

6. Click below the line for the sample title and type a sample post, using some font and color effects, such as **This is a sample post using <u>underlining</u> and *italic* text.**

7. It is a good idea to save your blog entry as you work. Press Ctrl+S or click Save now and name your blog entry (this example is named blogentry.docx).

At this point, you need to set up a blog account so that Word knows where to post the blog entry. To do so, follow these steps:

1. Choose Blog Post ⇨ Manage Accounts ⇨ New to launch the blog registration wizard shown in Figure 11.2. This wizard walks you through the steps of registering your blog with Word.

**Figure 11.2.** Launching the blog registration wizard

**Inside Scoop**

Click Set As Default in the Blog Accounts dialog box to set your default blog, if you have more than one, to save time when posting.

2. Select your blog host from the list of providers in the New Blog Account dialog box and click Next. (If your provider isn't listed, click the My provider isn't listed link to learn about what information you need from your blog host to manually enter settings.)

3. In the next dialog box that is specific to your blog host, the information you need differs depending on your blog host. You may need a user or space name and a password or secret word. To upload images, you need a destination address for the images from your blog host. Some blog hosts also require a blog URL. In this example, I use Blogger: type the user name provided to you by your blog host in the User Name field and type the password in the Password field.

4. When you finish you should get a message saying that registration was successful. Click OK to close the dialog box. You should see the Blog Accounts dialog box shown in Figure 11.3.

5. Click Close to accept current settings and close the dialog box.

**Figure 11.3.** You can manage several blogs from the Blog Accounts dialog box.

You are now ready to send your sample post. You have two choices: You can publish the post directly to the blog for public view by choosing Blog Post ⇨ Publish ⇨ Publish, or you can choose Blog Post ⇨ Publish ⇨ Publish as Draft to post the entry to your blog for your eyes only prior to review and public posting.

**Hack**

If Word doesn't support images for your blog host's format, select Publish as Draft and add your photos and other images to the post with your blog host's editor.

**Hack**

To compose in Word and send in Outlook, open the document in Word, press Ctrl+A to select the entire document, open Outlook and start a new message (Ctrl+N), click in the body of the message and press Ctrl+V to paste the Word document. Outlook to Word works the same way.

If you want to work with a post that has already been sent to your blog, choose Blog Post ⇨ Open Existing. You can select the appropriate blog from the drop-down list and then work with individual posts.

## Sending your document as e-mail

In previous versions of Office, it was possible to select Word as the default e-mail editor. This was useful because the basic e-mail editing capabilities of Outlook were rudimentary compared to Word. In Office 2007, selecting Word as the e-mail editor is no longer possible, although the Outlook 2007 Editor is, in effect, a slightly stripped-down version of Word 2007 with some additional features specific to working with e-mail.

I won't cover the Outlook Editor in detail here, but here's a summary: You have access to all the basic character and paragraph formatting commands of Word, along with find/replace commands and proofing tools. With the Outlook Editor you can also insert many types of document objects you find in Word: tables, pictures, clip art, SmartArt, charts, shapes, hyperlinks, bookmarks, text boxes, quick parts, WordArt, equations, and symbols. Themes and Quick Styles also function in the Outlook Editor. The key limitations have to do with fundamental differences between creating a paper document with a fixed page size and one that has to work with variable width and height of e-mail messages. Therefore, columns, page margins, headers, and footers are unavailable in the Outlook Editor.

## Sending your document as an attachment

You can send your document as an attachment in e-mail without having to leave Word with just a few clicks or keystrokes. Before I describe how, though, you should know a few things about sending documents as attachments. The first item relates to security. If you are sending something that contains confidential, sensitive, or embarrassing information in hidden form, don't assume it will stay that way. Chapter 21 shows you

**Watch Out!**

Although your message may eventually be sent in HTML, if you save it as HTML format in Word and then use the send feature, it will convert the file to Word 2007 document format (*.docx) automatically.

how to use Word features to protect yourself from letting out the wrong information inadvertently. The second item relates to compatibility. If you know your recipients have the latest version of Word, no further preparation is required. If you think that it is in any way likely that they have an earlier version of Word or that they don't have Word at all, you need to consider saving to a more readily available or older format. This is discussed in more detail later in this chapter. If the recipient just needs to be able to read the document, you can take advantage of the Email as PDF Attachment or Email as XPS Attachment option, described later in this section.

To send a Word document in e-mail, you must have an e-mail application installed that is working properly. These steps assume you have installed Microsoft Office Outlook 2007 and that you have a document that is ready to send that you created in Word. To send a Word document as an e-mail attachment, follow these steps:

1. Open the document you want to send. If you make any changes to the document, save them before performing the send operation. If you are sending to someone who doesn't have Word 2007, use the Save As command to select an earlier format such as Word 97 - 2003 (*.doc) or Rich Text Format (*.rtf).

2. Choose Microsoft Office ⇨ Send ⇨ Email as shown in Figure 11.4.

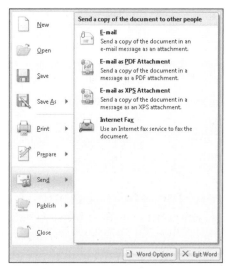

**Figure 11.4.** Sending a Word document as an e-mail attachment

**3.** Word launches Outlook, opens a new message file, adds the Word document's filename as the Subject line, and adds the Word document as an attachment, as shown in Figure 11.5. In the To field, type the e-mail address of the intended recipient (or click the To button to select an address from your contacts list). Do the same in the Cc field for anyone to whom you wish to send a copy of the file.

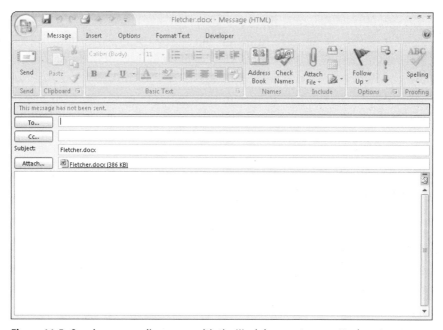

**Figure 11.5.** Opening an e-mail message with the Word document as an attachment

**4.** If you want to substitute your own Subject line, triple-click the filename that has been automatically entered in the Subject field to select it and type a new Subject line.

**5.** Type any cover message you want to accompany the Word document attachment in the message field.

**6.** Click Send to send the e-mail message containing the Word document as an attachment. Outlook closes automatically. Your Word document remains open.

If your recipient does not need to modify the document you are sending, you can click Microsoft Office ⇨ Send ⇨ E-mail as PDF Attachment or Microsoft Office ⇨ Send ⇨ E-mail as XPS Attachment. PDF and XPS readers are publicly available and free to download. To learn more about PDF and XPS format, see Chapter 2.

## Sending your document via fax

There are two ways to send a fax using Word (apart from printing your document and putting it in the fax machine). One, printing to a fax machine, is explained in Chapter 9. If you have installed an Internet fax service add-in, you can send your document as a fax. To do so, choose Microsoft Office ⇨ Send ⇨ Internet Fax. The Microsoft Office Fax Service opens a new document window with some fax-related options, as shown in Figure 11.6. You can fill in the pertinent information such as the recipient's name, the destination fax number, an optional cover sheet, and so on. When you are finished adding information, you will be asked to click Send to send the document as a fax.

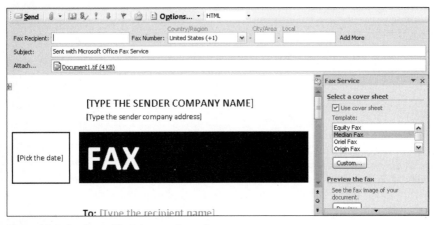

**Figure 11.6.** Sending a Word document as a fax

## Embedding fonts to preserve your document's look

If you want to send a document to another person and you want to make sure that the document retains the fonts that you selected, Word has an option to allow you to embed your selected fonts within the document to guarantee that the document's recipient can see the fonts as you intended. To access this feature, choose Microsoft Office ⇨ Word Options ⇨ Save.

Select the Embed fonts in the file option to enable this feature, as shown in Figure 11.7. Embedding fonts in a document allows anyone opening the document to use the embedded fonts, even when

**Figure 11.7.** Embedding fonts in a Word document

the fonts are not installed on the PC used to open the document.

Embedding fonts increases the size of your file. For example, a sample single page with two fonts with a file size of 13KB is 307KB with the fonts embedded. With the size of today's hard drives and other storage devices, combined with the reduced size of Word 2007's XML-based files, this is not likely to become an issue unless you have very large documents, a large number of documents, a great number of fonts, or need to send several documents in e-mail. If file size is an issue for you, you can select the Embed only the characters used in the document option. This significantly reduces the file size. However, it limits the use of the font by recipients if they don't already have the font. By default, Word doesn't bother to embed common system fonts such as Arial and Times New Roman. If you have some reason to embed them, deselect the check box for the Do not embed common system fonts option.

You can choose to turn the font-embedding feature on for the current document or for all new documents by choosing the scope of the change in the drop-down list Preserve fidelity when sharing this document. When you finish with any setting changes, click OK to accept the changes.

# Working with Compatibility Mode

Chapter 2 covers Compatibility Mode in some detail. In this section, I describe general strategies for working with this mode while retaining maximum functionality.

## Preserving complex formatting and using all of Word 2007's features

If you want to take advantage of Themes, Quick Styles, and other Word 2007-only features, you can work in Word 2007's native mode until you get everything as you want it. Then save the file as a Word 97 - Word 2003 file. An alternative, if you are collaborating with someone who has Word 2003, is for your colleague to download a file converter from Microsoft so

> ## Backward Compatibility in Macros
>
> Even working in Compatibility Mode when you create macros is no guarantee that they will work in earlier versions. If you have an important project, you need to test it with the earlier versions of Word. In testing even very simple macros, I find that additional functionality in Word 2007 easily confuses earlier versions of Word when they try to run macros. Fortunately, the Visual Basic debugger appears and highlights the offending code. Even if you have only a beginner's knowledge of programming (or are simply fearless), you can often fix the macro by stripping out superfluous macro code that only applies to Word 2007 functionality so that it will run in an older version of Word.

that Word 2003 can recognize Word 2007 files. Once the file is opened, the formatting will be intact, although certain "live" elements such as Themes and Quick Styles will be converted to static elements (see Chapter 2 for a list). If you receive the document back again, it will have your Quick Styles converted to static styles, but the formatting will be intact. You can then work in Compatibility Mode or convert the document back to Word 2007 format. This will not, however, convert the now-static elements back to live elements. In other words, if you use Quick Styles, send the file to a Word 2003 user who modifies the file and then sends it back, and you in turn open the file, the Quick Styles remain static styles unless you manually apply Quick Styles again.

## What happens to macros?

If you want to add macros to documents or templates in Compatibility Mode that will be usable by others with earlier versions of Word, you can do so assuming you are writing or recording macros that take advantage of commands available in earlier versions of Word. Make sure to save the macro or macros to the document or template you are sending (not Normal.dotm). When recipients of the document or template with macros open the file, they receive a warning that the document or template contains macros. They can click Enable to allow the macros to run. See Chapter 23 for more details on macros.

## Adding content controls

You can still add content controls in Compatibility Mode as well, although the newer controls are not available. Choose Microsoft Office ⇨ Word Options ⇨ Personalize and click the Show Developer tab in the Ribbon. You can select from the legacy tools (legacy forms and ActiveX controls) in the Controls group of the Developer tab, as shown in Figure 11.8. The new content controls are grayed out and unavailable in this mode.

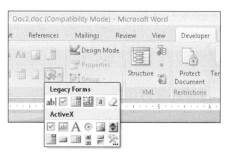

**Figure 11.8.** Adding legacy controls to a document in Compatibility Mode

## Allowing maximum back and forth collaboration

If you know you are going to be constantly working with an older version of Word, you can always set the default file save format to that of an earlier version. Choose Microsoft Office ⇨ Word Options ⇨ Save and select the appropriate alternative format from the drop-down list for the Save files in this format option.

Working in Compatibility Mode is the simplest way that you can maximize collaborative work with others using older but recent versions of Word or other current word processors. In general, keeping your documents simpler helps avoid problems when sending material back and forth. For best results, avoid:

- Macros
- Picture effects
- Embedded objects such as Excel spreadsheets when possible
- Complex formatting such as multicolumn text

# Sending your document in other file formats

If it is important to you that your document's appearance is preserved when viewed by the recipient, you have several ways of guaranteeing that he or she sees what you see on the page. The first option is to save the document as a PDF or XPS file. Creating a PDF or XPS file is a way to guarantee that any copy of the file that is viewed or printed will have a uniform and predictable look, retaining all your formatting, text, and graphics. PDF files, a widely adopted standard, can be viewed with the freely downloadable Adobe Reader. XPS files are Microsoft's new alternative format (also with a freely downloadable viewer, albeit for Windows PCs only) that incorporates Microsoft Rights Management and is not as yet widely used. See Chapter 2 for more details about these options.

If you want the recipient of your document to be able to modify the document, however, save it in a word processing file format. Even if the recipient of your document does not have Microsoft Word 97 through Word 2003, Compatibility Mode, which is discussed earlier, may still be the best option; for example, OpenOffice.org Writer 2.0 and WordPerfect 12 open files saved in Compatibility Mode. Most formatting translates correctly when switching between Word in Compatibility Mode and these word processors, and you can also open Word templates, add bookmarks, pictures, and so on. Don't expect custom toolbars and macros to operate, however. If you have a complex document that uses lots of special features, it is a good idea to do some testing with your recipient and his or her word processor to make sure everything works as you expect it to, or at least makes an acceptable conversion.

If the intended recipient of your document is working with old software, you may need to work with a simpler file format. If the recipient does not have one of the various earlier Microsoft Word or Works formats, the best hope is Rich Text Format (*.rtf), which will preserve most formatting. If all else fails, you can save your document as a Plain Text (*.txt) file, which contains no formatting.

## Just the facts

- Create posts to your blog with the New blog entry feature.
- Use the Send command to transmit your document as an e-mail attachment or Internet fax.
- Embed fonts in your document to guarantee the recipient sees what you see.
- Work with Compatibility Mode to render your Word 2007 document readable by those with earlier versions or other word processing software.

GET THE SCOOP ON...
Keeping track of revisions ▪ Using comments ▪ Keeping
track of versions ▪ Comparing different versions of the
same document ▪ Sharing a document workspace ▪
Collaborating with others online

# Collaborate with Others

Chapter 12

In this chapter, I describe the ways you can collaborate with others on a document. The aspects of collaboration I cover are tracking changes made, noting who made the changes and when, protecting a document from revisions or restricting what kinds can be made and by whom, keeping track of versions (which draft is it?), and posting the document to a commonly accessible location. (I covered sending documents in e-mail in Chapter 11.)

Word allows you to keep track of changes made by more than one person, taking note of the date and time of each change. You have quite a degree of control over who can make changes and what they can change. You can also add text comments (or, if you have a Tablet PC, voice or ink comments). You can compare two versions of the same document or combine multiple versions of the same document, highlighting the differences, and take advantage of collaboration sites (such as Microsoft Office Live Collaboration, and to a limited degree, MSN Groups) and document management servers (such as Microsoft Office SharePoint Server) to deal with version control.

## Reviewing your document

One thing that Microsoft organizes well is the commands relating to the review cycle of a document. All the pertinent commands are located on the Review tab of the Ribbon, shown in Figure 12.1. You can type comments (or add voice or handwritten comments if you have a Tablet PC), track revisions, accept or reject changes, compare two versions of the same document, combine multiple versions of the same document, and protect aspects of the document from changing.

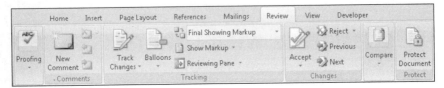

**Figure 12.1.** The Review tab brings together all commands relating to document review in one place.

You also have a good degree of control over what you see when reviewing the document. If you want to see the revised version as clean copy, you can do so. Alternatively, you can view all changes, just revisions, just comments, just one reviewer's comments, and so on. You can also choose to have changes shown in balloons at the right margin or to have them shown inline with the text.

## Tracking changes

I start out with something that may seem obvious, but is nevertheless sometimes misunderstood: Don't turn Track Changes on for your first draft of a document. If you do, every word appears as a change (because it is a change from the blank document you opened). Once you have a first draft, you can begin the process of tracking changes. To do so, press Ctrl+Shift+E or click Review and click the icon above the phrase Track Changes. This is a toggle command. You can turn it on and off by repeating it. You can tell that Track Changes is activated because the button becomes a different color from the background color of the Ribbon. For additional options, choose Review ⇨ Track Changes to see the menu shown in Figure 12.2.

**Watch Out!**
Many Office users don't bother to add names and initials when personalizing copies of the software. If you have not done so, revisions you make will be tagged as revisions made by User1. Choose Microsoft Office ⇨ Word Options ⇨ Personalize to verify that you have the correct User name and Initials.

Page Layout
References
Mailings
Review
Final Showing Markup
Show Markup
Reviewing Pane
Track Changes
Balloons
Track Changes
Change Tracking Options...
Change User Name...

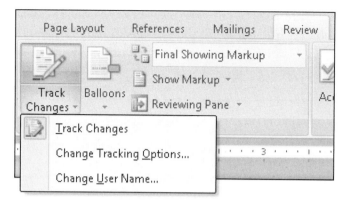

**Figure 12.2.** The Track Changes menu options

If you have Track Changes turned on, the default way changes appear depends on the document view you select. Draft view is designed for use when creating and revising documents, and focuses on content more than form or formatting. In this view (and in Outline view), all insertions and deletions are by default indicated inline in red. Text that is moved from one location within the document to another is indicated in green. Word uses strikethrough to indicate a deletion, underline to indicate an insertion, double strikethrough to indicate moved text, and double underline to indicate moved text where it is inserted. (Table cell changes are denoted with different colors; see Figure 12.6.) A change bar also appears at the left indicating whenever there is a change on that line. Formatting changes are not indicated in red or green, although the change bar appears at the left for any formatting changes. Figure 12.3 illustrates changes in Draft view.

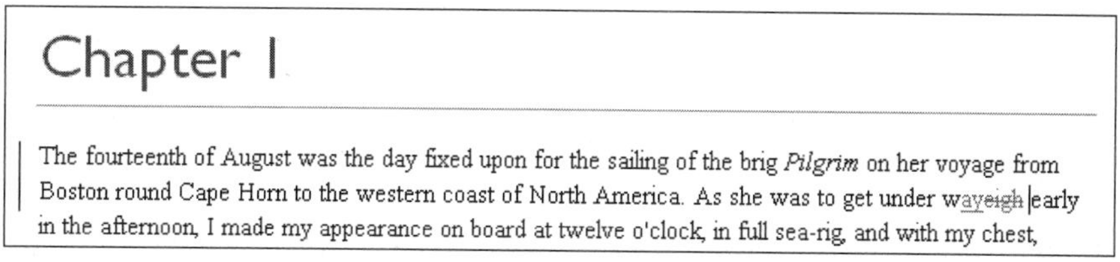

Chapter I
The fourteenth of August was the day fixed upon for the sailing of the brig Pilgrim on her voyage from
Boston round Cape Horn to the western coast of North America. As she was to get under wayeigh early
in the afternoon, I made my appearance on board at twelve o'clock, in full sea-rig, and with my chest,

**Figure 12.3.** Changes tracked using Word's default settings in Draft view

In all other views, the change bar still appears at the left indicating that there is a change on that line, and on the right a balloon indicates the action taken, and any formatting changes are also indicated with a balloon, as shown in Figure 12.4. In any view, you can determine the person who made the change, the nature of the change, and the time and date of any change by hovering over the change with the mouse, as shown in Figure 12.5.

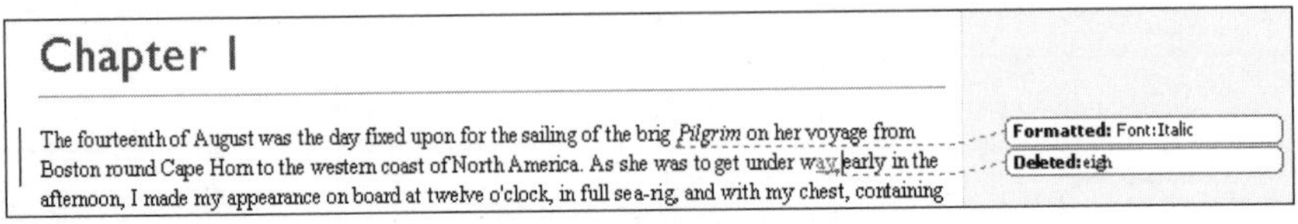

**Figure 12.4.** Changes tracked using Word's default settings in Draft view

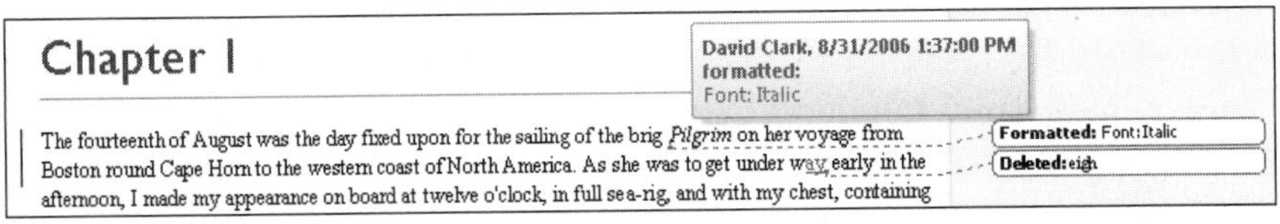

**Figure 12.5.** Hovering over a change with the mouse gives you information about the change.

You can customize almost every aspect of how changes are displayed. If it's just a matter of switching between inline change display and balloon change display, choose Review ⇨ Balloons, and select from the three options listed:

- Show revisions in balloons
- Show all revisions inline
- Show only comments and formatting in balloons

If you want to change other aspects of how change tracking is displayed, choose Review ⇨ Track Changes ⇨ Change Tracking Options to see the dialog box shown in Figure 12.6.

Many settings that you can change are self-explanatory, and I won't take up space with those things here. However, note that you can turn off change tracking of moves (as opposed to insertions and deletions) by deselecting the Track moves check box, and you can turn off formatting change tracking by deselecting the Track formatting check box. You can also control the page layout when printing if you are printing your draft document with changes displayed.

**Figure 12.6.** The Track Changes Options dialog box

## Working with comments

You can add comments to your document. They serve as virtual sticky notes that allow you to comment on the text without interfering with it. You can add text comments and, if you have a Tablet PC, voice or hand-written comments. Using comments instead of embedding comments within text is smart for several reasons. You isolate comment from content so that you don't accidentally publish private comments (as noted in the sidebar earlier), you can browse through comments only to make reviewing the document more efficient, and you can turn the display and printing on and off.

**Inside Scoop**

If the name or initials listed when you add a comment are incorrect or simply show User instead, you can't edit the comment to correct this. However, you can quickly fix the problem by choosing Review ⇨ Track Changes ⇨ Change User Name and updating the username and initials.

## Adding a text comment

To add a text comment to a document, you first need to decide where you want the comment to appear. It is attached to a specific insert point or selected block of text. After positioning the cursor at the appropriate insertion point or selecting the appropriate block of text, choose Review ⇨ New Comment. The selected text is highlighted, and a line is drawn out to a balloon in the margin where you can type your text comment. Your comment is prefaced with "Comment [*your initials*1]:" where your initials are those that you indicated when you personalized Word or Office upon installation. The number is the comment number — if you add two comments, they are numbered consecutively (such as DJC1, DJC2, and so on). When you hover the mouse over the comment, the message includes your username and the date and time, as shown in the example in Figure 12.7. The comment appears in the body font of the current theme in a reduced size, but you can change the font and add italics, bold, highlighting, color, and so on to a comment. You cannot change the size.

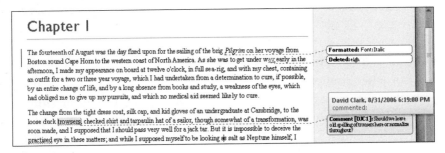

**Figure 12.7.** Adding a text comment to a document

## Adding a voice comment or handwritten comment

If you have a Tablet PC, you can add voice comments or ink comments to the document. To add voice comments, first add the Insert Voice command to your Quick Access Toolbar (QAT). To do so, follow these steps:

1. Choose Microsoft Office ⇨ Word Options ⇨ Customization.

2. In the Choose commands from drop-down list, choose Commands Not in the Ribbon.

3. Scroll through the list to find Insert Voice, and click it to select it.

**4.** Click Add to add it to your QAT and then click OK to confirm the changes.

Once you have added Insert Voice as a button on your QAT, you can use it to add a voice comment. To do so, follow these steps:

**1.** Click Insert Voice on the QAT to add a voice comment. A sound recording dialog box appears, as shown in Figure 12.8.

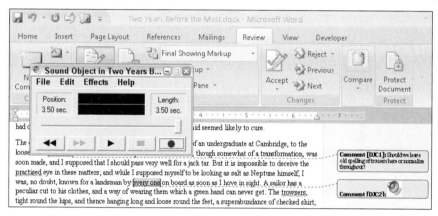

**Figure 12.8.** Recording a voice comment

**2.** Click the red button to start recording and make your voice comment. (Speak slowly and clearly.)

**3.** Click the square to stop recording. A speaker icon appears in the comment balloon to indicate that the comment is a voice comment.

Once you add a voice comment, you can right-click the comment and choose Sound Recorder Document Object ⇨ Play to hear the comment, as shown in Figure 12.9.

To add handwritten comments using a Tablet PC, choose Review ⇨ New Comment and write in the comment bubble.

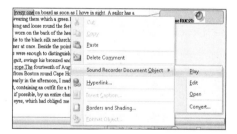

**Figure 12.9.** Playing a voice comment

**Hack**

You can also add the Edit Comment command (which doesn't appear anywhere on the Ribbon) to your QAT by choosing Microsoft Office ⇨ Word Options ⇨ Customization. Select All Commands and then add Edit Comment from the list. The command takes you to the comment associated with the currently selected text.

### Finding comments

To efficiently move through comments, you have two options. Use the Next or Previous buttons in the Comments group on the Review tab if you want to use the Ribbon. The alternative method is to use the vertical slider's object browser (see Chapter 4). Press Ctrl+Alt+Home and select Browse by Comment from the object gallery.

### Deleting comments

To delete a comment, you can either select it and choose Review ⇨ Delete in the Comments group, or right-click the comment and click Delete Comment from the pop-up menu. If you want to delete all comments in the document, click the list arrow next to the Delete button and in the Comments group of the Review tab, and then click Delete All Comments in Document.

### Deleting the comments from select reviewers

If you want to delete comments of select reviewers, not all reviewers, follow these steps:

1. Choose Review ⇨ Show Markup ⇨ Reviewers.
2. Deselect the check marks from any reviewers whose comments you want to keep, so that only the comments of the reviewers you want to delete are displayed.
3. Choose Review ⇨ Delete ⇨ Delete All Comments Shown.
4. Choose Review ⇨ Show Markup ⇨ Reviewers again and reselect the reviewers whose comments you want to keep so that they reappear.

## Reviewing changes

The process of reviewing changes can be accomplished in several ways. You may have a review cycle that encourages those reviewing your work to add comments to which you respond or to which you respond by altering the text. You may have a situation where others directly modify the text and you accept or reject their suggested changes. Because I do this for a living all day long, both as a writer and as an editor, I feel I can offer some experienced tips on reviewing a marked-up document:

- Separate content from form when reviewing. Address format changes separately from textual changes, preferably in a separate pass through the document.

- Take full advantage of comments to indicate that you have responded to comments and queries from reviewers.

- View extensive and complex textual changes at least once with all change marks hidden to make sure that the final wording makes sense.

- Do a spelling and grammar check at the end of the review cycle to guard against new errors that may be introduced during the review cycle.

### Display for Review

Word allows you to select different stages of the review cycle with the Display for Review list. You can choose from Final Showing Markup (the default setting), Final, Original Showing Markup, and Original. These selections are not entirely self-explanatory, but Table 12.1 clarifies the function of each setting. These different settings give you the display flexibility you need to review a document without having to open two separate file versions of the same document to compare the changes.

**Table 12.1.** Display for Review settings

| Setting | Description |
| --- | --- |
| Final Showing Markup | Displays additions, formatting, and moves in text, noting deletions and formatting in balloons when balloons are displayed |
| Final | Displays latest changes with no change indicators visible |
| Original Showing Markup | Displays deleted text in strikethrough in text, noting additions, formatting changes, and moves in balloons when balloons are displayed |
| Original | Displays original document before any changes were made (but does not actually remove the changes) |

## Show Markup

In addition to the display settings mentioned above, you can also choose types of markup you want to display by choosing Review ⇨ Show Markup to display the options shown in Figure 12.10. By default, all markup elements and reviewers are displayed. However, you can deselect the check boxes of any of the elements to focus on one type of change at a time. You can also select individual reviewers or select all reviewers. When you clear the check box of a specific reviewer, that reviewer's comments are

**Figure 12.10.** Show Markup options

hidden. However, any textual and formatting changes are still displayed if you have Final Showing Markup or Original Showing Markup selected.

## The Reviewing Pane

The Reviewing Pane allows you an additional way to keep track of changes. By default, this pane is turned off — I personally find it too distracting. However, it has the benefit of showing comments in a larger font size, and allows you to make changes to document changes and comments without working in the document itself. You can turn the Reviewing Pane on to display at the left mar-

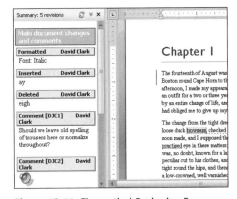

**Figure 12.11.** The vertical Reviewing Pane

gin by choosing Review ⇨ Reviewing Pane ⇨ Reviewing Pane Vertical, as shown in Figure 12.11, or at the bottom with Review ⇨ Reviewing Pane ⇨ Reviewing Pane Horizontal, as shown in Figure 12.12. To update the revision number, click what looks like the Refresh button on a Web

### Bright Idea

When you review a complex revision with lots of changes, set the display for review to Final when things appear overwhelming. You can read a clean copy with no marks visible. You can then switch back to Final Showing Markup to accept or reject changes.

browser (the two arrows chasing each other). To see a detailed summary of the number of insertions, deletions, comments, and so on, click the chevron. To close the Reviewing Pane, click the pane's Close button.

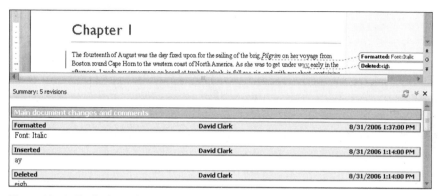

**Figure 12.12.** The horizontal reviewing pane

## *Locating, accepting, and rejecting changes*

You can accept or reject changes, locate changes, or move between them using the commands in the Changes group of the Review tab on the Ribbon. Note that this process takes you to every change shown, be it a comment, insertion, deletion, or move. To begin reviewing, accepting, and rejecting changes in a document, follow these steps:

1. Position your cursor at the part of the document where you want to start reviewing changes. (Press Ctrl+Home to move to the beginning of your document.)

2. Choose Review ➪ Next to move to the first change in the document.

3. If you want to accept the change as it stands and move to the next change, choose Review ➪ Accept. The change becomes permanent and balloons, change bars, font color, or other change indicators disappear and Word moves to the next change. To reject a change as it stands and move to the next change, choose Review ➪ Reject.

**Hack**

You can undo an accept or reject operation during a change review by clicking Undo on the QAT or pressing Ctrl+Z.

**Watch Out!**
Accepting all changes finalizes the changes but does not entirely clean up your document. Comments remain unless you specifically invoke the Delete All Comments in Document command.

If you want to accept or reject a change but you also want to modify the change before moving on, click the arrow below the Accept button or adjacent to the Reject button to see more options. Figure 12.13 shows the menu of Accept options; those for Reject are identical. Select Accept Change to accept the change (or Reject Change, as the case may be) without moving to the next

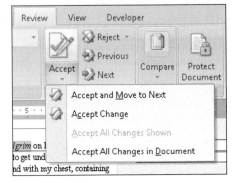

**Figure 12.13.** Additional Accept Change menu options

change in the document. Make any modifications to the change as needed. If you don't want the modified accepted change or rejected change to appear as a new change, make sure that Track Changes is turned off (Ctrl+Shift+E). When you are satisfied, choose Review ➪ Next to move on to the next change in the document.

Although you should exercise caution using the commands, you can always accept or reject all changes in the document. If you have filtered out some reviewers or types of changes using Show Markup settings, you also have the option of accepting or rejecting all changes shown, which is a good way to delete all changes from one reviewer, accept all formatting changes only, and so on.

## Protecting the document from changes

Prior to sending your document out for review, you can restrict various types of changes. To do so, choose Review ➪ Protect Document ➪ Restrict

**Watch Out!**
Restricting all styles doesn't prevent users from changing document themes or changing the Quick Style set.

Reviewing Options to display the Protect Document pane shown in Figure 12.14. Restrictions are categorized as either formatting or editing restrictions. After you decide what to restrict, you must specifically initiate document protection for the restrictions to begin, as described later in this section.

### Restricting formatting changes

Word offers you the ability to exert control over every aspect of formatting and allows you great flexibility in what you want to restrict, because you can restrict changes down to the style level. To restrict formatting changes, select the Limit formatting to a selection of styles option in the Restrict Formatting and Editing pane, and then click Settings to see the dialog box shown in Figure 12.15.

By default, all styles are allowed. Basic options are to allow no style changes (click None) or a subset (click Recommended Minimum). If you want to reset the style restrictions so that all may be changed once more, click All.

There are a few additional options. If you desire, you can select the Allow AutoFormat to override formatting restrictions

**Figure 12.14.** The Restrict Formatting and Editing pane

**Figure 12.15.** The Formatting Restrictions dialog box

option. You can also select the Block Theme or Scheme switching option, or the Block Quick Style Set switching option.

### Restricting editing

Word provides you with several ways to limit editing, rather than just all or none. Select the Allow only this type of editing in the document option to choose what type of editing you want to restrict. Table 12.2 explains the four options.

**Table 12.2.** Types of editing restrictions

| Type | Description |
| --- | --- |
| Tracked changes | Allows document reviewers to change the document, but all changes are tracked. Track Changes cannot be turned off. |
| Comments | Allows document reviewers only to add comments to the document. |
| Filling in forms | Allows document reviewers only to supply data in fields, but does not allow them to change fields or other text in the document. |
| No changes (Read only) | Allows document reviewers to make no changes to the document. |

If you have certain sections of your document that you want to protect and others that you want to allow others to edit, you can use the Exceptions feature. This allows you to select a group of users or individuals that have editing options for selected sections of the document. To allow everyone to edit a selected section of the text, select the text in the document and select the check box next to Everyone. Use the same techniques if you have other groups available to choose from.

You can also select exceptions to restrictions for individual users. To add someone to the list, click More users and type the user account name (if you are on a network) or an Internet e-mail address. You can then select text and select the check box next to each user's name, as shown in Figure 12.16.

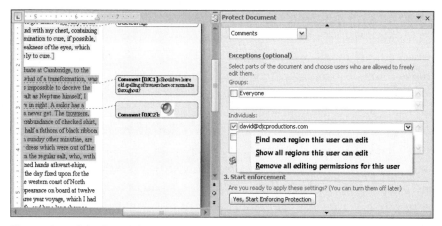

**Figure 12.16.** Selecting editing restriction exceptions

## *Enforcing protection*

Once you select your restrictions, you can begin protecting the document by choosing Review ⇨ Protect Document ⇨ Restrict Formatting and Editing ⇨ Yes, Start Enforcing Protection. You are asked to select a password and to retype the password. It is important to remember not to rely on this method of protecting your document in critical situations, however, because a sufficiently knowledgeable user can override these safeguards. Instead, use the user authentication option (if available), which only allows users with appropriate permissions to remove document protection, and which also encrypts the document and enables the Do Not Distribute feature. This option takes advantage of Windows Information Rights Management (IRM). See Chapter 21 for more details on IRM.

To remove document protection, choose Review ⇨ Protect Document ⇨ Restrict Formatting and Editing ⇨ Stop Protection. If you used a password to protect the document, you are asked to type the password to authorize removal of document protection.

---

**Watch Out!**

The Mark As Final feature is informational and is intended to help prevent accidental modifications to final documents. It is not a security feature. If the user wants to remove the Final status, he or she can do so by simply choosing Microsoft Office ⇨ Prepare ⇨ Mark As Final again to turn the Final status off.

## Marking the document as final

After completing your document, you can mark it as final and prevent further editing by choosing Microsoft Office ⇨ Prepare ⇨ Mark As Final. This is a toggle command that can be turned back off if you want to revise the document later. When you mark the document as final, someone reading the document will receive the message "This modification is not allowed because the selection is locked" when he or she attempts to make changes to the document. If the user attempts to remove document protection, a message appears stating that it is not possible to disable document protection because the document is marked Final. The Status property for the document also appears as Final.

# Comparing and combining document versions

If you are faced with the situation of several people working in parallel on the same document rather than making changes in sequence in the same file, you may need to compare separate versions. Fortunately, Word provides you with a pair of features that allow you to do this in a relatively painless way.

## Comparing two versions of a document

You may find yourself in the situation where you need to know what is different in two versions of the same document. This is particularly useful if you have an updated version of a document with no change tracking, or when comparing business contracts during negotiations. To compare two versions of a document, follow these steps:

1. Choose Review ⇨ Compare ⇨ Compare ⇨ Compare. The Compare Documents dialog box appears.

2. Click More to view all the available options, as shown in Figure 12.17.

3. Click the Original document drop-down list to select from a list of recently opened documents, or click the Browse

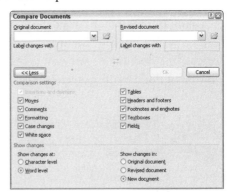

**Figure 12.17.** The expanded Compare Documents dialog box

**Inside Scoop**

It's been my experience that the Reviewing Pane and the Compared Document pane are sufficient to perform the comparison. I close the original and revised document panes to free up the screen by choosing Review ⇨ Compare ⇨ Show Source Documents ⇨ Hide Source Documents.

for Original button to the right of the list box to browse to find the original file.

4. Follow the same procedure for the Revised document drop-down list (or use the Browse for Revised button).

5. Once you select a revised document, the Label changes with field is populated with your name (the current username). You can type a different text string here if you want.

6. By default, all changes to the document are shown. You can deselect check boxes for any changes you don't care to take note of (such as formatting, if you are focusing on content).

7. By default, Word shows you changes at the word level. You can elect to show changes at the character level if you want to see just exactly what changed character by character (useful perhaps for numerical data).

8. Finally, you can show changes in the original document, the revised document, or a new document. I recommend creating a new document, which is the default setting, for the sake of proper version control.

9. Click OK to start the document comparison.

Once you click OK, a screen something like that shown in Figure 12.18 appears. As you can see, the Reviewing Pane is launched, the new document appears in the center pane, the original document appears at the top right, and the revised document appears at the bottom right. At this point, you can use the commands in the Changes group of the Review tab to accept or reject changes in much the same way that you would if you were reviewing a single document with Track Changes turned on. When you finish with the review process, click Save or press Ctrl+S, assign the Compare Result version a new name, and click Save.

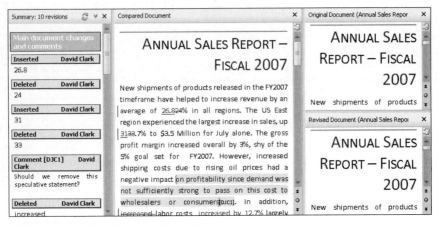

**Figure 12.18.** Viewing the comparison of two documents

## Combining revisions from multiple authors into one document

In certain situations, you will need to compare revisions made by more than two authors to the same document. With Word, you can combine revisions from two authors at a time — you simply repeat the process for additional authors. To do so, follow these steps:

1. Choose Review ⇨ Compare ⇨ Compare ⇨ Combine. The Combine Documents dialog box appears.

2. Click More to view all the available options. The options are the same as those for comparing two documents (shown in Figure 12.17).

3. Click the Original document drop-down list to select from a list of recently opened documents, or click the Browse for Original button to the right of the list box to browse to select the first file. (Because you are combining multiple documents, you needn't select the original document here. You can choose the first of the revised versions.)

4. Once you select an original (first revised) document, the Label unmarked changes with field is populated with the username or the document's reviser. You can type a different text string here if you want.

5. Follow the same procedure for the Revised document drop-down list (or use the Browse for Revised button) to select the next revised version of the document.

6. As with the Compare Documents feature, all changes to the document are shown by default. You can deselect check boxes for any changes you don't care to take note of (such as formatting, if you are focusing on content).

7. By default, Word shows you changes at the word level. You can elect to show changes at the character level if you want to see just exactly what changed character by character (useful perhaps for numerical data).

8. Finally, you can show changes in the original document, the revised document, or a new document. As with the Compare Documents feature, I recommend creating a new document, which is the default setting, for the sake of proper version control.

9. Click OK to start combining the document versions.

Once you click OK, a screen something like that shown in Figure 12.19 appears. As you can see, the Reviewing Pane is launched, the new document appears in the center pane, the original (or first revised) document appears at the top right, and the second revised document appears at the bottom right. At this point, you can use the commands in the Changes group of the Review tab to accept or reject changes in much the same way that you would if you were reviewing a single document with Track Changes turned on. When you finish with the review process, click Save or press Ctrl+S, assign the Combine Result version a new name, and click Save. Repeat the process to add additional document versions.

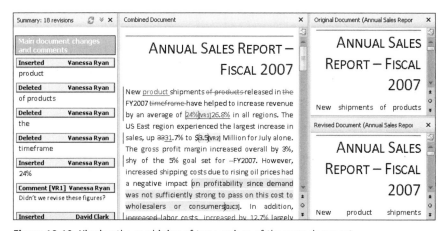

**Figure 12.19.** Viewing the combining of two versions of the same document

# Sharing a document workspace

If you work in a networked corporate or organizational environment with Microsoft Office SharePoint Server, you can take advantage of SharePoint versioning capabilities to check in and check out documents to and from a shared, centralized network location. You need to rely on your own IT organization and administrator for network address location information, access rights, and other information in order to use such features. I cover the Word commands that relate to this in a general way.

To save a document to an existing document workspace on a document management server, choose Microsoft Office ⇨ Publish ⇨ Document Management Server. When you see the Save As dialog box, choose the appropriate network location or choose Tools ⇨ Map Network Drive to add a network share location if necessary. Once you have used SharePoint, you should be able to click the appropriate server location the next time you use Word.

If you have the necessary SharePoint permissions on your network, you can also create a new Document Workspace site from within Word as you save your document to the network. To do so, choose Microsoft Office ⇨ Publish ⇨ Create Document Workspace. The Document Management pane appears to the right of your document, as shown in Figure 12.20. By default, the new Document Workspace name will be that of your document unless you type a different name. Type a new URL in the Location for new workspace box. Click Create to create the new document workspace.

**Figure 12.20.** Creating a new document workspace

You can also use your Web browser to navigate to your SharePoint site. You can set up shared documents so that document editors must check files in and out to ensure a single latest version. Clicking the drop-down list for the document allows you to check it in or out, or edit it in Word, among other things, as shown in Figure 12.21. To add version history and check in/out functionality to Shared Documents in SharePoint, choose Settings ⇨ Document Library

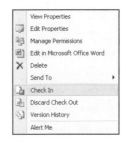

**Figure 12.21.** Working with a document on a SharePoint site

**Hack**

Hovering over the document's icon shows the version history for that document.

Settings from the Shared Documents screen, and from the Customize Shared Documents screen, click Versioning settings. The versioning settings allow for content approval, version numbering style, limiting the allowable number of versions, check in and check out, and security settings.

# Online collaboration on the Web

If you work with business partners or others who do not share your local area network, you can take advantage of shared sites such as Microsoft Office Live Collaboration to check in and check out documents to and from a shared Web site. Although not as fully featured, managed shared-interest sites such as MSN Groups also allow you to post and share documents.

## Document collaboration with Microsoft Office Live Collaboration

If you have Microsoft Office Live Collaboration, which charges a monthly fee to host the site, you can set up a business collaboration site that also includes a document library. Use your Web browser to manage the site and upload or download documents (checking them in or out as needed). Microsoft manages site login security, and you can add users and manage access. Users must have a Passport account (such as an MSN account or Hotmail account). Users can have Administrator, Editor, or Reader status. You can filter your displayed list of documents or add custom columns with additional information.

Clicking the drop-down list for the document allows you to check it in or out, edit properties, and review version history, among other things. You can only check a document out if it is checked in, and vice versa. Clicking Version History allows you to see the document's version history, as well as delete individual versions or modify versioning settings.

## Document collaboration with MSN Groups

If you have an MSN account, you can use MSN Groups to create a document library, albeit one with less capabilities. If you set up the account and have Manager status, you can upload files and perform all administrative tasks. Although the features are limited, you can make the group restricted to invitees only, if you wish, and the group is protected to some extent, although I don't recommend using such groups for highly sensitive information. If you assign an invitee Assistant Manager status, that person can also upload and download documents. Figure 12.22 shows a sample document library in MSN Groups. Note that the user currently logged in has assistant manager status and as such has full file access to the documents in the library.

| TechWriting@groups.msn.com | | | Welcome ☻ VKR1 (assistant manager) |
|---|---|---|---|
| **Documents** | | | |
| 📄 **Add File**   📂 **Create Folder**   ✖ **Delete** | | | 📁 **My Storage** |
| 📋 **Copy**   📑 **Move**   🔧 **Settings** | | | |
| **Name** | **Size** | **Posted By** | **Modified** |
| 📁 | | | |
| 📂 Documents | | | 📝 9/3/2006 10:02 AM |
| 📄 Annual Sales Report - VR.docx | 159 K | ☻ VKR1 | ☑ 9/3/2006 12:06 PM |
| 📄 Annual Sales Report Update.docx | 159 K | David | ☑ 9/3/2006 11:39 AM |
| 📄 Business Plan 2007.docx | 44 K | David | ☑ 9/3/2006 11:41 AM |
| 📄 Shipping Manifest.docx | 9 K | David | ☑ 9/3/2006 11:41 AM |

**Figure 12.22.** An MSN Groups document library

To add a file or files to the document library, click Add File. You may be asked to allow MSN to install an ActiveX control first. This ActiveX control allows you to browse through your computer's files and select any files you want to upload to the MSN Groups document library. You are given a space limit to how many files you can upload — 3MB in this example — and a storage meter at the bottom of the window displays how much space you have to work with as you select files, as shown in Figure 12.23.

**Watch Out!**

MSN Groups does not have version control or check in/check out functionality. You can only choose between allowing download-only (Members) or full document access (Manager or Assistant Manager), in which case documents with the same filename can be overwritten.

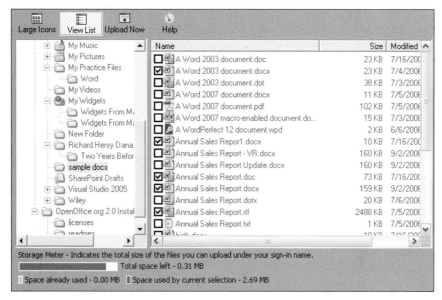

**Figure 12.23.** Uploading files to an MSN Groups document library

# Just the facts

- Use Track Changes to keep track of document drafts and see just what was changed, when, and by whom.

- Save yourself some grief by preparing for and closely tracking versions with a solution suitable to the scope of your document revision.

- Use the Protect Document feature to restrict revision of all or certain aspects of your document.

- Use a document management server such as Office SharePoint Server to manage group document updates and revisions.

- If possible, take advantage of versioning and check in/check out features of a document management server when numerous revisers or drafts are required.

- Use a Web-based collaboration site such as Microsoft Office Live when the collaborators don't share your local area network.

**GET THE SCOOP ON...**
Creating a form to fill out in Word ▪ Adding controls to
streamline data entry and eliminate typos ▪ Preventing
users from editing a form ▪ Creating a printed form ▪
Creating a checklist

# Create Forms

There are many different ways to approach the gathering of information. What I *don't* show you in this chapter is how to jury-rig Word so that you can use it as a front end for a database. Microsoft and other vendors have better tools for that purpose, including Microsoft InfoPath, a rich-client form application that is designed to work with XML-based database systems, and Microsoft Access, the relational database management system that comes with Microsoft Office.

However, Word is well suited to the task of creating forms that need to be printed out eventually for some reason, such as work orders, contracts, and so on. You can design forms to be electronic forms, printed forms, forms that you fill in electronically and then print out and sign, or some hybrid form that allows electronic or printed versions. I start by describing the features you can take advantage of with electronic forms and then move on to designing printed forms.

Before going through the exercise of showing you how to create a form from scratch, however, I'll mention that there are a number of very good forms available as templates through Microsoft Office Online. To review these templates, choose Microsoft Office ⇨ New ⇨ Forms. The Forms category templates are divided into the following subcategories:

▪ Academic

▪ Business

Chapter 13

- Community
- Employment
- Healthcare
- Legal
- Personal

You can choose a form template from among these subcategories, download it and use it or modify it first to suit your needs. (Many templates not in the Forms category available from Microsoft Office Online could be used as forms as well.) Most of these forms are intended to be customized for your use and then printed, but some forms have online versions that allow users of the form to fill them out in Word.

I cover the basics of creating a form in this chapter, but you can learn how to add more functionality to electronic forms with macros in Chapter 23. (Some basic form automation requires macros if you need the form to be filled out using an earlier version of Word.) You can design the form more readily by making full use of the table features (see Chapters 15 and 16) as I do later in this chapter.

## Creating an electronic form

To create a form that users can fill out by typing data into fields using Word, you can take advantage of several Word features to make your job easier. First, however, you need to be able to answer several questions:

- Which version(s) of Word can you expect the recipient of the form to have?
- Will the form be filled out and returned electronically or printed and signed?
- Which areas of the form need to be protected from modification by the user?
- Do any of the blank fields in the form require additional explanation?

**Inside Scoop**

Use common system fonts if possible, or if size is not an issue, embed fonts to ensure proper form alignment by choosing Microsoft Office ⇨ Word Options.

**Watch Out!**

If you suspect that some of the form users will have an earlier version of Word, use Compatibility Mode and save the file in Word 97 - 2003 (*.dot) format. This blocks the use of the new controls but also prevents the user from having problems with the form.

## Designing an electronic form

Once you have the answers to these questions, you can proceed. If you intend to have the form filled out by the user each time, it makes sense to design your form as a template. The following example demonstrates the use of some Word 2007 content controls and shows how to assure that only the data entry fields are modified.

In this example, you create a simple change-of-address form, and it is assumed users have Word 2007. To do so, follow these steps:

**1.** Choose Microsoft Office ⇨ New ⇨ Blank document.

**2.** Press F12 (or choose Microsoft Office ⇨ Save As).

**3.** Double-click in the File name field and type **AddressChangeForm**.

**4.** In the Save as type drop-down list, select Word Template (*.dotx).

**5.** Click Trusted Templates in the Save in field and click Save.

**6.** Press Ctrl+* or choose Home ⇨ Show/Hide Paragraph so that paragraph marks are displayed.

**7.** Type **Change of Address Form**.

**8.** Click to the left of the text so that it is all selected, including the paragraph mark; press Ctrl+E (to center the paragraph); select 24 as the font point size; click Outside Borders from the Borders button; and for shading, select the second gray in the first column (White, Background 1, Darker 15%). Your document should look something like Figure 13.1.

**9.** Press the right arrow key, and then press Enter to move to the next line.

**10.** Click Clear Formatting in the Font group of the Ribbon to revert the new paragraph back to Normal style.

Change·of·Address·Form¶

**Figure 13.1.** Adding a title to the form

**Inside Scoop**

To maximize the likelihood of compatibility with the user's printer, avoid narrow margins if possible.

## Using table features in a form

At this point, you use Word's table feature to create fields for labels and for data entry:

1. Choose Insert ⇨ Table ⇨ Insert Table to see the dialog box shown in Figure 13.2.

2. Type **3** in the Number of columns field, **14** in the Number of rows field, and click OK.

3. Type the labels as indicated in Figure 13.3.

4. Click to the left of the row containing Old address and choose Table Tools ⇨ Layout ⇨ Merge Cells. This combines the contents of each row into one table-wide cell. (Each separate compartment of the table is a *cell*.)

**Figure 13.2.** Inserting a table into the form

5. Repeat Step 4 for the row containing New address, for both rows containing Street address, and for the row below each instance of Street address, so that your table looks like Figure 13.4.

6. Click to the left of the row containing First name. Hold the Ctrl key down and click to the left of every other row that has a label in it.

7. When all the rows of the table with text have been selected, choose Home ⇨ Shading and select the second gray in the first column (White, Background 1, Darker 15%). Your form should now look like Figure 13.5.

8. Click Save or press Ctrl+S to save your changes.

| First·name:¤ | Last·name:¤ | Date:¤ |
|---|---|---|
| ¤ | ¤ | ¤ |
| Old·address¤ | ¤ | ¤ |
| Street·address¤ | ¤ | ¤ |
| ¤ | ¤ | ¤ |
| City¤ | State¤ | ZIP¤ |
| ¤ | ¤ | ¤ |
| New·address¤ | ¤ | ¤ |
| Street·address¤ | ¤ | ¤ |
| ¤ | ¤ | ¤ |
| City¤ | State¤ | ZIP¤ |
| ¤ | ¤ | ¤ |
| Effective·date:¤ | Effective·until·{if·temporary}:¤ | ¤ |
| ¤ | ¤ | ¤ |

**Figure 13.3.** Adding labels to the form

| First·name:¤ | Last·name:¤ | Date:¤ |
|---|---|---|
| ¤ | ¤ | ¤ |
| Old·address¤ | | |
| Street·address¤ | | |
| ¤ | | |
| City¤ | State¤ | ZIP¤ |
| ¤ | ¤ | ¤ |
| New·address¤ | | |
| Street·address¤ | | |
| ¤ | | |
| City¤ | State¤ | ZIP¤ |
| ¤ | ¤ | ¤ |
| Effective·date:¤ | Effective·until·{if·temporary}:¤ | ¤ |
| ¤ | ¤ | ¤ |

**Figure 13.4.** Using Merge Cells to clean up the form

## Change·of·Address·Form¶

| First·name:¤ | Last·name:¤ | Date:¤ |
|---|---|---|
| ¤ | ¤ | ¤ |
| Old·address¤ | | |
| Street·address¤ | | |
| ¤ | | |
| City¤ | State¤ | ZIP¤ |
| ¤ | ¤ | ¤ |
| New·address¤ | | |
| Street·address¤ | | |
| ¤ | | |
| City¤ | State¤ | ZIP¤ |
| ¤ | ¤ | ¤ |
| Effective·date:¤ | Effective·until·{if·temporary}:¤ | ¤ |
| ¤ | ¤ | ¤ |

**Figure 13.5.** Adding shading to the label cells of the table

## Adding Controls to a form

Now that you have created a table with some labels, you can begin adding fields to the form. To do so, you need to have the Developer tab visible on the Ribbon:

1. Choose Microsoft Office ⇨ Word Options ⇨ Personalize, check the option Show Developer tab in the Ribbon, and click OK.

2. Click in the table cell immediately below the one containing First name, and then click the Developer tab.

3. Click Text in the Controls group on the Developer tab (the second of the two Aa buttons) to insert a plain text control. If you are curious why you need to bother adding fields that just contain text, it's because this makes it easier to protect the rest of the form from alteration later in the process. Developers can also use these fields to extract the data.

4. Repeat the process for the cells immediately below the text containing the labels Last name, Street address, City, and ZIP, so that your form's table looks like Figure 13.6.

| First·name:¤ | Last·name:¤ | Date:¤ |
|---|---|---|
| Click·here·to·enter·text.¤ | Click·here·to·enter·text.¤ | ¤ |
| Old·address¤ | | |
| Street·address¤ | | |
| Click·here·to·enter·text.¤ | | |
| City¤ | State¤ | ZIP¤ |
| Click·here·to·enter·text.¤ | ¤ | Click·here·to·enter·text.¤ |
| New·address¤ | | |
| Street·address¤ | | |
| Click·here·to·enter·text.¤ | | |
| City¤ | State¤ | ZIP¤ |
| Click·here·to·enter·text.¤ | ¤ | Click·here·to·enter·text.¤ |
| Effective·date:¤ | Effective·until·(if·temporary):¤ | ¤ |
| ¤ | ¤ | ¤ |

**Figure 13.6.** Adding Text controls to the form

5. Click in the cell immediately below the cell containing Date, and then click Date Picker from the Controls group of the Developer tab. This displays a pop-up calendar from which the user can select a date, as shown in Figure 13.7.

6. Repeat the process for the cells immediately below the cells containing Effective date and Effective until (if temporary), so that your form's table looks like Figure 13.8.

**Figure 13.7.** With Date Picker, the user can select a date by clicking on a calendar.

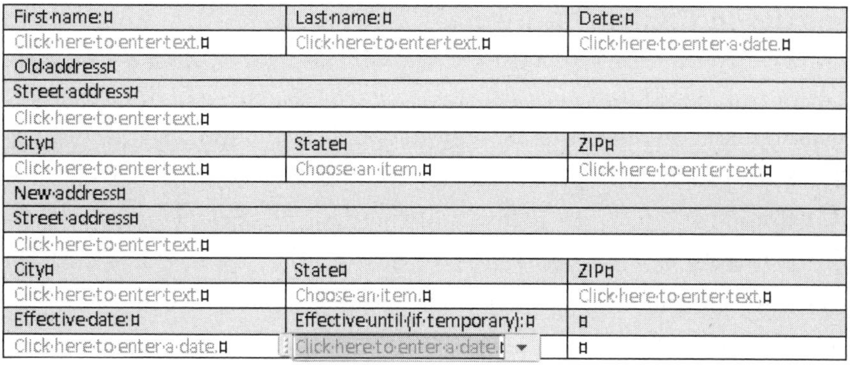

| First·name:¤ | Last·name:¤ | Date:¤ |
|---|---|---|
| Click·here·to·enter·text.¤ | Click·here·to·enter·text.¤ | Click·here·to·enter·a·date.¤ |
| Old·address¤ | | |
| Street·address¤ | | |
| Click·here·to·enter·text.¤ | | |
| City¤ | State¤ | ZIP¤ |
| Click·here·to·enter·text.¤ | Choose·an·item.¤ | Click·here·to·enter·text.¤ |
| New·address¤ | | |
| Street·address¤ | | |
| Click·here·to·enter·text.¤ | | |
| City¤ | State¤ | ZIP¤ |
| Click·here·to·enter·text.¤ | Choose·an·item.¤ | Click·here·to·enter·text.¤ |
| Effective·date:¤ | Effective·until·(if·temporary):¤ | ¤ |
| Click·here·to·enter·a·date.¤ | Click·here·to·enter·a·date.¤ ▾ | ¤ |

**Figure 13.8.** Adding the Date Picker control to the form

7. The Date Picker control has several options for date format to be displayed once selected by the user. Click the first of the Date Picker controls in your form, and then choose Developer ➪ Properties to see the Content Control Properties dialog box for the Date Picker control, as shown in Figure 13.9.

8. Select the third option, October 28, 2006, in this example (although yours will have the current date). The Display the date like this field should display MMMM d, yyyy. Click OK.

9. Repeat Steps 7 and 8 for the remaining two date fields.

10. Click Save or press Ctrl+S to save your changes.

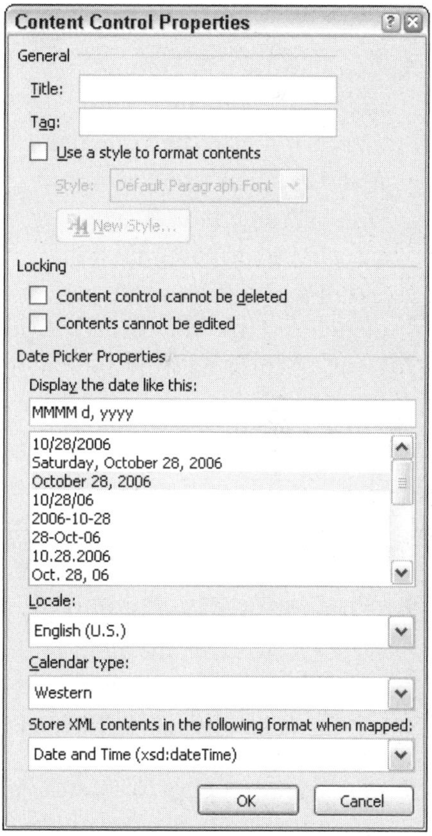

**Figure 13.9.** The Content Control Properties dialog box for the Date Picker control

## Modifying Control properties

You have not yet done anything with the State fields. Add a Dropdown List control so that the user can select a state (I use three in this example, assuming my organization is regional and not national). To add a Dropdown List control, follow these steps:

1. Click in the cell of the form's table immediately below the cell containing the first instance of State.

2. Click Dropdown List in the Controls group of the Developer tab.

3. Click Properties to see the Content Control Properties dialog box for the Dropdown List control.

4. Click Add to display the Add Choice dialog box. In the Display Name field, type **California**.

5. As you can see in Figure 13.10, the Value field automatically fills in the same text string that you typed for the Display Name field. In this case, however, you want a different text string to actually

**Figure 13.10.** Adding an item to the Dropdown List control

be entered into the form: the postal abbreviation for the state. Delete California from the Value field and type **CA** in its place. Click OK. The new item now appears in the list.

6. Repeat Steps 4 and 5, replacing California and CA with Oregon (OR), and Washington (WA), respectively. (If you notice you've made a mistake during your data entry, you can click Modify to edit an existing list entry or Remove to delete the entry.)

7. When you are satisfied with your list, click OK.

8. Click the arrow to the right of the list to see how the drop-down list will operate. You should see a list like the one shown in Figure 13.11. Click the arrow again to close the list without making a selection.

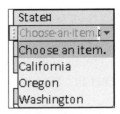

**Figure 13.11.** A Dropdown List control added to a form

9. With the Dropdown List control still selected, press Ctrl+C (or right-click the control and click Copy in the pop-up menu).

**10.** Click in the cell of the form's table immediately below the cell containing the second instance of State.

**11.** Press Ctrl+V (or choose Home ⇨ ) to paste a copy of the State Dropdown List control into the second state field. Press Esc to clear the Paste Options icon from the screen.

**12.** Click Save or press Ctrl+S to save your changes.

## Locking the form for data entry only

You now have the completed form. However, as it stands now, anything can be modified in the form, including the title and labels. In order to lock out all but the data entry fields, follow these steps:

**1.** If Design Mode is still enabled, disable it now by clicking Design Mode. The Properties button should be disabled (grayed out).

**2.** Choose Developer ⇨ Protect Document ⇨ Restrict Formatting and Editing.

**3.** Under Editing Restrictions in the Restrict Formatting and Editing pane, select the Allow only this type of editing in the document option.

**4.** In the drop-down list immediately below this option, select Filling in forms.

**5.** Under Start enforcement, click Yes, Start Enforcing Protection.

**6.** In the Start Enforcing Protection dialog box, select Password as the protection method. (A change-of-address form is not sensitive, so the relatively weak password method of protection is adequate. Use User authentication if you are working with more sensitive documents or documents more likely to be tampered with, such as legal forms and contractual agreements.)

**7.** Type a password in the Enter new password field and retype it in the subsequent field to confirm the password. Click OK to protect the form.

**8.** You now have a protected template. Click Save or press Ctrl+S to save your work.

## Using the electronic form

To use the form, you can choose Microsoft Office ⇨ New and select AddressChangeForm.dotx from your Trusted Templates. You can also save this form as a document. Either way, only the data entry fields can be modified. In fact, the user cannot even select any fields that are not form fields. To make changes later, open the template and choose Developer ⇨ Protect Document ⇨ Stop Protection. Type the password in the Unprotect Document dialog box when prompted and click OK to unprotect the document.

## Adding a digital signature and/or signature line

Microsoft has partnered with some security vendors to incorporate digital signatures into its documents. Digital signatures may not be valid in every jurisdiction. Whether you opt to include digital signature capabilities to your document or not, you can add a signature line. (You can always ask the user to print the document, sign it, and return it to you physically or via fax.) To do so, follow these steps:

1. Choose Insert ⇨ Signature Line. An informational dialog box appears.

2. If you need to set up signature services, click the related button; otherwise, click OK to view the Signature Setup dialog box shown in Figure 13.12.

3. Type the data for the fields in the dialog box. In this example, a specific signer and signer's title are included along with instructions on how to sign the signature line electronically with the title field: **David J. Clark, Author (double-click to sign electronically)**.

**Figure 13.12.** Setting up a signature line

4. Click OK to see the signature line, as shown in Figure 13.13.

When users receive the document and double-click the signature line, they first see the informational dialog box mentioned earlier, and then the Sign dialog box shown in Figure 13.14. Note that the user can type his or her name or select an image (such as an image file containing the user's handwritten signature). The user then clicks Sign to sign the document digitally. When successfully added, a Signature Confirmation dialog box lets the user know that his or her signature has been added, and that it becomes invalid if the document is subsequently modified.

Once the user clicks OK at the Signature Confirmation dialog box, the signature is filled out, either with the printed name or the image, along with a date of signature. A Signatures pane appears, as shown in Figure 13.15, which allows you to review and manage signatures.

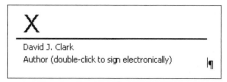

**Figure 13.13.** Adding a signature line

**Figure 13.14.** Signing a Word document electronically

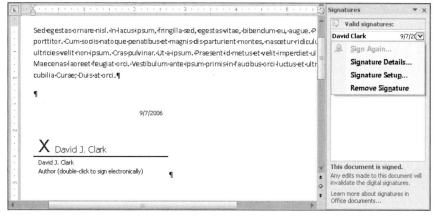

**Figure 13.15.** The Signatures pane allows you to review and manage signatures.

**Hack**

Word 2007 has no new check box control. Add a check box by clicking Check Box Form Field from Legacy Forms in the Controls group. When this form field is double-clicked, the user clicks the Default value radio button Not checked or Checked and clicks OK.

# Creating a printed form

If you want to create your own custom-printed form, it's a good idea to have a look at the various form templates offered through Microsoft Office Online to give you an idea of how to construct a form. I show you how to use individual Word 2007 features that are useful in creating forms, but I won't create a single example.

## Adding blank lines with instructions within a paragraph

If you want to print a form where the recipient fills out a form with text, typing information in the blank lines between other words, you can activate underlining and press Tab several times to create a blank within the body of a paragraph. It is impractical and awkward looking to add instructions immediately below the line within a paragraph in Word. However, adding fill-in instructions in a very light shade of gray right where the text is to be typed works well. To try this technique, follow these steps:

1. Create a blank space using the Tab key, and underline the entire section as just described.

2. Add the descriptive text in the middle of the underlined tabs. It's a good idea to render the descriptive text in boldface and/or all caps to guarantee readability.

3. Select the descriptive text, and change its font color to the lightest gray that will still be legible when printed. (This may take a few trial printings.) When you do this, the underlining also changes to gray, but don't worry, you can change that.

4. With the descriptive text still selected, click the arrow next to the Underline button and click Underline Color.

5. Select Black (not Automatic). Your blank should now look like Figure 13.16.

**Bright Idea**

For additional clarity you can raise the descriptive text a bit above the line by selecting the text and clicking the Font dialog box launcher on the Home tab. Click the Character Spacing tab, click Raised in the Position list (the default 3 points is usually sufficient), and click OK. The descriptive text appears raised slightly above the line.

**Figure 13.16.** Instructions appear in gray above the blank line.

## Adding boxes to be filled in

There are several ways to add boxes to be filled in with information. You can always use a table as the basis for your printed form as you did with the electronic form. You can select the format of the border of each side of each cell in a table (described in more detail in Chapter 15), or elect to have no visible borders. Another way to add a box is to select a set of tabs or hard spaces (spaces you enter with the Spacebar) and then choose Home ⇨ Outside Borders. This is most useful when you need to add a box within a paragraph of text.

The most flexible way to create boxes for text is to use the Text Box feature. Choose Insert ⇨ Text Box ⇨ Draw Text Box, and then click and drag down and to the right to create a box. When you are satisfied with the size of the box, release the mouse button. You can resize and make any number of changes to text boxes. To learn more about this feature, see Chapter 20.

## Adding check boxes

To add a box to check on a printed form, the easiest way is to insert the symbol for a blank check box. To do so, choose Insert ⇨ Symbol ⇨ Symbols and select a square such as the one shown in Figure 13.17. Click Insert to insert the symbol into your form. There are equivalent symbols showing a check mark or X.

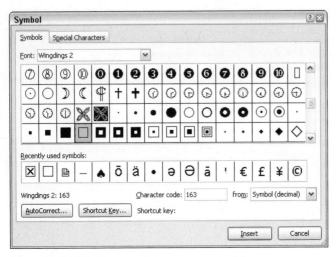

**Figure 13.17.** Selecting a symbol to use as a check box

## Creating a printed checklist

If you are creating a checklist, you may want to use an easier method than the one just described for creating boxes next to each item. Format your checklist as a bulleted list with each item on the list separated by a paragraph mark (press Enter after each item). Select the list, and then click the arrow next to Bullets in the Paragraph group of the Home tab. Choose Define New Bullet ⇨ Symbol to select the appropriate check box symbol, much as you would for inserting a symbol into a document. Click OK when you decide on the appropriate check box design for your bullet, and you have a checklist.

## Adding signature lines

You can use the ready-made signature lines described in the earlier section on electronic forms to add a signature line. Simply ignore the electronic signature details. If you want more control over the format, the easiest way to compose a signature line is to use the method described earlier with the Tab key and underlining for adding blank lines. You can add an X in the line to indicate that it is a signature line or add some other instructions. (Many people type a row of underscore characters, but this method can cause problems and is cumbersome when you are trying to align things vertically.) Several examples of signature lines appear in Figure 13.18. Example a shows what was just described above. Example b shows a simple line constructed with underlined tabs. In order for the instruction line below the signature line to appear sufficiently close, I chose Home ⇨ Line spacing ⇨ Remove Space After Paragraph. In Example c, underlined tabs are used, as in Example a, but an instruction line is added and I chose Insert ⇨ Shapes to add a

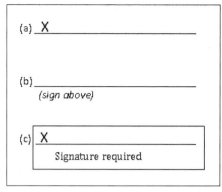

**Figure 13.18.** Some ways to display a signature line

rectangle to surround the signature line. I chose Drawing Tools ⇨ Format ⇨ Arrange ⇨ Text Wrapping ⇨ Behind Text to position the rectangle behind the signature text. (For more on adding Shapes to your document, see Chapter 17.)

## Using footers to add version details

If you need to track the revision cycle for your forms, you can use the footer (or header) feature in combination with existing document properties to print an unobtrusive message at the bottom that indicates information about the form. To do so, follow these steps:

1. Choose Insert ⇨ Footer ⇨ Edit Footer.

2. Type **Author:**, and then choose Header & Footer Tools ⇨ Design ⇨ Quick Parts ⇨ Properties ⇨ Author. Your footer should look something like Figure 13.19. You can also use the Title field in the document property for the form number.

**Figure 13.19.** Adding document properties to the form's footer

3. Click Save to save the file, naming it however you choose.

4. Press Tab to move to the center of the footer, and type **Last Saved:**.

5. Choose Header & Footer Tools ⇨ Design ⇨ Quick Parts ⇨ Field ⇨ Info.

**6.** In the Info categories list, click SaveDate. The date and time of the last Save operation appears, as shown in Figure 13.20. (If you subsequently save during the same session, press F9 to update the field.)

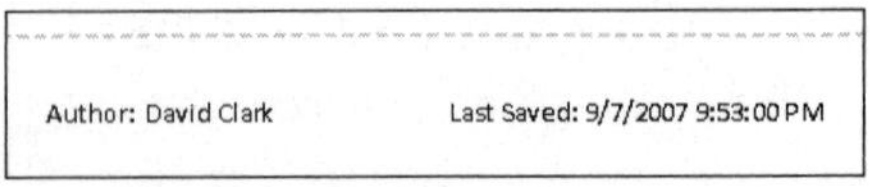

Author: David Clark　　　　　　　　Last Saved: 9/7/2007 9:53:00 PM

**Figure 13.20.** Adding the last-saved date and time to the form

## Just the facts

- Many ready-made forms are already available as templates through Microsoft Office Online.

- Establish whether the form will be filled out electronically or printed or a combination of the two before you design your form.

- Content controls available in Word 2007 make data entry in electronic forms a snap.

- You can add digital signature capabilities to your forms in Word 2007.

- Customize a bulleted list to create a checklist in seconds.

How a mail merge works ▪ Using the Mail Merge Wizard ▪
Printing form letters ▪ Sending an e-mail blast ▪ Printing
envelopes and labels ▪ Working with rules ▪ Creating a
directory with merge printing

# Create E-Mail Blasts, Mass Mailings, and Directories

O ne of the most frequent reasons users go to the Help screen or to a book is to help them out with merge printing of mass mailings, commonly referred to as a mail merge. However, creating mass mailings, e-mail blasts, and directories are simply operations that require several steps to complete. Once you understand the basic principles of a mail merge operation, you can apply what you learn to the various related activities covered in this chapter. There have not been significant changes in mail merges from earlier versions of Word, apart from the location of the related commands in the user interface. The Mail Merge toolbar has been removed, but all the commands related to mail merges have been collected on the Mailings tab of the Ribbon shown in Figure 14.1.

I start by describing the process of a mail merge in general terms to give you a context, and then use the creation of a form letter to walk through the process. Later, I follow with how to create form e-mails and send them, how to print envelopes and labels, how to create directories, and how to work with merge rules for more sophisticated use of mail merges.

*Chapter 14*

**Figure 14.1.** The Mailings tab brings together all merge-related commands.

# How a mail merge works

A mail merge takes data from fields in one source, such as an Access data-base file, Excel spreadsheet, or Outlook Contacts list, and adds the data into corresponding fields in a Word document so that multiple versions of the document can be created automatically. This is called *merging data*; merging data at print time is called *merge printing*. Each instance of the set of data fields that corresponds to the recipient in the list is referred to as a *record*. A record corresponds to each row in a spreadsheet or to a record in a database. Once you create or choose an existing recipient list, you can manipulate it to select or ignore individual records that you want to merge.

Because data from two different sources is being combined on the fly, some types of errors won't appear until you perform the merge. Fortunately, Word allows you to preview the merge and check to make sure that everything is running as expected, and it also performs an auto-matic check for errors. You can make changes to individual records as necessary in the recipient list.

Finally, you complete the merge. You can edit individual letters at this point or go directly to printing them. Merge operations that are not for printed form letters have some differences to the process that I summa-rize here and cover in more detail in the pertinent sections. With merges that are intended to go out as e-mails instead of as printed letters, you need to have an e-mail address for each recipient, of course, so that you can send the e-mail message, and some additional information is required at the end of the merge process. Also, you do not have the opportunity to edit individual e-mails. You can merge print labels and envelopes in much the same way you print form letters, although there are a few differences that I describe later. You can also print individual labels and envelopes easily with the corresponding commands.

Merge rules are conditional commands that you can insert into a form letter or other merge document to cause a specific action to occur when a certain condition is met. This allows you to send one type of letter to one recipient and a different type of letter to another, depending on information specific to that recipient, among other things.

One last item that you can create using the merge feature in Word is a directory. You can take advantage of the mass mailing tools to generate a directory of names and addresses listed in a single document. I include this item after merge rules because it is useful to have an understanding of merge rules before creating a directory.

## Using the Mail Merge Wizard

The Mail Merge Wizard is essentially the same as in the last few versions of Word, and is invoked by choosing Mailings ⇨ Start Mail Merge ⇨ Step by Step Mail Merge Wizard. This displays the Mail Merge pane shown in Figure 14.2. A *wizard*, in Microsoft parlance, is a set of instructions integrated with commands that walk you through some multistep procedure in the application. The Mail Merge Wizard divides the mail merge process into six steps:

1. Select document type.

2. Select starting document.

3. Select recipients.

4. Write your letter or e-mail message, or arrange your envelope, label, or directory.

5. Preview your letters, e-mail messages, envelopes, labels, or directory.

6. Complete the merge.

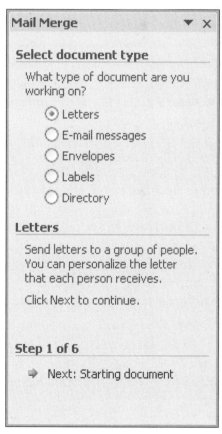

**Figure 14.2.** The Mail Merge Wizard opens the Mail Merge pane.

Each step gives you a set of options, explaining each one. The navigation arrows at the bottom allow you to move to the previous step if necessary or move on to the next step when ready. You can close the Mail Merge pane at any time by clicking its Close button.

# Creating a form letter

You can create a form letter by invoking individual commands or by using the Mail Merge Wizard. I walk you through the process with the wizard, indicating the alternative commands as we go along.

## Starting a mail merge

To start a mail merge, choose Mailings ⇨ Start Mail Merge ⇨ Step by Step Mail Merge Wizard to use the wizard, which brings you to the first step in the process: selecting the type of document you want to create with the mail merge. Alternatively, you can select the type of document directly from the menu by choosing Mailing ⇨ Start Mail Merge and then clicking one of the following options:

- Letters
- E-mail messages
- Envelopes
- Labels
- Directory
- Normal Word Document

To create a form letter for a mass mailing, select the Letters radio button in the Mail Merge Wizard, and then click the Next: Starting document link (or choose Start Mail Merge ⇨ Letters). A screen like that shown in Figure 14.3 appears. Notice that most of the commands in the Mailings tab are disabled at this point. Don't worry; this is just because you haven't selected any recipients yet.

At this point, you can elect to use the current document, open an existing document, or use a template. We'll use the current document in this example.

**Inside Scoop**

Don't bother with the Previous and Next navigation arrows in the wizard if you need to go back a few steps, such as the case where you need to change a letter mailing to an e-mail mailing after you are nearly done. Just select the appropriate command in the Start Mail Merge group of commands.

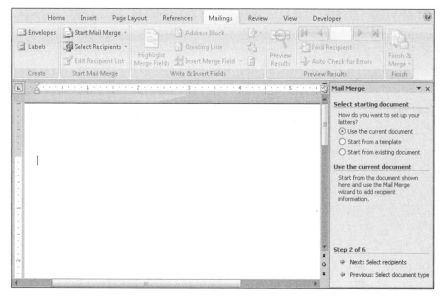

**Figure 14.3.** Selecting a starting document

## Adding a recipient list

In the Mail Merge pane, click Next: Select recipients. You have three choices: You can open an existing list (such as a list generated previously in Word, an Access database file, or an Excel spreadsheet); select from an Outlook contacts list; or you can type a new list in Word. You can accomplish the same task by choosing Mailings ⇨ Select Recipients and choosing Type New List, Use Existing List, or Select from Outlook Contacts on the menu.

### Creating a recipient list

You can create a recipient list in Word, which is saved in Microsoft Office Address List format (*.mdb). This is best if the information you want to type is typical of a mailing (with name, address, and other standard contact information), and if you intend to perform minimal database maintenance (although you can certainly open the file and manipulate it in Access if need be, because it is in fact in a standard Microsoft database file format). If you work with a very large list (in terms of the number of data fields, the number of records, or both), it is better to work with

Access or a server database management system such as SQL Server. Although creating a list in Word provides you with a ready-made list of common data fields, you can add or remove individual data fields to customize your list. If you create a long list, you can use the Find command if necessary to find specific data in the list. To create a list in Word, follow these steps:

1. Select the Type a new list radio button in the Mail Merge pane and then click Create (or choose Mailings ⇨ Select Recipients ⇨ Type New List on the Ribbon). The New Address List dialog box appears, as shown in Figure 14.4. Each row represents a record (a recipient), and each column represents a data field.

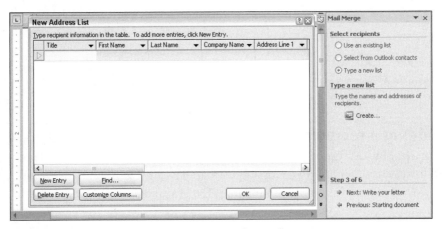

**Figure 14.4.** Typing a new address list of recipients for a mail merge

2. Click Customize Columns. The Customize Address List dialog box appears, as shown in Figure 14.5.

3. Delete columns you don't need by selecting the field name and clicking Delete. For this example, delete Company Name, Address Line 2, Country or Region, Home Phone, and Work Phone. Click Yes to confirm each deletion.

**Figure 14.5.** Customizing the address list

**Watch Out!**

If you delete a column in your address list that already contains data, any data in that column will also be deleted.

**4.** To add your own custom field (column), click Add and type the name of the field — in this case, type **Customer Type** and click OK.

**5.** Move this new field to the beginning of the list. Click Move Up eight times (until Customer Type is the first field name in the list). Your list of field names should now look like the one in Figure 14.6.

**6.** To add the data to the list, click in the first field (the first row of the first column of the list) and type the appropriate information. In this example, type **Repeat** in the Customer Type field.

**7.** Press Tab to move to the next field. (Press Shift+Tab to move to the previous field if you need to go back.) Type

**Figure 14.6.** The customized address lists with fields removed and added

the appropriate information and press Tab again to move until you get to the end. If you want to use the sample data found in this chapter, fill in the data as shown in Table 14.1, clicking New Entry when you finish a row to proceed to the next recipient on the list.

**8.** When you finish with the address list, click OK.

**9.** Assign the list a name (by default the file is stored in My Data Sources, although you can specify a different folder). For this example, type **Customer** and click Save, which displays the Mail Merge Recipients dialog box shown in Figure 14.7.

**10.** Because you are going to use everyone on your sample list, you can just click OK for now. You return to managing the recipient list later in this chapter.

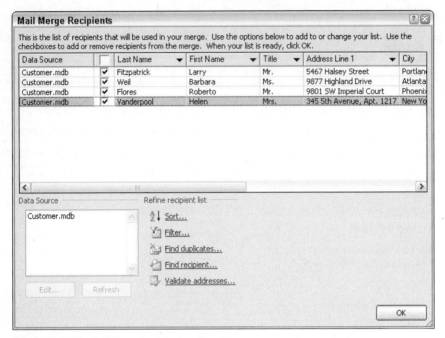

**Figure 14.7.** The Mail Merge Recipients dialog box

## Table 14.1. Sample data for the recipient list

| Customer Type | Sample Customer Data |
|---|---|
| Repeat | Mr. Larry Fitzpatrick<br>5467 Halsey Street<br>Portland, OR 97222<br>lfitzpatrick@example.com |
| New | Ms. Barbara Weil<br>9877 Highland Drive<br>Atlanta, GA 30308<br>weilfamily@example.com |
| New | Mr. Roberto Flores<br>9801 SW Imperial Court<br>Phoenix, AZ 85021<br>rlflores@example.com |
| Repeat | Mrs. Helen Vanderpool<br>345 5th Avenue, Apt. 1217<br>New York, NY 10016<br>helen_vanderpool@example.com |

Note that most of the commands on the Mailings tab of the Ribbon are now enabled. Before moving on to the next step, I describe how you can extract your recipient list from other data sources.

## Using an existing list

You can pull your data from any number of types of data sources, from e-mail contact lists to server database systems. In this section, I describe how to pull data from your Outlook Contacts list, an Excel spreadsheet, an Access database, and a server database (in general terms).

### Selecting from Outlook Contacts

You can take advantage of your existing Contacts list in Microsoft Outlook to create a recipient list for a mass mailing. To select recipients from an Outlook Contacts list, follow these steps:

1. Click Select from Outlook contacts in the Mail Merge pane (Step 3 of the Mail Merge Wizard) and click Choose Contacts Folder. Alternatively, you can choose Mailings ⇨ Select Recipients ⇨ Select from Outlook Contacts from the Ribbon.

2. You are asked to choose a Profile name. The default name is Outlook. If this is the only profile in your list, go ahead and click OK. Otherwise, choose the profile that contains the Contact list you need.

3. From the list of Contact folders in the Select Contacts dialog box, select the desired list and click OK (most people will only have one list to choose from). This brings you to the Mail Merge Recipients dialog box.

4. At this point, you can decide who from your Contact list should receive your mass mailing. You can just click OK for now. You return to managing the recipient list later in this chapter.

### Using an Excel spreadsheet

You can use data from a spreadsheet in a Microsoft Excel Workbook to create a recipient list for a mass mailing. The spreadsheet can be from an Excel 2007 Workbook or from Excel 97-2003 (*.xls). To select recipients from an Excel spreadsheet, follow these steps:

1. Select the Use an existing list radio button in the Mail Merge pane (Step 3 of the Mail Merge Wizard) and click Browse. Alternatively, you can choose Mailings ⇨ Select Recipients ⇨ Use Existing List from the Ribbon.

2. In the Select Data Source browser window, find the Excel Workbook file that contains the spreadsheet data you need and click Open. The Select Table dialog box shown in Figure 14.8 appears.

3. If you have named the range that contains your recipient list data, select the named range from the list. If your spreadsheet data just begins at the top of the first sheet with no named range, select Sheet1$, as shown in Figure 14.8. (If the first row contains the names for the columns of data, select the First row of data contains column headers option.) Click OK.

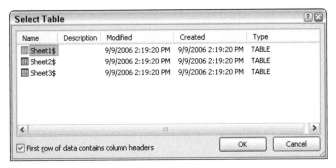

**Figure 14.8.** Selecting data from an Excel Workbook

### Using an Access database file

You can use data from a Microsoft Access database file to create a recipient list for a mass mailing. The database file can be from an Access 2007 file or from Access 97-2003 (*.mdb). To select recipients from an Access database file, follow these steps:

1. Select the Use an existing list radio button in the Mail Merge pane (Step 3 of the Mail Merge Wizard) and click Browse. Alternatively, you can choose Mailings ⇨ Select Recipients ⇨ Use Existing List from the Ribbon.

2. In the Select Data Source browser window, find the Access database file that contains the data you need and click Open. This displays the Mail Merge Recipients dialog box.

3. At this point, you can decide who from your Contact list should receive your mass mailing. You can just click OK for now. You return to managing the recipient list later in this chapter.

### Using a server database such as SQL Server

You can use a server database as a data source for your recipient list. If you already have established a connection, simply choose the data source from the My Data Sources list. If you need to establish a new connection, click New Source in the Select Data Source dialog box to launch the Data Connection Wizard shown in Figure 14.9. Follow the steps in this wizard to establish a connection to the appropriate database. Note that you need appropriate user access rights and server path information from your IT administrator to complete this wizard and establish the connection to the data source.

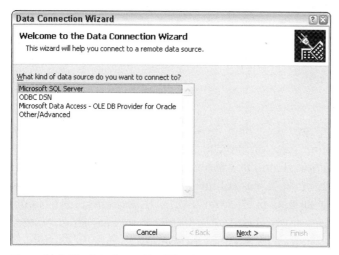

**Figure 14.9.** The Data Connection Wizard

## Managing the recipient list

Once you have a data source selected for your recipient list, you can sort it, filter it, find duplicate recipients, and, if you have an address validation service, you can ensure that addresses are valid. Unless you type a short list for a mail merge, you are often faced with the task of picking a subset of recipients from a larger list. The list of recipients that appears in the mail merge recipients list should be the list of people you actually want to receive your mailing. The tools in the Mail Merge Recipients dialog box allow you to make the choices necessary to narrow down the list. You can take advantage of filtering and sorting features to use rules to narrow down your selection of recipients or you can click the check box

**Inside Scoop**

Because the Mail Merge Recipients dialog box shows you a static view of the data source, it is always a good idea to click the Refresh button to guarantee that you are working with the most recent data in the data source before you perform a sort, filter, or merge operation.

next to any individual recipients to add them or clear the check box to remove them from the list. Finally, if you see something that needs to be changed in the data source itself, such as a typo or other error, you can select the data source and click Edit to edit the data source file (assuming you have appropriate permission).

To manage the recipient list, click Edit recipient list in the Mail Merge pane (Step 3 of the Mail Merge Wizard) or choose Mailings ⇨ Edit Recipient List. The Mail Merge Recipients dialog box shown earlier in Figure 14.7 appears.

## Sorting

You have two ways to sort your data for the mail merge. You can either sort by clicking a column, or you can click Sort to access the Sort Records tab of the Filter and Sort dialog box for multilevel sorts.

If you click on the Last Name column, for example, the records are sorted in ascending alphabetical order (A-Z). If you click Last Name again, the records are re-sorted in descending alphabetical order (Z-A).

For a more complex sort, such as by Last Name and then by Customer Type, click Sort, choose Last Name from the field name list for Sort by, and then choose Customer Type from the field name next to Then by, as shown in Figure 14.10. Note that you can select Ascending or Descending for each level of a multilevel sort.

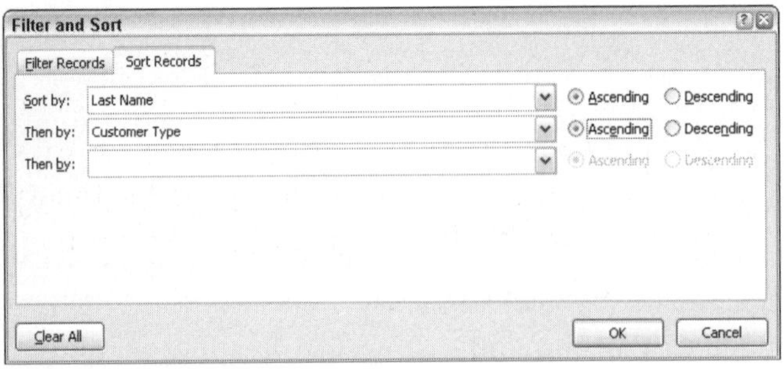

**Figure 14.10.** Sorting records for the mail merge list

**Inside Scoop**

To clear a sort and go back to the original sort order, click Sort ⇨ Clear All in the Sort Records tab of the Filter and Sort dialog box.

## Filtering

As with sorting, you have two ways to filter your data for the mail merge. You can either click the arrow on a specific column to show a list of non-repeating values to filter by, or you can click Filter to access the Filter Records tab of the Filter and Sort dialog box for more complex filtering operations.

If you click the arrow on the Last Name column, for example, a pull-down menu like the one shown in Figure 14.11 appears. Along with the sort options, every unique string in that data field category is displayed, as well as four additional options:

- All: Shows all records
- Blanks: Shows only blank records
- Nonblanks: Shows only records that are not blank
- Advanced: Allows you to specify a matching value for each field

If you have a field that tends to have a few values that repeat, such as New and Repeat in your Customer Type example, it is a simple matter to click the field's arrow and select one of these values to filter your list to show only all new or all repeat customers. For a more complex filtering operation, such

**Figure 14.11.**
Selecting a filtering option for mail merge recipients

as all new customers residing in the state of Georgia (GA), click Filter from the Mail Merge Recipients dialog box or click Advanced from the pull-down menu of one of the columns. Next, choose the columns you want to filter and select a string to match or compare with the value for each record, as shown in Figure 14.12. You can choose from among the following ways to compare the filter string with the data in individual records:

- Equal to
- Not equal to
- Greater than or equal
- Is blank

- ▪ Less than
- ▪ Greater than
- ▪ Less than or equal

- ▪ Is not blank
- ▪ Contains
- ▪ Does not contain

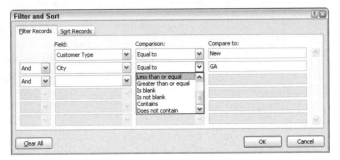

**Figure 14.12.** Selecting more advanced mail recipient filter criteria

Click OK to perform the filter operation. The goal of all this filtering is to come up with a list of only those who you intend should receive your mass mailing. As you step through the mail merge process, you have additional chances to remove individual recipients from the list if need be. You can remove blank or incomplete records from the list with filtering, or you can use filtering to select the specific subset of a larger list to whom you want to send your mailing.

### Finding duplicate recipients

Although it is possible to find duplicate records using the sorting and filtering abilities, Word provides a duplicate finding command already built in. This command is particularly useful and much more efficient if you have a database of any length or if you are working from a data source that has combined information from several sources. To find duplicates, click Find duplicates in the Mail Merge Recipients dialog box. If there are any duplicates, they appear in a window of the Find Duplicates dialog box, as shown in Figure 14.13. Choose the record you want to keep and delete the others.

**Inside Scoop**

As with sorting, to clear filtering and go back to displaying all records, choose Filter ⇨ Clear All in the Filter Records tab of the Filter and Sort dialog box.

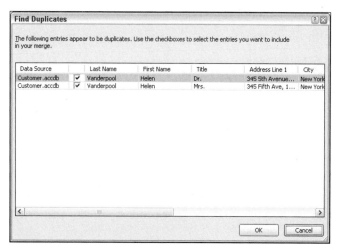

**Figure 14.13.** Finding duplicate recipients

### Finding recipients

To find a recipient or other piece of data quickly in your recipient list, click Find recipient in the Mail Merge Recipients dialog box. You can type a text string in the Find field such as a name or customer number. By default, Word searches all fields, but you can narrow the search to a specific field (which you should do if it is a large list and you know the field that contains the string). Click Find Next to start the search. Word moves to the first record containing the search string. Clicking Find Next again takes you to the next instance of the search string (if the search string occurs twice in the same record, you will still find yourself in the same record). When you are through searching, click Cancel or the Close button.

### Validating recipient addresses

If you have address validation software, you can validate addresses at this point. If you do not, Microsoft asks if you want to be directed to address validation software vendors via the Microsoft Office Web site.

## Adding merge fields and rules

When you are satisfied with your recipients list, you can move on to writing your form letter (Step 4 of the Mail Merge Wizard). A form letter is composed of blocks of unchanging text and fields that correspond to data fields in your data source, called merge fields. Word saves you some time by making some assumptions about data and creating two special types of merge fields: the address block and the greeting line. In the course of creating a form letter, I show you how to use both as well as how to add other merge fields. To write a form letter with merge fields, follow these steps:

1. If paragraph marks are not showing, press Ctrl+* so that they are displayed. Press Ctrl+R or click Align Right.

2. Choose Insert ⇨ Insert Date and Time, select a format and click OK to insert the current date into the letter.

3. Press Enter three times to move down the page, and press Ctrl+L or click Align Left to change the alignment in preparation for the address and letter content.

At this point you can add your return address or a header that serves as your stationery letterhead, if necessary.

### Adding an address block

Proceeding from the previous section, follow these steps to add and format an address block:

1. Click Address block in the Mail Merge pane (if still visible) or choose Mailings ⇨ Address Block. The Insert Address Block dialog box shown in Figure 14.14 appears. On the left side of the dialog box are settings pertinent to how you want to have the address presented. If you have data fields for nickname, spouse's name, company name, and so on, you have a great degree of flexibility in how you want to address the recipient, from the very casual to the very formal. If you are performing an international mass mailing, you may want to change some of the default settings by deselecting the Insert postal address check box and selecting the appropriate radio button option below it.

2. On the right side of the dialog box shown in Figure 14.14 you can preview how the address will appear for each of your recipients. Use the arrow keys to preview each address and make sure that each address and recipient's name appears as it should. (The Match Fields command is covered later in this section.)

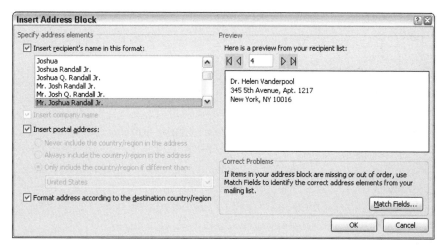

**Figure 14.14.** The Insert Address Block dialog box allows you to make decisions about how the recipient's address appears.

3. When you are satisfied with the address block format, click OK to insert it into your form letter. AddressBlock appears between double angle brackets to indicate that it is a merge field, as shown in Figure 14.15. You can format the merge field just as you can with any text.

«AddressBlock»¶

4. Press Enter three times to move to the greeting line.

**Figure 14.15.** The AddressBlock merge field inserted into the form letter

### Adding a greeting line

As with the address block, the greeting line is a ready-made merge field that saves some steps in a common task in writing form letters. To add a greeting line, follow these steps:

1. Click Greeting line in the Mail Merge pane (if still visible) or choose Mailings ➪ Greeting Line. The Insert Greeting Line dialog box shown in Figure 14.16 appears.

2. You can start with Dear, To, or type your own greeting (such as Hi for an informal e-mail message to a friend).

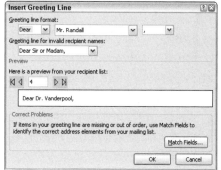

**Figure 14.16.** The Insert Greeting Line dialog box allows you to format the greeting for your form letter.

**Inside Scoop**

Choose Mailings ⇨ Highlight Merge Fields to have Word show a gray background behind merge fields so that you can more readily locate text that will be inserted from the recipient list upon performing the merge. This command is a toggle; click it again to turn it off.

You can select a name format (much like the address block) or choose punctuation. Use a comma for personal or casual business communication. A colon is for formal correspondence. Accept the defaults for this example, but type an alternate greeting line for invalid recipient names: Instead of the default Dear Sir or Madam, type **Dear Valued Customer,** in the corresponding field.

3. In the Preview area, use the arrow keys to preview each recipient and make sure that each recipient's name appears as it should. When you are satisfied, click OK. The GreetingLine merge field is now inserted into your form letter.

4. Press Enter twice to add space before typing more text.

5. At this point, it is a good idea to save your form letter. Press Ctrl+S or click Save, and name the document **FormLetter.docx**.

### Adding other merge fields

Now that you have added an address and a greeting, you can begin typing a letter. You can add any field in the data source as a merge field or choose from the standard set of merge fields. To insert a merge field in the body of the letter, follow these steps:

1. Type the body of your letter up to the point at which you want to customize it with data for the recipient. For our example, type **We value you as a customer. That's why we are offering you a 20 percent discount on all merchandise at our**.

2. Click More items in the Mail Merge pane (if still visible) or choose Mailings ⇨ Insert Merge Field. The Insert Merge Field dialog box shown in Figure 14.17 appears.

3. Click City to select the City merge field.

4. Click Insert to insert the City merge field into the form letter, and click Close.

5. Type the remainder of the sentence: **store only.**

6. Add one more merge field and finish the letter. Press Enter and type **Present this letter at our**, and then click the arrow next to Insert Merge Field on the Mailings tab. Click City to add the merge field again.

7. Finish the sentence and remainder of the letter by typing **store to receive your discount. This offer is good through December 2007.**

8. Press Enter several times and close with typing **Thank you,** and press Enter again. Type **The Management**.

9. Press Ctrl+S or click Save to save your document.

**Figure 14.17.** The Insert Merge Field dialog box

## *Matching fields*

Word provides you with a way to match fields in a data source with standard merge fields to make your work easier. You can click Match Fields to link a field in your recipient list with the appropriate built-in address field so that address blocks and greeting lines work correctly. Word does a good job of guessing at such things, but if your address fields have nonstandard names you can use the Match Fields feature to link fields correctly. To do so, choose Mailings ⇨ Match Fields (or click Match Fields in the dialog box for inserting an address block, greeting line, or merge field). The dialog box shown in Figure 14.18 appears. For each field that you want to match, click the drop-down list for the built-in address field name that best fits that of your data source field and then select the

**Bright Idea**

If you want to use your form letter more than once and you suspect you will be pulling data from more than one source, consider using the Address fields for your merge fields if possible, as opposed to the database fields.

**Hack**

Match Unique Identifier to unique customer ID numbers and Department to customer categories to guarantee maximum flexibility when working with data sources.

corresponding field in your data source from the list. You can select the check box at the bottom of the dialog box to remember this matching set for all data sources on your computer.

### Adding electronic postage

If you have an electronic postage service, you can add the postage at this time in the merge by clicking Electronic postage in the Mail Merge pane (Step 4 of the Mail Merge Wizard). If you do not have an electronic postage service, clicking this link takes you to a dialog box that asks if you want to be directed to electronic postage software vendors via the Microsoft Office Web site.

**Figure 14.18.** Matching fields from your data source to the standard merge field names

## Previewing the merge operation

Once you open or start a new document, add a recipient list, and insert merge fields into your form letter, you can preview the merge. This is useful to verify that everything looks as it should before printing. To preview the merge, click Next: Preview your letters in the Mail Merge pane if the Mail Merge Wizard is still open or choose Mailings ➪ Preview Results (this is a toggle command; you can click it again to turn off the Preview Results view and return to the form letter with field names).

At this point you can view each letter as it will appear. Use the arrow keys in the Preview Results group of the Mailings tab on the Ribbon or in the Mail Merge pane to navigate between individual records, or click

Find Recipient (or Find a recipient on the Mail Merge pane) to locate a specific recipient record. At this point, it is not too late to edit the recipient list. If you are using the Mail Merge Wizard and the Mail Merge pane is open, you can click Exclude this recipient to exclude the recipient currently displayed from the merge operation (this is equivalent to deselecting the check box in the Mail Merge Recipients dialog box).

Click Auto Check for Errors (or press Alt+Shift+K) to choose the way Word deals with errors during a merge operation. The errors referred to here are not bugs in the Word application software but errors generated by the person designing the form letter — if you are not using merge rules it is unlikely that you will encounter any errors. Nevertheless, you have three ways to deal with the errors. You can simulate the merge prior to the final merge and report any errors in a new document; complete the merge, pausing to report each error as it occurs; or complete the merge without pausing, generating an error report in a new document.

## Completing the merge operation

After you preview results, go ahead with the merge operation. You have two ways to do this: You can either merge directly to the printer, or you can merge the results into a single large file that allows you to edit individual letters, printing them all as one big document when finished with the editing. This second alternative is also useful if, before printing, you want to transport the merge results to another computer that doesn't have access to the data source you used to create the mail merge.

### Merging directly to the printer

To merge directly to the printer, click Print in the Mail Merge pane (Step 6 of 6 in the Mail Merge Wizard), choose Mailings ⇨ Finish & Merge ⇨ Print Documents, or just press Alt+Shift+M. The Merge to Printer dialog box appears, as shown in Figure 14.19. You can print all records, the current record, or a specified range of

**Figure 14.19.** Selecting the records to merge to the printer

records. Click OK to proceed to printing. Make any necessary settings in the Print dialog box and click OK.

### Merging to a new document

To merge your results to a single new document in which you can edit individual letters before printing the mail merge as a large single document, click Edit individual letters in the Mail Merge pane (Step 6 of 6 in the Mail Merge Wizard), choose Mailings ⇨ Finish & Merge ⇨ Edit Individual Documents, or just press Alt+Shift+N. This command performs the mail merge, inserting the results into a new document (Letters1 by default if you are creating a form letter) and opening the document. It is a good idea to use the Save As command to rename this file as something that is easier to remember. Note that in this example your first field, the current date, has an exclamation point, to draw your attention to it. If you mouse over the exclamation point it shows Update F9 to remind you that you can press F9 to update to the current date.

You can edit each letter as you go through the merged letters document, customizing or correcting as necessary. Be sure to save frequently as you go. When you are satisfied with the document, you can print it using the standard Print command. When you are done, you can close the document. The form letter document will remain open in a separate window until you close it separately.

## Creating an e-mail blast

To create a form e-mail to send as a mass electronic mailing, commonly referred to as an e-mail blast, select the E-mail messages radio button in the Mail Merge Wizard and then click the Next: Starting Document link (or choose Start Mail Merge ⇨ E-mail messages). As with letters and other types of merges, most of the commands in the Mailings tab are disabled at this point because recipients aren't selected yet.

Click Next: Starting document if you are using the Mail Merge Wizard. At this point, you can elect to use the current document, open an existing document, or use a template. (If you are using the Ribbon

---

**Watch Out!**

Electronic mass mailings don't have any further chances to correct mistakes before sending out e-mail messages. I recommend taking care in the Preview Results phase. Also, choose Mailings ⇨ Auto Check for Errors and select the simulation option to do a trial run before sending your e-mail, or put yourself in the recipient list and merge just your record to e-mail to do a trial run.

commands, presumably you've already made this decision.) Note also that the document view switches to Web Layout view.

Click Next: Select recipients (using the wizard) or choose Mailings ⇨ Select Recipients. You have the same options as with a form letter mail merge here. One critical distinction between e-mail merges and print merges is that you need to have a field that contains an e-mail address for an electronic mail merge. Each recipient must have an e-mail address for the electronic mail merge to function properly.

Once you select and edit your recipient list as needed, click Next: Write your e-mail message (using the wizard) or proceed directly to writing the e-mail if you are working with the Ribbon commands. You can use the same merge fields as with form letters. It is not essential to include the e-mail address field in the actual e-mail message itself.

After you create your e-mail message, click Next: Preview your e-mail message (using the wizard) or choose Mailings ⇨ Preview Results if you are working with the Ribbon commands.

When you are ready to send out your electronic mass mailing, click Next: Complete the merge (using the Wizard), and then click Electronic Mail. If you are using the Ribbon commands, choose Mailings ⇨ Finish & Merge ⇨ Send E-mail Messages. The final Merge to E-mail dialog box appears, as shown in Figure 14.20. In the To field, specify the field name that contains the recipient's e-mail address. In the Subject line, type the subject line that will appear in the message header. For mail format, accept the default of HTML if you want to retain any measure of character or paragraph formatting in your message. Choose plain text if formatting is

**Figure 14.20.** Add a subject line and mail format at merge time.

unimportant, and choose Attachment if you want the document to be sent as a Word document file attachment to the e-mail message. If you use this last option, consider saving the form e-mail message in Word 97 - 2003 (*.doc) format if you suspect some of the recipients won't have Word 2007.

**Hack**

Word doesn't support multiple Subject lines in a single merge to e-mail, but you can sort your recipient list and then merge ranges of record numbers separately with different Subject lines to get around this.

# Creating envelopes and labels

If you are doing a mass mailing, chances are you will be doing a mass printing of envelopes or labels with it. This section shows you how to use Word's Envelopes and Labels features to help print these special items. I start with how to print individual envelopes and labels, and then move on to using a mail merge to print them.

Unfortunately, Microsoft has removed the POSTNET bar code and FIM-A code from Word's Envelopes and Labels features that allow you to prepare for bulk mailing. (Although the bar code field code is still available, it cannot be pasted into an envelope or label, and the options have been removed from the dialog boxes.) The reason given is that the United States Postal Service may change the way it calculates bar codes, and "to avoid providing bar codes that may become obsolete, Microsoft has removed this feature from Word 2007."

The only current workaround is to purchase the services of address verification software, such as that provided by Stamps.com or other vendors. When you invoke address verification, you are provided with a bar code. For more information, go to http://office.microsoft.com/en-us/marketplace/default.aspx.

# Printing single labels and envelopes

You can take advantage of the label and envelope printing features to print individual labels or envelopes. If you are creating a custom letter (not a form letter) and you want to print the envelope when you're done, you can choose Mailings ⇨ Envelopes and Word pulls the name and address information from the top of your letter. If you have stored your return address, you can also add this to your envelope or label.

## Storing your return address

If you have not yet done so, you can store your return address in Word. Choose Microsoft Office ⇨ Word Options ⇨ Advanced. Under the General tab, type your address in the Mailing address box. Word does not pull your name from the user name field for this option, so if you want your name to appear at the top of the return address, include it as well.

### Envelopes

You can print an individual envelope in Word by choosing Mailings ⇨ Envelopes. This displays the Envelopes tab of the Envelopes and Labels dialog box. If you have already created a letter, Word pulls the recipient address from the letter and inserts it in the Delivery address field. If you have already saved a return address, it appears in the Return address field, as shown in Figure 14.21. Note that the delivery address retains the font and other formatting of the recipient address in the letter.

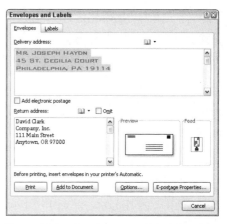

**Figure 14.21.** Creating an envelope using the recipient address from the current document

If you create an envelope that is not associated with an addressed letter in Word, you can either type a delivery address in the appropriate field or select the address from an Outlook Address Book or Contacts list. The same holds true for the return address. If you have not yet saved a return address in Word, you are asked whether Word should save the return address typed here as your default return address.

If you have installed electronic postage software, click Add electronic postage to add it to your printed letter. If you want to omit a return address (or if you have preprinted envelopes that already include it), select the Omit check box above the Return address field.

At the bottom of the dialog box are four buttons: Print, Add to Document, Options, and E-postage Properties. If you are ready to print and have already inserted a blank envelope in your printer's feeder tray, click Print. This Print button sends the envelope data directly to the printer — no Print dialog box appears beforehand, so make sure you are ready to print before clicking it. When you print an envelope this way, the envelope is not saved as a Word document. If you make a mistake or have a printer problem, you must re-create the envelope.

If you click the Add to Document button, Word adds the envelope as a new first page at the beginning of your document (with different page settings and so on). If you perform a Print Preview, your letter and envelope would look something like Figure 14.22. This way, you can save the envelope information, either to print the letter and envelope later or to avoid re-creating it if you have a printer problem.

**Figure 14.22.** Adding an envelope to a letter document

Clicking the Options button takes you to the Envelope Options dialog box, with Envelope and Printing Options tabs. (You can also get to the Envelope Options tab by clicking the picture of the envelope in the Preview window. Click the envelope feeding diagram to get to the Printing Options tab.) The Envelope Options tab is where you set the envelope size. The default is a standard U.S. business envelope: size 10 (4⅛ x 9½ inches). Select an envelope size from the drop-down list or select Custom size. This displays a dialog box where you can specify the width and height. As with other dimensions in Word, if you specify metric measurements, they are automatically converted. The minimum envelope dimensions are 6.4 x 2.13 inches. The maximum envelope dimensions are 22 x 22 inches, but it is best to switch to an adhesive label for larger format envelopes.

You can change the font attributes for the delivery or return address by clicking the corresponding Font button. (Avoid using ornate display fonts for addresses — using a simple standard font is the safest way to ensure that the postal service machines that read the delivery addresses on envelopes will do so correctly.)

You can also adjust the location of the return and delivery addresses. The Auto setting works well in most cases, but if you feel you need to

**Bright Idea**

If you add the envelope to the document and you need to print just the envelope, print page 1 of the document only.

> **Hack**
> You can also change the font attributes of the delivery or return address by selecting the address, right-clicking it, and clicking Font to display the standard Font dialog box.

change them, you can use the up or down arrows to adjust the settings or type a value to change the distance that each address appears from the left or top edge of the envelope. The Preview window shows you how the two addresses will appear.

Click the Printing Options tab to change the feeder tray or the direction of printing. In most cases, Word gets this correctly, but if for some reason things are backward or reversed, you can change the tray, whether you feed the envelope face up or down, or whether the envelope is rotated clockwise or counterclockwise in this dialog box.

Clicking the E-postage Properties button on the Envelopes tab of the Envelopes and Labels dialog box allows you to adjust your e-postage settings. If you click this button before setting up electronic postage, you will be asked whether you want to be directed to the Microsoft Office Web site to learn about electronic postage add-ins.

### Labels

The Labels command is actually used for any type of printed piece that fits more than one to a sheet. Thus, laser-cut business cards, tent cards, and name tags can also be printed using this command. You can print an individual label in Word by choosing Mailings ⇨ Labels. This displays the Labels tab of the Envelopes and Labels dialog box. If you have already created a letter, Word pulls the recipient address from the letter and inserts it in the Address field, as shown in Figure 14.23. Note that the address retains the font and other formatting of the recipient address in the letter. Select and

**Figure 14.23.** Creating a label using the recipient address from the current document

right-click the text in the Address field and click Font to change font attributes and Paragraph to change paragraph attributes. Unlike with envelopes, if you check the return address box, the Address field is filled in with just the return address (replacing the recipient address if there was one).

If you are creating an address label that is not associated with an addressed letter in Word, you can either type an address in the appropriate field or select the address from an Outlook Address Book or Contacts list. The same holds true for the return address. (As with envelopes, if you have not yet saved a return address in Word, you are asked whether Word should save the return address entered here as your default return address.) If you create a different type of label, such as a name tag, CD label, and so on, type the appropriate information in the Address field (even though it may not be an address, this is where you type the label text). If you create an address label and have installed electronic postage software, click Add electronic postage to add it to your printed letter.

When printing a single label, you can either elect to print a full page of them (as you might with a return address label, for example), or you can specify the row and column of the label to be printed. This is particularly useful when you use precut adhesive label sheets, because you can reuse a sheet this way one label at a time until they have all been printed.

If you are ready to print and already have labels in your printer's feeder tray, click Print at the bottom of the Envelopes and Labels dialog box. This Print button sends the label data directly to the printer — no Print dialog box appears beforehand, so make sure you are ready to print before clicking it. As with envelopes, when you print a label this way, it is not saved as a Word document. If you make a mistake or have a printer problem, you must re-create the label.

If you click New Document, Word creates a new document containing the label (or the sheet of duplicate labels if you choose that option). Using this feature, you can save the label information, either to modify or print later or to avoid re-creating it if you have a printer problem or want to reprint the label or set of labels.

Clicking the Options button takes you to the Label Options dialog box shown in Figure 14.24. (You can also get to the Label Options dialog box by clicking the picture of the label in the Label window.) Word provides two lists of label products, one for continuous-feed printers and one for page printers. Continuous-feed printers are older printers that use long rolls or perforated sheets of labels fed into the printer continuously. Page printers (most laser and inkjet printers) are selected by default. You can select the tray if more than one is available for your page printer.

**Figure 14.24.** You can change label settings in the Label Options dialog box.

Clicking the E-postage Properties button on the Labels tab of the Envelopes and Labels dialog box allows you to adjust your e-postage settings. If you click this button before setting up electronic postage, you will be asked whether you want to be directed to the Microsoft Office Web site to learn about electronic postage add-ins.

The label products are listed first by manufacturer and then by model number. If you need to see the detailed specifications, click Details to see a preview with all pertinent dimensions. If you want to create a custom label size (or if you have labels that are not in the list), click New Label to see the dialog box shown in Figure 14.25. Add the measure information in the various fields, type a name in the Label name field, and click OK to add your custom label to the list.

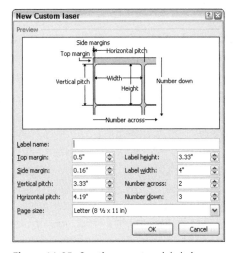

**Figure 14.25.** Creating a custom label size

## Merge printing envelopes

To print envelopes for a mass electronic mailing, click Envelopes in the Mail Merge Wizard and then click the Next: Starting document link (or choose Start Mail Merge ⇨ Envelopes). As with letters and other types of merges, most of the commands in the Mailings tab are disabled at this point because you haven't selected any recipients yet.

If you are using the wizard, click Next: Starting document. At this point, you can elect to change the document layout or start with an existing document. (If you are using the Ribbon commands, presumably you've already made this decision, and the Envelope Options dialog box appears.) Click Envelope options. Make any setting changes as described previously for printing individual envelopes. When you click OK, you are taken to the next phase if using the wizard: Select recipients. If you are using the Ribbon, choose Mailings ⇨ Select Recipients. You have the same options as with a form letter mail merge here.

Once you select and edit your recipient list as needed, click Next: Arrange your envelope (using the wizard) or proceed directly to adding recipient information if you are working with the Ribbon commands. You can use the same merge fields as with form letters. Unlike when you create an individual letter, you must insert the address block. To do so, click in the area of the delivery address and click Address block in the Mail Merge pane (using the wizard), or choose Mailings ⇨ Address Block. If you are using electronic postage, click Electronic postage in the wizard now.

After arranging the envelope, click Next: Preview your envelopes (using the wizard), or choose Mailings ⇨ Preview Results if you are working with the Ribbon commands.

After you preview results, go ahead with the merge operation. As with a form letter, you have two ways to do this: You can either merge directly to the printer, or you can merge the results into a single large file that allows you to edit individual envelopes, printing them all as one big document when finished with the editing. This second alternative is also useful if, before printing, you want to transport the merge results to another computer that doesn't have access to the data source you used to create the mail merge.

### *Merging directly to the printer*

To merge directly to the printer, click Print in the Mail Merge pane (Step 6 of 6 in the Mail Merge Wizard), choose Mailings ⇨ Finish & Merge ⇨ Print Documents, or just press Alt+Shift+M. You can print all records, the current record, or a specified range of records. Click OK to proceed to printing. Make any necessary settings in the Print dialog box and click OK.

### *Merging to a new document*

To merge your results to a single new document in which you can edit individual envelopes before printing the mail merge as a large single document, click Edit individual envelopes in the Mail Merge pane (Step 6 of 6 in the Mail Merge Wizard), choose Mailings ⇨ Finish & Merge ⇨ Edit Individual Documents, or just press Alt+Shift+N. This command performs the mail merge, inserting the results into a new document (Envelopes1 by default), and opening the document. It is a good idea to use the Save As command to rename this file to something that is easy to remember.

You can edit each envelope as you go through the merged envelopes document, customizing or correcting as necessary. Be sure to save frequently as you go. When you are satisfied with the document, you can print it using the standard Print command. When you are done, you can close the document.

## Merge printing labels

To print labels for a mass mailing, click Labels in the Mail Merge Wizard and then click the Next: Starting document link (or choose Start Mail Merge ⇨ Labels). As with letters and other types of merges, most of the commands in the Mailings tab are disabled at this point because you haven't selected any recipients yet.

If you are using the wizard, click Next: Starting document. At this point, you can elect to change the document layout or start with an existing document. (If you are using the Ribbon commands, presumably you've already made this decision, and the Label Options dialog box

**Inside Scoop**

Choose Mailings ⇨ Update Labels to make sure you are using the most current information from your data source.

appears.) Click Label options. Make any setting changes as described previously for printing individual labels. When you click OK, you are taken to the next phase if using the wizard: Select recipients. If you are using the Ribbon, choose Mailings ⇨ Select Recipients. You have the same options as with a form letter mail merge here.

Once you select and edit your recipient list as needed, click Next: Arrange your labels (using the wizard) or proceed directly to adding recipient information if you are working with the Ribbon commands. You can use the same merge fields as with form letters. Unlike when you create an individual letter, you must insert the address block. To do so, click Address block in the Mail Merge pane (using the wizard) or choose Mailings ⇨ Address Block. When you have the first label as you like it, click Update all labels to copy the information to the other labels. Note that if you are doing this manually (without the wizard), make sure that you insert the address block field code immediately after «Next Record» in the other labels on the sheet. This code is a merge rule that inserts the next record in the list and is essential to print your labels correctly. If you are using electronic postage, click Electronic postage in the wizard now.

After arranging the label, click Next: Preview your labels (using the wizard) or choose Mailings ⇨ Preview Results if you are working with the Ribbon commands.

After you preview results, go ahead with the merge operation. As with a form letter, you have two ways to do this: You can either merge directly to the printer, or you can merge the results into a single large file that allows you to edit individual labels, printing them all as one big document when finished with the editing. This second alternative is also useful if, before printing, you want to transport the merge results to another computer that doesn't have access to the data source you used to create the mail merge.

## Merging directly to the printer

To merge directly to the printer, click Print in the Mail Merge pane (Step 6 of 6 in the Mail Merge Wizard), choose Mailings ⇨ Finish & Merge ⇨ Print Documents, or just press Alt+Shift+M. You can print all records, the current record, or a specified range of records. Click OK to proceed to printing. Make any necessary settings in the Print dialog box and click OK.

### *Merging to a new document*

To merge your results to a single new document in which you can edit individual labels before printing the mail merge as a large single document, click Edit individual labels in the Mail Merge pane (Step 6 of 6 in the Mail Merge Wizard), choose Mailings ⇨ Finish & Merge ⇨ Edit Individual Documents, or just press Alt+Shift+N. This command performs the mail merge, inserting the results into a new document (Labels1 by default), and opening the document. It is a good idea to use the Save As command to rename this file to something that is easy to remember.

You can edit each label as you go through the merged labels document, customizing or correcting as necessary. Be sure to save frequently as you go. When you are satisfied with the document, you can print it using the standard Print command. When you are done, you can close the document.

# Working with rules

Word provides merge rules that allow you to set conditions under which a specific action should be performed during a merge. This allows you a great deal of control for your merge operation. For example, if you want to include different wording depending on the customer type in a marketing mailing, you can use merge rules to send one type of information to one type of customer and a different piece to another customer. Or, you can create a merge that asks you to type specific information as you go. Table 14.2 summarizes the merge rules available to you.

| Table 14.2. Word merge rules | |
| --- | --- |
| **Merge Rule** | **Description** |
| Ask | This rule prompts the user during merge to type text, which is stored in a bookmark. You must specify a bookmark name and a prompt. You may optionally supply default bookmark text. Click Ask once for the answer to the prompt to apply to all records, otherwise user is asked at each record. |
| Fill-in | This rule prompts the user during merge to type text, which is added to the document. You may optionally supply default fill-in text. Click Ask once for the answer to the prompt to apply to all records, otherwise user is asked at each record. |

*continued*

## Table 14.2. *continued*

| Merge Rule | Description |
| --- | --- |
| If...Then...Else... | If the content of a specified field meets a certain condition (for example, Customer Type is equal to Repeat), then a string of text is inserted. If the condition is not met, an alternate string of text is inserted. |
| Merge Record # | This rule inserts the merge record number (including those you exclude from the recipient list). |
| Merge Sequence # | This rule inserts the actual number of records merged (does not include those you exclude from the recipient list). |
| Next Record | This rule inserts the next record where you insert the Next Record rule. This is particularly useful for labels and directories where more than one record appears on a page. |
| Next Record If | This rule is a variant of the Next Record rule. It inserts the next record if a condition is met (for example, Next Record If Last Name is not blank). |
| Set Bookmark | This rule assigns information to an assigned variable name. Use this in conjunction with Ref field code to store and manipulate values during a merge. |
| Skip Record If | This rule allows you to skip a record if a condition is met (for example, Skip Record If Last Name is blank). |

## Creating a directory

To print a directory using Word's mail merge feature, click Directory in the Mail Merge Wizard and then click the Next: Starting document link (or choose Start Mail Merge ⇨ Directory). As with letters and other types of merges, most of the commands in the Mailings tab are disabled at this point because you haven't selected any recipients yet.

If you are using the wizard, click Next: Starting document. At this point, you can elect to change the document layout or start with an existing document. (If you are using the Ribbon commands, presumably you've already made this decision.) Click Next: Select recipients if you are using the wizard. If you are using the Ribbon, choose Mailings ⇨ Select Recipients. You have the same options as with a form letter mail merge here. Take care that you sort the recipients so that they appear in a logical sequence (such as ascending alphabetically by last name).

Once you select and edit your recipient list as needed, click Next: Arrange your directory (using the wizard) or proceed directly to adding recipient information if you are working with the Ribbon commands. You can use the same merge fields as with form letters. More manual work is required for creating a directory, though. First, insert the merge fields that you want to see for the first record. Next, add the Next Record merge rule. (You may also use Next Record If and Skip Record If merge rules here.) Add the same merge fields as you did for the first record and repeat until you have enough fields to print the directory, as shown in the example in Figure 14.26. I suggest using the table feature to simplify your work.

| «AddressBlock»¶ | «Next·Record»«AddressBlock»¶ |
|---|---|
| ¤ | ¤ |
| «Next·Record»«AddressBlock»¶ | «Next·Record»«AddressBlock»¶ |

**Figure 14.26.** Arranging a directory to be prepared using the Mail Merge feature

After arranging the directory, click Next: Preview your directory (using the wizard) or choose Mailings ➪ Preview Results if you are working with the Ribbon commands.

After you preview results, go ahead with the merge operation. This merges your results to a single new document in which you can edit any part of the directory before printing it. To do so, click To New Document in the Mail Merge pane (Step 6 of 6 in the Mail Merge Wizard), choose Mailings ➪ Finish & Merge ➪ Edit Individual Documents, or just press Alt+Shift+N. This command performs the mail merge, inserting the results into a new document (Directory1 by default), and opening the document. It is a good idea to use the Save As command to rename this file something that is easy to remember. You can edit each entry in the directory as you go through the merged version, customizing or correcting as necessary. Be sure to save frequently as you go. When you are satisfied with the directory, you can print it using the standard Print command. When you are done, you can close the document.

## Just the facts

- You can create mass printed or electronic mailings using Word's Mail Merge feature.
- The Mail Merge Wizard walks you through the six steps of completing a merge.
- All the mail merge commands are now located on the Mailings tab of the Ribbon.
- Merge fields allow you to add data from a list or database into a form letter, label, e-mail message, envelope, or directory.
- Merge rules allow you to control how a merge performs based on conditions that you set.

# Add Tables to the Mix

# PART IV

# Create and Manage Tables

Tables are an efficient and compact way to display information, and they make their way into almost any written report that needs to present a matrix of data. Creating tables with a word processor used to be a time-consuming and fussy exercise involving numerous tab settings and printing by trial and error. Things have improved greatly, and now it is relatively easy to create a table in Word. However, tables are by their nature somewhat complex, so the topic is divided into two chapters.

In this first chapter about tables, I show you several ways to go about creating a table, how to format a table, and how to work with cells, rows, and columns. Chapter 16 covers more advanced topics such as importing tables, splitting tables across several pages, and ways to make everything fit on the page.

## Creating a table

When you first examined the Ribbon tabs in Word 2007, you may have searched in vain for a Table tab. Word 2007 provides you with table commands grouped together on a command tab, but not until you insert a table into your document. There are numerous ways to add a table to your document. I show you how to do each one, because each method has its advantages and disadvantages.

343

# Creating a table from scratch

To create a new table, position your insertion point where you want the table to appear in your document and choose Insert ⇨ Table to see the menu shown in Figure 15.1. At this point, you have several ways to create a table, depending on your preferences. I describe the advantages of each one separately. In general, it's easiest to design a table when you know how many rows and columns you'll have. You can always add rows or columns later, however. Also consider the nature of the data you are presenting and things like the orientation of your paper.

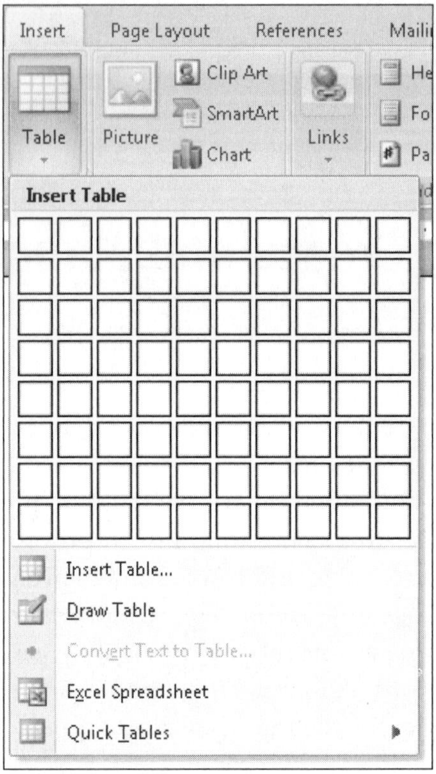

**Figure 15.1.** Inserting a table into a document

## *Inserting a table using the grid and mouse*

If you want an on-the-fly preview of how things will look, this is a good way to insert a table. This method was available in prior versions of Word, but in Word 2007 you can see the table as it will appear before you decide on the number of rows and columns. To use this method to insert a table, choose Insert ⇨ Table and then move your mouse over the grid until you have a table with the number of rows and columns you want. The menu grid changes color to indicate graphically how many rows and columns you have currently chosen, and text appears at the top to confirm, as shown in Figure 15.2. Underneath the menu, you see how the table will appear in your document (prior to making any adjustments). When you are satisfied with the dimensions of your table, click the mouse.

After you confirm the table's dimension, it is inserted into the document. Notice that the Table Tools' Design tab now appears on the Ribbon, as shown in Figure 15.3.

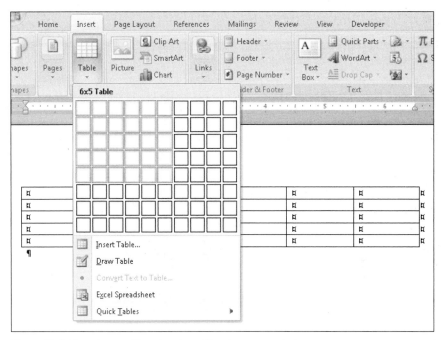

**Figure 15.2.** Inserting a table using the grid and mouse method

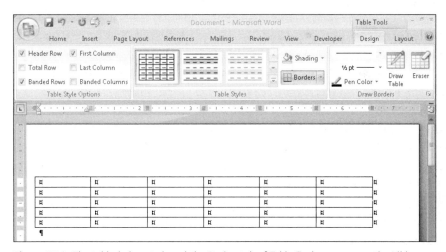

**Figure 15.3.** The table is inserted, and the Design tab of Table Tools appears on the Ribbon.

## Inserting a table using the dialog box

If you want to insert several tables with similar dimensions or AutoFit rules, this is a good way to insert a table. To use this method to insert a table, choose Insert ⇨ Table ⇨ Insert Table. The Insert Table dialog box, shown in Figure 15.4, appears. You can use the arrows keys or type a value for the number of rows and columns you want. The AutoFit behavior section allows you to control table cell dimensions. By default, the Fixed column width option is selected, with Auto as the width. This divides the text width of the page within the margins by the number of columns: Inserting a table with 4 columns onto a page with 6 inches between margins would yield a column width of 1.5 inches for each column. (Unless otherwise specified, the row height is determined by the font size.) If you select a specific measurement, each column will be of that fixed width. Selecting the AutoFit to contents option adjusts the width to the cell's contents. Selecting the AutoFit to window option adjusts the width to the window size (used for Web pages).

**Figure 15.4.** The Insert Table dialog box

## Drawing a table

If you want to draw a table that is not a simple grid, the easiest way is to use the Draw Table feature. To do so, choose Insert ⇨ Table ⇨ Draw Table. The insert point cursor converts to a pencil. Click and drag to create a rectangle and release the mouse button to insert the rectangle onto the page. Dashed lines at the vertical and horizontal rulers indicate the exact coordinates of your pencil as you drag it. I usually create a large rectangle that indicates the outside limits of the table, and then draw lines from one side of the rectangle to the other to divide it. Figure 15.5 shows a table created with this method. You can clear lines by clicking the eraser and erasing lines.

**Hack**

When Draw Table is turned on, you can also temporarily convert the Pencil to an Eraser by holding down the Shift key.

The Draw Borders command group also includes Line Style, Line Weight, and Pen Color commands. You can set these as you draw or change them later.

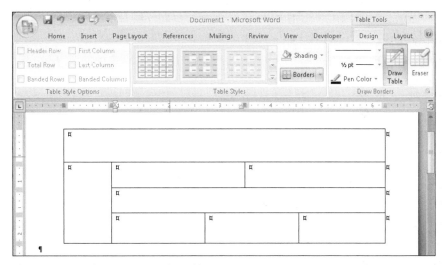

**Figure 15.5.** Drawing a more complex table

## Inserting an Excel spreadsheet

If you are inserting a table in which you want to take advantage of Excel's mathematical formulas and calculation capabilities, this is the option to use. Although it was possible to insert an Excel spreadsheet into a Word document in earlier versions, you can now do so by choosing Insert ⇨ Table ⇨ Excel Spreadsheet. This inserts a spreadsheet into your document, as shown in Figure 15.6, in which you can insert values, formulas, and so on, using the Excel interface and

**Figure 15.6.** Inserting an Excel Spreadsheet as a table in your Word document

commands. This command saves you the trouble of launching Excel and saving a separate file if you intend to input the data and formulas while creating a Word document. You can also insert an existing Excel spreadsheet; I show you how to do that in Chapter 16.

## Creating a table using Quick Tables

A new feature in Word 2007 is the ability to insert a ready-made table into a document. These tables are known as *Quick Tables,* and they are designed to integrate stylistically with the Quick Styles. Quick Tables have sample data already placed in each cell to give you an idea of what sort of data they are suitable for and how they will look when populated with data.

To insert a Quick Table into your document, choose Insert ⇨ Table ⇨ Quick Tables. Select the style of table from the Quick Tables Gallery shown in Figure 15.7.

Once you insert the table, you can clear the sample data from the table without deleting the table itself by selecting the table and pressing Delete. (Don't use Backspace — that deletes the whole table.)

**General**

**Double Table (Basic)**

| Element | Symbol | Weight | Element | Symbol | Weight |
|---------|--------|--------|---------|--------|--------|
| Lithium | Li | 3 | Cesium | Cs | 55 |
| Beryllium | Be | 4 | Barium | Ba | 56 |
| Sodium | Na | 11 | Francium | Fr | 87 |
| Magnesium | Mg | 12 | Radium | Ra | 88 |
| Potassium | K | 19 | Aluminum | Al | 13 |
| Calcium | Ca | 20 | Gallium | Ga | 31 |
| Rubidium | Rb | 37 | Indium | In | 49 |

**Double Table (Style 20)**

| Element | Symbol | Weight | Element | Symbol | Weight |
|---------|--------|--------|---------|--------|--------|
| Lithium | Li | 3 | Cesium | Cs | 55 |
| Beryllium | Be | 4 | Barium | Ba | 56 |
| Sodium | Na | 11 | Francium | Fr | 87 |
| Magnesium | Mg | 12 | Radium | Ra | 88 |
| Potassium | K | 19 | Aluminum | Al | 13 |
| Calcium | Ca | 20 | Gallium | Ga | 31 |
| Rubidium | Rb | 37 | Indium | In | 49 |

Save Selection to Quick Tables Gallery...

**Figure 15.7.** The Quick Tables gallery

**Bright Idea**

If you create a table that you want to use again, select the table and then choose Insert ⇨ Table ⇨ Quick Tables ⇨ Save Selection to Quick Tables Gallery.

# Moving and deleting tables

You can move a table around on a page as a unit. To do so, move the mouse pointer over the table until the table's move handle appears (the square containing up, down, right, and left arrows). Then hold down the right mouse button and drag the table to its new location. The table can "float" on the page. It is not necessary to insert blank lines to place it lower on the page. If you move a table over a paragraph of text, the text of the paragraph flows around the table. You cannot move a table outside the printable area of a page. If you move a table to the bottom of the page it may split into two sections, one on each page.

## Resizing a table

If you need to resize an entire table once you have inserted it into your document, you can do so by first selecting the table by clicking its move handle. Next, click and drag the resizing square in the lower-right corner of the table up, down, left, or right until the table's external rectangular dimensions are how you want them.

## Cutting and pasting a table

If you prefer to cut and paste the table to its new location, select the table by clicking its move handle. Press Ctrl+X or choose Home ➪ Cut to remove the table from your document and copy it to the Clipboard. Next, position your cursor at the point in the document where you want to insert the table, and press Ctrl+V or choose Home ➪ Paste to paste it into the new location.

## Deleting a table entirely

If you want to delete an entire table (not just the contents of its cells), select the table by clicking its move handle. Press Ctrl+X or choose Home ➪ Cut to remove the table from your document and place it in the Clipboard, or choose Table Tools ➪ Layout ➪ Delete ➪ Delete Table to delete the table completely without copying it to the Clipboard. You can also select the table and then press Backspace.

# Formatting tables

Once you insert a table, you have many ways that you can modify its visual appearance to give it the look you want. Word creates two custom tabs of Table Tools on the Ribbon, the Design tab, and the Layout tab. These Table Tools tabs only appear when a table is selected.

The Design tab has commands that have to do with style, such as shading and line color, line width, and style, and whether there should be a special treatment for certain common table design elements, such as header and total rows. The Design tab appears in Figure 15.8.

**Figure 15.8.** The Table Tools Design tab on the Ribbon

The Layout tab contains the commands that relate to manipulating the cells, rows, and columns of the table, such as inserting rows and columns, cell size, and text alignment within cells. This tab also contains commands for manipulating cell data: sorting, repeating header rows, converting tables to text, and adding formulas to cells. The Layout tab appears in Figure 15.9.

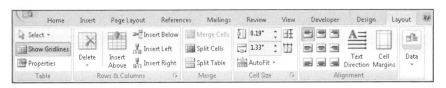

**Figure 15.9.** The Table Tools Layout tab on the Ribbon

# Working with table styles

If you used earlier versions of Word, you may recall the Table AutoFormat feature. This has been replaced by the Table Styles feature. With table styles, you can select from a gallery of table styles and select which table elements should get a differentiating design treatment. In earlier versions of Word, you could select ready-made styles to which you could apply special formatting for a heading row, last row, first column,

**Inside Scoop**

I find I get a better idea of what the table will really look like if I wait to apply styles until after I enter data into the table.

and last column. With Word 2007 Table Style options, you can apply special formatting to all of these categories (*last row* has been renamed *total row*) as well as have the option to add banded columns or rows. Banded columns or rows have alternating colors or shading every other column or row to allow you to more readily line up the data visually.

To select a table style, you must first insert a table into your document. Select the table by clicking its move handle and choose Table Tools ⇨ Design. Move your mouse over one of the table styles in the gallery to see a live preview of what your table will look like. When you find one that you like, click the style to apply it to your table, as shown in Figure 15.10. You can also modify an existing style, clear the table style (so that the table reverts to a "plain vanilla" look, or create a new table style from this menu).

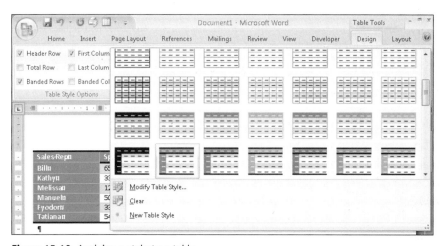

**Figure 15.10.** Applying a style to a table

## Table style options

You can select which table elements get special treatment when applying a table style, depending on your needs. You may want to use a table style that has banded rows but you don't want to use them. In that case, deselect the

**Hack**
You can access most common table commands by right-clicking inside the table and choosing from the commands on the pop-up menu.

Banded Rows check box and the rows appear in a single color or shading. If you have selected a style that doesn't treat the final row as a total row, you can do so by selecting Total Row. This inserts a special treatment for the final row of the table. The special design treatment or formatting will vary depending on the table style selected. The two plain table styles, Table Grid (with plain line borders) and Table Normal (with no printed borders), have no extra formatting, so if you select one of these styles, the Table Style Options don't apply any special formatting to special rows or columns even if selected.

## Shading and borders

You can always make additional changes to the shading and borders of tables using the Shading or Borders commands in the Table Styles group of the Design tab. These function just as they do for paragraphs, as described in Chapter 7. To change the font color of the text in individual cells, select all the text to which you want to apply the color change, and then choose Home ⇨ Font Color and select the new color.

## Working with cells, rows, and columns

What many Word users find frustrating about working with tables is that manipulating cells, rows, columns, and the data inside them is not predictable. You expect a certain behavior when working in Word, and with tables the procedure is different. This is also true if you are used to working with Excel all day and then have occasion to work with tables in Word instead.

Taking a few minutes to go over the basic elements of entering data, moving around within a table, and manipulating cells, rows, and columns will save you lots of grief.

## Showing gridlines

By default, gridlines are turned on. *Gridlines* are nonprinting horizontal and vertical lines indicating the boundaries of each cell. These appear on the screen to help you while you create and work with your table (although they do not appear in Full Screen Reading view). They are distinct from Borders, which are the printing and always-visible horizontal and vertical boundaries that you can elect to add to your table. Figure 15.11 shows a sample Quick Table with gridlines showing. Figure 15.12 shows the same table with gridlines hidden. It's a good idea to keep gridlines turned on when you are manipulating tables and turn them off to see how things will look on the printed page. The Show Gridlines command is a toggle command. To turn gridlines on or off, make sure that your insertion point is within a table so that the Table Tools tabs are visible, and choose Table Tools ⇨ Layout ⇨ Show Gridlines.

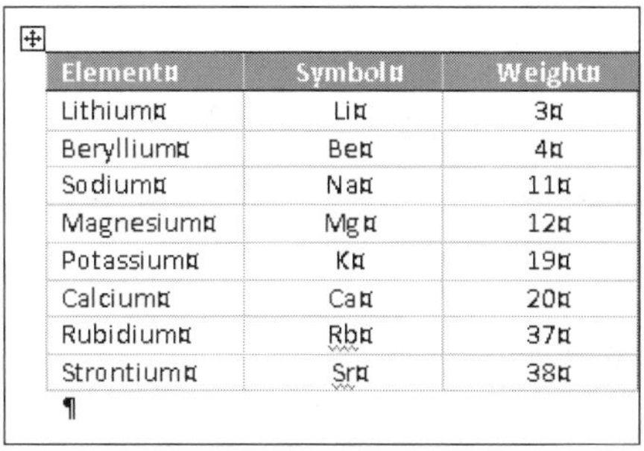

| Element¤ | Symbol¤ | Weight¤ |
|---|---|---|
| Lithium¤ | Li¤ | 3¤ |
| Beryllium¤ | Be¤ | 4¤ |
| Sodium¤ | Na¤ | 11¤ |
| Magnesium¤ | Mg¤ | 12¤ |
| Potassium¤ | K¤ | 19¤ |
| Calcium¤ | Ca¤ | 20¤ |
| Rubidium¤ | Rb¤ | 37¤ |
| Strontium¤ | Sr¤ | 38¤ |

¶

**Figure 15.11.** A table with gridlines displayed

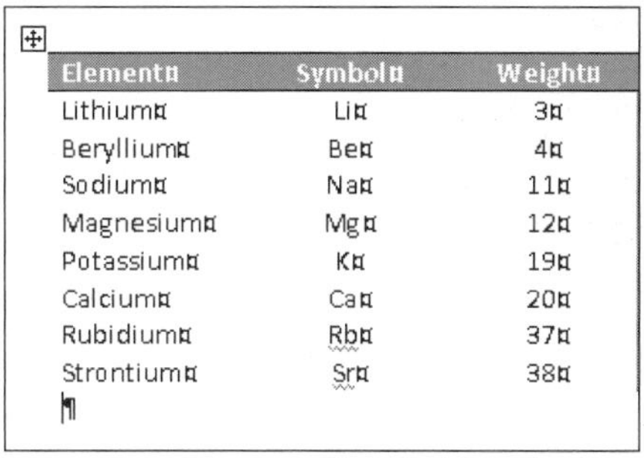

| Element¤ | Symbol¤ | Weight¤ |
|---|---|---|
| Lithium¤ | Li¤ | 3¤ |
| Beryllium¤ | Be¤ | 4¤ |
| Sodium¤ | Na¤ | 11¤ |
| Magnesium¤ | Mg¤ | 12¤ |
| Potassium¤ | K¤ | 19¤ |
| Calcium¤ | Ca¤ | 20¤ |
| Rubidium¤ | Rb¤ | 37¤ |
| Strontium¤ | Sr¤ | 38¤ |

¶

**Figure 15.12.** A table with gridlines hidden

## Typing data and moving around in a table

To type text into a cell, click in the cell and begin typing. To move to the next cell, press Tab — this selects the entire contents of the cell. (Each column is like a tab stop: you can't have tab stops within a cell.) To move back a column, press Shift+Tab — this also selects the entire contents of the cell. You can always click in a cell to move to that cell, of course, but note that this moves the insertion point into the cell, it does not select the contents. Table 15.1 shows the keyboard keys for moving around in a table.

**Table 15.1.** Table navigation key combinations

| Keyboard | Function |
|---|---|
| Tab | Move to and select contents of next cell in row |
| Shift+Tab | Move to and select contents of previous cell in row |
| Up Arrow | Move up one row |
| Down Arrow | Move down one row |
| Alt+Page Up | Move to first cell in column |
| Alt+Page Down | Move to last cell in column |
| Alt+End | Move to last cell in row |
| Alt+Home | Move to first cell in row |
| Alt+Shift+Up Arrow* | Move to and select entire row above current row |
| Alt+Shift+Down Arrow* | Move to and select entire row below current row |

* Use the plain arrow keys, not those on the numeric keypad. Using the Up and Down Arrow keys on the numeric keypad moves the entire contents of the row up or down rather than moving to and then selecting the new row.

## Selecting tables, columns, rows, and cells

There are several ways to select tables and their elements. The easiest to describe are the commands on the Ribbon. You can select a table, column, row, or cell by choosing Table Tools ⇨ Layout ⇨ Select and then clicking Select Table, Select Column, Select Row, or Select Cell. Your insertion point must be somewhere inside the table element you are selecting in order for this to work.

To select an entire table with your mouse, move the mouse over the table until the move handle (described earlier in this chapter) appears and click it. To select an entire column, move your mouse to the top of the column until a downward-pointing arrow appears over the column, and then click the mouse. To select an entire row, click to the left of the row. To select an entire cell, move the mouse cursor to the lower-left corner until an arrow pointing up and to the right appears and click the left mouse button; triple-clicking the cell should also work.

You can also select cells or blocks of cells by holding down the Shift key and pressing the up-, down-, left-, and right-arrow keys to extend the selection by one cell at a time.

## Moving the contents of one cell to another

You can move one cell's contents into another cell by selecting the cell's contents and dragging it into the target cell, or you can cut (select the data and press Ctrl+X) and paste the data from the source cell into the target cell (by pressing Ctrl+V). If there is already data in the target cell, the data from the source cell is added to that of the destination cell.

If you want to keep the data in the source cell and copy it to the new cell as well, select the data from the source cell and drag it to the new location while holding down the Ctrl key, or copy the data from the source cell (select it and then press Ctrl+C) and then paste it into the target cell (press Ctrl+V).

## Moving several selected cells

If you want to move several cells all at once, you can move them to another location within the table by selecting the group of cells and then dragging the contents to the new location, much as you would do with the contents of an individual cell. The cut-and-paste method also functions in the same way. However, the contents of the selected source cells overwrite any data that may already exist in the target cells. The same holds true for copying data from a group of selected cells into a group of target cells.

## Moving or copying a column

To move a column to another location in the table, select the column by moving the mouse cursor to the top of the column you want to move or copy until the mouse cursor becomes a downward-pointing arrow, indicating that it is in column selection mode. Click to select the current column, or click and drag to the left or right to include more columns in the selection.

Once you select the column or group of columns, click and drag it to where you want to move the column or group of columns and release the

**Inside Scoop**

To move or copy a column so that it is the last column, drag the column to the right of the outside border of the last cell.

mouse button. The columns move to the new location. Note that the columns do not erase the data from any existing columns, they just change the column order. You can perform the same operation using the Cut and Paste commands.

To copy a column or group of columns, follow the same procedure as above but hold the Ctrl key down while dragging the column or columns to the new location. You can perform the same operation using the Copy and Paste commands.

## Moving or copying a row

To move or copy a row, select the entire row by clicking to the left of the row, or click and drag it up or down to include more rows in the selection.

Once you select the row or group of rows, click and drag it to where you want to move the row or group of rows and release the mouse button. The rows move to the new location. Note that the rows do not erase the data from any existing rows, they just change the row order. You can perform the same operation using the Cut and Paste commands.

To move or copy a row successfully among other rows that already have data in their cells, select the entire row by clicking to the left of the row, not by selecting all cells in the row (doing so causes weird things to happen — Word adds the entire row and pushes everything to the right).

To copy a row or group of rows, follow the same procedure as explained previously, but hold the Ctrl key down while dragging the row or rows to the new location. You can perform the same operation using the Copy and Paste commands.

**Inside Scoop**

To move or copy a row so that it is the last row, drag the row down past the bottom border of the last row.

# Inserting cells, columns, and rows

You insert additional cells, rows, and columns into an existing table not from the Insert tab, as you might expect, but from the Rows & Columns group of the Layout tab of Table Tools on the Ribbon.

## Inserting cells

You can insert individual cells into a table, but do so with care: If you have data already arranged in such a way that each row and column is sorted in some way, you can throw things off by adding a cell in the middle of everything. To insert cells into an existing table, move the insertion point to the cell in the table where you want to insert a new cell. Choose Table Tools ⇨ Layout, and then click the dialog box launcher in the lower-right corner of the Rows & Columns group, as shown in Figure 15.13. The Insert Cells dialog box offers four ways to insert a cell. The default here is to insert a cell and shift the existing cells down a row. You can also select the Shift cells right option to move everything in that row only over one column. You can also use this dialog box to insert a row above or column to the left of the insertion point.

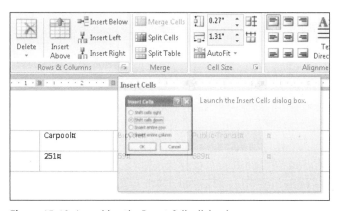

**Figure 15.13.** Launching the Insert Cells dialog box

## Inserting columns

To insert a column to the left of the insertion point in an existing table, choose Table Tools ⇨ Layout ⇨ Insert Left. To insert a column to the right of the insertion point in an existing table, choose Table Tools ⇨ Layout ⇨ Insert Right.

If you want to insert more than one new column, select as many as you want to add (up to the entire table), and then choose Table Tools ⇨ Layout ⇨ Insert Left (or Right) to insert the new blank columns into the table. It is usually necessary to make adjustments to column widths after such an operation, which I show you how to do later in this chapter.

### Inserting rows

To insert a row above the insertion point in an existing table, choose Table Tools ⇨ Layout ⇨ Insert Above. To insert a row below the insertion point in an existing table, choose Table Tools ⇨ Layout ⇨ Insert Below.

If you want to insert more than one new row, select as many as you want to add (up to the entire table), and then choose Table Tools ⇨ Layout ⇨ Insert Above (or Below) to insert the new blank rows into the table.

## Deleting cells, columns, and rows

You can delete cells, columns, and rows in several ways. The easiest way is to select the cell, row, or column, and press Backspace. However, you can also access deletion commands on the Layout tab of Table Tools on the Ribbon.

### Deleting cells

You can delete individual cells from a table, but do so with care: If you have data already arranged in such a way that each row and column is sorted in some way, you can throw things off by deleting a cell in the middle of everything. (If you just want to delete the contents of the cell or cells, select the cell or cells that you want to empty and press Delete.)

**Figure 15.14.** The Delete Cells dialog box

To delete a cell or cells in a table, click in the cell or select the group of cells and choose Table Tools ⇨ Layout ⇨ Delete ⇨ Delete Cells to see the dialog box shown in Figure 15.14. The default option is to shift cells left after a deletion, but you can also shift cells up or delete an entire row or column.

### Deleting columns

To delete a column, click in the column you want to delete and choose Table Tools ⇨ Layout ⇨ Delete ⇨ Delete Columns. If you want to delete more than one column at a time, select the columns you want to delete, and choose Table Tools ⇨ Layout ⇨ Delete ⇨ Delete Columns.

### Deleting rows

To delete a row, click in the row you want to delete and choose Table Tools ➪ Layout ➪ Delete ➪ Delete Rows. If you want to delete more than one row at a time, select the rows you want to delete and choose Table Tools ➪ Layout ➪ Delete ➪ Delete Rows.

### Clearing cells of data

To delete the contents of the cell or cells, select the cell or cells that you want to empty and press Delete. This works with entire rows, columns, or tables as well.

## Merging and splitting cells

You can combine table cells or split them apart as needed. The most common reason for merging cells is for headings that span more than one column (or row). Cells are often split to create subdivisions under various headings.

### Merging cells

To merge two or more cells together, select the cells you want to merge into one cell, right-click in the selected cells, and click Merge Cells. Alternatively, you can select the cells you want to merge into one cell and choose Table Tools ➪ Layout ➪ Merge Cells. Note that the cells must be directly adjoining in order to merge. Figure 15.15 shows a table before merging the top two cells together. Figure 15.16 shows the table after the cells in the top row have been merged.

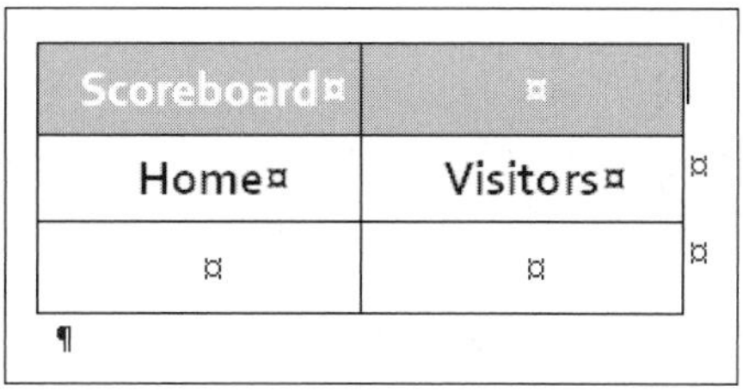

**Figure 15.15.** A table before merging two cells together

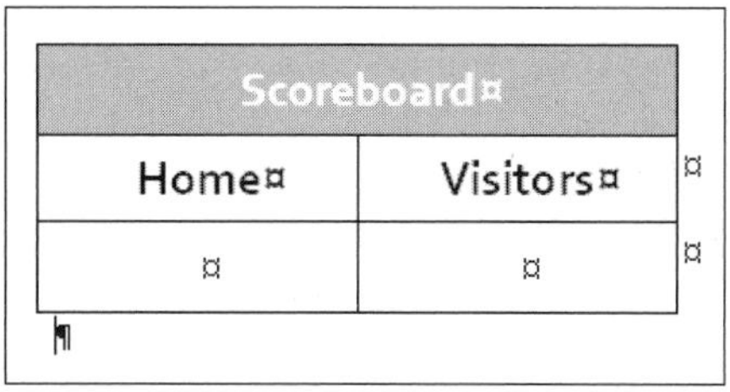

**Figure 15.16.** A table after merging the two cells in the top row together

If you merge two or more cells together that each contain text, then the first cell (top or leftmost) text appears above the second cell (bottom or rightmost) text, separated by a paragraph, and so on.

**Bright Idea**

If you already know that you are going to have cells that don't line up in an even grid as you design the table, use the Draw Table feature to skip the merging and splitting operations altogether.

If you have a lot of cells to merge or simply prefer using the mouse instead of menus, you can also choose Table Tools ⇨ Design ⇨ Eraser and erase the boundaries between cells to merge them together.

### Splitting cells

To split a single cell into two or more cells, right-click in the cell and click Split Cells from the pop-up window, or click in the cell and choose Table Tools ⇨ Layout ⇨ Split Cells. To split several cells into two or more cells, select the cells and choose Table Tools ⇨ Layout ⇨ Split Cells. In either case, the Split Cells dialog box appears, as shown in Figure 15.17.

The Split Cells dialog box gives you the opportunity to determine the way in which the split is performed. You can take one cell and split it into two columns in one row, two rows in one column, two rows in four columns, and so on. If you select the Merge cells before split option, any content in the cells is first merged together and then split, so that the cells containing content remain together. For example, Figure 15.18 shows a table with four cells (two rows, two columns). After splitting the four cells into two rows of four columns with the Merge cells before split option selected, the four cells appear together across the top, as shown in Figure 15.19. However, splitting the four cells into two rows of four columns without the option selected gives you the entirely different result shown in Figure 15.20.

**Figure 15.17.** The Split Cells dialog box

| Summer | Fall |
|--------|------|
| Winter | Spring |

**Figure 15.18.** A table with two rows and columns prior to splitting cells

| Summer | Fall | Winter | Spring |
|--------|------|--------|--------|
|  |  |  |  |

**Figure 15.19.** The effect of merging cells before a split

**Figure 15.20.** The effect of not merging cells before a split

> **Hack**
>
> If you want to split empty cells, it is sometimes easier to choose Table Tools ⇨ Design ⇨ Draw Table and simply draw lines to split cells apart.

## Splitting a table

You can split a table into two (or more) separate tables with the Split Table command. (If you want to split the same table across more than one page with repeating headings, there is a different command designed just for that purpose, which I describe in Chapter 16.) To do so, position your insertion point in the first cell of the row that you want to be the first row of the new table, as shown in Figure 15.21. Choose Table Tools ⇨ Layout ⇨ Split Table. Your table is separated by a blank line, as shown in Figure 15.22.

| Q1 FY07 | Q2 FY07 | Q3 FY07 | Q4 FY07 |
| --- | --- | --- | --- |
| $789,879 | $1,235,879 | $549,772 | $1254,666 |
| Q1 FY08 | Q2 FY08 | Q3 FY08 | Q4 FY08 |
| $549,888 | $1,622,224 | $546,546 | $1,900,123 |

**Figure 15.21.** Positioning the insertion point where you want to split the table

| Q1 FY07 | Q2 FY07 | Q3 FY07 | Q4 FY07 |
| --- | --- | --- | --- |
| $789,879 | $1,235,879 | $549,772 | $1254,666 |

| Q1 FY08 | Q2 FY08 | Q3 FY08 | Q4 FY08 |
| --- | --- | --- | --- |
| $549,888 | $1,622,224 | $546,546 | $1,900,123 |

**Figure 15.22.** The table is split into two tables separated by a blank line.

# Adjusting cell size

There are many ways to adjust the dimensions of individual cells to the height of rows and to the width of columns. The most commonly used methods are covered here.

## Setting row or cell height

By default, Word determines the cell or row height based on the size of the text that is typed into the cell. If you type more text than will fit within the cell from left to right, the line wraps and the cell and row height is increased to accommodate the additional line or lines of text. The same thing happens if you add other items such as shapes, illustrations, WordArt, or equations to a cell.

If you want to change the row height using your eye to determine what looks right, move the mouse over the cell border (or gridline if you don't have visible borders). Drag the cell boundary up or down when the mouse pointer is directly over the cell border or gridline and changes to

**Inside Scoop**

If you have cells that run across in rows of equal height, your cell height adjustments affect the entire row. If cells do not align vertically across the table, your adjustments only apply to the selected cells.

a double rule with up and down arrows. You can accomplish the same thing by selecting the row and dragging the corresponding cell margin bar in the vertical ruler on the left side of your screen.

If you want to specify measurements for selected cells or rows, you also have two ways to do this. The simplest way is to use the arrow keys or type a value in the Height list box in the Cell Size group of the Layout tab of Table Tools, as shown in Figure 15.23. By default, the value in the list box determines the minimum height of the cell in inches. In other words, if you have a lot of text in a cell and you specify a cell height that won't allow the text to fit, the text cell height is only reduced to the smallest size that displays all the contents of the cell. Select the entire table first if you want all cells in the table to have equal height. If you want the height of the rows to be distributed evenly within the table, choose the Distribute Rows command immediately to the right of the Height list box.

**Figure 15.23.**
Commands for adjusting the cell height in a table

If you want more options for defining row height, click the dialog box launcher in the bottom-right corner of the Cell Size group of the Layout tab of Table Tools. This displays the Row tab of the Table Properties dialog box shown in Figure 15.24. You can specify the height of each row in the table. (The row indicator shows Row 1 in Figure 15.24, but if you select the entire table, Rows is displayed indicating that your choice here affects all rows. The row indicator can also spec-

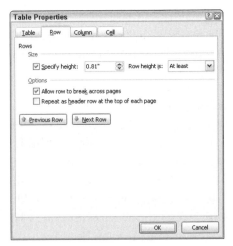

**Figure 15.24.** The Row tab of the Table Properties dialog box

ify a range of selected rows.) Select the Specify height option, and type or use the arrow keys to select a value. If you accept the default Row height

**Bright Idea**

Use the Previous Row and Next Row buttons to specify height for each row in your table without leaving the dialog box.

is At least selection, the value you specify is used unless it is too small for the cell contents. If you select Exactly, the value you enter is used whether all the contents can by displayed or not. When you are satisfied with the row height for any rows you want to modify, click OK.

### Setting cell or column width

When you insert a table into a document, the default cell or column width is the width of the table divided by the number of columns. You can, however, adjust this in many ways. By default, when you type more text than will fit within the cell from left to right, the line wraps and the cell and row height is increased to accommodate the additional line or lines of text, but the column width remains the same. However, if you add other items such as shapes, illustrations, WordArt, or equations to a cell, the column width expands to fit the object that you insert.

If you want to change the cell or column width using your eye to determine what looks right, move the mouse over the cell border (or gridline if you don't have visible borders). Drag the cell boundary left or right when the mouse pointer is directly over the cell border or gridline and the pointer changes to a double rule with left and right arrows. You can accomplish the same thing by clicking in a cell in the column and dragging the corresponding cell margin bar in the horizontal ruler at the top of your screen.

If you want to specify measurements for selected cells or columns, you also have two ways to do this. The simplest way is to use the arrow keys or type a value in the Width list box in the Cell Size group of the Layout tab of Table Tools, as shown in Figure 15.25. By default, the value in the list box determines the minimum width of the cell in inches. Select the entire table first if you want all cells in the table to have equal width specified in the Width list box. If you want the width of the columns to be distributed evenly within the table and you want to allow Word to determine what the width needs to be, choose

**Figure 15.25.**
Commands for adjusting the cell width in a table

**Bright Idea**

Use the Previous Column and Next Column buttons to specify width for each column in your table without leaving the dialog box.

the Distribute Columns command immediately to the right of the Width list box.

If you want more options for defining column width, click the dialog box launcher in the bottom-right corner of the Cell Size group of the Layout tab of Table Tools. This displays the Column tab of the Table Properties dialog box shown in Figure 15.26. You can specify the width of each column in the table. (The column indicator shows Columns in Figure 15.26, indicating that the entire table is selected. If you have column 2 selected, the column indicator displays this. The

**Figure 15.26.** The Column tab of the Table Properties dialog box

column indicator can also specify a range of selected columns.) Check the Preferred width box and type in or use the arrow keys to select a value. If you accept the default Measure in Inches selection, the value you specify is measured in inches. If you select Percentage, the value you enter assigns the column width a percentage of the table's entire width. For example, if you want column 1 to be one-half the width of the entire table, specify 50 percent here. When you are satisfied with the column width for any columns you want to modify, click OK.

### Fixed column width versus AutoFit

When you insert an empty table into your document, it has cells (and columns) of equal width. By default, Word assumes you want to use a fixed column width. However, you can also have the column change its width depending on the cell contents. To do so, choose Table Tools ⇨ Layout ⇨ AutoFit ⇨ AutoFit Contents. When you use this option, the columns adjust as you type data into each cell, giving the column containing the cell with the most text the greatest width.

If you create a Web page, you can choose AutoFit Window, which sizes the table's columns to fit across the window where the document is being viewed. To do so, choose Table Tools ⇨ Layout ⇨ AutoFit ⇨ AutoFit Window.

You can revert to fixed column width at any time by choosing Table Tools ⇨ Layout ⇨ AutoFit ⇨ Fixed Column Width.

## Changing table alignment settings

In addition to adjusting the size of cells, rows, and columns, you can also determine how text is aligned within a cell, what margins should exist within cells, whether there should be any spacing between cells, and what direction the text should flow in a cell.

### Setting text alignment in cells

By default, any text within a cell is aligned at the top left corner of the cell. You can change the text alignment of any cell, row, column, or block of selected cells by clicking one of the nine possible alignment choices in the Alignment group of the Layout tab of Table Tools, as shown in Figure 15.27. You can choose top, center, bottom vertically, and left, center, right horizontally.

**Figure 15.27.**
Commands to choose text alignment within a cell

### Setting text direction

Occasionally you will want to have a sideways label to present your information in the best way. In Word (in the U.S.-English version), text in tables is displayed left to right by default. You can also have text in a cell display top-to-bottom or bottom-to-top. To do this, select the cell that you want to change and choose Table Tools ⇨ Layout ⇨ Text Direction. The first time you click Text Direction the text changes from left-to-right to

**Watch Out!**

Don't use the AutoFit Contents command until you have data in your table. If you click AutoFit Contents with an empty table, the table shrinks to its smallest possible size because there is no data. Click Undo or press Ctrl+Z to reverse this problem (clicking Fixed Column Width does not repair the problem).

**Bright Idea**

If you need to print a table broadside (landscape) within a document that has headers and/or footers, you can keep the headers and footers at the top and bottom of the page and still have the table print sideways by changing the text direction of the entire table and making column and row adjustments accordingly.

top-to-bottom. Clicking Text Direction again changes the text to bottom to top. When you change text direction, all the cell alignment commands change direction also, and the cell dimensions change to accommodate the new text direction. You may need to make adjustments to the row and column dimensions to get the look you want.

## Setting cell margins and spacing

By default, Word sets a left and right margin of 0.08 inches for each cell so that some space separates the data contained in each cell. There is no default top or bottom margin because the font spacing takes care of that for you. If you want to make changes to these settings, select the entire table or the cells, rows, columns, or blocks of cells you want to affect and choose Table Tools ⇨ Layout ⇨ Cells Margins. The Table Options dialog box appears, as shown in Figure 15.28. Use the arrow keys or type a value to change the cell margins. Click OK to apply your changes.

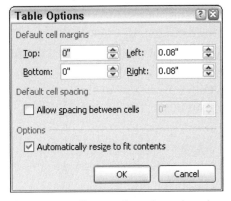

**Figure 15.28.** Change cell margins and spacing in the Table Options dialog box.

You can also add space between cells (as opposed to adding margins within cells) by selecting the Allow spacing between cells option in the Table Options dialog box, and then using the arrows keys or typing a value for the space between cells. Click OK to apply your changes.

## Just the facts

- You can add a table to your document by choosing Insert ⇨ Table on the Ribbon.

- Quick Tables provide you with ready-made tables of several types populated with sample data to allow you to get a sense of what they will look like.

- Table styles provide a quick and easy way to create professional-looking tables.

- You can choose from among several methods for creating a table, from drawing with the mouse, to selecting using a grid tool, to inserting an Excel spreadsheet.

- The Layout tab of Table Tools on the Ribbon provides many commands for working with cells, rows, and columns.

GET THE SCOOP ON...
Converting text into a table, and a table into text ▪
Sorting table data ▪ Importing data into tables ▪ Using
formulas in tables ▪ Making tables cross the page barrier

# Advanced Table Features

In Chapter 15, I showed you several ways to go about creating a table, how to format a table, and how to work with cells, rows, and columns. This chapter covers more advanced topics such as converting tables to text and back again, sorting tables, splitting tables across several pages, working with formulas, and ways to make everything fit on the page.

## Converting between tables and text

You can convert text into a table in Word and vice versa. The commands are by necessity located in different parts of Word's user interface, however.

### Converting text into a table

To convert text into a table, you must have each group of text separated by a unique marker. The marker is usually a tab, although a paragraph mark, comma, or character that you specify can work. In general, if you have tabular text that you have created by setting tabs in Word with a paragraph mark at the end of each line, you have all the information Word needs to convert the data into a table because you have separators for both rows and columns. If you have a string of data separated by paragraph marks alone, you will have a table of a single row. A common way to extract data to and from different database and spreadsheet applications is to have data that corresponds to different fields

369

separated by commas and individual records by a return (if a database) or columns separated by commas and rows by a return (if a spreadsheet).

For example, if you have text separated by tabs that you want to convert into a table, select the text you want to convert and choose Insert ⇨ Table ⇨ Convert Text to Table. The Convert Text to Table dialog box appears, as shown in Figure 16.1. Here you can specify the number of rows and columns, the AutoFit behavior (as described in Chapter 15), and the text separator. When you have made any

**Figure 16.1.** The Convert Text to Table dialog box

changes to the settings, click OK to convert the selected text into a table.

Word makes certain assumptions when you convert from text to a table. For example, if you use the Auto setting for the Fixed column width option, Word uses the tab settings you had for the text before and then makes the last column reach to the left margin of your current page settings. Word does not convert special tabs into the corresponding cell alignment type. In other words, if you have a tabbed list with center tabs, the new table will not present the contents of the table's cells as centered, but will rather use the default left top alignment setting.

## Converting a table into text

You can convert a table into text as well. One common reason for doing this is to convert data into a form that can be read by a database or spreadsheet program. To do so, select the table (or part of a table) and choose Table Tools ⇨ Layout ⇨ Data ⇨ Convert to Text. The Convert Table to Text dialog box appears, as shown in Figure 16.2. You can specify one of the common text separators or select Other and specify a character of your own choosing. Note that if you have a nested table, you have the

**Figure 16.2.** The Convert Table to Text dialog box

option of converting nested tables (tables within tables) or just the outer table. This option is disabled unless you have tables nested within cells of the table you want to convert to text.

# Advanced table data manipulation

Word provides you with some additional features for working with data within tables. You can sort data in a table in several different ways. You can also add formulas to automate numerical tables.

## Sorting items in a table

You can perform a sort of up to three levels on a table or on an individual column. One limitation here is that you can only sort rows using column sorting criteria — you cannot sort columns using row criteria. The sort can be of the type Text (alphabetical), Number, or Date, and it can be ascending or descending. To perform a sort on a table or part of a table, select it and choose Table Tools ⇨ Layout ⇨ Data ⇨ Sort. The Sort dialog box shown in Figure 16.3 appears. If you have a header row, select the Header row option. This allows you to sort using the name of the column. If your table has no header rows, select the No header row option. You can select the sorting column or columns by number, such as Column 1, Column 2, and so on. In the Sort by list, select the first column you want to sort. Choose Text, Number, or Data in the Type field, and select Ascending or Descending. If you want to then sort by an additional criterion, select the column containing that sort criteria in the first Then by list, followed by the third sort criterion in the second Then by list.

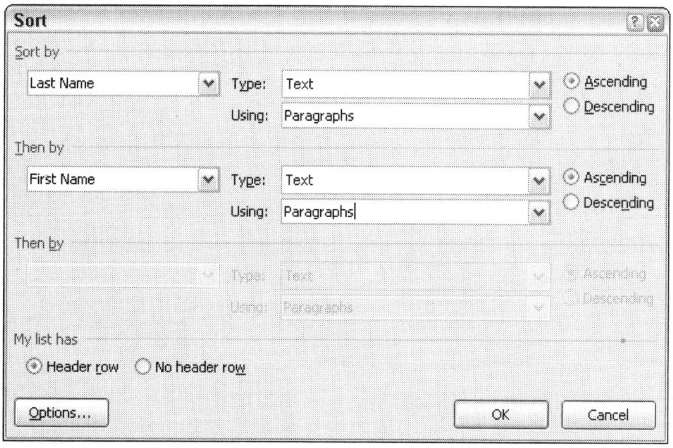

**Figure 16.3.** Sorting a table

If you have a column that contains more than one item that you want to sort by, you can accomplish this using the Options button in the Sort dialog box. For example, if you have a Names column, you can sort by last name and then by first name. To do so, make sure that the names take the form Last, First as in Smith, Jane in the column. Click Options in the Sort dialog box to display the Sort Options dialog box, as shown in Figure 16.4. Select the Commas option and click OK. Note that this dialog box also allows you to perform case-sensitive sorts and column-only sorts where applicable, and to choose a different sorting language if need be.

**Figure 16.4.** The Sort Options dialog box

## Adding formulas to tables

If you are using a table in a form that contains numbers, such as an invoice or tally of some kind, you may find the Formula feature useful. To insert a formula into a table cell in Word, choose Table Tools ⇨ Layout ⇨ Data ⇨ Formulas to display the Formula dialog box, as shown in Figure 16.5. You can type a formula using the same syntax you would in Microsoft Excel, beginning the expression with an equal sign (=). You can specify the value of any given cell using a spreadsheet-style coordinate system, where the first

**Figure 16.5.** Inserting a formula into a table cell

**Hack**

If you have merged cells while creating your table, it cannot be sorted. You will receive a message saying "Cannot sort a table containing merged cells." You can get around this by copying the table or section of table that you want to sort into a new table and sort the new table.

column is A, the second B, the first row is 1, the second 2, so that the value in the second column of the second row is B2, as shown in Figure 16.6. Alternatively, you can assign a bookmark name to a cell and the numeric value contained in the cell. You can also paste certain mathematical and logical functions into the formula, such as SUM, PRODUCT, AVERAGE, and so on. You can choose from a list of number formats here as well.

| A1 | B1 | C1 |
| A2 | B2 | C2 |
| A3 | B3 | C3 |

**Figure 16.6.** The spreadsheet-style coordinate system used to specify table cells in formulas

To insert a formula that takes the quantity of items as shown in the sample table in Figure 16.7 and multiplies it by the item price into a cell that displays the item total, follow these steps:

| Item | Quantity | Item Price | Item Total |
| Chair | 2 | 349.99 | |
| Ottoman | 1 | 375.00 | |
| Lamp | 2 | 95.00 | |

**Figure 16.7.** A sample table with a calculation to perform

1. Click in the cell where you want to insert the formula (cell D2, the item total for Chair, in this example).

2. Choose Table Tools ⇨ Layout ⇨ Data ⇨ Formula.

3. Note that Word attempts to guess what you want to do (add everything to the left of the cell selected using the expression =SUM(LEFT)). In this case, you want to perform a different operation, so delete everything to the right of the equal sign in the Formula field.

4. In the Paste function list, click PRODUCT.

5. Notice that the Formula field now reads =PRODUCT(). Now type **B2:C2** inside the parentheses to add the cell range for which you want to receive the product of the multiplication operation. (Note that I used this example to show you how to include a function, but you could simply have used =B2*C2 here to get the same result.)

**Watch Out!**

If you add columns or rows you must recalculate the formulas in your table. To do this, press F9.

**6.** Click OK to insert the formula into your table. The Item Total column for the item Chair now displays the calculated total, as shown in Figure 16.8.

| Item | Quantity | Item Price | Item Total |
|------|----------|-----------|-----------|
| Chair | 2 | 349.99 | 699.98 |
| Ottoman | 1 | 375.00 | |
| Lamp | 2 | 95.00 | |

**Figure 16.8.** Adding a formula that displays results in the table

**7.** To fill out the remainder of the cells in the column, repeat the procedure for each cell, replacing the appropriate row number in the cell range for each one. The next row would have the formula =PRODUCT(B3:C3).

# Advanced table formatting

Chapter 16 describes basic ways to add formatting to your tables. This section describes ways to address some common formatting problems and tricky things about tables.

## Automating data entry tasks in tables

If you have a predictable series to add in a large table, there are several ways that you can simplify your task.

### Using Excel's AutoFill feature to save time in Word

I used to say to myself "If only Word had Excel's AutoFill feature!" whenever I had to type in the months of the year, days of the week, or any other obvious series. At some point, I realized that although Microsoft wasn't getting around to adding an AutoFill feature to Word, it would be very easy to use Excel's feature and paste the data into Word in just a few keystrokes or mouse clicks. (I should stress that this is quick and easy if you are running Office 2007 on a PC with sufficient memory, processor speed, and hard drive space to handle the software. If you have shoe-horned Office 2007 onto an older PC that barely meets the system requirements, launching Excel while Word is running may be a slow process and not worth the wait.)

To use the AutoFill feature to add a row or column of data in a series from Excel into a Word table, follow these steps:

1. Launch Excel and type the first item in the series of numbers, days, months, quarters, as appropriate, in the format you choose, such as **Jan** for January.

2. You may need to enter data into more than one cell to make your pattern apparent. For example, if you used *Feb* as the second item in the series beginning with *Jan,* the remainder of the series would be the subsequent months. If you made the second item *Mar,* the series would be bimonthly: Jan, Mar, May, Jul ..., as shown in Figure 16.9.

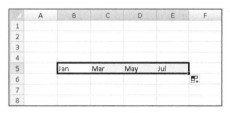

**Figure 16.9.** Using the AutoFill feature in Excel to generate a series for a table

## Save Yourself Some Grief: When to Use Excel Instead

It's great that Word allows you to add formulas to tables, but this is a limited feature that hasn't changed in several versions and isn't particularly easy to use. The Word formula feature is suited for performing basic mathematical calculations in a simple table. It's fine for basic invoices and other such items, but it is not suited to more advanced calculations. For more complex calculations, filtered data, data validation, and so on, use an Excel spreadsheet instead. You have the benefit of more functions, more extensive help, formula replication, and more. You can either create the spreadsheet first in Excel and then paste it into Word or choose Insert ⇨ Table ⇨ Excel Spreadsheet to embed a simple spreadsheet into your document without leaving Word.

3. Drag the lower-right corner of the cell to the right to autofill a row the required number of cells or downward to autofill a column.

4. Select the series of cells in Excel. Press Ctrl+C or right-click the selection and select Copy.

5. Open a Word document (or switch to an open document in Word).

6. If you are starting a new table, press Ctrl+V or choose Home ⇨ Paste to insert the row or column as a table in Word. If you are entering the series into existing blank cells in a Word table, select the destination series of blank cells and choose Home ⇨ Paste ⇨ Paste Cells.

7. Once you add the series to Word, you can close Excel.

### Numbering rows in a table

If you need to number the rows in your table, you can certainly use the method of cutting and pasting from Excel, but you don't need to. Select the column in which you want to add numbering to the rows and choose Home ⇨ Numbering. You can click the arrow next to the Numbering button to choose a number format. This method also allows you to assign a number to the beginning of text in a populated cell, but if you have any paragraph marks within the cell, each new paragraph gets a new number.

## Fitting everything on one page

In this section, I've collected some tips on how to fit everything on a page. However, if you have trouble fitting everything on the page in a table, you may be defeating the purpose of this form of displaying information. After all, the whole idea is to have a concise summary of important information organized in a way that also displays relations between bits of data. If you make the table work too hard (or make the reader work too hard by squinting to see fine print), you have defeated the purpose of the table. If you have too much information to fit in the table comfortably, here are a few strategies that work for me that don't involve formatting and squeezing:

■ Omit less critical details from the table — if you need to include it somewhere, put it in later textual information.

■ Break up a table into several tables; have a summary table and then follow it with details for each column or row.

- If you have a grid of related numerical data, consider converting it into a chart.

- Pull extra materials like titles, definitions of terms, table notes, and data sources out of the body of the table.

### Making everything fit horizontally

There are several ways you can squeeze text so that more fits horizontally on the page. If your table doesn't need to fit in a portrait orientation, the easiest way may be to flip the paper to a landscape orientation. To do so, choose Page Layout ⇨ Orientation ⇨ Landscape. You can then stretch the table to the right to add more room, making changes to the widths of individual columns as necessary.

If you have a printer that accepts U.S. Legal-size paper (8½ x 14 inches), you can further extend your table in landscape mode by selecting the longer paper size by choosing Page Layout ⇨ Size ⇨ Legal.

You can extend a table outside your normal print margins (as long as you stay within the printable area of the page for your printer) by dragging the entire table to the left and then stretching the right side.

Additional ways to make things fit horizontally are to reduce cell margins, reduce or eliminate space between cells, or reduce font size of text within cells. With the last technique, you can either manually reduce the font size of text within selected cells, or right-click the selected cell range or table, choose Table Properties ⇨ Cell ⇨ Options, and check Wrap text and/or Fit text. Wrap text, which is selected by default, allows text to wrap within the cell to the next line; Fit text reduces the font to allow the text to fit within the cell. One other way to reduce font size is to select the cell range or table and launch the Font dialog box from the Home tab of the Ribbon and click the Character Spacing tab. From here you can reduce the font size of all selected cells or the entire table by a percentage (Scale), or you can select Condensed in the Spacing list to have individual characters moved more closely together.

**Inside Scoop**

To stretch just the right column, drag the right border to the right with the mouse. To stretch the entire table proportionally, drag the square in the lower-right corner of the table.

> **Watch Out!**
> Word will let you drag your table boundaries to the page edge, which will most likely be outside the printable area of your printer. Be sure to check this by choosing Microsoft Office ⇨ Print ⇨ Print Preview if you are coming close to the edge.

If you want to preserve the proportions of your table, you can reduce (or enlarge) its width by percentage. To do so, choose Table Tools ⇨ Layout ⇨ Properties (or right-click the row and click Table Properties). Click the Table tab. Select the Preferred width option in the Size section, and select Percentage in the Measure in list. Type the percentage reduction (less than 100 percent) or enlargement (greater than 100 percent), and click OK to see your changes.

### Making everything fit vertically

If you want to avoid having to break your table across a page and want everything to fit, you have several techniques at your disposal. First, you can extend the table past the top and bottom page margin. Take care here, however, to stay within the printable area of the page for your printer (particularly large unprintable areas exist at the top and bottom margin of the page with some inkjet printers). You can check your work using the Print Preview command as described in the previous section. If you have headers and/or footers, consider suppressing them for the page containing the table if possible, or reducing their size.

You can also use the various font size reduction methods described in the previous section. If you have space to spare on the horizontal edge, widen your table to flatten it out and give you more vertical room. Disable the Wrap text option for cells to reduce vertical height, if practical. If you need to have wrapped text, select the table or cell range, and choose Home ⇨ Line spacing to reduce the line spacing to the minimum spacing that preserves legibility.

## Splitting tables across pages

Certain tables need to split and span across multiple pages. Word has developed some features that make such splits easy to deal with.

## *Repeating header rows*

If you have a table that needs to continue onto the next page or onto several subsequent pages, you can have a selected row repeat so that the columns containing data are labeled on each page. To do so, select the row that contains the header text and choose Table Tools ⇨ Layout ⇨ Properties (or right-click the row and click Table Properties). This displays the Row tab of the Table Properties dialog box, as shown in Figure 16.10. Select the Repeat as header row at the top of each page option, and click OK.

**Figure 16.10.** Header rows can be repeated across the top of each page automatically.

## *Preventing rows from splitting across a page*

By default, Word allows rows to break across pages. In other words, if you have a table cell containing more than one line of text, it can begin on one page and end on another. You can, however, keep all lines of a row together: This moves the entire row to the next page when you reach the end of the page. To keep rows together, select the rows for which you want this condition to apply and choose Table Tools ⇨ Layout ⇨ Properties (or right-click the row and click Table Properties). This displays the Row tab of the Table Properties dialog box, as shown earlier in Figure 16.10. Deselect the Allow row to break across pages option, and click OK.

# Table width, alignment, and text wrapping

Up to this point, you've seen how to move tables around with the move handle (described in Chapter 15). However, you can determine a preferred width for a table, align the outer borders of the table relative to the text, or indent by a fixed amount. You can also control how tables and text wrapping behave. To access these settings, choose Table Tools ⇨ Layout ⇨ Properties (or right-click the row and click Table Properties). Click the Table tab to see the options shown in Figure 16.11.

To specify the table's width in inches, choose Table Tools ⇨ Layout ⇨ Properties (or right-click the row and click Table Properties). Click the Table tab. Select the Preferred width option in the Size section, and select Inches in the Measure in list. Type the desired measurement, and click OK to see your changes.

To change alignment of the table relative to page margins, choose Table Tools ⇨ Layout ⇨ Properties (or right-click the row and click Table Properties). Click the Table tab. Click Left, Center,

**Figure 16.11.** The Table tab of the Table Properties dialog box controls table size, alignment, and text wrapping.

or Right. To indent the table from the page margin, use the arrows or type a value in the Indent from left list. Typing a negative value creates a

hanging indent (or outdent). If you create a hanging indent, be sure that it is still within your printer's printable page.

You can adjust how text wrapping works with tables and text by choosing Table Tools ⇨ Layout ⇨ Properties (or right-clicking the row and clicking Table Properties). Then click the Table tab, and select None to prevent any text from appearing to the right or left of the table, or select Around to allow text to flow around the table. If you select Around, click Positioning to see additional options shown in Figure 16.12. You can position the table horizontally relative to column, page, or margin. You can

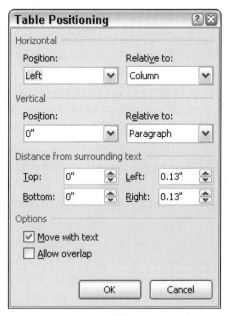

**Figure 16.12.** Additional table-positioning options

position the table vertically relative to margin, page, or paragraph. You can specify the distance that separates the table from surrounding text. You can have the table move with the text when the text is moved or have it stay put. You can also allow overlap of text and table. When you finish making any changes in this dialog box, click OK to apply the changes.

## Nesting tables

There may be times when you want to have tabular material appear within tables. Such tables within tables are called nested tables. Nested tables are sometimes used when designing pages, where you have a single large table for the page, and the contents of each cell are other elements. An example of such a table is shown in Figure 16.13. To create a table within a table, position the cursor inside the cell where you want to create the new table, and choose Insert ⇨ Table. To copy a table from the Clipboard to a cell within another table, choose Home ⇨ Paste ⇨ Paste as Nested Table.

**Figure 16.13.** Using a nested table to create a page layout

# Just the facts

- You can convert text into a table by selecting the text and choosing Insert ⇨ Table ⇨ Convert Text to Table. Conversely, you can convert a table back to text by selecting the table and choosing Table Tools ⇨ Layout ⇨ Data ⇨ Convert to Text.

- You can sort rows in a table by choosing Table Tools ⇨ Layout ⇨ Data ⇨ Sort.

- You can add simple formulas and expressions using functions to tables by choosing Table Tools ⇨ Layout ⇨ Data ⇨ Formula, but use Excel for more complex computations and just embed the spreadsheet in the Word document.

- Use Excel's AutoFill feature to generate common series such as months of the year or days of the week, and then paste them into your Word table.

- You can reduce or condense the font size or scale the table down by a percentage to fit it on a page.

- Use the Repeat header rows option to have the column headings repeat at the top of each page in a multipage table.

# Punch It Up with Graphics and Page Design

PART V

GET THE SCOOP ON...

Creating diagrams using ready-made shapes in Word ■
Giving diagrams a professional look with Shape Styles ■
Making your point quickly with SmartArt graphics

# Illustrate Your Point with Shapes and SmartArt

Sometimes the best way to communicate a concept is with an illustration. In this chapter, I show you how to take advantage of Word's diagram drawing capabilities. You can work with an extensive collection of shapes and lines, draw freehand, or work with ready-made graphic images commonly used to illustrate concepts with SmartArt graphics. The graphics described in this chapter are all *vector graphics*. That is, they are composed of lines that can be manipulated, as opposed to bitmap graphics, which are sets of dots in a pattern.

## Create illustrations using shapes

You can insert shapes from a gallery of ready-made common shapes. The gallery also includes lines and freehand drawing options. If you are working with text and want to insert an illustration in a standard rectangular form, like a painting canvas, you can also insert a drawing that gives you the blank but sizable rectangular "canvas" within which you can insert shapes, lines, and so on. You access these features by choosing Insert ⇨ Shapes, which shows you the menu in Figure 17.1. As you can see, they are grouped by category.

**Inside Scoop**

Word's drawing tools are great for simple things. If you want to create complex technical illustrations, save yourself some grief and use software intended for that purpose, such as Microsoft Visio. Visio integrates well with Word if you need to integrate your illustrations with a report.

## Inserting a new drawing into your document

If you are using your illustration in combination with text in a report or article, you will probably want to insert a rectangle (referred to in Word as a *drawing canvas*) and then add shapes, lines, and text within the rectangle to form your illustration. This allows you to more readily size and move the completed illustration as a unit. Also, if you are using connecting lines between different shapes (such as in a flowchart), you can only connect them to shapes so that the lines stretch when you move the shapes if you are doing this within a drawing canvas.

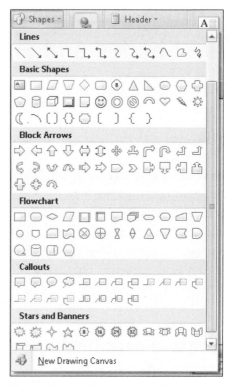

**Figure 17.1.** Ready-made shapes that you can use to create drawings in Word

To insert a new drawing, choose Insert ⇨ Shapes ⇨ New Drawing. You see the outline of a rectangle that is your new drawing canvas inserted onto your page, with the Format tab of Drawing Tools displayed, as shown in Figure 17.2 (some of the command groups may have more detail on your own screen depending on the screen resolution of your monitor). By default, the background of the drawing canvas is white and the borders are invisible. However, you can select a shape style for the drawing canvas from the Shape Styles gallery, or click Shape Fill (the button with a paint bucket) to select a fill color or Shape Outline (the button with a pencil drawing a rectangle) to select an outline color.

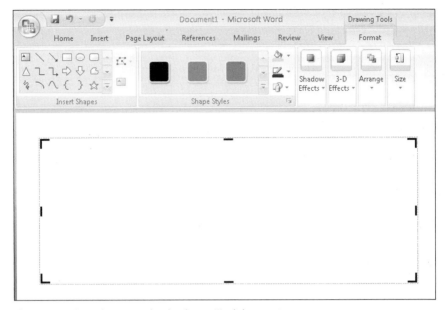

**Figure 17.2.** Inserting a new drawing into a Word document

The corner and side indicators can be dragged to resize the outside dimensions of the drawing. Dragging one of the corners reduces or enlarges the rectangle of the drawing canvas while preserving its *aspect ratio* (the ratio of height to width). Dotted lines indicate the size of the new drawing canvas, as shown in Figure 17.3. Release the mouse when you are happy with the canvas's new size. To make the rectangle wider or narrower, drag the vertical bars on the borders of the drawing canvas from left to right. To make the drawing canvas taller or shorter, drag the horizontal bars on the borders of the drawing canvas up or down.

**Figure 17.3.** Resizing a new drawing

**Hack**

You can also resize a drawing by using the arrows or typing a value for the height or width of the drawing canvas.

**Bright Idea**

If you leave the Lock aspect ratio option checked, as it is by default, then you preserve your drawing's height and width ratio. You can deselect this option if you want to stretch or compress your drawing horizontally or vertically.

For more extensive size controls, click the dialog box launcher in the lower-right corner of the Size group of the Format tab of Drawing Tools to display the Size tab of the Format Drawing Canvas dialog box shown in Figure 17.4. You can set the absolute height or width in linear units (inches), or you can select the Relative radio button to specify a percentage of some other element of the document. You can select from Margin, Page, Top Margin, Bottom Margin, Inside Margin, or Outside Margin for height, and Margin, Page, Left Margin, Right Margin, Inside Margin, or Outside Margin for width. You can scale the dimensions by percentage as well.

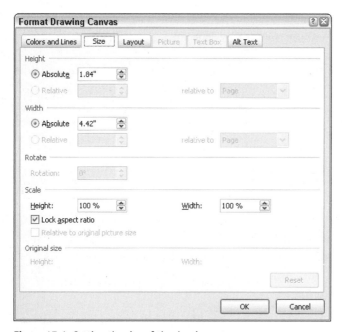

**Figure 17.4.** Setting the size of the drawing canvas

## Inserting shapes and lines

You can insert shapes and lines into a document by choosing Insert ⇨ Shapes and then selecting the appropriate shape or line. You can insert a shape into the document or you can insert it onto an existing drawing canvas. The following example shows you how to start a simple flowchart within a drawing canvas. To do so, follow these steps:

1. Open a new blank document.

2. Choose Insert ⇨ Shapes ⇨ New Drawing Canvas. (In the following figures, I've made the drawing canvas narrower so that you can see it in the illustrations — this is optional.)

3. Choose Insert ⇨ Shapes ⇨ Flowchart ⇨ Terminator.

4. Drag the plus sign (+) to create a terminator shape like the one shown in Figure 17.5.

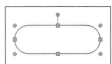

**Figure 17.5.** Inserting a shape for a flowchart

5. Right-click the shape and click Add Text (or choose Drawing Tools ⇨ Format ⇨ Edit Text located in the Insert Shapes group).

6. Type **Car won't start.** At this point, you could modify the text's font and other attributes using the usual commands.

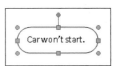

**Figure 17.6.** Adding text to a shape and resizing it

7. Resize the shape using the handles that surround it (the blue dots and squares) so that it fits nicely around the text, as shown in Figure 17.6.

8. Add another shape: Choose Insert ⇨ Shapes ⇨ Flowchart ⇨ Decision. Use the dot handles to size the Decision diamond shape so that it is somewhat larger than the terminator shape. You can also move the entire shape by holding the mouse over the shape until you see a four-way directional arrow cursor. Drag the entire shape to where you need it to be. Your drawing should now look something like Figure 17.7.

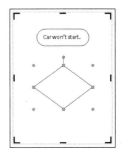

**Figure 17.7.** Adding another shape to the flowchart

9. Right-click the Decision shape, click Add Text, and type **Is car in Park?**

**Hack**

To make the shape fit the size of the text inside it, choose Text Box Tools ⇨ Format, and click the Text Box Styles dialog box launcher. Click the Text Box tab of the Format AutoShape dialog box and select the Resize AutoShape to fit text option.

**10.** Choose Insert ⇨ Shapes ⇨ Lines ⇨ Arrow. Draw a line downward from the bottom of the terminator shape by clicking and dragging it downward. Release the mouse button when your drawing looks something like Figure 17.8. You should see two red dots, indicating that the line is connected to both shapes. When you move one of the shapes, the line stays connected and stretches or shrinks as needed.

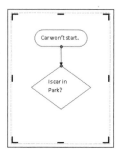

**Figure 17.8.** Connecting a line to a shape

## Drawing freeform shapes and lines

You can include freehand line drawings in Word. Choose Insert ⇨ Shapes ⇨ Lines ⇨ Freeform to create a freeform shape like the one shown in Figure 17.9. Drag the mouse pointer to draw a shape. To draw a shape that has an enclosed interior space, drag the mouse pointer until you intersect a line you have already drawn to enclose the shape. If you release the mouse button before you enclose the shape, a new line starts from the point where you release the mouse, and Word assumes you want this to be a fixed point in your freeform shape. You can cancel this last line by pressing Esc.

**Figure 17.9.** A freeform shape drawn with the mouse

Choose Insert ⇨ Shapes ⇨ Lines ⇨ Scribble to create a freeform line. Once you create a freeform shape or line, you can stretch and manipulate it as you would any other shape or line.

**Inside Scoop**

Freehand drawing works best if you have a Tablet PC or drawing stylus, but you can still create shapes using a mouse as well. If you intend to create more sophisticated drawings, I highly recommend using a drawing program such as FreeHand MX instead of Word.

# Changing shapes and lines

Once you insert shapes or lines into your document, you can manipulate them in many ways. You can replace one shape with another, stretch or rotate a shape, arrange them from back to front, and group them together or separate them.

## Changing an existing shape

To change an existing shape, first click on the shape so that the handles are displayed, as shown in Figure 17.10. Every shape has nine handles. Four blue dots are at the four corners surrounding the shape, forming a rectangle. The corner dots allow you to stretch or squeeze the shape vertically and horizontally at the same time. The two squares on the vertical borders allow you to stretch or squeeze the shape horizontally. The two squares on the horizontal borders allow you

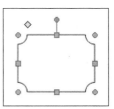

**Figure 17.10.** The handles allow you to resize and position the shape.

to stretch or squeeze the shape vertically. The top green dot is used for rotating the shape. If you mouse over this top dot, you see an arrow indicating that you can use it to rotate the shape. When you drag the dot, the shape pivots around its center.

In addition to the handles surrounding a shape, some shapes have a yellow diamond handle. This handle is used to adjust the size of some additional detail in the shape, such as the size of the arrowhead, or in the case of the sample shape shown in Figure 17.10 (the plaque shape), the diamond adjusts the size of the cutaway curve. Figure 17.11 shows how the same shape looks after dragging the yellow diamond to increase the size of the cutaway curve.

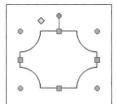

**Figure 17.11.** The yellow diamond handle moves interior lines in a more complex shape.

## Replacing a shape with another shape

To change an existing shape and replace it with another shape, click the shape, choose Drawing Tools ⇨ Format ⇨ Change Shape in the Shape Styles group, and click a new shape. (If you have added text to your shape, it is now a text box, in which case you choose Text Box Tools ⇨ Format ⇨ Change Shape and click a shape. If you have added text, you can't convert your shape to a line or freeform shape.) The new shape replaces the old one, retaining the same approximate dimensions and any style or formatting from the earlier shape.

## Resizing shapes

I described earlier how you can use the handles around the shape to stretch or squeeze it to the desired size. For more extensive size controls, click the dialog box launcher in the lower-right corner of the Size group of the Format tab of Drawing Tools to display the Size tab of the Format AutoShape dialog box shown in Figure 17.12. You can set the absolute height or width in linear units (inches), or you can select the Relative radio button to specify a percentage of some other element of the document. You can select from Margin, Page, Top Margin, Bottom Margin, Inside Margin, or Outside Margin for height, and Margin, Page, Left Margin, Right Margin, Inside Margin, or Outside Margin for width. You can specify the shape's rotation (select or type a number between 0 and 360 degrees). You can scale the dimensions by percentage as well.

**Figure 17.12.** Adjusting the size controls of a shape

**Bright Idea**

If you want to create multiple shapes of the same size, first create one and then copy and paste the shape to create more shapes of exactly the same size.

## Arranging shapes

Word has several ways to arrange shapes on a page. You can determine the shape's position relative to the entire page, move it in front of or behind other text or shapes, or determine how or whether text wraps around the shape. You can also align a shape or shapes or distribute more than one shape evenly, either vertically or horizontally. You can use a nonprinting visual grid to aid you in determining how shapes should align. You can also group shapes together so that they move as one or ungroup them to manipulate them individually. Finally, you can flip shapes at right angles.

### Positioning shapes or drawings on a page

There are several commands available to you for positioning a shape on the page. In addition to moving the shape by dragging it with the mouse, you can use the keyboard shortcuts summarized in Table 17.1. These commands also work for SmartArt shapes described later in this chapter. To position the shape or drawing relative to the page, choose Drawing Tools ⇨ Format ⇨ Position, and select the desired position.

**Table 17.1.** Keyboard commands for shapes and SmartArt

| Keyboard | Function |
| --- | --- |
| Tab | If a shape is selected, moves to the next shape |
| Shift+Tab | If a shape is selected, moves to the previous shape |
| Escape | Undoes the selection of a shape |
| Left arrow | Nudge the shape to the left |
| Right arrow | Nudge the shape to the right |
| Up arrow | Nudge the shape upward |
| Down arrow | Nudge the shape downward |

If you select Inline with Text, this places the shape or drawing at the left margin. If there is text on the page, the text appears above and below the shape or drawing but does not wrap around it. The With Text Wrapping options tightly wrap text around the shape. You can choose from nine positions for the shape on the page within this set of options, including top left, middle right, and so on.

Choose Drawing Tools ⇨ Format ⇨ Position ⇨ More Layout Options to display the Advanced Layout dialog box. Click the Picture Position tab to see the many picture position settings shown in Figure 17.13.

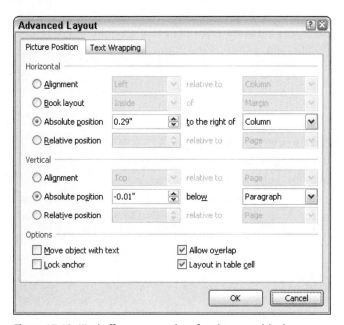

**Figure 17.13.** Word offers many settings for picture positioning.

## Text wrapping

If you insert a shape or drawing into a document that also contains text, the text can wrap around the shape or drawing in any number or ways. To select the text wrapping method, click the shape or drawing to select it and choose Drawing Tools ⇨ Format ⇨ Text Wrapping to see the options displayed in Figure 17.14. (Your screen may look slightly different depending on your PC's screen resolution.) Most of the text-wrapping options are self-explanatory, but a few require a bit of clarification beyond the little dog in the command button.

**Watch Out!**

Once you put a shape or drawing behind text, you can't get at it without removing the text. Make sure to move the shape or drawing behind the text as your last change.

The option In Line with Text wraps text until it encounters a shape or drawing, resuming the text at the lower-right edge of the shape or drawing. This text wrapping style rarely looks good. I recommend avoiding it if possible. The Square option wraps text around the shape leaving a rectangle (not necessarily a square). This is useful with irregular shapes, where wrapping text around the shape makes it hard to read without skipping a line. The Tight and Through options are almost the same, except that Tight wraps text only up to the right and left edges of the shape, where Through also inserts text into any space within the shape. The Behind Text setting places the shape or drawing behind the text as a background. It's a good idea to render the shape semitransparent (see later in this chapter) to aid legibility of the text. Obviously, the same applies to putting a shape in front of text, unless the text is intended only as a design element and is not intended to be read.

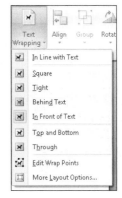

**Figure 17.14.** Text-wrapping options

Use the Edit Wrap Points option to finely tune how closely the text wraps on each line. You can move existing points along the shape without changing the shape itself to adjust how closely the text moves in toward the shape. You can also click to add additional wrap points for more precision, as shown in Figure 17.15.

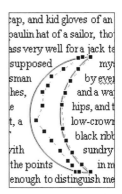

**Figure 17.15.** Adding wrap points to adjust text wrapping around a shape

### Moving a shape forward or backward

If you have overlapping shapes or shapes and text, you need to be able to move something toward the foreground (or the top layer) or toward the background (or the bottom layer). To move a shape to the foreground, choose Drawing Tools ⇨ Format ⇨ Bring to Front. To move a shape forward one level, choose Drawing Tools ⇨ Format ⇨ Bring to Front ⇨ Bring Forward. To bring a shape in front of text, choose Drawing Tools ⇨ Format ⇨ Bring to Front ⇨ Bring in Front of Text. To move a shape to the background, choose Drawing Tools ⇨ Format ⇨ Send to Back. To move a shape backward one level, choose Drawing Tools ⇨ Format ⇨ Send to Back ⇨ Send Backward. To send a shape in back of text, choose Drawing Tools ⇨ Format ⇨ Send to Back ⇨ Send Behind Text.

### Aligning shapes

You can align shapes relative to each other, to the page, or to the margins. You can align one shape, one group of shapes, or several individually selected shapes. To align a shape or shapes, select the shape or shapes and choose Drawing Tools ⇨ Format ⇨ Align to display the menu shown in Figure 17.16. Because alignment is relative, check and see which setting is appropriate for you: Align to Page, Align to Margin, or Align Selected Objects (if you have more than one object selected). Next, you can choose to align the shapes left, right, center, top, bottom, or middle. Alternatively, you can distribute the shapes horizontally or vertically (as you would rows or columns in a table).

**Figure 17.16.** Shape alignment commands

If you have lots of small shapes to align, such as in an organizational chart, it's best to use a grid to help you align and order your presentation. To do so, first choose Drawing Tools ⇨ Format ⇨ Align ⇨ Show Gridlines. Your document page now looks like a piece of graph paper. The gridlines are there to aid you in your page layout — they won't be printed. Next, choose Drawing Tools ⇨ Format ⇨ Align ⇨ Grid Settings to see the Drawing Grid dialog

**Hack**
To select more than one shape, hold down the Shift key while clicking each shape.

box shown in Figure 17.17. When gridlines are displayed, objects align to the nearest gridlines. This is especially useful when drawing rectangular shapes. Select the Snap objects to grid when the gridlines are not displayed option to align shapes to the nearest gridlines when the gridlines are not displayed. Select the Snap objects to other objects option to make it easier to connect lines to boxes, and so forth. Figure 17.18 shows a sample of a drawing created using gridlines, with the rectangles and lines snapping the gridlines.

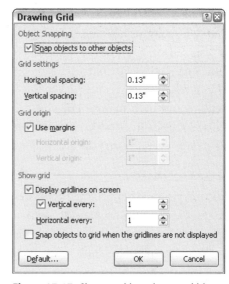

**Figure 17.17.** Change grid settings to aid in aligning objects in your drawing.

### Grouping shapes

You can group shapes together to form more complex drawings. Once grouped, you can perform actions upon the group, such as resizing, moving, and formatting. To group shapes together, select them by holding down the Shift key and clicking each one until all shapes (and lines) are selected that you want to group together. You can tell that you have selected them because all of the move handles are visible, as shown in Figure 17.19. Choose Drawing Tools ⇨ Format ⇨ Group ⇨

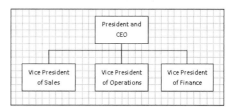

**Figure 17.18.** An organizational chart created using gridlines

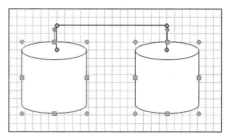

**Figure 17.19.** Shapes and lines selected prior to grouping

Group to group the selected shapes together. Notice that all the grouped shapes are now treated as one large shape with one set of handles, as shown in Figure 17.20. If you want to make a change to one of the shapes after grouping, choose Drawing Tools ⇨ Format ⇨ Group ⇨ Ungroup. You can make a change and then choose Drawing Tools ⇨ Format ⇨ Group ⇨ Regroup to regroup the shapes back together again.

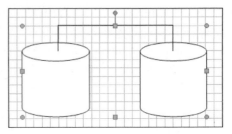

**Figure 17.20.** Shapes and lines after grouping

### Flipping or rotating shapes

Besides using the top handle to rotate the shape around 360 degrees, you can also rotate the shape 90 degrees to the left or right by selecting the shape and choosing Drawing Tools ⇨ Format ⇨ Rotate ⇨ Rotate Left 90° (or Rotate Right 90°). You can also flip the shape along the vertical (or horizontal) axis by choosing Drawing Tools ⇨ Format ⇨ Rotate ⇨ Flip Vertical (or Flip Horizontal). Choosing Drawing Tools ⇨ Format ⇨ Rotate ⇨ More Rotation Options displays the Size tab of the Format AutoShape dialog box, where you can specify a rotation amount by degrees from 0 to 360.

## Working with shape styles

You can choose from a large assortment of ready-made shape styles to add color, borders, and shading to your shapes. To do so, select a shape or group of shapes and choose Drawing Tools ⇨ Format. Click the More arrow in the list of shape styles to see more of the shape styles available, as shown in Figure 17.21. Note that as you move your mouse over the shape style, the selected shape or

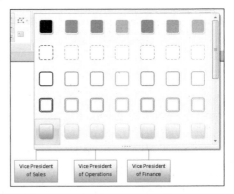

**Figure 17.21.** The Shape Styles gallery

group of shapes changes to give you a preview of what the shape will look like in the new style. Click the shape style to apply it to your selected shape or group of shapes. Figure 17.22 shows the plain organizational chart after a shape style has been applied to it. There is no "plain" shape style — once you select shape styles, you cannot switch back to plain lines except by clicking Undo (or pressing

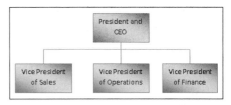

**Figure 17.22.** A simple organizational chart with shape styles applied

Ctrl+Z). You can, however, make changes to the preset shape styles (including changing things back to plain lines) using the formatting commands described in the next section.

## Formatting shapes

Besides the ready-made styles available to you in the Shape Styles gallery, you can make changes to the color or fill pattern of a shape and change the color, pattern, or weight of its border lines. Special effects also allow you to add shadows and three-dimensional perspective to your shapes.

### Changing the shape's color or fill pattern

To change the background color or fill pattern, select a shape or group of shapes and choose Drawing Tools ⇨ Format ⇨ Shape Fill. Clicking the paint bucket itself fills the entire shape with whatever is currently selected (just like the Paint Bucket tool in the Windows Paint accessory or many other graphics tools). If you click on the arrow, you can select a color, picture, gradient, texture, or pattern from the menu.

Figure 17.23 shows gradient options previewed by moving the mouse over the selection. If you choose a theme color, your color changes along with the other aspects of your document when you change themes. If you choose a gradient, the gradient's color also changes with a theme change. Clicking More Gradients displays the Fill Effects dialog box shown in Figure 17.24. Note that if you select the Preset radio button in the Colors option, you can choose from a long list of gradient options. The Transparency slider can be used to make the shape more or less transparent. This is especially useful to make text within the shape more legible by rendering the gradient fill more transparent. The More Colors menu selection on the Shape Fill command also has a transparency option.

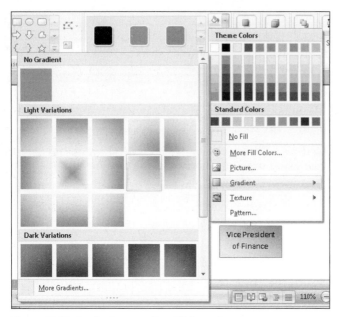

**Figure 17.23.** Previewing a gradient fill for a shape

The Texture menu option on the Shape Fill menu in the Shape Styles group allows you to include a photorealistic texture pattern, such as burlap, linen, marble, wood grain, and so on. The Pattern menu option is a remnant from the past that shows bitmap fill patterns familiar to paint program users of early Macs and PCs, such as tiles, checkerboards, and interlocking bricks, which are good for giving that mid-1980s Apple ImageWriter look to something. You can also include a picture file as a background image. If

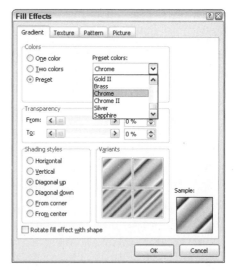

**Figure 17.24.** Selecting a preset gradient fill color set

you want Word to squeeze the entire picture into each shape, choose the Picture menu option. If you have a picture of something that you intend to use as a texture (such as a picture of a rock wall or the ocean waves), use the Texture menu option and then click More Textures. Select your picture in the dialog box that follows.

## Changing the shape's lines

You can change the way a shape's outline is displayed or the way a line appears by choosing Drawing Tools ⇨ Format ⇨ Shape Outline. Clicking the shape outline button itself changes the color of the outline. If you click on the arrow, you can select a color, weight, dash, arrow, or pattern from the menu, as shown in Figure 17.25. If you choose a theme color, your color changes along with the other aspects of your document when you change themes.

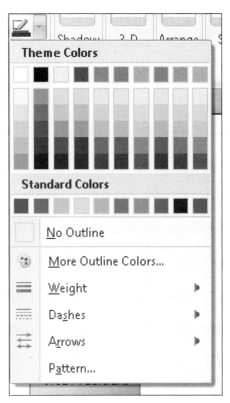

**Figure 17.25.** Changing the border or line style

## Adding special effects to shapes

Apart from adding colors and fills and rotating shapes around, Word has provided some additional effects to help you give your illustrations more visual interest: shadow and 3-D effects.

### Shadow effects

To add shadow effects to your shape, select your shape or group of shapes, choose Drawing Tools ⇨ Format ⇨ Shadow Effects, and click the arrow to

---

**Watch Out!**

If you have a group of shapes with lines, ungroup them first because Word treats shape outlines and connecting lines in the same way. For example, if you want to remove borders from shapes, it will also remove any connecting lines.

see the options shown in Figure 17.26. Note that as you move your mouse over a shadow effect, the effect is previewed live for your selected shape. Drop shadows give the appearance of the shape hovering over the page. Perspective shadows show the shape in perspective with a vanishing point. You can also select Shadow Color to select a color other than gray for your shadow. You can also choose a semitransparent rather than an opaque shadow from the Shadow Color option.

Choose Drawing Tools ➪ Format ➪ Shadow Effects ➪ Shadow On/Off to toggle between shadow and no shadow, as shown in Figure 17.27. The surrounding buttons allow you to nudge the shadow up, down, right, or left.

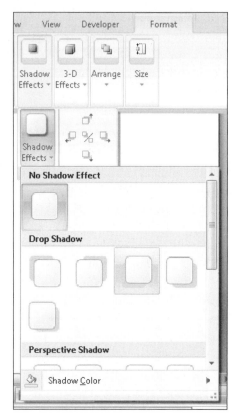

**Figure 17.26.** Selecting a shadow effect

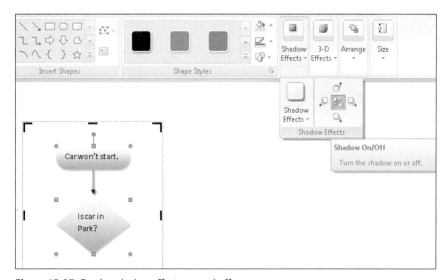

**Figure 17.27.** Turning shadow effects on and off

## 3-D effects

To add 3-D effects to your shape, select your shape or group of shapes, choose Drawing Tools ➪ Format ➪ 3-D Effects, and click the arrow to see the options shown in Figure 17.28. Note that as you move your mouse over a 3-D effect, the effect is previewed live for your selected shape. Parallel 3-D effects give the appearance of technical illustrations, while Perspective 3-D effects show the shape in perspective with a vanishing point. Select 3-D Color to select a color other than gray for your shaded sides of the 3-D shape. Select Depth to choose the depth of the three-dimensional shape. The depth is measured in points, from 0 to 288 if you have a parallel representation of three dimensions, or from 0 to infinity if you have perspective representation of three dimensions. This Infinity setting goes close to a vanishing point, as shown in Figure 17.29. Select Direction to choose from which angle you view the 3-D shape, and whether parallel or perspective. Select Lighting to pick a light source direction and a brightness setting (Bright, Normal, or Dim). Select Surface to choose what type of surface the three-dimensional shape will have: the choices are Matte, Plastic, Metal, and Wire Frame.

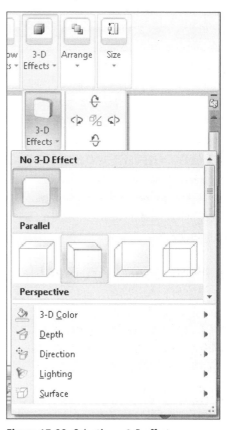

**Figure 17.28.** Selecting a 3-D effect

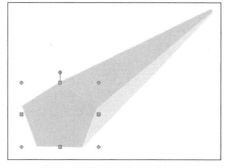

**Figure 17.29.** A shape with the depth set to Infinity

**Watch Out!**

If you select a shape that is already three-dimensional, such as Cube, you won't be able to apply 3-D effects and will have fewer things to work with. Instead, use the two-dimensional equivalent (such as a square) and apply 3-D effects to get the most control over the shape. Unfortunately, you can't make a sphere — applying 3-D effects to a circle makes a cylinder.

Choose Drawing Tools ⇨ Format ⇨ 3-D Effects ⇨ 3-D On/Off to toggle between two and three dimensions. The surrounding buttons allow you to tilt the 3-D shape forward, backward, right, or left.

# Taking advantage of SmartArt graphics

SmartArt graphics in Word 2007 evolved from ready-made diagrams available in earlier versions of Word. The diagram gallery is greatly expanded, the graphics have more features, and the colors, fonts, and effects change to match your current theme.

## Adding a SmartArt graphic to your document

To insert a SmartArt graphic, choose Insert ⇨ SmartArt to display the dialog box shown in Figure 17.30. Click the category list at the left to see a specific type of SmartArt graphic, and then click the specific graphic you want to use in your document. To add a SmartArt graphic to your document, follow these steps:

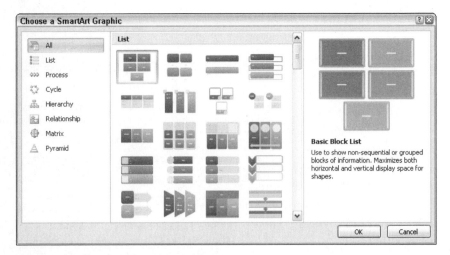

**Figure 17.30.** Choosing a SmartArt graphic

1. Choose Insert ⇨ SmartArt.

2. Click a category (Process for this example).

3. Click a SmartArt graphic (Basic Process for this example). You see a description of the graphic in the window to the right.

4. Click OK. The SmartArt graphic is inserted into your document, as shown in Figure 17.31. The grips (areas with little dots) at the corners and sides of the SmartArt graphic frame act as handles to size the graphic on the page. You can also select individual shapes within the SmartArt graphic and modify them as you would other shapes.

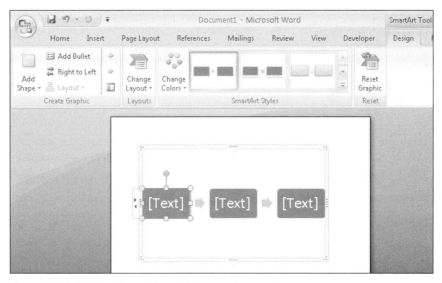

**Figure 17.31.** Adding a SmartArt graphic to your document

5. To add text, you can either click on each text section in the graphic and type text, or click the arrow on the left side of the graphic frame to show a text window, as shown in Figure 17.32. The second method is used here.

6. Type **Testing** in the first line. Notice that it appears in the first box and the font is sized appropriately.

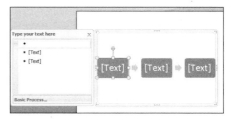

**Figure 17.32.** Adding text to the SmartArt graphic in the text window

7. If you press Enter at this point, another box is added for additional processes. However, you want to keep just three, so click in the next box in the text window marked *[Text]* and type **Deployment**. Notice that the text in this and the first box both are reduced in size. The longer word, *Deployment*, fits in the box, and the word *Testing* is reduced in size so that the font sizes match for each box.

8. Click in the last box in the text window marked [Text] and type **Maintenance**, and click the close box for the text window. Your graphic should look like Figure 17.33.

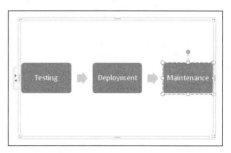

**Figure 17.33.** A SmartArt graphic with text added

At this point, you can add more boxes to the graphic, add bullets, or change the direction of the process to right-to-left. Click Change Layout to select a different process graphic (your text transfers over to the new graphic). Click Change Colors to choose different colors. If you make lots of changes and want to revert to the original, click Reset Graphic. This retains your text but undoes any additional formatting. You can edit the text at any time by clicking text within the graphic or by expanding the text window and editing the text there.

## Working with SmartArt Styles

You can add to the visual impact of your SmartArt graphics by applying SmartArt styles. To do so, click the SmartArt style. You can preview what your graphic will look like by moving your mouse over the different styles while your graphic is selected. Click the More arrow to see the entire list of styles. Figure 17.34 shows the SmartArt graphic created in the earlier example after applying the Bird's Eye Scene SmartArt style.

**Figure 17.34.** Adding a SmartArt style for visual impact

## Just the facts

- You can create illustrations using shapes and lines in Word 2007.

- Inserting a drawing canvas into your document allows you to manipulate the background and outer dimensions of an illustration more readily.

- SmartArt graphics offer a ready-made set of typical diagrams that can be used quickly and easily.

- You can take advantage of the Shape and SmartArt styles to add polish and visual impact to your illustrations.

GET THE SCOOP ON...
How to create charts ▪ Choosing the right chart type ▪
Modifying chart data ▪ Linking charts to Excel spread-
sheets ▪ Chart layouts and styles

# Add Charts to Present Your Data

*Chapter 18*

Sometimes you need to graphically display data to best convey its meaning. Word provides you with a wide range of chart styles to help you accomplish this. Because the Microsoft Office application best suited to the manipulation and analysis of data is Excel, Word 2007 integrates directly with Excel to help you create charts. If you don't have Excel installed or need to use Compatibility Mode, Microsoft Graph provides you with more rudimentary data sheet tools.

Word 2007 has a large number of chart layouts available, as well as ready-made chart styles that you can select from a gallery. One very useful improvement is that when you insert a chart, it already includes sample data so that you can see what the chart will look like. It's easy to replace the sample data with real data of your own.

## Creating charts

There are several ways to create a chart and include it in Word, depending on how you get the data for your chart. If you are creating a chart by typing data as you create your document, you can choose Insert ⇨ Chart to see the Insert Chart dialog box with chart styles grouped by type, as shown in Figure 18.1.

## Selecting a chart type

In the list of chart types shown in Figure 18.1, you can choose whatever type best conveys the information about your data. Table 18.1 summarizes the various chart types. For each chart type, there are several chart subtypes. Most chart types require at least two series of data to compare. Some chart types are intended to show more series (such as bubble charts).

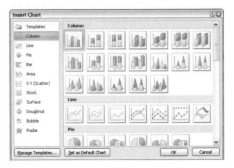

**Figure 18.1.** Choosing a chart type

### Table 18.1. Chart types and their uses

| Type | Typical Function |
| --- | --- |
| Column | Use to compare data or show changes over time. |
| Line | Use to compare data and identify trends. |
| Pie | Use to show proportional allocation of a resource. |
| Bar | Use to compare data; better than column to show wide variations in data along x-axis. |
| Area | Use to show the collective effect of a value over time. |
| XY (Scatter) | Use to help identify patterns. |
| Stock | Use to show stock performance. |
| Surface | Use to show optimum results with various combinations of data. |
| Doughnut | Use to show proportional allocation like a pie chart, but over time. |
| Bubble | Use to compare values using x and y values and a bubble size to indicate a third value. |
| Radar | Use to compare aggregate values of several data series. |

**Inside Scoop**

If you want to use one of the more modern charts in Word 2007 but want to distribute your document electronically to someone with an earlier Word version, you can still do this as long as the recipient doesn't need to edit the chart: it gets converted into a picture.

The following procedure assumes you have Excel installed and are working in Word 2007 format. To add a new chart to your document and customize it with your own data, follow these steps:

1. Open a document, and choose Insert ⇨ Chart.

2. Click the chart type. In this example, click Column.

3. Click the chart subtype. In this example, click 3-D Cylinder.

4. Click OK to insert the chart into your document. Word resizes the document window to the left half of your screen and opens an Excel spreadsheet window in the right half, as shown in Figure 18.2.

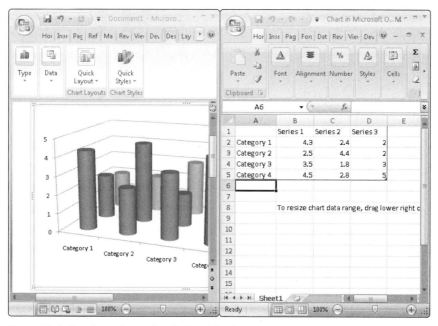

**Figure 18.2.** Creating a chart using Word and Excel

5. The chart contains sample data. You can modify the existing labels and data to fit your own data. For this example, click in the Excel spreadsheet cell A2 containing Category 1 and type **North**, and press Enter. Notice that the corresponding chart label in the Word document changes as well.

6. Repeat the operation for Categories 2 through 4, replacing them with **South**, **East**, and **West**.

7. Click in the Excel spreadsheet cell B1 containing Series 1 and type **2007**.

8. Repeat the operation for Series 2 and 3, replacing them with **2008** and **2009**.

9. To add an additional series, click in the cell E1 (column E, row 1) in the Excel spreadsheet and type **2010**. Note that the chart's data range automatically extends to the next column.

10. Next, add sample data in cells E2, E3, E4, and E5 by typing **4**, **4**, **5**, and **3** into the respective cells.

11. Click the Close box in the spreadsheet window. Your chart should now look like Figure 18.3.

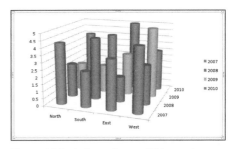

**Figure 18.3.** A chart after modifying and adding data

## Using a chart template

If you want to save a chart's formatting and layout to use for future charts, select the chart and choose Chart Tools ⇨ Design ⇨ Save As Template. Assign the chart a name and click Save. It is stored in a separate template file with the file extension .crtx. When you want to use the chart template again, choose Insert ⇨ Chart ⇨ Templates and select it by locating it in the My Templates area. When you mouse over a chart template, the name you chose for it appears over a thumbnail representation of the chart, as shown in Figure 18.4. Choose Insert ⇨ Chart ⇨ Manage Templates to manage your chart template files.

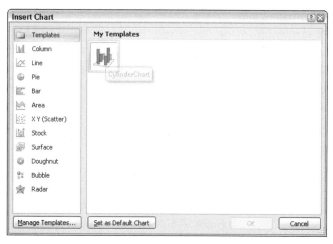

**Figure 18.4.** Selecting a chart template

## Adding a chart using Microsoft Graph

If you have not installed Excel or are working in Compatibility Mode, your charting capabilities are somewhat limited. When you choose Insert ⇨ Chart in such a case, your screen will look something like Figure 18.5.

You can select from a variety of chart types by choosing Chart ⇨ Chart Type from the pull-down menu to see the Chart Type dialog box shown in Figure 18.6. While the charts available using Microsoft Graph are not as visually polished, all the chart types listed earlier in Table 18.1 are available, and most of the settings for data formatting are there as well. If you need to have backward compatibility for recipients of the chart who have earlier versions of Word, this is a viable option. If professional graphics are important and the chart does not need to be edited by recipients, create the

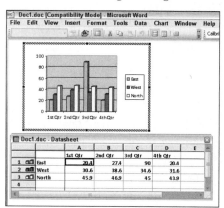

**Figure 18.5.** Creating a chart using Microsoft Graph

graph in Word 2007 using the new chart styles and save the file in Word 97 - 2003 format. The chart appears visually as it would in Word 2007, but it is only a picture in the older file format.

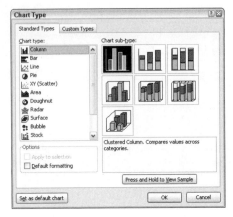

**Figure 18.6.** Selecting a chart type using Microsoft Graph

# Working with chart data

You can modify chart data of an existing chart in several ways. You can select a data range, edit the content of individual data cells, or change the chart axes. You can also link a chart in Word to an external Excel spreadsheet. An external Excel spreadsheet can, in turn, be linked to other external sources of data, such as network database servers, relational database files, and other sources.

## Selecting a data range

To select a data range to chart within an existing datasheet in Word, select the chart and choose Chart Tools ⇨ Design ⇨ Select Data. A screen something like Figure 18.7 appears. Much like when you first insert a chart, Word resizes the document window to the left half of your screen and opens an Excel spreadsheet window in the right half, with the data range selected. In addition, the Select Data Source dialog box appears.

The screen becomes fairly confusing at this point, especially if you are not an Excel guru. I'll describe each element. First, in the Select Data Source dialog box, you can specify the chart range in the Chart data range field. By default, this is the named data table =Table1[#All]. The parameter [#All] indicates that all rows and cells are included in the chart. You can specify another table or named range by typing the table or named range after an equal sign. You can also specify a cell range, such as =Sheet1!$A$1:$E$5 in our example and Figure 18.8. Clicking the Collapse Dialog button (the tiny spreadsheet with a red arrow selecting a cell) in the right side of the Chart data range field allows you to select the range by dragging it with the mouse, as shown in Figure 18.8, in which only the first four rows and columns are selected. Notice how the Chart data range field now has the range =Sheet1!$A$1:$D$4 and that the chart in the underlying window has fewer rows of cylinders. To accept such a modification to the data range, click the Expand Dialog button (with a rectangle and a downward pointing red arrow in the right side of the Chart data range field where the Collapse Dialog button was) and click OK.

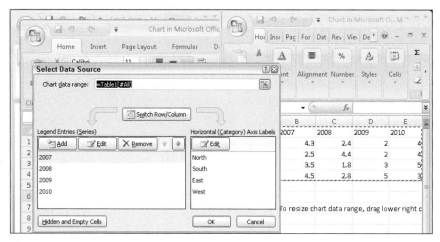

**Figure 18.7.** Selecting a data range for a chart

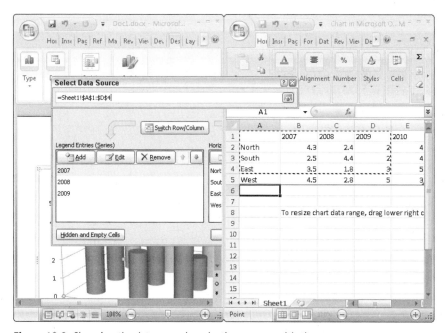

**Figure 18.8.** Changing the data range by selecting a range with the mouse

## Switching row/column that forms chart axis

You can swap the row and column that form the series (legend entries) and the category (horizontal axis labels). To do so, select the chart and choose Chart Tools ⇨ Design ⇨ Switch Row/Column.

## Editing chart data

If you need to change chart data after inserting it into the document, you can do so easily. To edit an individual series or category, select the chart and choose Chart Tools ⇨ Design ⇨ Select Data. With the series, you can add, edit, or remove the legend entries as well as the data by clicking the corresponding button in the dialog box. With the category, you can only edit the horizontal axis labels. To go directly to the spreadsheet to edit the data directly, select the chart and choose Chart Tools ⇨ Design ⇨ Edit Data.

## Determining how to handle hidden and empty cells

You can change settings for how hidden or empty cells are handled by choosing Chart Tools ⇨ Design ⇨ Select Data ⇨ Hidden and Empty Cells. By default, empty cells are shown as gaps because you can also give them a zero value, and with some chart types, connect the surrounding data points with a line (as if to indicate a trend). By default, Word hides data in hidden rows and columns but you can select the check box for this option to display the hidden data.

## Pasting a chart from an Excel spreadsheet

When you have a situation where you frequently create a report in a Word document format that includes data that you pull from a specific Excel spreadsheet, you can create your chart in Excel and then paste the chart into your Word document. The Word document is then *linked* to the Excel spreadsheet; if you make changes to the data in the Excel spreadsheet, the chart is updated in the Word document. You can also create a chart in Excel and paste it along with the values into Word with no link, if you don't need to update data from the Excel spreadsheet but want access to the data once in Word. This is called *embedding* the chart. Finally, you can paste a chart you create in Excel simply as a picture, where no data manipulation is possible. This feature is useful if the chart is final or if you don't want the recipients to manipulate it. To paste a chart into Word from Excel, follow these steps:

1. Start Excel and select the data range for which you want a chart.

2. Create the chart in Excel by clicking the chart type from the Charts group of the Insert menu.

3. Select the chart and press Ctrl+C, or choose Home ⇨ Copy to copy the chart to the Clipboard.

4. Open your destination Word document and position your cursor where you want to insert the chart.

5. In Word, press Ctrl+V or choose Home ⇨ Paste to paste the Excel chart from the Clipboard into your Word document.

6. Click the Paste Option button, as shown in Figure 18.9.

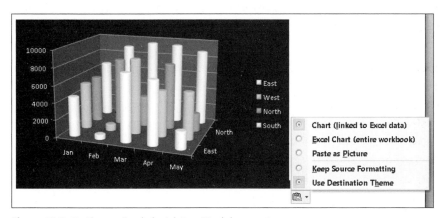

**Figure 18.9.** Pasting an Excel chart into a Word document

7. To paste the chart with a link to the spreadsheet, select the Chart (linked to Excel data) option. To embed the chart, select the Excel Chart (entire workbook) option. To paste the chart as a picture, select the Paste as Picture option. By default Word uses the document theme of the Word document (the destination theme), but you can elect to preserve formatting from the Excel chart instead by selecting the Keep Source Formatting radio button.

If you have linked a chart to an Excel spreadsheet, choose Chart Tools ⇨ Design ⇨ Refresh Data in the Word document after the Excel spreadsheet has been updated to ensure that you have the latest data displayed in your chart. When you choose Chart Tools ⇨ Design ⇨ Edit Data in a chart that is linked to an Excel spreadsheet, the spreadsheet from which the data is pulled opens so that you can edit the data in Excel.

**Bright Idea**

To create charts based on data from server databases, Access, and other data sources, create a spreadsheet in Excel and use the External Data command to pull in the data. Then create a chart, and paste it as a linked chart into your Word document.

# Formatting your charts

You can change the look of individual charts in many ways. Apart from selecting a chart subtype, you can also decide how much information to display in the chart and how to arrange the data. This is referred to as the chart layout. The colors, textures, and so on are referred to as the chart style. There are both Quick Layouts and Quick Styles to save you time, or you can change individual layout or style elements to suit your needs.

## Selecting a chart layout

The easiest way to select a chart layout is to select the chart and then choose Chart Tools ⇨ Design ⇨ Quick Layout and pick one of the ready-made chart layouts from the thumbnail views, as shown in Figure 18.10. For some Quick Layouts you may need to supply additional information, such as a title. Placeholder labels appear in your chart, as shown in Figure 18.11, in which Chart Title and Axis Title appear as placeholders. Click in the text box for each placeholder and replace it with appropriate text to complete the chart.

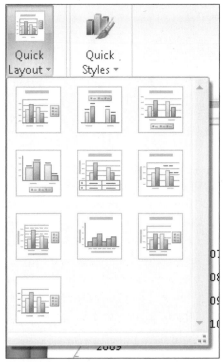

**Figure 18.10.** Selecting a Quick Layout for a chart

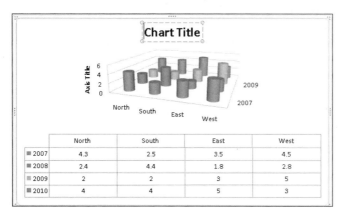

| | North | South | East | West |
|---|---|---|---|---|
| ▪ 2007 | 4.3 | 2.5 | 3.5 | 4.5 |
| ▪ 2008 | 2.4 | 4.4 | 1.8 | 2.8 |
| ▪ 2009 | 2 | 2 | 3 | 5 |
| ▪ 2010 | 4 | 4 | 5 | 3 |

**Figure 18.11.** Replace placeholder text when selecting a Quick Layout with additional labels.

If you want to make more specific changes or just don't find the layout you like in the Quick Layout section, select the chart and then choose Chart Tools ⇨ Layout to see the commands shown in Figure 18.12 (your tab may differ slightly in appearance depending on your screen resolution). This tab gives you literally dozens of command settings for your chart, almost anything you could think of. I suspect this feature is so rich because charting is so critical for Microsoft program managers (especially for PowerPoint presentations), and Word users get the benefit of this richness of features because charting is an integrated component in Office. Rather than walking through each feature, I will summarize them here and give one step-by-step example to give you a feel for how the Layout tools work.

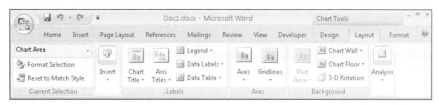

**Figure 18.12.** The Layout tab of Chart Tools provides many options for displaying your chart's data.

The Current Selection group of commands allows you to choose a specific part of the chart to work on. The Insert group allows you to add a picture, shape, or text box to your chart. The Labels group provides you with a way to add labels to various parts of the chart, and allows you to add a data table (a *data table* in this context is a tabular display of the data that is presented to accompany the graphical representation of the data). The Axes group allows you to choose from numerous axis display options and to determine whether the chart should display gridlines and if so what kind. The Background group allows you to make changes to the chart's background features, such as the plot area, chart wall, chart floor, or its 3-D rotation. The Analysis group provides commands that can highlight data features, such as trend lines, and up/down bars.

Among the many features provided on the Layout tab is the ability to add a data table to your chart. To do so, follow these steps:

1. Select the chart.

2. Choose Chart Tools ⇨ Layout ⇨ Data Table so see the options displayed in Figure 18.13.

3. Click Show Data Table with Legend Keys from the Data Table menu to insert the data table into your chart, as shown in Figure 18.14. Note that as the data table is added, the graphical element

**Figure 18.13.** Displaying a data table in your chart

of the chart is reduced to make room for the data table while the surrounding frame of the chart remains the same size.

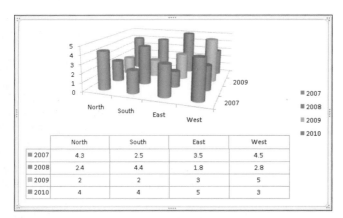

| | North | South | East | West |
|---|---|---|---|---|
| ▪ 2007 | 4.3 | 2.5 | 3.5 | 4.5 |
| ▪ 2008 | 2.4 | 4.4 | 1.8 | 2.8 |
| ▪ 2009 | 2 | 2 | 3 | 5 |
| ▪ 2010 | 4 | 4 | 5 | 3 |

**Figure 18.14.** A chart with a data table added

**4.** Choose Chart Tools ⇨ Layout ⇨ Data Table ⇨ More Data Table Options to see various additional options. Make any desired changes, and then click Close to return to the chart.

## Selecting a chart style

The easiest way to select a chart style is to select the chart and choose Chart Tools ⇨ Design ⇨ Quick Styles and pick one of the ready-made chart styles from the thumbnail views, as shown in Figure 18.15. If you choose from among the Quick Styles, your chart colors and fonts will be compatible with your current document's theme, and will change along with the rest of your document if you change the document theme.

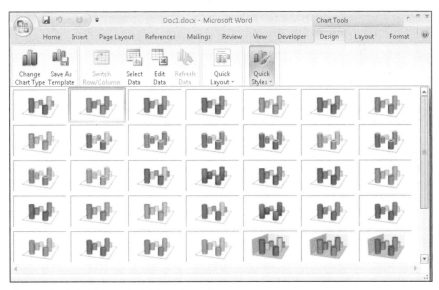

**Figure 18.15.** Selecting a Quick Style for a chart

If you want to change the look of individual aspects of the chart or just don't like the choices in Quick Styles, select the chart and choose Chart Tools ⇨ Format to see more options, as shown in Figure 18.16. To modify the formatting of any section of the chart, first select that section. To do so, you can either click on the section you want to modify with the mouse so that the move handles appear, as shown in Figure 18.17, or pick the area of the chart you want to modify by selecting it from the list in the Current Selection group of the Format tab, as shown in Figure 18.18. To change visual formatting elements to a selected area of the chart, select that area and then click Format Selection to see the relevant options for that selection. The Format [selection] dialog box that corresponds to the chosen chart area usually has some positioning options specific to that chart area and a menu of additional formatting options such as Fill, Border Color, Border Styles, and so on, as indicated in the example in Figure 18.19, shown for the vertical axis chart area. Click Close to close the Format dialog box when you are done.

**Figure 18.16.** The Format tab of Chart Tools gives you many formatting options.

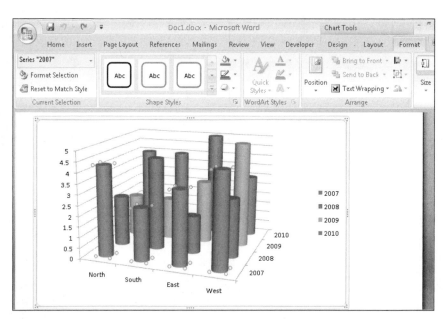

**Figure 18.17.** Selecting an area of the chart to format with the mouse

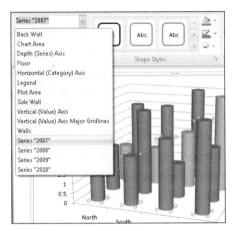

**Figure 18.18.** Selecting an area of the chart to format from the selection menu

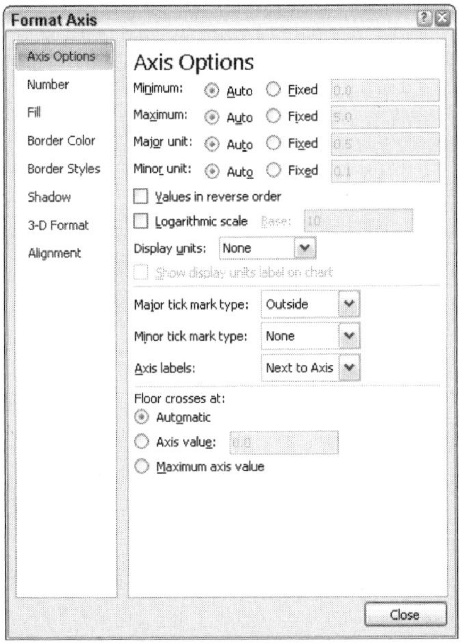

**Figure 18.19.** Formatting options for the Axis chart area

You can also use Shape Styles to change the look of shapes used in the chart or use Shape Styles to change the background of the chart. These change with the document theme. If you want to make changes to any text elements of the chart, first select the chart element that contains the text you want to change, or select the entire chart to change all text in the

**Bright Idea**

When you change format options for a chart area, the changes are made immediately. Drag the formatting dialog box to the side of the chart so that you can view the changes and adjust as necessary before closing the dialog box.

chart. Next, choose Home ⇨ Fonts and select the font you want to use, the point size, and any font attributes you want to change. If you choose from the theme fonts, they will change to match any new document theme you choose. Alternatively, you can take advantage of Word's WordArt Styles for special text treatment. (Chapter 20 covers WordArt in more detail.) Select the chart element containing text and then click Quick Styles from the WordArt Styles group to pick a ready-made text style or click Text Fill, Text Outline, or Text Effects to make individual changes to the text displayed.

Last, you can arrange how a chart appears on a page. You can determine the chart's position relative to the entire page, move it in front of or behind other text or objects, or determine how or whether text wraps around the chart. You can also align a chart to the page or the margin. You can use a nonprinting visual grid to aid you in determining how the chart should align. To set the chart's position relative to text on the page, choose Chart Tools ⇨ Format ⇨ Position and choose one of the options. To determine how or whether text wraps around the chart, choose Chart Tools ⇨ Format ⇨ Text Wrapping and choose one of the options. To align the chart to the page or margin, choose Chart Tools ⇨ Format ⇨ Align and click Align to Page or Align to Margin. The gridlines settings are also on this menu.

## Just the facts

- Word 2007 has a huge selection of charts and many ready-made ones with sample data that you can edit quickly for charts in minutes.
- You can link a chart in Word to Excel spreadsheet data so that the Word document updates when you modify the Excel spreadsheet.
- Word's Quick Layouts for charts provide many ready-made styles to choose from.
- Choosing a Quick Style for charts allows you to keep to a document theme so that the chart's colors and fonts change with the document when you change themes.

# Adding Pictures to Your Document

The advent of digital photography for the consumer has made the inclusion of photographs and other illustrations commonplace and expected in everything from Web pages to printed documents. In this chapter, I show you how to include pictures in your Word documents. You can insert your own digital photographs or work with an extensive collection of clip art.

Word has some convenient details in how it handles pictures. I particularly like how it handles compression of pictures. You can set the amount of detail based on whether your document will be viewed on-screen or on paper or sent as an e-mail attachment. Also, you can insert a caption easily (and automatically, if you like).

## A word about photographs, clip art, and copyright

I'm not a lawyer, so I'm not going to give you a precise description of when it's okay to use an image. When in doubt, consult an expert. However, seriously consider any issues of copyright if you work with photographic images that you didn't create yourself. And if you did create them, consider protecting them. Also, in general, you need to have someone's permission to photographically reproduce his or her image. This permission is usually referred to as a model release form, and many sample forms are available on the Web.

If you are using clip art or stock photos that you have purchased, you usually have the right to reuse them freely, but check the fine print if you are unsure about any limitations that may exist on the images you want to use.

## Adding pictures to your document

You can add digital photographs or other images from a digital image file to your document by choosing Insert ⇨ Picture. By default, Word opens your My Pictures folder in Windows and displays all picture file formats in Thumbnail view, as shown in Figure 19.1. Click Insert to insert the picture directly into your document. If you have a large document with many pictures, you may wish to insert a link to the image file rather than inserting it directly into a document. To do this, click the More arrow next to the Insert button and click Link to File. You can also insert the image file *and* link it to the external file. This is useful if you want to have the image contained within the Word document but want to update if necessary. To use this feature, click the More arrow next to the Insert button and click Insert and Link.

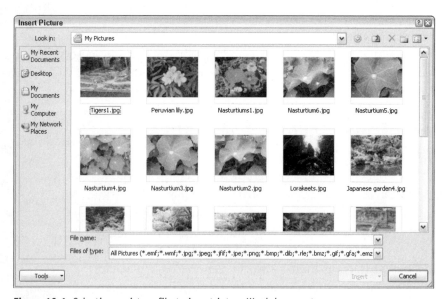

**Figure 19.1.** Selecting a picture file to insert into a Word document

**Inside Scoop**

If you want to make changes to links to image files after inserting them into your document, choose Microsoft Office ⇨ Prepare ⇨ Edit Links to Files.

Once you insert a picture into a document, it appears with sizing handles and a rotation handle, as shown in Figure 19.2, much like a shape, SmartArt, or chart. The Ribbon displays the Format tab for Picture Tools.

**Figure 19.2.** An image file inserted as a picture into a document

# Working with pictures in Word

The Format tab of Picture Tools on the Ribbon provides you with most commands you need to work with pictures in Word. The Adjust group has controls for brightness, contrast, color, compression, changing pictures, and a Reset Picture button (showing a picture with a blue arrow pointing to the left) to return everything to how it was when you inserted the picture. The Picture Styles group has a gallery of preset frame styles, a picture shape option (in which you can select a shape as the frame for your picture), a picture border command, and a set of picture effects. The

---

## Working with Digital Photographs Using Microsoft Office Picture Manager or Other Photo Software

If you are working with a larger group of digital photographs, it makes sense to use the Microsoft Office Picture Manager tool. You can access this tool from Windows by choosing Start ⇨ All Programs ⇨ Microsoft Office ⇨ Microsoft Office Tools ⇨ Microsoft Office Picture Manager. You can crop and rotate pictures. You can also correct color and remove red eye (things not possible from within Word itself). You can perform most of these operations on more than one file at a time, which makes for easier batch processing of images before you bring them into Word.

If you want to do extensive image retouching or manipulation, consider purchasing photo-editing software, such as one of Adobe's Photoshop products.

---

Arrange group allows you to arrange the picture's position on the page and adjust text-wrapping behavior, rotation, and alignment. Finally, the Size group allows you to crop the picture or to specify linear dimensions for the picture on the page (if you prefer this to sizing it with the mouse).

### Adjusting brightness and contrast

To adjust the brightness of a picture, select the picture and choose Picture Tools ⇨ Format ⇨ Brightness. This displays the menu shown in Figure 19.3. This allows you to change the brightness by +/− 40 percent in 10 percent increments. This is really all the practical range you need, but if for some reason you want to specify something outside the range or at smaller increments, click the Picture Corrections Options command on the Brightness menu and use the arrows, slider, or the keyboard to enter a value in the Brightness field.

To adjust the contrast of a picture, select the picture and choose Picture Tools ⇨ Format ⇨ Contrast. A menu similar to the one for Brightness appears from which you can change the contrast by +/− 40 percent in 10 percent increments. As with brightness, this is really all the practical range you need, but if for some reason you want to specify something outside the range or at smaller increments, click the Picture

Corrections Options command on the Contrast menu and use the arrows, slider, or the keyboard to enter a value in the Contrast field.

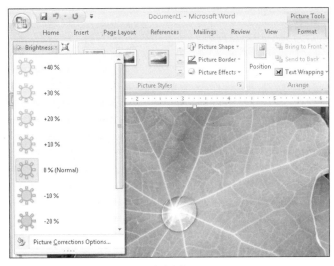

**Figure 19.3.** Adjusting a picture's brightness

## Adjusting colors

Apart from changing brightness or contrast, you can also recolor the picture for a special design treatment by selecting the picture and then choosing Picture Tools ⇨ Format ⇨ Recolor. The menu shown in Figure 19.4 appears. Because this figure is shown here in grayscale, I'll clarify that the color modes are grayscale, sepia (a warm brown tone like an old photograph), washed out, and black and white (extremely high contrast). The dark and light variations are color tints based on the theme colors, so that they change as you change a document's theme.

You can also set a color to be transparent (as in blue or green screen in television and films) so

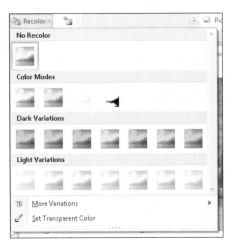

**Figure 19.4.** Picture recoloring options

that the color drops away. This only works with images that have large solid color fields or high contrast. To use this feature, select the picture and then choose Picture Tools ➪ Format ➪ Recolor ➪ Set Transparent Color. The mouse pointer changes to a stylus pointing to a crop mark. Click the picture on the color you want to become transparent. The color drops out of the picture, giving you something like Figure 19.5, in which the blue-sky background has largely dropped out. (The remaining sky is a slightly different blue, so it does not become transparent.)

**Figure 19.5.** Setting a transparent color in a picture

## *Adjusting picture compression*

By default, Word performs data compression on embedded image files upon saving the document. This does not lose any information about the picture but it does allow Word to keep the file size smaller. It does not compress the picture beforehand, because having the full picture in memory allows you to manipulate it more easily. Also by default, the cropped areas of your pictures are deleted to save space. Finally, Word assumes that you want the highest quality resolution of 220 pixels per inch (ppi), which is sufficiently sharp for printed documents and high-resolution monitors.

You can invoke compression before saving the file by selecting the picture or pictures and choosing Picture Tools ➪ Format ➪ Compress Pictures. You might want to do this if you have a document with many large pictures that is hard to scroll through due to the large file size, or if you are using small sections cropped from large image files. You can compress all pictures using the default settings by clicking OK, or click Options to see the settings shown in Figure 19.6. Select the Screen

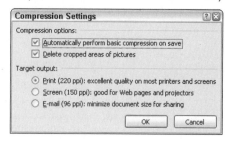

**Figure 19.6.** Adjusting picture compression settings

(150 ppi) setting for smaller picture file sizes that are still the right resolution to appear sharp on Web pages and projection screens. Select
E-mail (96 ppi) for the smallest picture file size. This will still appear
sharp on computer screens of up to 1024 by 768 pixels.

### Changing the picture

If you adjust your page layout, picture frame, and so on, and you just
want to swap the current image for one from another image file while
maintaining the current picture dimensions and picture style settings in
your document, select the picture and choose Picture Tools ⇨ Format ⇨
Change Picture. Select a replacement picture and click Insert to insert
the new picture into the picture frame.

### Resetting picture formatting

If you want to remove any formatting changes you made to a picture,
select the picture and choose Picture Tools ⇨ Format ⇨ Reset Picture.
This removes any brightness, contrast, recoloring, or picture style
changes you have made. It will not undo the Change Picture command,
so if you have added a replacement picture from a new image file, it
remains, but with any formatting changes removed.

## Working with picture styles

Word 2007 provides any number of professional-looking ready-made picture styles if you are looking for something more interesting than a bor-
derless rectangle. You can choose from a gallery of styles by selecting your
picture and then clicking the
thumbnail image of a style in the
picture style gallery in the Picture
Styles group of the Format tab
of Picture Tools. Click the More
arrow to see the entire gallery.
Figure 19.7 shows one of the new
styles (Bevel Perspective). Apart
from this selection of ready-made
styles, you can also make changes
to the picture's shape or border,
or take advantage of other effects.

**Figure 19.7.** Adding a picture style

**Watch Out!**
Using Change Picture doesn't transfer any Brightness, Contrast, or Recolor settings, and if the replacement picture does not have the same aspect ratio (height/width ratio) as the old picture, it matches the widest dimension.

## Picture shape

You can choose from many shapes to form the outside border of your picture. To do so, select the picture and then choose Picture Tools ⇨ Format ⇨ Picture Shape. Pick a shape by clicking it from the shape gallery. Figure 19.8 shows a picture with a hexagon shape. If you are familiar with some graphics and drawing software, you may assume that the picture might wrap around a 3-D shape. This is not the case, although there are some 3-D effects that I discuss later in this chapter.

**Figure 19.8.** Changing the picture shape to a hexagon

## Picture border

You can choose from many borders for your picture. By default, the border of a picture has no outline. However, you can choose to add a visible border to form an outline around your picture. To do so, select the picture and choose Picture Tools ⇨ Format ⇨ Picture Border. To pick a simple line, click Weight (for line weight) and select a line weight measured in points, as shown in Figure 19.9. Note that the line weight you choose is previewed around your picture. You can choose from several multiple-line styles by clicking More Lines from the Weight menu. Alternatively, you can choose a dashed line style by choosing Picture Tools ⇨ Format ⇨ Picture Border ⇨ Dashes. Once you select a border line or dash, you can select a color other than black if you want by choosing Picture Tools ⇨ Format ⇨ Picture Border and clicking a color.

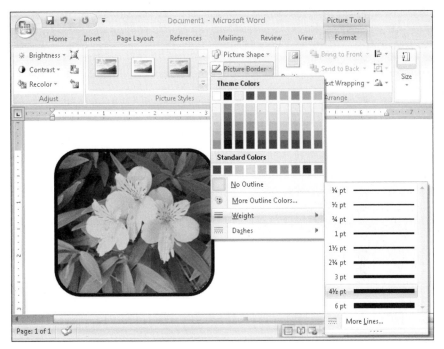

**Figure 19.9.** Adding a border to a picture

## Picture effects

Word provides many picture effects to give your illustration a new look. If you don't want to spend a lot of time playing with these settings, you can choose from one of the Preset effects settings. To choose a preset picture effects setting, select the picture and choose Picture Tools ⇨ Format ⇨ Picture Effects ⇨ Preset to see the gallery of preset options shown in Figure 19.10. Note that the preset effect is previewed as you move your mouse over it. Click the thumbnail of the effect to apply it to your picture. In addition to the preset options, you can choose from six effects or combine several effects. Table 19.1 summarizes these effects.

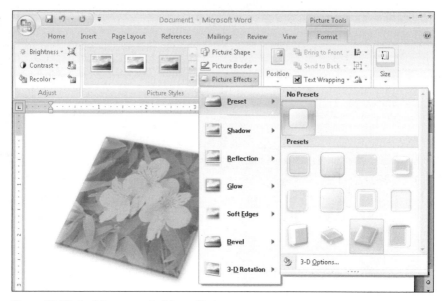

**Figure 19.10.** Applying a preset picture effect

## Table 19.1. Picture effects

| Effect | Description |
|---|---|
| Shadow | Adds a shadow to the picture. Choose from nine different light sources for an outer or inner shadow, or five light sources for a perspective effect. Additional Shadow Options settings include transparency, size, blur, angle, distance, and color. |
| Reflection | Adds a reflection to your picture (as if it is standing on a mirrored surface). Choose from nine variations. |
| Glow | Adds a colored glow around your picture. Choose from 24 variations based on color and width of glowing border or choose additional colors with More Glow Colors. |
| Soft Edges | Adds a soft edge or fade to your picture. Choose from a soft edge width of 1, 2.5, 5, 10, 25, or 50 points. |
| Bevel | Adds a beveled edge to your picture. Choose from 12 bevel styles and click 3-D Options to adjust surface material, lighting, angle, color, and contour. |

| Effect | Description |
| --- | --- |
| 3-D Rotation | Adds a three-dimensional appearance to your picture (as if it were in a physical picture frame or box). Choose from 10 parallel styles, 11 perspective styles, and 4 oblique styles. Click 3-D Rotation Options to adjust rotation along the x-, y-, or z-axis, change the perspective, or adjust picture's position from the "ground." |

### Arranging your picture on the page

You can arrange how a picture appears on a page. You can determine the picture's position relative to the entire page, move it in front of or behind other text or objects, or determine how or whether text wraps around the picture. You can also align a picture to the page or the margin. You can use a nonprinting visual grid to help determine how the picture should align. To set the picture's position relative to text on the page, choose Picture Tools ⇨ Format ⇨ Position and select one of the options. To determine how or whether text wraps around the picture, choose Picture Tools ⇨ Format ⇨ Text Wrapping and select one of the options. To align the picture to the page or margin, choose Picture Tools ⇨ Format ⇨ Align and select Align to Page or Align to Margin. The gridlines settings are also on this menu.

### Sizing and cropping a picture

The corner and side handles of the picture's frame can be dragged to resize the outside dimensions of the picture. Dragging one of the corners reduces or enlarges the picture while preserving its aspect ratio. To make the picture wider or narrower, drag the square handles on the left or right borders of the picture. To make the picture taller or shorter, drag the square handles on the top or bottom borders of the picture up or down. If you use the side or top and bottom handles to resize the picture, the picture will appear distorted accordingly. You can also use the arrows or type a value in the shape height or width box in the Size group of the Format tab of Picture Tools. Clicking the Size dialog box launcher

**Inside Scoop**

You can also add a caption to a picture such as the ones you see throughout this book. To do so, right-click the picture and click Insert Caption. For more information on captions, see Chapter 22.

gives you additional options, as shown in Figure 19.11. You can specify the height or width in inches or in percentage of original size. You can lock the aspect ratio or stretch the picture horizontally and or vertically to match the required dimensions. The picture's dimensions change as you modify the settings. Click the Alt Text tab to specify a text description as an alternative for Web browsers when no graphics display and for users with disabilities. By default, the alternative text is the image file's name.

If you are inserting a picture from an image file and you only want to use part of the image file, you can digitally crop your picture by selecting the picture and choosing Picture Tools ⇨ Format ⇨ Crop. You can then drag the cropping handles in the corners and on the sides to trim off the parts of the image that you don't want to include in your picture, as shown in Figure 19.12. By default, the area trimmed away from the picture during the crop operation is trimmed when the picture is compressed to reduce file size. (The original image file is not affected.)

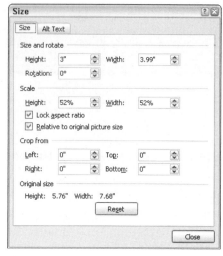

**Figure 19.11.** Picture sizing options

**Figure 19.12.** Cropping a picture

# Adding clip art to your document

You can add clip art to your document in Word, in the form of illustrations, photographs, video, or audio clips. You can download and store collections of clip art organized by theme, and you can search online as well. Microsoft provides over 150,000 images and sounds at no cost, and provides links to other stock photo and image services. Once you insert clip art into your document, you can format it or edit it as needed. To insert clip art into your document, choose Insert ⇨ Clip Art. This opens the Clip Art pane shown in Figure 19.13. You can then use one of the following methods to pick your clip art.

**Figure 19.13.** The Clip Art pane allows you to search for clip art to insert into your document.

## Finding the right clip art

There are several ways to find the right clip art, depending on how much you know about what you want. If you have a very precisely defined need that you can put into a word or two, such as toaster or angry man, then you can probably find your clip art best by typing keywords in the search field. If you prefer to browse through images, you can view thumbnail images of clip art before inserting it into your document, by media type, category, or source. The size of the clip art collection makes a difference, too. If you search Office Online, you might want to narrow your search with keywords. If you are just looking in the clip art media on your PC, the collection may be small enough to browse through it to find what you need.

At the risk of invoking a cliché, you get what you pay for with clip art. While you may have paid a substantial amount to get Microsoft Office, I suspect a much smaller piece of your budget has been given over to developing compelling clip art. The drawings and photographs are fine in their way for departmental reports, school projects, volunteer activities, and the like, but if you are going to incorporate graphics into an advertising flyer or anything more professional, I suggest investing in a subscription to a stock image service.

### Searching with a text string to find the right clip art

Type a keyword or keywords to search for a certain type of image in the Search for field of the Clip Art pane. Try to strike a balance between being too specific and too vague. For example, if you want a picture of a boat, don't type *ketch* — you won't find anything. Don't type *sea*, either, unless you want to look through all the pictures related to the sea. Instead, type **boat**. Click Go when you are ready to start your search.

**Figure 19.14.** Adjusting the scope of your clip art search

You can adjust the scope of the search by clicking the Search in list and choosing from the choices listed in the window, as shown in Figure 19.14. You can click a check box in the list to select the collection and all its subcategories. Click the plus sign to expand a collection to see individual categories. Click the Everywhere check box to search all available collections. You can also select specific media types to look for. Click the Results should be list to limit your search to select types, as shown in Figure 19.15. You can choose from the four basic categories of Clip Art (vector graphic images made of shapes), Photographs (in bitmap formats such as JPEG, PNG, TIFF, or Windows Bitmap), Movies, or Sound files. Movies or sound files can be viewed in your document by double-clicking the filename.

**Figure 19.15.** Selecting a clip art media type to search for

Once you find a candidate clip art file, you can insert it directly into your document by clicking the thumbnail picture, or you can get more information by clicking the More arrow that appears to the right of the thumbnail picture of the clip art when you move your mouse over it. A menu like the one shown in Figure 19.16 appears. Click Preview/Properties to get a larger view of the clip art and find out all the details about it. Figure 19.17 shows a sample.

**Figure 19.16.** Viewing clip art selection details

**Figure 19.17.** Previewing clip art and viewing property details

**Watch Out!**

Practically speaking, it doesn't make much sense to include movies or sound files in Word documents. If you include animated GIF files (those animated Web images), they will only be animated if you save your document as an HTML file and view it with a Web browser.

## Working with the Clip Organizer

If you want to spend some time organizing your clip art, click the Organize clips link in the Clip Art pane. This displays a larger window for browsing and organizing your clip art, as shown in Figure 19.18.

**Figure 19.18.** The Clip Organizer

## Working with Office Online clips

If you want to look for new clip art online or investigate commercial stock photo and clip art services, click the Clip art on Office Online link on the Clip Art pane. This link takes you to the clip art section of Microsoft Office Online, which shows the latest clip art and clip art services. Select the clip art you want and download it to insert it into your document.

## Editing and formatting clip art

Once you insert clip art into your document, you can edit and format it according to the media type. You can use the Picture Tools commands for all images. If the clip art is a vector graphics image file (composed of shapes), you can manipulate individual shapes within the drawing by right-clicking the clip art and clicking Edit Picture. Click on the shape in the clip art that you want to edit and the move handles will appear indicating that it is selected. As an example, Figure 19.19 shows a clip art drawing before and after removing the background shape's color. The image on the left is the original image. The image on the right shows the same image after selecting the background shape, clicking Shape Fill, and selecting No Fill.

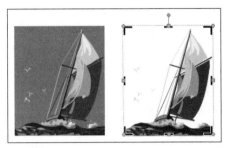

**Figure 19.19.** Editing individual shapes within a clip art image

# Just the facts

- You can easily add pictures to Word documents.

- Use Microsoft Office Picture Manager to manage many pictures at a time. Use photo-editing software such as Adobe Photoshop to do retouching and extensive image manipulation.

- Many picture effects are available, including tints that change color to match the document theme.

- You can insert clip art and manipulate it from within Word.

GET THE SCOOP ON...
Using text boxes to create sophisticated page layouts ■
Using building blocks to save time and reduce repetition ■
Adding symbols, special characters, and equations ■
Adding bold messages with WordArt ■ Inserting a drop
cap into your document

# Advanced Text Formatting

In this chapter, I describe how to take advantage of some more advanced page layout features and other more specialized features. Text boxes are shapes containing text that you can use to control the flow of text on the page. The boxes themselves can be invisible frames within which the text can flow, or they can be visible objects with borders and shading that you incorporate into the design of your document. Text boxes are not new to Word, but they function slightly differently in Word 2007. Word 2007 also ships with 36 built-in text boxes, so that you can add a sidebar or a pull quote without reinventing the wheel.

I also describe building blocks in this chapter. In Word, building blocks are existing sections of documents that you can add quickly and easily to your document. They are stored in the Building Blocks template. Many of Word's built-in document elements are stored in this template, such as cover pages, equations, page numbers, headers, footers, text boxes, and watermarks.

Finally, I cover the equation tools (much improved from earlier versions in terms of usability), special characters, symbols, WordArt (the tool that allows you to treat text with graphic effects for use in posters, banners, and so on), and adding a drop cap to a paragraph.

# Making an impact with text boxes

You can use paragraph formatting and columns to control how text flows on the page to some degree. However, if you are creating a document where page layout is critical, such as a poster, newsletter, advertisement, or Web page, you can take advantage of Word's text box feature to gain more control of how the text flows, particularly if you have a separate, floating piece of text. In Word 2007, text boxes behave differently than they did in earlier versions of Word in that you can insert a text box onto the page without a surrounding drawing canvas. To insert a text box into your document, choose Insert ⇨ Text Box to display the menu shown in Figure 20.1.

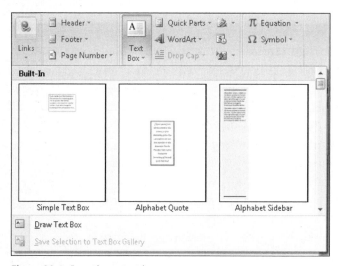

**Figure 20.1.** Inserting a text box

# Selecting a text box from the text box gallery

You can select a built-in text box, one that you have added to the gallery, or create one from scratch. The text box gallery has text boxes grouped by design name and then by type of text box. Apart from the basic model (called Simple Text Box), the designs have names like Austere, Cubicles, Mod, and Tiles. The types of text box are simple text box, quote, and sidebar. You can use a sidebar style as a quote or vice versa; there is no material difference. However, some of the designs offer several styles, and this distinguishes them. To select an existing text box and insert it into a document, follow these steps:

**Inside Scoop**

If you use one of the built-in styles, the colors and fonts of the text box change along with the rest of the document if you change the document theme.

1. If you are inserting the text box onto a page that already contains text, position your cursor approximately where you want the text box to appear (you can adjust its exact position later).

2. Choose Insert ➪ Text Box.

3. Click the thumbnail view of the text box to insert it into the document. If you hold your mouse over a text box in the gallery, a ToolTip appears giving a summary description of the selected text box. In this example, click Austere Quote (a text box centered on the page in brackets). Your text box is inserted into the document, as shown in Figure 20.2.

**Figure 20.2.** Inserting a text box into a document

4. Type (or copy and paste) the text into the text box. The sample text disappears as you type or paste in the new text. If you paste in the text, be sure to click the Paste Option button to the lower right of the text and select Match Destination Formatting. The text box

**Figure 20.3.** A text box using the Austere Quote text box style

will resize itself to accommodate your text. Your text box will look something like Figure 20.3.

Once you insert the text box and add the text to it, you can resize the text box using the move handles surrounding the text box. They behave much as they do for shapes and pictures discussed in earlier chapters: The blue dots in the corners and blue squares at the sides resize the text box when you click and drag them with a mouse. If you resize your text box after you add text, you need to adjust it in such a way that the text box is large enough to contain the text and also not too large for the text. You can rotate the text box, but the text itself will not rotate with it. You can change the text direction (as with a table cell) by choosing Text Box Tools ⇨ Format ⇨ Text Direction. Click the Text Direction button to cycle through the three available text directions: down, up, and left to right.

## Drawing a new text box

To draw a new text box, choose Insert ⇨ Text Box ⇨ Draw Text Box. The mouse cursor changes to a large plus sign (or crosshairs, if you prefer). Click and drag your mouse to create a new text box, releasing the left mouse button when the box is the desired size. A box like the one shown in Figure 20.4 appears. Click in the text box to type the text. You must size the text box manually; although Word knows to wrap the text at the border of the text box, it doesn't automatically increase the size of the text box to fit your text as it might with a table cell.

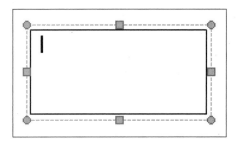

**Figure 20.4.** Drawing a new text box

## Linking text boxes

If you want to have running text that flows from one text box to the next, you can link the text boxes together. To do so, follow these steps:

1. Select the first text box containing text.

2. Choose Text Box Tools ⇨ Format ⇨ Create Link. Your mouse cursor becomes a measuring cup filled with letters.

**Bright Idea**

If you want to create multiple text boxes of the same size, first create one and then copy and paste the text box to create more text boxes of exactly the same size.

3. Move the cursor to the second text box into which you want the text to flow (your cursor converts into a measuring cup pouring out letters).

4. Click in the second text box to link it to the first. Figures 20.5 and 20.6 show two text boxes before and after linking.

**Figure 20.5.** Two text boxes prior to linking

You can link multiple text boxes if need be, so that you have several in a chain. You can also remove a link. Select the first box and choose Text Box Tools ⇨ Format ⇨ Break Link.

**Figure 20.6.** Two text boxes after linking

## Resizing text boxes

I described earlier how you can use the handles around the shape to stretch or squeeze it to the desired size. For more extensive size controls, click the dialog box launcher in the lower-right corner of the Size group of the Format tab of Text Box Tools to display the Size tab of the Format Text Box dialog box shown in Figure 20.7. You can set the absolute height or width in linear units (inches), or you can select the Relative radio button to specify a percentage of some other element of the document. You can choose from Margin, Page, Top Margin, Bottom Margin, Inside Margin, or Outside Margin for height and Margin, Page, Left Margin, Right Margin, Inside Margin, or Outside Margin for width. You can scale the dimensions by percentage as well, or lock the aspect ratio.

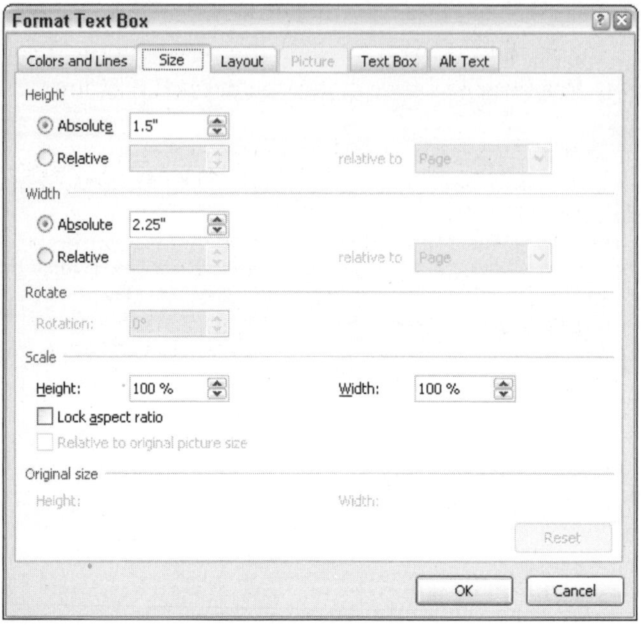

**Format Text Box**

| Colors and Lines | Size | Layout | Picture | Text Box | Alt Text |

Height
- ⦿ Absolute  1.5"
- ○ Relative            relative to  Page

Width
- ⦿ Absolute  2.25"
- ○ Relative            relative to  Page

Rotate
Rotation:  0°

Scale
Height:  100 %        Width:  100 %
☐ Lock aspect ratio
☐ Relative to original picture size

Original size
Height:        Width:

Reset

OK      Cancel

**Figure 20.7.** Adjusting the size controls of a text box

## Arranging text boxes

Word has several ways to arrange text boxes on a page. You can determine the text box's position relative to the entire page, move it in front of or behind other text or graphics, or determine how or whether text wraps around the text box. You can also align text boxes. You can use a nonprinting visual grid to aid you in determining how text boxes should align. You can also group text boxes and other objects together so that they move as one or ungroup them to manipulate them individually.

### Positioning text boxes on a page

There are several commands available to you for positioning a text box on the page. (They are the same commands used for positioning other objects.) In addition to moving the text box by clicking and dragging it with the mouse, you can use the keyboard shortcuts summarized in Table 20.1. To position the shape or drawing relative to the page, choose Text Box Tools ➪ Format ➪ Position, and then select the desired position.

**Table 20.1.** Keyboard commands for text boxes

| Keyboard | Function |
|---|---|
| Tab | If a text box's frame is selected, moves to the next text box or other object. |
| Shift+Tab | If a text box's frame is selected, moves to the previous text box or other object. |
| Escape | Undoes the selection of a text box. |
| Left arrow | Nudges the text box to the left. |
| Right arrow | Nudges the text box to the right. |
| Up arrow | Nudges the text box upward. |
| Down arrow | Nudges the text box downward. |

If you select In Line with Text, this places the text box at the left margin. If there is text on the page, the text appears above and below the text box but does not wrap around it. The With Text Wrapping options tightly wrap text around the text box. You can choose from nine positions for the text box on the page within this set of options, including top left, middle right, and so on.

Click Text Box Tools ➪ Format ➪ Position ➪ More Layout Options to bring up the Advanced Layout dialog box. Click the Picture Position tab to see the many picture position settings shown in Figure 20.8.

**Advanced Layout**    ? ✕

Picture Position | Text Wrapping

Horizontal

○ Alignment    Left ∨    relative to    Column ∨

○ Book layout    Inside ∨    of    Margin ∨

◉ Absolute position    0.38"  ⬍    to the right of    Column ∨

○ Relative position    ⬍    relative to    Page ∨

Vertical

○ Alignment    Top ∨    relative to    Page ∨

◉ Absolute position    4.75"  ⬍    below    Paragraph ∨

○ Relative position    ⬍    relative to    Page ∨

Options

☐ Move object with text    ☑ Allow overlap

☐ Lock anchor    ☑ Layout in table cell

OK    Cancel

**Figure 20.8.** Word offers many settings for picture positioning.

## Text wrapping

**Figure 20.9.** Text-wrapping options

If you insert a text box into a document that also contains text, the text can wrap around the text box in any number or ways. To select the text-wrapping method, click the text box to select it and then choose Text Box Tools ⇨ Format ⇨ Text Wrapping to see the options displayed in Figure 20.9. (Your screen may look slightly different depending on your screen resolution.) Most of the text-wrapping options are self-explanatory, but a few require a bit of clarification.

The In Line with Text option wraps text until it encounters a shape or drawing, resuming the text at the lower-right edge of the text box. This text-wrapping style rarely looks good. I recommend avoiding it if possible. The next option, Square, actually wraps text around the text box leaving a rectangle (not necessarily a square). This is useful with irregular text box shapes, where wrapping text around the text box shape makes it hard to read without skipping lines. The Tight and Through options are almost the same, except that Tight wraps text only up to the right and left edges of the text box; Through also inserts text into any space within the text box's shape (if it is not rectangular). The Behind Text, In Front of Text, and Edit Wrap Points settings are not very useful or practical to use with text boxes — I suspect they appear merely because they make sense for other types of objects such as drawings and pictures.

### Moving a text box forward or backward

If you have overlapping text boxes and shapes, you need to be able to move something toward the foreground (or the top layer) or toward the background (or the bottom layer). To move a text box to the foreground, choose Text Box Tools ⇨ Format ⇨ Bring to Front. To move a text box forward one level, choose Text Box Tools ⇨ Format ⇨ Bring to Front ⇨ Bring Forward. To bring a text box in front of text, choose Text Box Tools ⇨ Format ⇨ Bring to Front ⇨ Bring in Front of Text. To move a text box to the background (which you might do if you have a semi-transparent shape in front of it, for example), choose Text Box Tools ⇨ Format ⇨ Send to Back. To move a text box backward one level, choose Text Box Tools ⇨ Format ⇨ Send to Back ⇨ Send Backward. To send a text box in back of text, choose Text Box Tools ⇨ Format ⇨ Send to Back ⇨ Send Behind Text.

### Aligning text boxes

You can align text boxes relative to each other, to the page, or to the margins. You can align one shape, one group of shapes, or several individually selected shapes. To align a text box, select the text box and then choose Text Box Tools ⇨ Format ⇨ Align to display the menu shown in Figure 20.10. Because alignment is relative, check and see which setting is appropriate for you: Align to Page, Align to Margin, or Align Selected Objects (if you have more than one object selected). (If you need to change this setting, select the appropriate option, and choose Text Box Tools ⇨ Format ⇨ Align once more.) Next, you can choose to align the text box left, right, center, top, bottom, or middle.

**Figure 20.10.** Text box alignment commands

**Hack**

To select more than one text box, hold down the Shift key while clicking each text box.

If you have lots of small text boxes to align, such as in an organizational chart, it's best to use a grid to help you align and order your presentation. To do so, first choose Text Box Tools ➪ Format ➪ Align ➪ Show Gridlines. Your document page will now look like a piece of graph paper. The gridlines are there to aid you in your page layout — they won't be printed. Next, choose Text Box Tools ➪ Format ➪ Align ➪ Grid Settings to see the Drawing Grid dialog box shown in Figure 20.11. When gridlines are displayed, objects align to the nearest grid-

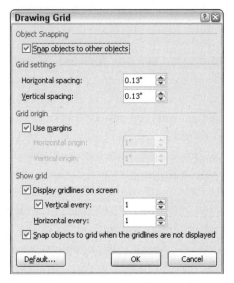

**Figure 20.11.** Change grid settings to aid in aligning text boxes.

lines. Select the Snap objects to grid when the gridlines are not displayed option to align text boxes to the nearest gridlines when the gridlines are not displayed. Select the Snap objects to other objects option to make it easier to connect lines to text boxes and so forth.

### Grouping text boxes and other shapes

You can group text boxes and other shapes together to form more complex drawings. Once grouped, you can perform actions upon the group, such as resizing, moving, and formatting. To group text boxes or shapes together, select them by holding down the Shift key and clicking each one until all text boxes (and shapes) are selected that you want to group together. You can tell that you have selected them because all of the move handles are visible. Choose Text Box Tools ➪ Format ➪ Group ➪ Group to group the selected objects together. If you want to make a change to one of the text boxes or other objects after grouping, choose Text Box Tools ➪

Format ⇨ Group ⇨ Ungroup. You can make a change and then choose Text Box Tools ⇨ Format ⇨ Group ⇨ Regroup to regroup the text boxes and other objects back together.

## Formatting text boxes

Besides the ready-made styles available to you in the text box gallery, you can also make changes to the shape, color, or fill pattern of a text box, and change the color, pattern, or weight or its border lines. Special effects also allow you to add shadows and three-dimensional perspective to your text boxes.

### *Changing the text box's shape*

You can change the shape of a text box in one of two ways. Adding text to a shape is described in Chapter 17. When you add text to a shape, it becomes a text box. However, you can also convert a standard rectangular text box into a different shape. Word isn't an advanced graphics program, though, and changing the outer shape of the text box still leaves a simple rectangle on the inside (it doesn't wrap around 3-D cylinders in perspective or anything like that). To change the text box's shape, select the text box, choose Text Box Tools ⇨ Format ⇨ Change Shape, and select a shape from the shape gallery. If you select a typical enclosed shape, the text box appears in roughly rectangular form within the shape. If you select a line, the text appears in the center of the sizing frame for that line. If you change a shape after adding text, you may need to resize the shape to make all the text visible. This is true even if you link the shape to other text boxes.

### *Changing the text box's color or fill pattern*

To change the background color or fill pattern, select a text box or group of text boxes and choose Text Box Tools ⇨ Format ⇨ Shape Fill. Clicking the paint bucket itself fills the entire text box's shape with whatever is selected (just like the Paint Bucket tool in the Windows Paint accessory or many other graphics tools). If you click the arrow, you can select a color, picture, gradient, texture, or pattern from the menu.

Figure 20.12 shows gradient options previewed by moving the mouse over the selection. If you choose a theme color, your color changes along with the other aspects of your document when you change themes. If you choose a gradient, the gradient's color also changes with a theme change. Clicking More Gradients displays the Fill Effects dialog box shown in Figure 20.13. If you select the Preset radio button in the Color section, you can choose from a long list of gradient options. The Transparency slider can be used to make the text box more or less transparent. This is especially useful to make text within the text box more legible by rendering the gradient fill more transparent. The More Colors menu selection on the Shape Fill command also has a transparency option.

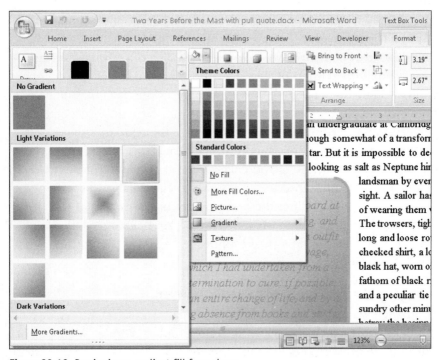

**Figure 20.12.** Previewing a gradient fill for a shape

The Texture menu option allows you to include a photorealistic texture pattern such as burlap, linen, marble, wood grain, and so on. The Pattern menu option is a remnant from the past that shows bitmap fill patterns familiar to paint program users of early Macs and PCs, such as tiles, checkerboards, and interlocking bricks that are good for giving that mid-1980s Apple ImageWriter look to something. You can also include a picture file as a background image. If you want Word to squeeze the entire picture into each text box, select the Picture menu option. If you have a picture of something that you intend to use as a texture (such as a picture of a rock wall or the ocean waves), use the Texture menu option and click More Textures. Select your picture in the dialog box that appears.

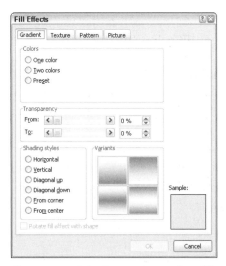

**Figure 20.13.** Selecting a preset gradient fill color set

### Changing the text box's borders

You can change the way a text box's outline is displayed or the way a line appears by choosing Text Box Tools ⇨ Format ⇨ Shape Outline. Clicking the Shape Outline button itself colors the text box outline with whatever color is selected. If you click the arrow, you can select a color, weight, dash, arrow, or pattern from the menu, as shown in Figure 20.14. If you choose a theme color,

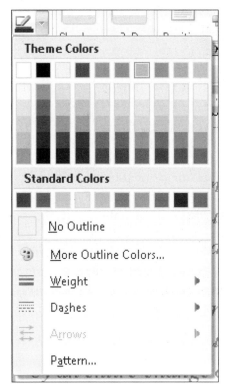

**Figure 20.14.** Changing the border or line style of a text box

**Watch Out!**

If you have a group of text boxes with connecting lines, ungroup them first because Word treats text box outlines and connecting lines in the same way. For example, if you want to remove borders from text boxes, Word also removes any connecting lines.

your color changes along with the other aspects of your document when you change themes.

## Adding special effects to text boxes

Apart from adding colors and fills, and rotating text boxes around, Word provides additional effects to give your text boxes more visual interest: shadow and 3-D effects.

### Shadow effects

You can add shadow effects to your text box. To do so, select your text box, choose Text Box Tools ⇨ Format ⇨ Shadow Effects, and click the arrow to see the options shown in Figure 20.15. As you move your mouse over a shadow effect, the effect is previewed live for your selected text box. Drop shadows give the appearance of the text box hovering over the page. Perspective shadows show the text box in perspective with a vanishing point. Click Shadow Color to select a color other than gray for your shadow. You can also choose a semitransparent rather than an opaque shadow from the Shadow Color option.

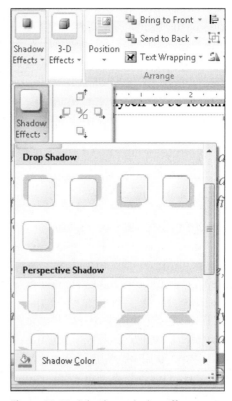

**Figure 20.15.** Selecting a shadow effect

Choose Text Box Tools ⇨ Format ⇨ Shadow Effects ⇨ Shadow Effects ⇨ Shadow On/Off to toggle between shadow and no shadow, as shown in Figure 20.16. The surrounding buttons allow you to nudge the shadow up, down, right, or left.

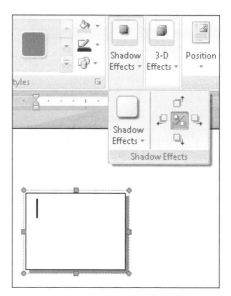

**Figure 20.16.** Turning shadow effects on and off

### 3-D effects

You can add 3-D effects to your text box. To do so, select your text box, choose Text Box Tools ⇨ Format ⇨ 3-D Effects, and click the arrow to see the options shown in Figure 20.17. As you move your mouse over a 3-D effect, the effect is previewed live for your selected text box. Parallel 3-D effects give the appearance of technical illustrations, while Perspective 3-D effects show the shape in perspective with a vanishing point. Select 3-D Color to choose a color other than gray for your shaded sides of the 3-D shape. Select Depth to choose the depth of the three-dimensional shape of your text box. The depth is measured in points from 0 to 288 if you have a parallel representation of three dimensions, or from 0 to infinity if you have perspective representation of three dimensions. This Infinity setting goes close to a vanishing point. Select Direction to choose from which angle you view the 3-D text box's shape, and

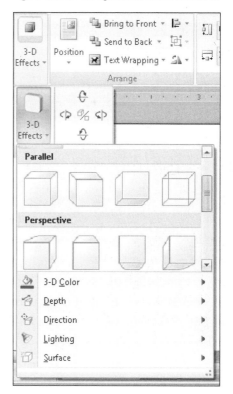

**Figure 20.17.** Selecting a 3-D effect

---

### When to Use Frames Instead of Text Boxes

In most cases with Word 2007, text boxes are the right option, and they have the most capabilities. However, there is another kind of text object that can be resized and moved around the page — a *frame.* It is an earlier type of text box that still has some uses in the current version of Word.

You can insert a frame into your document in one of two ways. The first way is to display the Developer tab and choose Developer ⇨ Legacy Tools ⇨ Insert Frame. The second way is to insert a text box, click the Text Box Styles dialog box launcher, click the Text Box tab, and then click Convert to Frame. Insert a frame instead of a text box when using the following Word reference features:

- Comments
- Footnotes or endnotes
- Fields used for numbering paragraphs in legal documents such as AUTONUM
- Table of Contents entries
- Index entries
- Table of Authority entries

To make formatting changes to a frame, right-click the selected frame and click Format Frame.

---

whether parallel or perspective. Select Lighting to pick a light source direction and a brightness setting (Bright, Normal, or Dim). Select Surface to choose what type of surface the three-dimensional text box shape will have; choices are Matte, Plastic, Metal, and Wire Frame.

Choose Text Box Tools ⇨ Format ⇨ 3-D Effects ⇨ 3-D Effects ⇨ 3-D On/Off to toggle between two and three dimensions. The surrounding buttons allow you to tilt the 3-D text box shape forward, backward, right, or left.

## Saving a text box to the text box gallery

If you create a custom text box that you want to use again, select the text box and choose Insert ⇨ Text Box ⇨ Save Selection to Text Box Gallery. The Create New Building Block dialog box appears, shown in Figure 20.18. You can then type a name and description. By default, the text box is assigned to the General category of the text box gallery. You can save the text box in Building Blocks.dotx or Normal.dotm. The following section has more information about building blocks.

**Figure 20.18.** Saving a text box to the text box gallery

# Using building blocks

You can build documents by putting together preformatted document parts called building blocks. Some built-in building blocks that I already described are cover pages, headers, footers, page numbers, tables, text boxes, and watermarks. There are also built-in building blocks for bibliographies, equations, tables of contents, and AutoText. I describe the built-in equations and discuss AutoText in this chapter. Bibliographies and tables of contents are covered in Chapter 22. I also show you how to add your own custom building block and how to search for new building blocks on Office Online.

## Working with the Building Blocks Organizer

To insert a building block into your document, choose Insert ⇨ Quick Parts ⇨ Building Blocks Organizer to see the organizer shown in Figure 20.19. As you can see, the organizer allows you to view the entire list of building blocks, most of which are stored in Building Blocks.dotx, although some are stored in Normal.dotm. The organizer lists all the building blocks and their properties. To edit a building block's properties, click Edit Properties from the organizer to see the Modify Building Block dialog box shown in Figure 20.20. You can change the building block's name, gallery, category, description, file location (normal.dotm or Building Blocks.dotx), or options. The options allow you to determine how the building block is added to the document: as content only, as content in its own paragraph, or as content on its own page. You can create a new category in the Category field if you want. To delete a building block from the list, select it and click the Delete button.

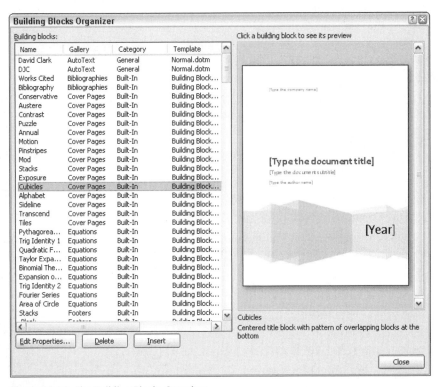

**Figure 20.19.** The Building Blocks Organizer

**Inside Scoop**

If you want to reset your building blocks back to the initial default list and remove any custom building blocks, delete your Building Blocks.dotx file, usually located in `C:\Program Files\Microsoft Office\Office 12\ Document Parts\`.

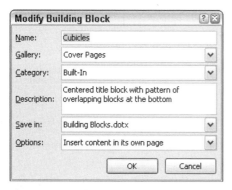

**Figure 20.20.** Editing the properties of a building block

## Adding custom building blocks to your building blocks list

If you have a piece of text or formatting that you use repeatedly in your work, you can add it to the building blocks list. To do so, follow these steps:

1. Create the text that you want to save as a building block, including any formatting that you want to add.

2. Select the text that you want to save as a building block.

3. Choose Insert ⇨ Quick Parts ⇨ Save Selection to Quick Parts Gallery. The Create New Building Block dialog box appears, as shown in Figure 20.21.

4. Word assigns the first word or two as the name of the building block by default (Copyright ©) in Figure 20.21). Edit the name so that it identifies your building block concisely and to your satisfaction.

**Figure 20.21.** Creating a new building block

5. Select a gallery to which the building block belongs. In this example, it would be AutoText, although you could just as easily create a cover page or table. Avoid choosing the top-level Quick Parts gallery because if you fill it with building blocks you won't be able to see

the other important types of Quick Parts such as document properties, fields, and so on.

6. Select a category or create a new one in the Category list.

7. Type a description for the building block. Include content and/or
formatting details.

8. In the Save in field, select Building Blocks.dotx or Normal.dotm.

9. In the Options field, choose whether to insert content only or in its
own paragraph or page.

10. Click OK. The building block is now saved to your building blocks list
and will be available to choose from the Building Blocks Organizer.

Once you create or modify building blocks, you'll see a message box
when you exit Word asking if you want to save your changes. Click Yes to
save the changes or No to abandon them.

## Bringing the AutoText feature back from the dead

In earlier versions of Word, one of my favorite features was AutoText (not
to be confused with AutoCorrect). I could choose from a list of common
phrases or add my own, and simply choose Insert ⇨ AutoText to select
one to insert into my document. Microsoft, in its infinite wisdom, has
removed the AutoText feature from Word 2007. However, buried several
levels down is an AutoText gallery in building blocks, so you can re-create
your own AutoText feature in a few minutes using the following Hack. If
you spend a long time creating AutoText phrases, be sure to make a
backup copy of your Building Blocks.dotx file, because that is where they
are stored by default.

## Inserting symbols and special characters

Word allows you to add symbols and special characters into your documents. The basic operation is very simple: to add a symbol, choose Insert
⇨ Symbol and select the appropriate symbol. However, because of the

**Hack**
Add a list of common phrases to your building blocks list's AutoText gallery as
described earlier. Choose Microsoft Office ⇨ Word Options ⇨ Customize. Select
Insert Tab in the Categories field and BuildingBlockOrganizer in the Commands
field. Press Ctrl+Alt+Ins (or any unassigned key combination) and click Assign.

way fonts work, additional care is required when sending documents with symbols to others.

## Things you should know about special characters, symbols, and fonts

When you work with the alphabet, punctuation, and numerals, you use characters that are reliably understood and replicated in different fonts and on different computer platforms. Special characters and symbols do not fall in this category. Although most special characters are included with most fonts, do not assume that they are. Elaborate display fonts are especially unreliable in this regard. Most symbols are created by including characters for symbol fonts — fonts created expressly for the purpose of providing specialty symbols.

Consequently, when using special characters and symbols, be sure to check that they are preserved if you change fonts or styles. If you send your document to others and you know you will be including symbols, it is a good idea to save the file with the fonts embedded. (To do this, choose Microsoft Office ⇨ Word Options ⇨ Save ⇨ Embed fonts in the file.)

## Adding symbols

To add a symbol, position your insertion point where you want to add the symbol and choose Insert ⇨ Symbol. You can select one of the commonly used symbols that display as shown in Figure 20.22. The Symbol menu lists 20 symbols: your most recently used symbols followed by other commonly used symbols. If you want to look for another symbol that isn't in the short list on the menu, choose Insert ⇨ Symbol ⇨ More Symbols to display the Symbols tab of the Symbol dialog box shown in Figure 20.23.

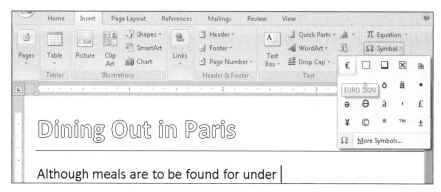

**Figure 20.22.** Selecting a frequently used symbol to insert into your document

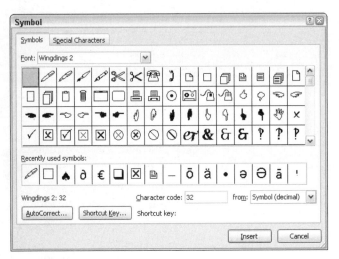

**Figure 20.23.** The Symbols tab of the Symbol dialog box

In the Symbols tab of the Symbol dialog box you can select a font. If the font selected is *(normal text)*, then the selected font in the document is displayed. You can choose any other font installed in Windows on your PC from the list. Some fonts are dedicated to supporting symbols, meaning that they have a fuller set of symbols, and you probably have a few of these fonts installed on your PC. Look for font names with *symbol* or *dingbat* in them. (A *dingbat* is a printing symbol or flourish.) Some fonts you may have on your list are Cambria Math, Symbol, Wingdings, and Zaph Dingbats.

After selecting a font, you can choose the font subset. The Basic Latin subset has the English alphabet (upper- and lowercase in most cases, except for certain decorative fonts), numerals, common punctuation symbols, and the few very basic symbols that you find on the standard U.S. English keyboard. In general, start looking for symbols in the Latin-1 Supplement subset onward. The subsets are grouped based on category. For example, if you need to display something in Russian characters, select Cyrillic. If you need to insert the currency symbol for Euro, select the Currency subset. In any case, you can scroll through the entire font (all subsets) with the scroll bar at the right of the symbols grid. To select a symbol, click it with the mouse. This does not insert it into the document. At the lower-left corner of the dialog box you will see its description. Its character code is displayed, which is useful information for programming and automation; the code is displayed in Unicode (in hexidecimal notation) or ASCII (in either decimal or hexidecimal notation).

**Inside Scoop**

If you want to choose a symbol for a bullet style, there is a different procedure. Choose Home ⇨ Bullets ⇨ Define New Bullet ⇨ Symbol. You can choose a bullet symbol from a dialog box similar to the one discussed here.

If you want to create a text string that is converted automatically to the selected symbol when typed, click the AutoCorrect button, type the text string you want to replace in the Replace field, and click OK. Alternatively, you can add a shortcut key combination. If one already exists, it is displayed. For example, pressing Alt+Ctrl+E inserts the Euro symbol. For a list of common symbols that already have assigned keyboard combinations, choose Microsoft Office ⇨ Word Options ⇨ Customize ⇨ Customize, then scroll down and click Common Symbols, which is the last item in the Categories list. Click any of the Common Symbols list items and look at Current keys to see which are already assigned.

Once you decide on a symbol, click Insert to insert it into your document; click Close to close the dialog box.

## Adding special characters

Special characters in Word are those characters that can't be found on the keyboard. They are either formatting characters that cannot simply be typed (such as a no-width optional break) or typographical symbols that are used somewhat less often than those on the keyboard.

To access the special characters, choose Insert ⇨ Symbol and click the Special Characters tab to see the dialog box shown in Figure 20.24. As you can see, most of the more common ones have a shortcut key equivalent (and they are listed on the tear-out card at the front of this book). You can also add an AutoCorrect or Shortcut Key sequence as you can with a symbol. To insert a special character, click Insert. After you insert a symbol, a Close button appears in the dialog box. Click it to close the dialog box.

**Inside Scoop**

To include a special character in a find or replace operation, press Ctrl+F for find or Ctrl+R for replace, click More in the Find or Replace dialog box if the larger version of the dialog box is not displayed, and then click Special to see a list of special characters to add to your search string.

**Figure 20.24.** Inserting a special character into your document

# Adding equations to your document

Word 2007 provides a new equation tool that is easier to use and more flexible than the Equation Editor of earlier versions. You can write an equation as you type using text and the Math AutoCorrect feature, you can insert an existing equation from Word, or you can insert a new equation that you create using the Design tab of Equation Tools.

## Inserting an equation

To add an equation to your document, choose Insert ⇨ Equation to see the Design tab of Equation Tools, part of which is shown in Figure 20.25. You can select from a set of built-in equations by clicking Equation in the Tools group of the Design tab. You can choose from a short list of equations that range from the elementary to the complex (the area of a circle to Fourier series). Click the desired equation to insert it into your document. You can also create an equation and then save it to this equation

---

**Hack**

Word's new built-in Equation tool does not integrate with equations created with Equation Editor in older documents. To work with an older equation, double-click the equation. Microsoft Equation 3.0 (the older equation editor) opens, and you can modify the equation using the older tool.

gallery by selecting the equation and choosing Equation Tools ⇨ Design ⇨ Equation ⇨ Save Selection to Equation Gallery. Figure 20.26 shows a built-in equation (the quadratic formula) inserted into a document.

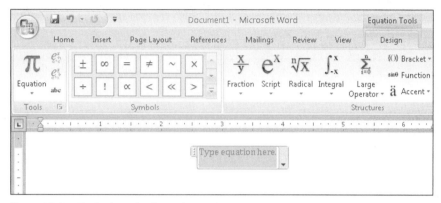

**Figure 20.25.** The Design tab of Equation Tools

## Changing equation display options

By default, Word centers an equation, offset from text paragraphs and stacked if necessary, as shown in Figure 20.26. This is referred to as Professional format, which is suitable for final display in a document. It is easier to understand and requires the reader to parse fewer nested items. However, it is easier to compose an equation using linear format, the format used when specifying a formula in Excel or a programming language, for example. To convert an equation to linear format, click the Equation Options arrow to the right of the equation to see the options shown in Figure 20.27. Figure 20.28 shows

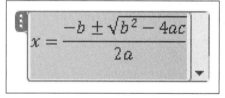

**Figure 20.26.** Adding a built-in equation to a document

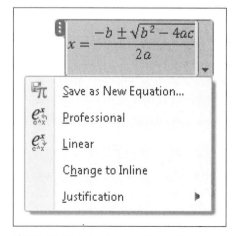

**Figure 20.27.** Selecting equation options

the quadratic equation of Figure 20.26 in linear form. Further, you can change the equation to run inline with text by selecting the Change to Inline option, so that it appears as shown in Figure 20.29.

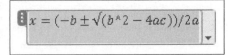

**Figure 20.28.** The quadratic equation in linear form

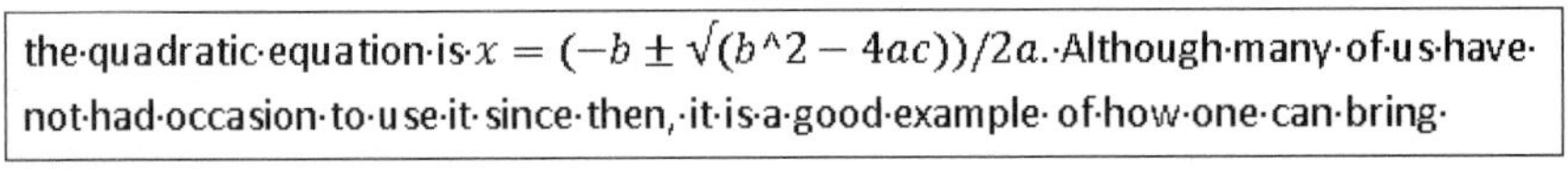

Once inline, you can change it back to being a separate object offset and movable from text by selecting the equation, clicking the Equation Options arrow, and clicking Change to Display. Finally, you can change the Justification options for the equation (if it is in Display and not Inline mode) by selecting Justification and choosing from one of four options: Centered as a Group (the default), Left, Right, or Centered.

the·quadratic·equation·is·$x = (-b \pm \sqrt{(b^2 - 4ac)})/2a$.·Although·many·of·us·have· not·had·occasion· to·use·it· since· then,·it·is·a·good·example· of·how·one·can·bring·

**Figure 20.29.** The quadratic equation displayed inline

Apart from the basic formatting options shown in the Equation Options menu, you have a very large group of settings available by clicking the Tools dialog box launcher in the Design tab of Equation Tools, which displays the Equation Options dialog box shown in Figure 20.30. It's beyond the scope of this book to go over all settings here. I will, however, explain a few things. Because Microsoft uses an XML format for Word document files, MathML (the mathematical markup language recommended by the W3C.org) is used to create the mathematical formulas shown in professional format. While most scientists and mathematicians

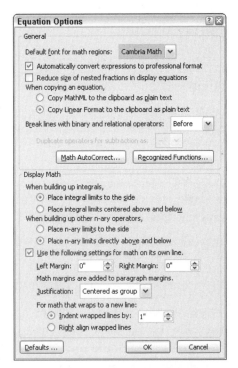

**Figure 20.30.** Expanded equation options

**Inside Scoop**

Cambria Math is the only font you can safely assume will work with esoteric symbols. However, if you just have fractions, radicals, and alphanumeric characters, you can change the font by choosing Equation Tools ⇨ Design ⇨ Normal Text. This is a toggle command. Clicking it again causes the equation to revert back to Cambria Math.

probably prefer TeX commands (more commonly in use in academia), they are not used in Word. Also, clicking MathAutoCorrect allows you to see the set of built-in conversions you can take advantage of when writing an equation, as shown in Figure 20.31. For example, if you type \**Sigma** it is automatically replaced with the capital Greek letter sigma, the symbol for summation.

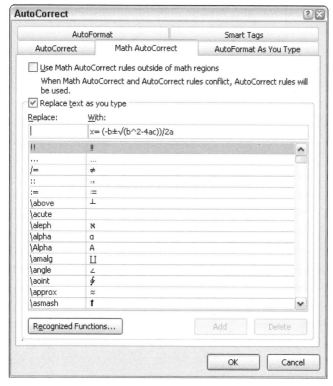

**Figure 20.31.** Viewing MathAutoCorrect settings

## Writing an equation from scratch

Of course, you can write your own equations using the tools provided. The Symbols group gives you several sets of symbols that you can click and insert as needed. Click the More arrow to see the Basic Math set. Click the arrow next to the Basic Math set to show other sets. Sets are provided for Greek letters, letter-like symbols, operators, arrows, negated relations, scripts, and geometry. In addition to the symbols, you can select from several equation structures in the Structures group. To choose from the gallery of predefined structures, click on a category, such as the Integral structure category shown in Figure 20.32, and click it to insert it into your document. You can click the outlined boxes to insert any necessary limits or parameters your equation may require.

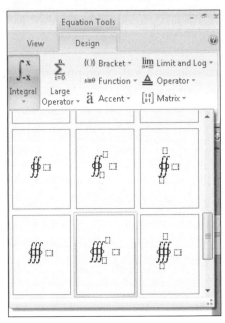

**Figure 20.32.** Adding a volume integral structure to an equation

## Using WordArt for visual impact

Word provides a quick and easy way to create decorative banner text: WordArt. To insert WordArt into your document, choose Insert ⇨ WordArt. A gallery of 30 styles of WordArt appears, as shown in Figure 20.33. Once you select a WordArt style, the Edit WordArt Text dialog box appears, where you can edit the text, select a font and a point size, and choose

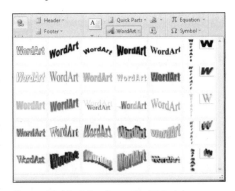

**Figure 20.33.** Selecting a WordArt style

**Watch Out!**

Word doesn't check the spelling of WordArt. It has been my experience that the larger the type, the more chance of a spelling error. If you are not sure about how to spell something you are displaying in WordArt, check it first and then apply WordArt.

whether the text should be bold or italic. If you have first selected text to apply the WordArt style to, it appears within the text frame. Otherwise the words *Your Text Here* appears: Type your text at this point if you didn't already select a text string. Click OK when you are satisfied with your settings.

Once you insert the WordArt, the WordArt is inserted into your document within a sizing frame and the Format tab of WordArt Tools appears, as shown in Figure 20.34. The Text group of commands allows you to edit the text, adjust spacing of characters, make all characters of even height, change the line spacing, or create vertical text (with one character on top of the other, as opposed to turning the word 90 degrees). The WordArt Styles group displays the available styles again, in case you want to change the style once inserted. The remaining format commands function as they do with shapes and text boxes.

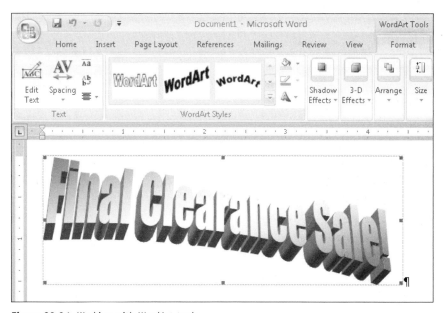

**Figure 20.34.** Working with WordArt tools

## Adding a drop cap to add sophistication

One final page layout element that Word provides is the drop cap. A drop cap is an initial capital that starts a document or major document section like a chapter. The capital is enlarged and often set in a different font, and is dropped into the paragraph or to the left of it. This tradition started in medieval illuminated manuscripts but has been carried forward into modern typography.

To insert a drop cap into your document, click the paragraph that you want to start with a drop cap and choose Insert ⇨ Drop Cap. Note that it is not necessary to select the first letter of the paragraph — Word figures this out. You can select from Dropped or In Margin options. As you move your mouse over the option, Word previews how the paragraph will look. Selecting Drop Cap Options allows you to select the font, the number of lines to drop, and the distance from the text. Once you insert the dropped cap, you can also resize it by dragging its frame.

## Just the facts

- You can use text boxes to move a section of text around on a page to create more interesting layouts and to present sidebars and pull quotes.
- Building blocks allow you to easily manage standardized text and designs.
- You can insert special characters and symbols into your document by choosing Insert ⇨ Symbol.
- You can write equations easily with Word's expanded equation tools.
- You can add visual impact and style with WordArt and drop caps.

# Special Features

# PART VI

# Control Issues

In Chapter 12, I describe ways to restrict editing or formatting of your documents and how to mark the documents as Final to prevent changes. In this chapter, I focus on how to make your documents more secure from tampering, how to restrict others from opening them, how to encrypt your documents, and how to strip out sensitive information that might be contained in parts of the documents that don't comprise the text of the documents such as comments, revisions, and document properties. Together these elements are referred to as *metadata*.

There are many reasons for keeping document access restricted, from the preservation of client or patient confidentiality to the protection of sensitive competitive information. Word has several ways to protect your data from unauthorized access.

First, however, let me make it clear that these are individual aspects of a broader security policy that you should consider implementing, whether you have particularly sensitive information or not. This broader security policy includes the physical security of your computer and storage media, operating system level security, and protection against viruses and other malware. These topics are beyond the scope of this book. A good starting place to look for more information is www.microsoft.com/security.

# Restrict access to your documents with RMS

Microsoft provides a way to track and restrict access to documents using a technique based on e-mail addresses and servers that verify users via e-mail called Windows Rights Management Services (RMS), which is available in Windows XP and Windows Vista. RMS gives you more control over access. You can permit selected recipients to read or change a document while preventing and prohibiting them from printing or cutting and pasting, for example. Most obvious ways of unauthorized copying are locked out. (For example, you can't just use the Print Screen command to print a restricted document.) You can give the document an expiration date so that it can't be read after a certain date. RMS has some limitations that Microsoft is at pains to make clear: Someone can always look at something and retype it in another document, take a picture of the computer screen, or use a third-party screen-capture program. Also, restricting access doesn't necessarily protect a document from being destroyed or stolen.

To protect your documents using this service, first install the RMS client on your computer. (If you work in a larger organization, this is likely taken care of by your network administrator, who can define rights templates for your organization.) To download the RMS client, go to `www.microsoft.com/windowsserver2003/technologies/rights mgmt`. Office 2007 also prompts you to download and install the client if you try to access a document protected with RMS.

To protect and restrict access to your current document, choose Review ⇨ Protect Document ⇨ Restrict Access (or choose Microsoft Office ⇨ Prepare ⇨ Restrict Permission ⇨ Restrict Access). Next, select the Restrict Permission to this document option in the Permission dialog box shown in Figure 21.1. If you click OK at this point, only you (or more to the point, someone logged in as you) have access permission. A notice appears above the document to make this clear, as shown in Figure 21.2. You can remove the access restriction by clicking Change Permission in the notice shown in Figure 21.2, which brings you back to the Permission dialog box, where you deselect the checkbox restricting permission and click OK to remove the restriction.

You can add users to the Read or Change list by typing their e-mail addresses in the corresponding boxes, separating each user's e-mail address with a semicolon (;). You can also select users from your Outlook address book or Contact list by clicking Read or Change. The Select Names dialog box appears, as shown in Figure 21.3. Select a user and click Read to allow Read permission or Change to allow Change permission. Click OK when done.

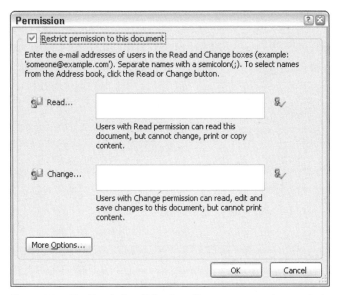

**Figure 21.1.** The Permission dialog box allows you to restrict permission to view the current document.

**Figure 21.2.** A notice showing that the document has restricted access

To assign full rights to a user, select the More Options radio button in the Permissions dialog box to see the expanded Permissions dialog box shown in Figure 21.4. From this box you can change each user's access level by clicking on his or her e-mail address from the list. You can choose Full Control, Read, or Change.

To make the document expire on a certain date, select the This document expires on option and type a date between the day after your current system date but before December 31, 2100. You can also allow users additional specific types of access as indicated by the various checkboxes in the expanded dialog box, which are self-explanatory. Click OK when done to confirm and apply any changes.

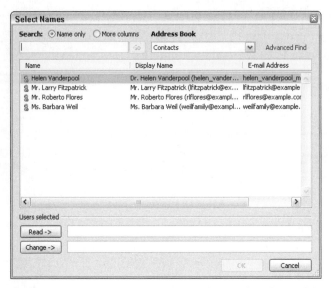

**Figure 21.3.** Selecting users and assigning them Read or Change rights

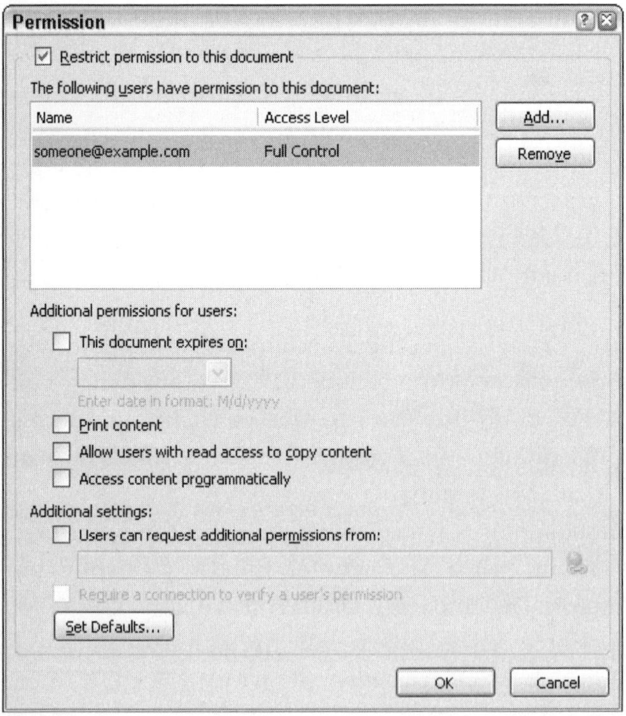

**Figure 21.4.** Additional access rights options in the expanded Permissions dialog box

# Inspect your document for hidden information

Before you send your document electronically to others, it's a good idea to "scrub" it of any sensitive information. You may think you would never do this sort of thing, but let me give you an example. Once, when I was reviewing an author contract, I turned on revision tracking to keep track of a change and it revealed another author's name and royalty advance amounts! Needless to say, this sort of thing can be embarrassing at the very minimum. Although it has been possible in the past to manually remove anything you might consider sensitive, I'm glad Microsoft has finally added the Document Inspector feature to remove hidden data and personal information.

To inspect the document, save the document and choose Microsoft Office ⇨ Prepare ⇨ Inspect Document. (If you don't save the document first, a warning message appears asking if you want to save because it is not always possible to restore data that the Document Inspector removes.) The Document Inspector dialog box appears, as shown in Figure 21.5. You can ignore any content category by clearing the corresponding checkbox. Click Inspect to inspect the document for the types of content listed. The Document Inspector shows you the results, as shown in the sample in Figure 21.6. If no items are found in a category, you will see a blue check mark. If items are found in a content category, you will see a red exclamation point. If you want to remove all content in that category, click Remove All. You may elect to leave some information in the document. For example, in the example shown in Figure 21.6, I don't want Word to remove the header from the document. I know what's in the header and it isn't sensitive, so I leave it alone. When you finish removing any suspect content, you can click either Reinspect to see what's left or Close to complete the operation.

---

**Watch Out!**

One disadvantage to the Document Inspector is that it doesn't allow you to review items first to see whether you mind that they are included in your document — it just gives you the choice of leaving them in or removing them. If you are unsure whether you want to retain the information, make a backup copy of the document or review it carefully first.

**Figure 21.5.** Select content to search for with the Document Inspector.

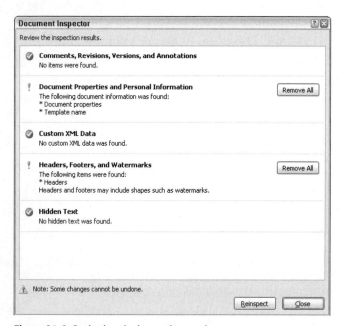

**Figure 21.6.** Reviewing the inspection results

# Adding a digital signature to a document

You may add a digital signature to a document to certify its authenticity. Once signed, any changes render the signature invalid. This is a way to ensure that no changes are made without your express authorization. Note that this is slightly different from adding an electronic signature line, which is covered in Chapter 13, although it uses the same technology.

To add a digital signature, you must install digital signature services. To add an invisible digital signature to your document, open the document and choose Microsoft Office ➪ Prepare ➪ Add a Digital Signature. The informational dialog box shown in Figure 21.7 appears. If you need to obtain signature services, click the corresponding button. If you already have signature services, click OK. You then see the Sign dialog box shown in Figure 21.8. You can add a line describing why you are signing the document. Click Change if you want to change the digital certificate you use to sign the document. When you finish making any changes, click Sign. Note that because the signature is certified by a digital signature verification service over the Internet, your computer must be connected to the Internet for this to work. You may see a progress bar in a window as your signature is being confirmed.

**Figure 21.7.** Information about digital signature services

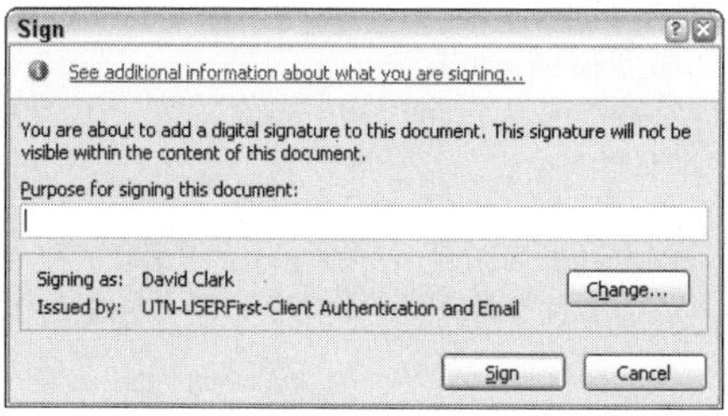

**Figure 21.8.** Digitally signing a document

**Inside Scoop**

You can't remove any items with the Document Inspector if your document is digitally signed and the document is also marked as final, so perform any inspections first.

Once successfully confirmed, a Signature Confirmation box appears. Click OK. You then see a Signatures pane at the side of your document, as shown in Figure 21.9. Click a name in the Valid signatures list to make changes, see details, or remove your signature. You can access the Signatures pane at any time by choosing Microsoft Office ⇨ Prepare ⇨ View Signatures. If you need to change the document after signing it, open the Signatures pane, select your signature, and click Remove Signature, or choose Microsoft Office ⇨ Prepare ⇨ Mark as Final to remove the Mark as Final designation (it's a toggle command), then click OK when asked if you are sure.

**Figure 21.9.** Manage signatures in the Signatures pane.

# Encrypt your document

You can encrypt your document in Word to increase document security. When you encrypt data, you scramble it in such a way that it is undecipherable without a key. The key, in this case, is a password that you provide. To encrypt a document, open the document and choose Microsoft Office ⇨ Prepare ⇨ Encrypt Document. The Encrypt dialog box appears, as shown in Figure 21.10. Type a password. According to Microsoft, passwords should be at least eight characters, although 14 or more characters is better, and you should mix upper- and lowercase letters (passwords are case-sensitive), numbers, and symbols (the ones on the keyboard). After typing a password (which appears as dots on the screen), click OK. You are then asked to

**Figure 21.10.** Adding a password when encrypting your document

**Watch Out!**

Document encryption is a two-edged sword. Once encrypted, the only way to decipher the document's content is by using the password. If you forget or lose the password, the content is inaccessible.

retype the password. Do so and click OK. (This is a way of making sure you have no typos when you do data entry. If the two passwords don't match, start over.) To remove encryption, choose Microsoft Office ⇨ Prepare ⇨ Encrypt Document after opening the document, delete the password, and click OK.

## Protecting or encrypting your document when you save it

As you can see, Microsoft provides many ways to control, encrypt, and restrict access to your documents. The features are scattered through the user interface. However, you do have access to several methods of controlling access to your document in one place when you save it. Press F12 or choose Microsoft Office ⇨ Save As. In the Save As dialog box, choose Tools ⇨ General Options to see the dialog box shown in Figure 21.11. When you type a password in the Password to open field, you encrypt the file and restrict all access to the file to those who know the password.

When you type a password in the Password to modify field, you prevent others from accidentally modifying the file. This method should only be used in such a context, because it can be easily circumvented. An even gentler version of this is to select the Read-only recommended option, which tells users when they open the document that it "should be opened as read-only unless changes to it need to be saved. Open as read-only?" The user can then click Yes, No, or Cancel.

**Figure 21.11.** Options for protecting and encrypting your document upon saving

Finally, the General Options has a Protect Document button, which takes you to the document protection options covered in Chapter 12.

## Just the facts

- You can take advantage of Windows Rights Management Services (RMS) to grant access rights to your document for individuals using their e-mail addresses.

- You can use the Document Inspector to remove personal data from a document before distributing it electronically.

- You can digitally sign a document to ensure its authenticity and prevent others from modifying it after you sign it.

- You can encrypt your document using a password for maximum document protection.

GET THE SCOOP ON...
Adding a table of contents ▪ Adding footnotes and endnotes ▪ Creating a bibliography ▪ Adding captions ▪
Adding cross-references to your document ▪ Making an
index ▪ Creating a table of authorities

# Create Reference Aids

I n this chapter, I describe how to add various types of reference aids to your document. You can add a table of contents, index, bibliography, footnotes, endnotes, citations, cross-references, captures, and, if you are in the legal profession, a table of authorities. By taking advantage of the automated versions of these reference aids, you can edit your document and move material around while Word keeps track of the changes and the implications they might have on, say, the page numbers of your table of contents. By using these built-in features, you can also have your reference aids match the formatting and look of the rest of your document because they are based on styles that change with your document's theme.

## Creating a table of contents

If you have a longer document, you may want to include a table of contents so that your reader can locate chapters within the document by finding the page number. There are two basic ways to create a table of contents in Word. You can take advantage of Word's automated table of contents, which keeps track of headings and which page they appear on, so that you can automatically generate a table of contents and update it when you make changes to your document. You can also create a table of contents manually.

## Inserting an automated table of contents

If you want to create an automated table of contents, you must first have contents to automate: You can't start with the table of contents and then write the document with this method (to do this, see the section on inserting a manual table of contents). If you use the built-in Heading styles (or styles built upon them) for the headings in your document, it is very easy to insert an automated table of contents. Simply move your cursor to the location where you want to insert the table of contents, choose References ⇨ Table of Contents, and select Automatic Table 1, Automatic Table 2, or Insert Table of Contents. If you select one of the automatic tables from the gallery, it is inserted at the cursor insertion point in your document, as shown in Figure 22.1. The automatic table is based on your current style and theme selection.

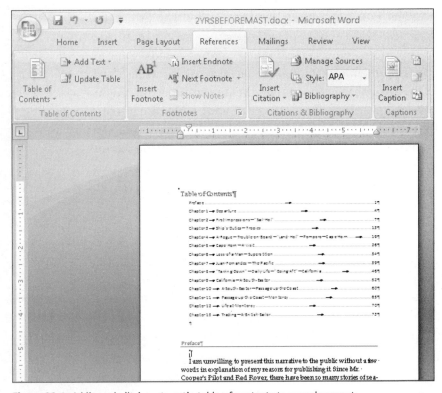

**Figure 22.1.** Adding a built-in automatic table of contents to your document

**Hack**

If you don't use built-in heading styles, you can still have Word identify them as headings. In the Indents and Spacing tab of Paragraph settings, set Outline level appropriately (not Body Text). The level must be high enough to be displayed by the table of contents (which only displays levels 1, 2, and 3 by default).

If you want to have your table of contents on a separate page, simply move your cursor to the line immediately following the table of contents and press Ctrl+Return or choose Insert ⇨ Pages ⇨ Page Break to make the following text start on the next page.

Once you insert a table of contents, it automatically includes hyperlinks to the sections referenced in it: When you Ctrl+Click on a heading, you are taken directly to the heading in the document.

### Formatting a table of contents

If you want to modify the settings for an existing table of contents, or if you want to insert a new automated table of contents that is not in the built-in list, choose References ⇨ Table of Contents ⇨ Insert Table of Contents to see the dialog box shown in Figure 22.2. (If you use this method to insert a new table of contents, it will not display the headings Contents or Table of Contents above the table of contents; you must add the heading yourself if desired.) Notice that you have different options for Web and Print Preview. In the Print Preview section, you can change how page numbers are treated. Deselect the Show page numbers option if you don't need to show page numbers. Deselect the Right align page numbers option if you want the page number to appear immediately after the chapter or heading name. The Tab leader list indicates what character should be used to lead the eye from the end of the heading name to the page number. You may also opt to have no tab leader.

In the General section of this dialog box, you can choose from several general formats besides the current template: Classic, Distinctive, Fancy, Modern, Formal, and Simple. Granted, the names aren't particularly

**Hack**

You can make quick and global changes to formatting of the table of contents by right-clicking the table of contents and then selecting a formatting command from the pop-up menu to apply to the entire table of contents.

helpful, but you can change the format and look in the Print and Web Preview windows to see how it will look in your document before committing to it. (Of course, you can always change it later on.)

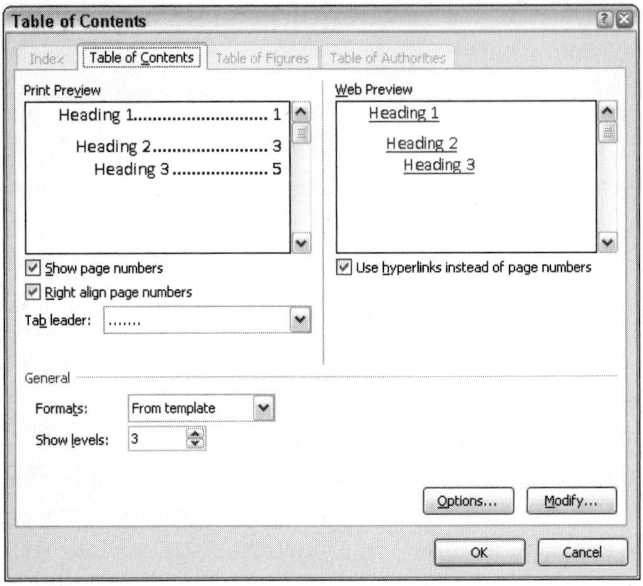

**Figure 22.2.** Adding a new table of contents or modifying settings

You can change how many levels are shown in the Show levels setting. Use the arrows or type a number from 1 to 9 here. If you have a longer document, remember to take into account levels for parts, sections, or chapters, as well as headings. If you notice that two heading levels appear at the same level in error in the table of contents, you can fix the problem by clicking Options to display the dialog box shown in Figure 22.3. You can select the criteria Word uses to build the table of contents in this box. By default, you use styles and outline levels (which shouldn't ordinarily conflict). However, you can assign different levels based

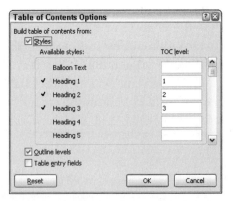

**Figure 22.3.** The Table of Contents Options dialog box

on style alone, outline level, or table entry field. This feature comes in handy if you have Heading 1 within a chapter, for example, but you have a long document divided into parts comprising chapters. You can assign the style for part names as level 1, the style for chapter names level 2, the Heading 1 style as level 3, and so on. Click OK when done or Reset to set things back to defaults.

You can modify styles of individual table of contents levels by clicking Modify. This displays the dialog box shown in Figure 22.4. Select a table of contents style (TOC 1, TOC 2, and so on, through TOC 9), and click Modify to make changes to font, paragraph, and other settings as you would with any other style.

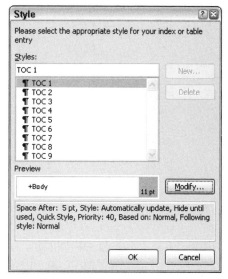

**Figure 22.4.** Modifying a table of contents entry style

Once you have the table of contents formatted as you would like it, I highly recommend saving your table of contents style to the Table of Contents gallery. To do so, select the table of contents and choose References ⇨ Table of Contents ⇨ Save Selection to Table of Contents Gallery. This allows you to save your settings as a building block in either your Building Blocks.dotx or Normal.dotm file. Once done, you can access your style from the Table of Contents gallery.

### Adding text to a table of contents

You may find occasion to add text to the table of contents. You can use this feature to add an additional level of heading or specify items that are not headings in the table of contents (such as initial content summaries, illustrations, tables, or key passages). You cannot add anything less than a paragraph, meaning that Word needs to see a paragraph mark delineating the end of the selection. To add text to the table of contents, select the paragraph and choose References ⇨ Add Text, as shown in Figure 22.5. Choose a level for the selected text. (There may be more levels to select from if you have elected to show more than three levels in your table of contents.) You can remove an entry you have added in this way by selecting it and then choosing References ⇨ Add Text ⇨ Do Not Show in Table of Contents. If you remove the entry by simply deleting it in the table of contents, it reappears if you update the table later.

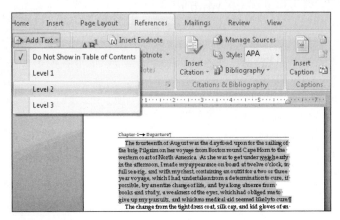

**Figure 22.5.** Adding text to the table of contents

## Updating a table of contents

If you create a draft of your document and you go on to make text or formatting changes, the pagination or heading phrasing may change. Word doesn't update the table of contents every time you make changes; you must choose References ⇨ Update Table (or click anywhere in the table and click Update Table). The dialog box shown in Figure 22.6 appears. This allows you to choose between updating only page numbers or updating everything else (in case you reword or change headings). If you know you are not changing headings you can select the Update page numbers only option (quicker in a very long document). Otherwise, select the Update entire table option to ensure you get all the changes. Click OK to proceed with the update.

**Figure 22.6.** Updating the table of contents

## Inserting a manual table of contents

If you want to include a table of contents that is independent from the document, move your insertion point to the point in your document where you want to add the table of contents and choose References ⇨ Table of Contents ⇨ Manual Table. Word inserts a table of contents in your document, as shown in Figure 22.7. To fill it out, click on each entry and type the desired text. (If you are using Draft document view, the blue shaded box will not appear, but you can still fill out the table of contents in the same manner.) You must copy and paste to add more entries. Although the Update Table button appears, it is not possible to update a manual table of contents — you receive an error message if you click this button.

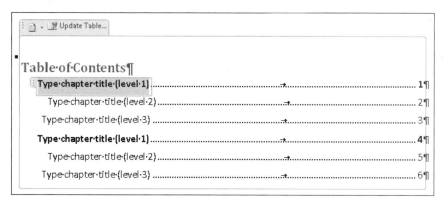

**Figure 22.7.** Adding a manually updated table of contents

## Removing a table of contents

You can't remove a table of contents by selecting it and pressing Delete. This empties the entries but leaves the empty table. To remove a table of contents, choose References ⇨ Table of Contents ⇨ Remove Table of Contents.

# Adding footnotes and endnotes

You can add footnotes or endnotes to your document in Word. A *footnote* is a note (often in smaller type) that appears at the foot of the page to indicate additional information that may be a digression or otherwise interrupt the flow of text if it were to occur in the body of the text. An *endnote* is similar to a footnote except that it appears at the end of a document. The reference point of the foot- or endnote is a superscript number or symbol in the text. You can have footnotes and endnotes in the same document, if necessary. In such a case, footnotes use arabic numerals and endnotes use roman numerals to differentiate the note types. Don't confuse a foot- or endnote with a bibliographical citation, another type of note that is handled differently. See the section on citations and bibliography later in this chapter for more information.

If you move text around, Word keeps track of the location of the foot- or endnote and renumbers in sequence automatically. You access the footnote and endnote features in the Footnotes group of the References tab on the Ribbon.

## Inserting a footnote

To insert a footnote using the default settings, move your cursor to the section of text for which you want to add a footnote and choose References ⇨ Insert Footnote. Word adds a superscript number at the point in the text where you insert the footnote, adds a rule to the foot of the page, adds the corresponding number beneath the rule, and moves the cursor immediately to the right of the number. You can now begin typing your footnote. Once you insert the footnote, it appears in a pop-up window if you hover over the footnote reference in the text. Figure 22.8 shows a sample of an initial reference in the text showing the pop-up window and Figure 22.9 shows the corresponding footnote. Note in the example that you can add font formatting to your footnote such as italic, but such formatting does not appear in the pop-up version.

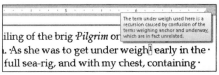

**Figure 22.8.** A footnote reference in text with the mouse over the note showing the footnote text in a pop-up window

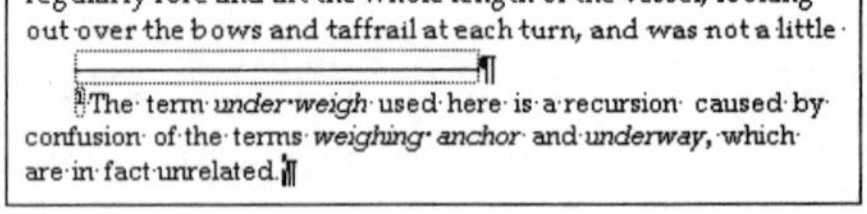

**Figure 22.9.** A typical footnote

**Hack**

You can add a footnote by pressing Alt+Ctrl+F. Add an endnote by pressing Alt+Ctrl+D.

## Inserting an endnote

To insert an endnote using the default settings, move your cursor to the section of text for which you want to add an endnote and choose References ⇨ Insert Endnote. As it does with footnotes, Word adds a superscript number at the point in the text where you insert the endnote. Word then adds a rule to the end of the document, adds the corresponding number beneath the rule, and moves the cursor immediately to the right of the number. You can now begin typing your endnote. Once you insert the endnote, it appears in a pop-up window if you hover over the endnote reference in the text. As with footnotes, you can add font formatting to your endnote such as italic, but such formatting does not show up in the pop-up version.

## Navigating between notes

To navigate between foot- or endnotes within a document, click a selection from the Next Footnote list in the Footnotes group of the References tab. Click Next Footnote to go to the next footnote. Click the arrow and select Previous Footnote, Next Endnote, or Previous Endnote. This takes you to the reference point in the text of your document. To go to the actual note itself, choose References ⇨ Show Notes. This is a toggle command; to go back to the reference in the text, click the Show Notes button again.

## Footnote and endnote options

If you want to use a different numbering system for your notes, convert endnotes to footnotes, or make other changes to the footnote and endnote settings, click the Footnotes dialog box launcher in the References tab to see the dialog box shown in Figure 22.10.

You can change the location of footnotes and endnotes. With footnotes, you can have the footnote appear at the foot of the page or the end of text on the page (so that the rule and footnote appear in the middle of the page, for example, if the page is only half filled with text). With endnotes, you can have them appear at the end of a document or the end of a section. This last option is particularly useful if you like to have your endnotes appear at the end of each chapter in a multichapter document. If you decide you want to convert all your endnotes to footnotes, or vice versa, click Convert in the Footnote and Endnote dialog box.

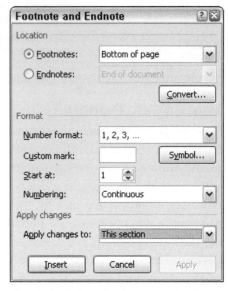

**Figure 22.10.** Changing footnote and endnote settings

You can choose from six Number formats: Arabic numerals (1, 2, 3, ...), lowercase letters, uppercase letters, lowercase Roman numerals, uppercase Roman numerals, and symbols (asterisk, dagger, double dagger, section mark, and so on).

By default, notes start numbering with 1 (or the first entry in the number format series, whatever that might be). You can change that by using the arrows keys to select a different starting point in the Start at box. Finally, your numbering can be continuous, it can start anew with each page, or it can start with each section. Click Apply to apply any changes made in this dialog box, or Insert to insert a new foot- or endnote.

## Removing footnotes and endnotes

To remove a footnote or endnote, select the reference number or symbol in the text and press Delete. (If you delete the text at the footnote or endnote area, the reference number or symbol and rule remain with a blank entry.)

**Inside Scoop**

You can choose a custom mark to use. Type the symbol in the Custom mark field, or choose a symbol by clicking Symbol.

# Adding citations and a bibliography

You can add citations and a bibliography to your document. This is particularly useful in academic and scientific writing. Word 2007 has added this greatly needed feature in a smart way. You can add sources as you write and select from a list to cite as you go. Because many documents refer to one source more than once, this can be a great timesaver. Because different disciplines have different standards for citation, Microsoft has built in several bibliography styles to accommodate these various disciplines so you can select the style that fits your discipline, and all the minor punctuation rules for your bibliography are taken care of by Word.

## Inserting a citation

To insert a citation, select the section of text you want to cite and choose References ⇨ Insert Citation. The menu shown in Figure 22.11 appears.

You have three options. First, you can click Add New Source to enter the details of a new source as you cite it, and the Create Source dialog box appears, as shown in Figure 22.12. The actual fields shown depend on your chosen bibliography style and type of source. To show all fields, select the Show All Bibliography Fields option. Specify a tag name for

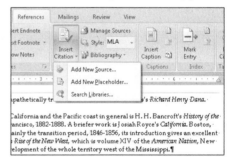

**Figure 22.11.** Inserting a citation into a document

this source (often the last name of the author or the title of a work). By default, Word assigns the tag name Placeholder1, Place-holder2, and so on. Assign a useful tag name that will appear in parenthesis in the text.

Your second option for inserting a citation is to tag your citation and add the information later. To do this, choose References ⇨ Insert Citation ⇨ Add New Placeholder. In the Placeholder name field, type a tag name. As with the previous option, assign a useful tag here; it will appear in parentheses in the text.

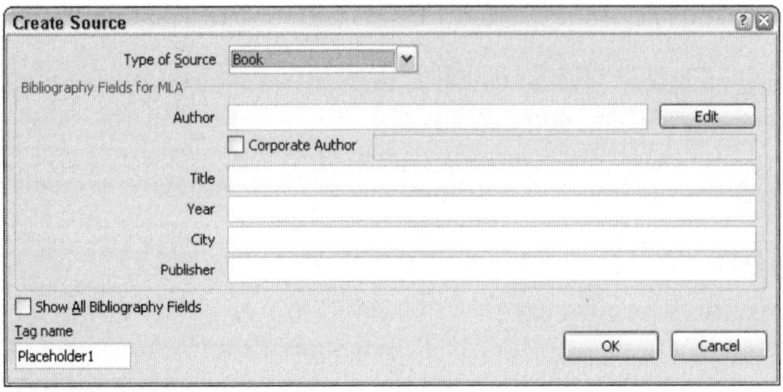

**Figure 22.12.** Creating a source for a bibliography in the MLA (Modern Language Association) style for a book

Last, you can search for your source online using Office's search capabilities. To do so, choose References ⇨ Insert Citation ⇨ Search Libraries, type the source title, author, or other search criteria in the Search for field of the Research pane and click the green arrow to begin the search, as shown in the example in Figure 22.13. This option just gets you to the information — you still need to use one of the other options to insert the citation tag into your document.

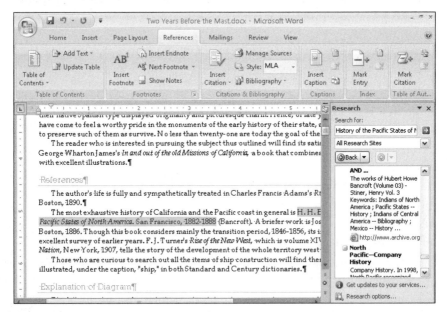

**Figure 22.13.** Searching online libraries to find a source

Once you insert the citation, it appears with the tag name in parentheses. In Print Layout view, if you click the citation, a frame appears. Click the arrow to see the options shown in Figure 22.14. You can edit the citation to include page numbers cited or suppress the author, year, or title, if included. Clicking Edit Source brings up a dialog box to edit the source (much like the Create Source dialog box). The last option converts the citation to static text. Use this option in the event that you don't intend to include a bibliography and you therefore want to add any citations inline.

**Figure 22.14.** Citation options

## Managing sources

You can manage sources cited, add new ones, and draw from an existing list by choosing References ⇨ Manage Sources. This displays the Source Manager, as shown in Figure 22.15. You can search for a source, create a master list, transfer sources from the master list to the current list (that of the current document), edit sources, and preview citations. The master list is stored as an XML file in the C:\Documents and Settings\[*your user name*]\Application Data\Microsoft\Bibliography.

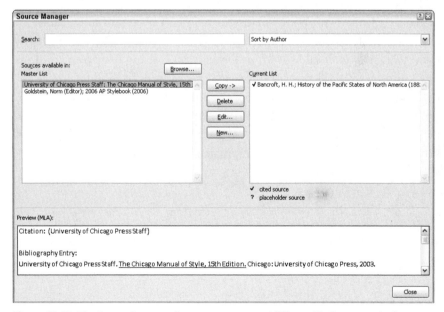

**Figure 22.15.** The Source Manager allows you to manage bibliographical sources cited.

## Selecting a bibliography and citation style

You can select a style that matches your field or discipline. For example, if you are writing a paper in college for an English literature class, select MLA for the Modern Language Association's style for citation and bibliography. If you are writing a nonfiction book for publication in the United States, choose Chicago to follow the style rules of the *Chicago Manual of Style*. If you are submitting your document for publication, the submission guidelines provided to you most likely specify a style guide to follow, or

your editor should know what bibliographical style is required. To select a bibliography and citation style, choose References ⇨ Style to see the choices listed in Figure 22.16. Note that the citation style changes when you make this selection (publication year may appear or disappear, a comma is added, the author name is replaced by a number, and so on).

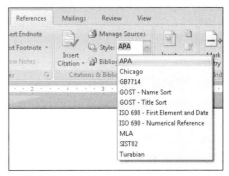

**Figure 22.16.** Selecting a citation and bibliography style

## Inserting a bibliography

When you finish with your document, you can insert a bibliography by choosing References ⇨ Bibliography. This displays the bibliography gallery like the example shown in Figure 22.17, using your own citations in the preview. Word provides two versions of built-in bibliographies for the selected style, one titled Bibliography and one titled Works Cited. Each bibliography style produces different built-in examples. The example in Figure 22.17 shows the MLA style. If you select the Insert Bibliography option, the bibliography is inserted without a title.

---

**Watch Out!**

Once you convert a bibliography to static text, you can't change bibliography style or update the bibliography entries automatically. You must edit the bibliography manually.

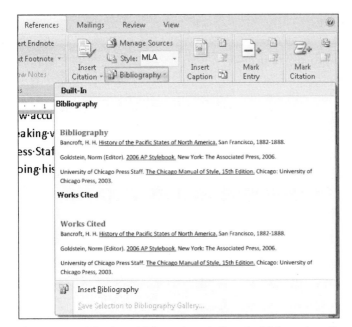

**Figure 22.17.** Selecting a bibliography style from the bibliography gallery

## Updating a bibliography

You can make changes to your document after inserting the bibliography. Just click in the bibliography, click the Bibliographies button at the top of the frame, and select Update Bibliography.

## Converting a bibliography to static text

If you want to convert a bibliography to static text, click the Bibliographies button at the top of the frame, and select Convert bibliography to static text.

## Adding captions

You can add captions to your document's illustrations, equations, or tables in Word. Using the caption feature allows you to automate the process of numbering these items, and keeping a label connected to the object you are labeling. If you use the caption feature, you can also generate a table of figures, tables, or equations that is updated along with the rest of the document.

## Inserting a caption

To insert a caption, select the illustration, equation, or table, and choose References ⇨ Insert Caption. A dialog box like the one shown in Figure 22.18 appears. By default, Word assigns the label Figure followed by a number for picture objects, such as Figure 1 in the example in Figure 22.18, Table 1 for tables, and Equation 1 for equations. To use the default label and numbering system, just type any additional caption text after the label and number in the Caption text box. Click OK to insert the caption below the selected object, as shown in Figure 22.19. You can use the frame handles around the caption to adjust its size. To delete a caption, click the caption and delete it.

**Figure 22.18.** Adding a caption to an illustration

**Figure 22.19.** A figure caption added to an illustration

## Setting caption options

You can change the label for the caption to Figure, Equation, or Table. If these choices aren't sufficient, you can add your own label name (such as Illustration, Exhibit, and so on) by clicking New Label and typing the new label's name. To delete a custom label once it has been added to the list, select it in the Label list and click Delete Label. You cannot delete the built-in label names. If you prefer to suppress labels of

**Bright Idea**

Captions are a type of text box. If you want to give your caption some additional design treatment, select the caption, choose Text Box Tools ⇨ Format, and make any changes to improve the caption's appearance. For font and paragraph changes, modify the Caption style.

any kind from your captions, select the Exclude label from caption option. This still leaves the consecutive number, however, which for some reason can only be removed manually once the caption is inserted into the document.

To change the relative position of the caption to the item selected, click the Position list and select to have the caption either above or below the selected item.

To change the numbering style, click the Numbering button in the Caption dialog box to display the Caption Numbering dialog box. You can choose from five Number formats: Arabic numerals (1, 2, 3, ...), lowercase letters, uppercase letters, lowercase Roman numerals, and uppercase Roman numerals. If you have sections or chapters that you want to include in your numbering system (as is done in this book), select the Include chapter number option. Your chapters must be numbered using a multi-level list style that includes headings in order for this to work. You must then select the style with which the chapter starts from the list and choose a separator, such as a hyphen or a period. In this book, for example, Arabic numerals are used for the figure numbering, with chapters included, separated with a period, for both tables and figures.

## Using the AutoCaption feature

To automatically include a caption when you insert an object type into your document, choose References ➪ Insert Caption ➪ AutoCaption to display the dialog box shown in Figure 22.20. In this example figure, Bitmap Image is checked. This means that any time a bitmap image file is added to the document, an accompanying figure caption is inserted. Note that you must select or create an appropriate label for any object type you select, otherwise Word assumes Figure in every case. Click OK when you are satisfied with your settings.

**Figure 22.20.** The AutoCaption dialog box

## Adding a table of figures

After adding captions to your illustrations, you can create a table of figures by choosing References ⇨ Table of Figures to see the dialog box shown in Figure 22.21. The Table of Figures options are very similar to those for a table of contents. Notice that you have different options for Web and Print Preview. In the Print Preview section, you can change how page numbers are treated. Deselect the Show page numbers option if you don't need to show page numbers. Deselect the Right align page numbers option if you want the page number to appear immediately after the chapter or heading name. The Tab leader list indicates what character should be used to lead the eye from the end of the figure caption to the page number. You can also opt to have no tab leader.

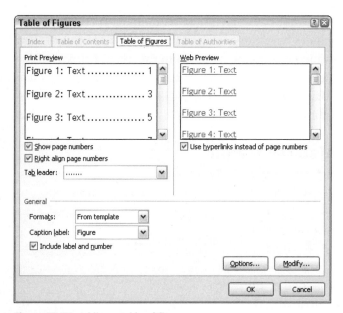

**Figure 22.21.** Adding a table of figures

In the General section of this dialog box, you can choose from several general formats besides the current template: Classic, Distinctive, Centered, Formal, and Simple. As with the table of contents formats, the names aren't particularly helpful, but you can change the format and look in the Print and Web Preview windows to see how it will look in your document before committing to it.

**Hack**

You can make quick and global changes to formatting of the table of figures by right-clicking the table of figures and then selecting a formatting command from the pop-up menu to apply to the entire table of figures.

You can select a caption category to display for your list in the Caption label setting. Use the arrows to choose a label from the list or choose no label. Deselect the Include label and number option if you want to remove the number and label from the table of figures. Click Options to select what criteria Word uses to build the table of figures in this box. By default, you use styles. However, you can assign different levels based on style alone or table entry field. Click OK when done.

You can modify the Table of Figures style by clicking Modify. Select a Table of Figures style (if you have more than one), and then click Modify to make changes to font, paragraph, and other settings as you would with any other style. Click OK when done.

In the Table of Figures dialog box, click OK when you are ready to insert the table into your document. This feature does not provide a built-in title — you must add your own such as Table of Figures, List of Illustrations, or some other title.

## Using cross-references

You can include cross-references in your document for two reasons: so that readers can click to go directly to a cross-reference when reading the document online, and so that you can keep your references automatically updated when you move things around. To insert a cross-reference, position your cursor at the point in the text where you want to include the cross-reference. Choose Insert ⇨ Link ⇨ Cross-Reference (or References ⇨ Cross-reference) to display the Cross-reference dialog box shown in Figure 22.22.

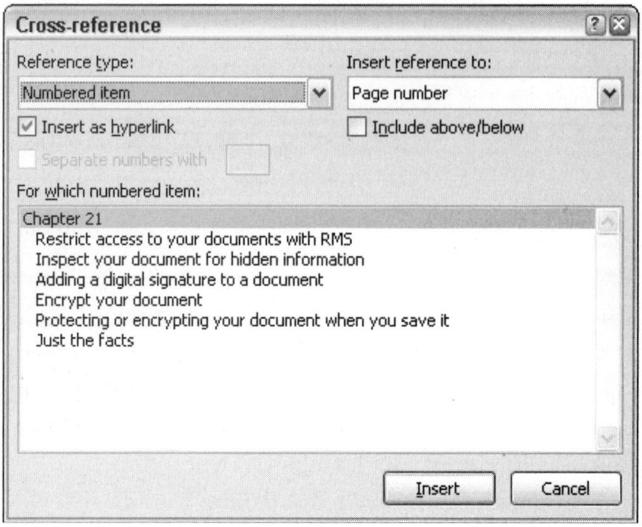

**Figure 22.22.** The Cross-reference dialog box

Select the reference type from the list. All the references of that type will be listed. For example, Figure 22.23 shows all the figure captions in the document.

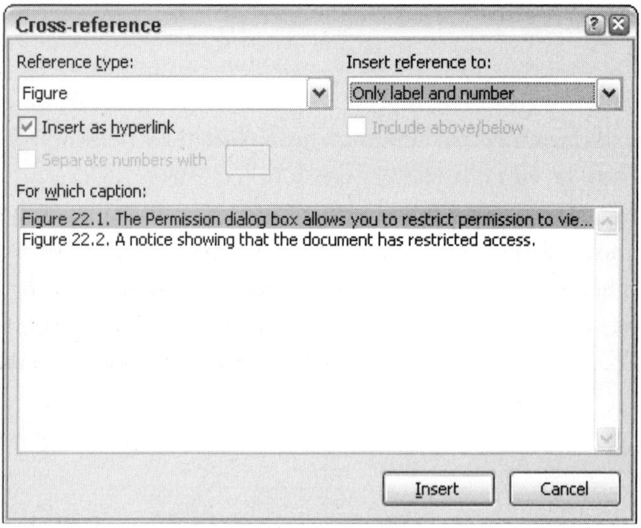

**Figure 22.23.** Selecting a cross-reference type

To add the reference, first choose what you want to insert into the text in the Insert reference to list: You can add the entire caption, only the label and number, only the caption text, the page number, or specify above/below. Next, click Insert to insert the reference. Figure 22.24 shows the cross-reference to a figure caption. Note that you can Ctrl+click to get directly to that figure's caption.

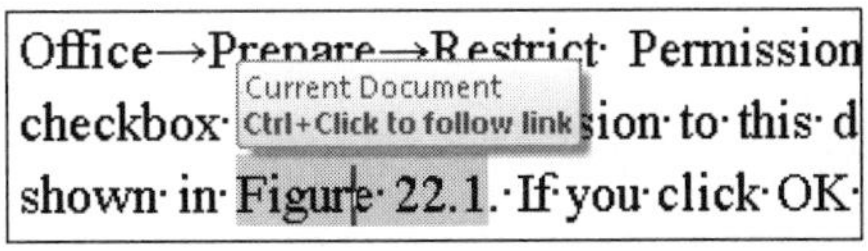

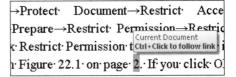

**Figure 22.24.** Inserting a cross-reference with label and number

Figure 22.25 shows a cross-reference to the same item, but this time the cross-reference is the page number.

**Figure 22.25.** Inserting a cross-reference using a page number

# Creating an index

You can create an index to your document in Word. To do this, you can either mark individual terms to include in the index, use an AutoMark file with a list of terms that Word will use to find and include in the index, or you can combine the two methods, using an AutoMark file for the obvious terms and then marking additional entries as needed.

If you know that your document will include an index, it is best to bear in mind important instances of terms, such as when a term is defined. You might elect to mark that instance of a term as you are writing. However, this might be too much to think about when you want to be concentrating on writing. In my experience, it's best to tag a document with index entries after the document is complete. That way, you can go through and mark index entries in a separate pass through the document. In the publishing industry, it is common to employ professional indexers who are experts at identifying key terms that belong in an index.

## Marking an index entry

To mark a term as an index entry, select the term and press Alt+Shift+X or choose References ⇨ Mark Entry. The Mark Index Entry dialog box appears, as shown in Figure 22.26. By default, the selected text is listed in the Main entry field. However, you can edit this field and the subentry field. For example, you may want *Atlantic spotted dolphin* to appear under the main entry *dolphin,* as a subentry *Atlantic spotted.* There would perhaps also be another subentry for the bottlenose dolphin.

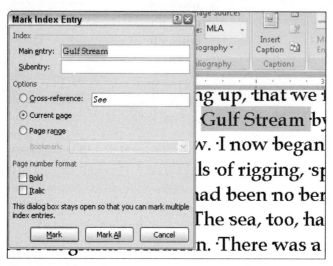

**Figure 22.26.** Marking an entry to include in the index

You can also choose to cross-reference another term. (This is not to be confused with the cross-reference feature mentioned earlier in this chapter.) For example, you might have an entry for one term that directs you to another one used more frequently in your document, such as "Car. *See* Automobile." Click Cross-reference and type your cross-referenced term after *See.* If you want to list the page where you have marked the entry, select the Current page option. To select a page range for an entry that is discussed over several pages, insert a bookmark at the end of the discussion, then go back and mark the beginning of the discussion and select the Page range option. Select the bookmark from the list of bookmarks to establish the beginning and end of the page range.

**Hack**

If you are displaying paragraph marks and other hidden formatting symbols, index entries will be visible in your document as field codes. If you find this distracting, press Ctrl+* or choose Home ⇨ Show/Hide Paragraph to hide the field codes and other marks.

If you want to include italic or bold in the page number (such as bold for the term defined or the main entry), select the corresponding checkbox as you make the entry. When you finish with the entry, click Mark. Click Mark All if you want to mark all instances of the selected term in the document. Take care with this last option if the term is common and you have a long document — having 40 entries for a term is rarely useful.

Figure 22.27 shows a document after having marked a term as an index entry. The index entry is inserted as a field code. The letter combination XE indicates

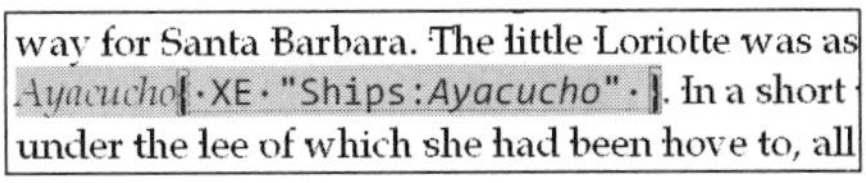

> way for Santa Barbara. The little Loriotte was as
> Ayacucho{·XE·"Ships:Ayacucho"·}. In a short
> under the lee of which she had been hove to, all

**Figure 22.27.** Text marked with an index entry

that it is an index entry. The actual entry is enclosed in double quotes. In the entry shown in Figure 22.27, the main entry is Ships and the subentry is one ship's name, *Ayacucho,* so the text of the index entry appears as "Ships:Ayacucho" in the field code. You can edit individual entries directly once they have been inserted into text if necessary.

Since the most common way to tag a document for indexing is to go through it all at once, this dialog box stays open after you mark an entry. If it gets in your way, click the Close button.

## Using an AutoMark file to mark up a document for an index

Besides going through and marking your index by hand, you can also develop a list of terms that you want to index. You can use just these terms or combine them with the terms you mark manually. First, create an AutoMark file. Open a new Word document and type your list of terms to be marked as index entries when found in your document, pressing Return after each term so that each is on its own line as its own paragraph. The terms do not need to be in any sort of order. Avoid using this method for terms that occur very frequently in your document because, like the Mark All command, this leads to the index entry with a meaninglessly large number of pages where the term appears. Be sure to check the spelling: If you misspell a word in the AutoMark file, it won't be tagged in the document (unless you have misspelled it there, too). Save and name the AutoMark file. Open the document you need to index and choose References ⇨ Insert Index ⇨ AutoMark, select the AutoMark file you created from the Open Index AutoMark File dialog box, and click Open. Word inserts an index entry for every instance of the words in your list.

## Adding the index

Once you finish tagging your document manually and/or with an AutoMark file, position your cursor in the document where you want to insert your index and choose References ⇨ Insert Index to see the dialog box shown in Figure 22.28. The Print Preview shows you what your index will look like (using its own sample text, not your document). The Indented type option indents subentries and the Run-in type option runs the subentries together in a hanging paragraph under the main entry, each separated by a semicolon. You can choose the number of columns: 1 through 4 or Auto. Auto allows Word to determine the best fit. The Language selection allows you to switch languages if you are using more than one. The Formats list allows you to work with your current template or to select Classic, Fancy, Modern, or Bulleted formats. The named formats all supply letter headings for each letter of the alphabet that appears in your index. The format using your template does not. If you use the Indented index type, you can select the Right align page numbers option and choose a tab leader, much as you would with a table of contents.

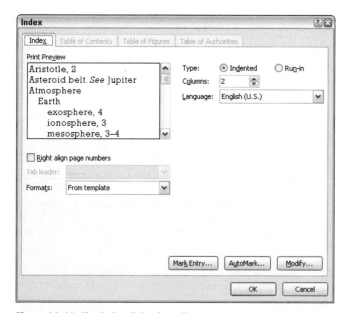

**Figure 22.28.** The Index dialog box allows you to set indexing options.

You can modify the index style by clicking Modify. Select an index style and click Modify to make changes to font, paragraph, and other settings as you would with any other style. Click OK when done.

Once you are done making any changes to format, style, and other settings, click OK in the Index dialog box to insert the index into your document.

## Updating the index

If you make changes to your document, the page location of index entries is likely to change. Fortunately, you can update your index so that the index matches the pagination of your document. To update the index, click anywhere in the index and choose References ⇨ Update Index.

# Creating a table of authorities

If you are writing a legal document, you may need to create a special type of reference list called a table of authorities. This feature works much like the index or bibliography features. First, mark each citation, be it case, statute, or other category, and then insert the table of authorities.

## Marking a citation

To mark a citation for a table of authorities, select the text to be cited and click Mark Citation to see the dialog box shown in Figure 22.29. Click Mark to mark the citation for inclusion in the table of authorities. Click Mark All to include every instance of this authority. You can choose a short and long citation form by editing the text in the correspon-ding text fields.

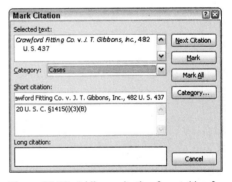

**Figure 22.29.** Adding a citation for a table of authorities

## Inserting a table of authorities

After you mark all authorities in your document, position your cursor where you want the table of authorities to appear in your document and choose References ⇨ Insert Table of Authorities. The dialog box shown in Figure 22.30 appears. You can choose a format: from the template, Classic, Distinctive, Formal, or Simple. You can select the Use passim option if you want to allow use of the term to denote that references are made throughout rather than list individual page references. Select the categories that you want to appear from the categories list, or select for all citations to appear. When satisfied with the settings, click OK to insert the table of authorities in your document.

**Figure 22.30.** The Table of Authorities dialog box

# Updating a table of authorities

If you make changes to your document, the page location of the table of authorities entries is likely to change. Fortunately, you can update your table of authorities so that it matches the pagination of your document. To update the table of authorities, click anywhere in the table of authorities and choose References ⇨ Update Table of Authorities.

## Just the facts

■ You can take advantage of Word's table of contents feature to automate the addition of this reference feature to your document, which can also function as an online navigation tool.

■ You can add footnotes or endnotes to your document.

■ You can add captions to your illustrations, tables, and equations. This also allows you to compile a list of illustrations, tables, or equations.

■ You can mark up your document for indexing or use a predefined list of terms.

■ You can add citations and compile a table of authorities for legal documents.

**GET THE SCOOP ON...**
How to be safe with macros ▪ How to record a macro ▪
How to write a macro using Visual Basic ▪ Working with
smart tags

# Save Time with Macros

Chapter 23

*M*acros are small command sequences, either recorded or programmed, that can be invoked to automate your work and save you from repetitive tasks. You can assign macros to key combinations to give you keyboard shortcuts, assign them to buttons that you can add to the QAT, or you can run them from the Macros window on the Developer tab. Before talking about how to create macros, it's important to discuss macro security. Then I give you a list of common tasks that you don't need to write a macro to automate, but that are not easily found in the Word interface. Next, I show you how to create macros by using the macro recorder technique. I also show you how to work with Visual Basic to review and modify macros, although teaching you how to program is beyond the scope of this book. Finally, I cover smart tags and how to take advantage of them to save yourself time. Smart tags are not macros, but they do fall under the heading of automating your work and timesaving, so I include them in this chapter.

## Macros and security

If you give a software program a truly powerful customization feature, it can unfortunately be used maliciously in a truly powerful way as well. You need to be able to create macros to save time and avoid repetitive tasks, but you also need a way to prevent untrustworthy people from using macros to cause you problems. Microsoft gives you several ways to handle this at the software application level. I heartily recommend keeping your security procedures in force and your antivirus software up to date, but I won't discuss those elements of the security environment here. You can get information on these topics from Microsoft by choosing Microsoft Office ⇨ Word Options ⇨ Trust Center and following the appropriate links. I limit myself to how Microsoft handles security with Word and macros in this chapter. Two concepts are used to help keep your Word documents protected: trusted sources and macro control.

To access the macro security settings for Word, choose Microsoft Office ⇨ Word Options ⇨ Trust Center ⇨ Trust Center Settings. The options shown in Figure 23.1 appear.

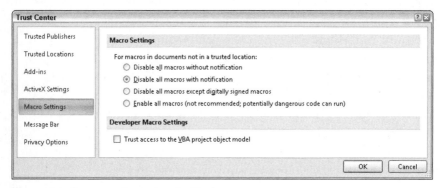

**Figure 23.1.** Macro security settings for Word

## Working with macros disabled

By default, Word disables all macros in files. What this means is that you receive a warning at the top of the document (below the Ribbon) notifying you that macros have been disabled. You receive this warning even if you created the macros yourself if this option is set when you first open a document. Clicking Options in the Warning message brings you further information, as shown in Figure 23.2. Select the Help protect me from unknown content (recommended) option, and click OK unless you created the macro yourself or you know and trust the source of the macros. If one of these conditions is met, select the Enable this content radio button and then click OK. If the document has a valid digital signature, you also have the option to trust all documents from this publisher. Select this option to add the publisher to your Trusted Publishers list (see the

**Hack**

You can also get to the macro security settings more directly if you have the Developer tab showing by choosing Developer ➪ Macro Security.

following section). If you do not enable macros, you can still view and work with the document — you just won't have access to the macros.

**Figure 23.2.** Viewing a macro security alert

If you want to routinely disable macros and don't want to see the warning message every time you open a document with macros, choose Microsoft Office ➪ Word Options ➪ Trust Center ➪ Trust Center Settings, and select the Disable all macros without notification option. You can work with the document without fear of any malicious macros being turned on. If you do try to run a macro with this option selected, you receive an error message letting you know that macros have been disabled.

## Working with trusted publishers and trusted locations

This is a chapter on macros, after all. You may actually want to *use* some of them. What tools does Microsoft give you to ensure that only the safe ones are available? You have two ways to efficiently manage macros that

**Watch Out!**
Don't include anyone in your trusted publishers list who doesn't have a digital certificate. Instead, store macros from this source in your trusted location (on your local drive, not a server location). That way, you are more protected from those posing as your trusted source.

you trust. You can trust a publisher (such as Microsoft — however you may feel about it, you can most likely put it on your trusted publishers list), or you can trust a macro and store it in a trusted location. All trusted macros by trusted publishers should have a digital certificate ensuring that they are who they say they are. If you have a document created by a trusted source but that source doesn't have a digital certificate (perhaps a colleague or your own IT department), you can store the document in a trusted location, such as your Trusted Templates folder. If you want to open documents containing macros that are trusted without first seeing the warning to enable the macros, adjust your Trust Center settings accordingly. To enable macros in documents or templates from trusted publishers or in trusted locations, choose Microsoft Office ⇨ Word Options ⇨ Trust Center ⇨ Trust Center Settings and select the Disable all macros except digitally signed macros option. I can see very few circumstances in which you would want to select the Enable all macros option, unless you are a security specialist or developer working under controlled conditions. It's best to forget about this option.

If you want to lock down your macros further, choose Microsoft Office ⇨ Word Options ⇨ Trust Center ⇨ Trust Center Settings ⇨ Trusted Locations. From this window, you can remove a specific trusted location, add one, or disable all trusted locations so that only trusted publishers are trusted. Choose Microsoft Office ⇨ Word Options ⇨ Trust Center ⇨ Trust Center Settings ⇨ Trusted Publishers to view or remove a trusted publisher from your list.

## Recording a macro

If you are going to create macros in Word, you can go about it in one of two ways: You can record the macro, or you can program it in Visual Basic. Either way, it's a good idea to choose Microsoft Office ⇨ Word Options ⇨ Popular and select the Show Developer tab in the Ribbon option (if this tab is not already displayed). Even if you don't think of

**Bright Idea**

I recommend displaying macro recording status on the status bar. It makes things easier to track and gives you another way to stop and start a macro. Right-click the status bar (immediately below the horizontal slider) and click Macro Recording. Click elsewhere in the document to close the menu.

yourself as a developer and you don't plan on using Visual Basic, the Developer tab gives you ready access to all the macro-related commands.

If you have no programming knowledge but have a very specific sequence of commands you want to be able to repeat, I suggest recording a macro. Before you begin, though, look at Table 23.1, which gives you a list of things you can do without having to record a macro.

**Table 23.1.** Things you don't need a macro for

| Task | Automation Technique |
|------|----------------------|
| Long sections of boilerplate text | Use the Building Blocks organizer for this. |
| Frequently used words or phrases | Add to the AutoCorrect list (Microsoft Office ⇨ Word Options ⇨ Proofing ⇨ AutoCorrect Options). |
| Easier access to an existing command | Add it to the QAT. |
| Adding your name or initials | Insert ⇨ Quick Parts ⇨ Field ⇨ UserName or UserInit. |
| Adding your address | Add your address in the Advanced section of Word Options, and then click Insert ⇨ Quick Parts ⇨ Field ⇨ UserAddress. |

## A sample macro assigned to a key combination

The easiest way to show you how to create a macro is to create a sample one. In this sample macro, you create a macro that finds all instances of a phrase and changes that phrase's formatting. The macro will be assigned to a keyboard combination so that it can be invoked whenever you need to use the macro by typing that key combination. You store the macro in your sample document. However, if you want to create a macro that you will have access to all the time, you can save it in Normal.dotm instead. To create the macro, follow these steps:

1. Open a new document.

2. Choose Developer ➪ Macro Security, and select Disable all macros except digitally signed macros. Click OK.

3. Type the following sample text: **Example, Inc.**

4. Press Ctrl+S. In the Save as type field, select Word Macro-Enabled Document (*.docm).

5. Type **MacroSample1.docm** in the File name field.

6. In the Save in list, select Trusted Templates and click Save.

7. Press Ctrl+Home to get to the beginning of the document.

8. Click the Record Macro button in the status bar (if displayed) or choose Developer ➪ Record Macro. The Record Macro dialog box appears.

9. In the Macro name field, type **ExampleNameFormat** as shown in Figure 23.3.

10. In the Store macro in field, select MacroSample1.docm (document).

11. In the description field, type **Finds Example, Inc. and changes format to dark blue, bold, small caps.**

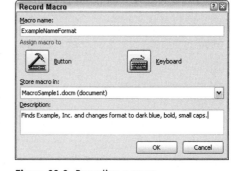

**Figure 23.3.** Recording a macro

12. Click Keyboard. The Customize Keyboard dialog box appears, as shown in Figure 23.4. Press Alt+Ctrl+4 (or some other key combination where the Currently assigned to line reads [unassigned]).

13. In the Save changes in field, choose MacroSample1.docm. Your screen should now look like Figure 23.4.

14. Click Assign (you could, at this point, add alternate key combinations) and then Close.

At this point, your cursor should look like an arrow with an audiocassette (indicating that you are recording). You now "record" the macro by invoking a series of Word commands. Any backpedaling and Undo commands are also added to the recorded macro, so try to go through these steps exactly:

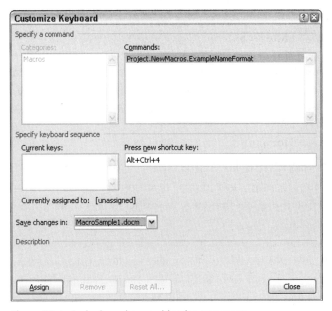

**Figure 23.4.** Assigning a key combination to a macro

1. Choose Home ⇨ Editing ⇨ Replace.

2. Click More.

3. In the Find what field, type **Example, Inc.**

4. In the Replace with field, also type **Example, Inc.**

5. Select the text you just typed in the Replace with field.

6. Choose Format ⇨ Font.

7. In the Font style list, click Bold.

8. In the Font color list, click Dark Blue from the Standard Colors list.

9. In the Effects list, select the Small caps checkbox.

10. Click OK.

11. Back in the Replace box, click Replace All.

12. Click OK to acknowledge that the replacements have been made.

13. Click Stop Recording on the status bar (or choose Developer ⇨ Stop Recording).

14. Although the Find and Replace dialog box remains open, it is not necessary to close it while recording the macro. Click Close in the Find and Replace dialog box now.

15. Click Save to save your changes so far.

To test the macro, delete the current text by selecting it and pressing Delete (don't use the Backspace key) and type **Example, Inc.** a few times in the document. Press Alt+Ctrl+4. The text string should convert immediately into bold, dark blue, small caps. If you don't save the file to a trusted location as we have in this example (Trusted Templates), this macro is disabled when you reopen the file unless you enable macros manually.

## A sample macro assigned to a button

In the next sample, I show you how to remove "shouting" in a document — the term used to describe the effect that large amounts of text in all uppercase letters has on the reader. You can do this by clicking a button, but you also change bold to normal and colored text to black for good measure. In this macro, you will have the macro apply to selected text only, and you assign it to a button rather than a key combination. In general, you should use this type of macro if you are adding it to your Normal.dotm file, because the button appears on your QAT whether you can access the macro or not. To create the macro, follow these steps:

1. Open a new document.
2. If you have not already done so, choose Developer ⇨ Macro Security, select Disable all macros except digitally signed macros, and click OK.
3. Type a brief paragraph of sample text in all uppercase letters in colors, with some bold. Optionally, you can type some other paragraphs before or after this text.
4. Press Ctrl+S. In the Save as type field, select Word Macro-Enabled Document (*.docm).
5. In the File name field, type **MacroSample2.docm** and click Save (saving it in Trusted Templates if you intend to use it again).
6. Select the paragraph with the text in all uppercase letters.
7. Click the Record Macro button in the status bar (if displayed) or choose Developer ⇨ Record Macro.
8. In the Macro name field, type **StopShouting**. (Don't include the period.)
9. In the Store macro in field, select MacroSample2.docm (document).

10. In the Description field, type **Converts selected text to sentence case, removes bold and color.**

11. Click Button. You will see the Customize screen of Word Options.

12. Click the new macro from your list at the left (it begins with Project.NewMacros.StopShouting).

13. Click Add. Your screen should now look something like Figure 23.5.

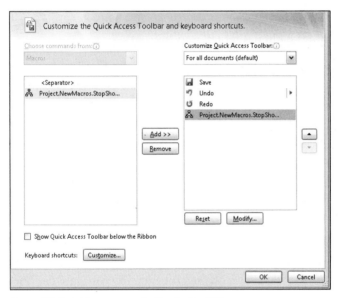

**Figure 23.5.** Adding a macro button to the QAT

14. Click the macro in the list at the right, and click Modify.

15. Choose an icon that best fits your macro from the symbols in the Modify Button dialog box shown in Figure 23.6 and click OK. I'll choose the red exclamation point in a box as the most appropriate here.

16. Click OK again to close Word Options.

**Figure 23.6.** Assigning an icon to a macro button

At this point, your cursor should look like an arrow with an audiocassette (indicating that you are recording), as with the previous example. You now record the macro by invoking a series of Word commands. Again, any backpedaling and Undo commands are added to the recorded macro, so try to go through these steps exactly. Your block of uppercase text should still be selected:

1. Choose Home ⇨ Font Color ⇨ Black (Text 1).

2. Click the Font dialog box launcher on the Home tab.

3. In the Font style field, click Regular, and then OK.

4. Choose Home ⇨ Change Case ⇨ Sentence case.

5. Click Stop Recording on the status bar (or choose Developer ⇨ Stop Recording).

To test your macro, click Undo (or press Ctrl+Z) three times to put your text back into its original color, bold, and uppercase form. Click the red exclamation point (or whatever button you have chosen) on the QAT to invoke the macro. This macro is disabled when you reopen the file unless you save it to a trusted location or enable macros manually.

## Working with macros in Visual Basic

If you create a macro and want to see the code underlying the macro or make minor changes without rerecording the macro, you can use the Visual Basic editor to view the macro and make changes. To do so, open the file containing the macro in question and press Alt+F8, or choose Developer ⇨ Macros to see the dialog box shown in Figure 23.7. From this screen, you can run a macro (useful if you have macros that you haven't assigned to a button or key combination), step into the macro (this allows you to view the macro one procedure at a time), edit the macro, create a new macro, or delete a macro. Click Organizer to move or copy macros from one file to another.

If you click Edit, the Visual Basic editor launches and you can see the code that your recorded macro has generated. Figure 23.8 shows the code generated from the first sample macro you created, which all fits in one subroutine. If you are familiar with programming code or are somewhat fearless, you can edit particularly obvious sections of the code (such as the text strings associated with .Text and .Replacement.Text in Figure 23.8).

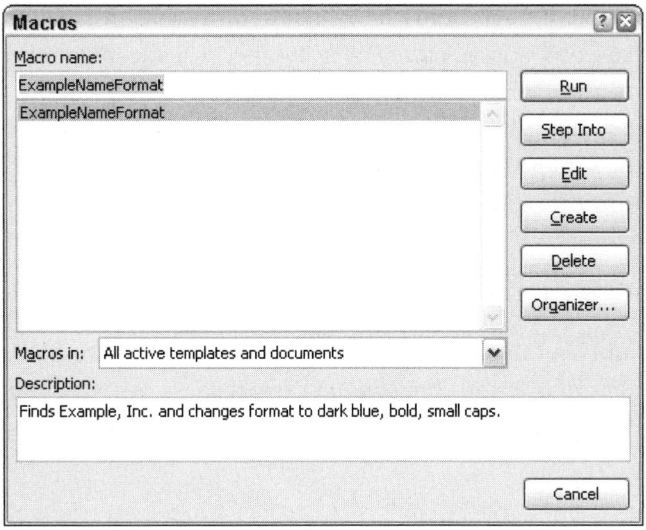


**Figure 23.7.** The Macros dialog box

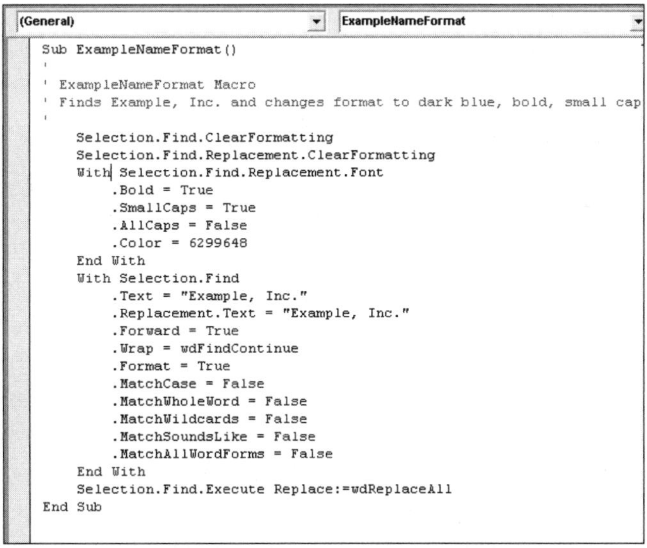

```
(General)                                   ExampleNameFormat
Sub ExampleNameFormat()
'
' ExampleNameFormat Macro
' Finds Example, Inc. and changes format to dark blue, bold, small cap
'
    Selection.Find.ClearFormatting
    Selection.Find.Replacement.ClearFormatting
    With Selection.Find.Replacement.Font
        .Bold = True
        .SmallCaps = True
        .AllCaps = False
        .Color = 6299648
    End With
    With Selection.Find
        .Text = "Example, Inc."
        .Replacement.Text = "Example, Inc."
        .Forward = True
        .Wrap = wdFindContinue
        .Format = True
        .MatchCase = False
        .MatchWholeWord = False
        .MatchWildcards = False
        .MatchSoundsLike = False
        .MatchAllWordForms = False
    End With
    Selection.Find.Execute Replace:=wdReplaceAll
End Sub
```

**Figure 23.8.** Viewing a macro in Visual Basic

# Smart tags

The smart tag feature has been in Office for several versions. With smart tags, Word looks for and attempts to identify certain text strings such as Outlook contact names, dates, addresses, and other data. Once identified, you can perform a short list of useful smart tag actions that pertain to that type of data (such as add a name to a contact list, or insert the address that corresponds to the name in your contact list).

However, in Word 2007, the smart tag feature is not turned on by default, and it is not something that you will find on one of the command tabs. To turn on the smart tag feature, choose Microsoft Office ⇨ Word Options ⇨ Proofing ⇨ AutoCorrect Options and click the Smart Tags tab. Select the Label text with smart tags option to turn on the feature. You see a list of available smart tag types, which have been given the strange, albeit appropriate, name Recognizers, as shown in Figure 23.9. The list shown in this figure shows just a few smart tags, but you can obtain more. Click More Smart Tags to go online to see additional commercial smart tags.

**Figure 23.9.** Enabling smart tags

When Word locates such a text string, it shows it with a dashed underscore in purple, much as it would show a grammar or spelling error. When you mouse over the tagged text, a small letter i in a circle (as commonly seen to symbolize information) appears above the text string. You can move over the information symbol and see the smart tag actions that pertain to that type of smart tag. For example, in Figure 23.10, Word identifies the sample name,

**Figure 23.10.** A smart tag type is recognized

Mr. Roberto Flores. Clicking the arrow to the right of the letter i gives me access to a set of actions that pertain to names, as shown in Figure 23.11. Because the name is in my contact list in Outlook, I can send Mr. Flores e-mail, schedule a meeting with him, open his contact entry in Outlook, add him to Contacts, or insert his address. I can also remove the smart tag, stop recognizing this text string, or go to the smart tag

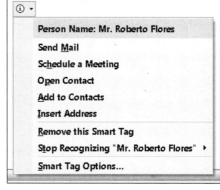

**Figure 23.11.** Smart tag actions menu

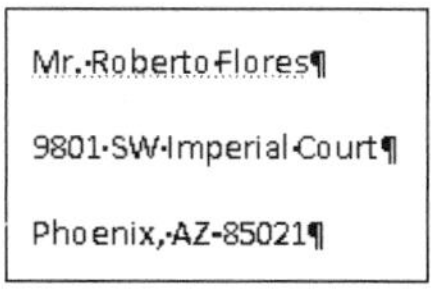

options (the Smart Tag tab of the AutoCorrect dialog box). Click Insert Address, for example, to insert the address that corresponds to Roberto Flores, as shown in Figure 23.12. Figure 23.13 shows how the measurement converter smart tag can provide instant help with U.S.-to-metric conversions.

> Mr. Roberto Flores¶
>
> 9801·SW·Imperial·Court¶
>
> Phoenix,·AZ·85021¶

**Figure 23.12.** An address inserted using the address from the Outlook Contacts list that matches the name

If you change smart tag settings, choose Microsoft Office ⇨ Word Options ⇨ Proofing ⇨ AutoCorrect Options ⇨ Smart Tags ⇨ Recheck Document to have Word reread the document and identify smart tags.

To remove smart tags from a document, choose Microsoft Office ⇨ Word Options ⇨ Proofing ⇨ AutoCorrect Options ⇨ Smart Tags ⇨ Remove Smart Tags.

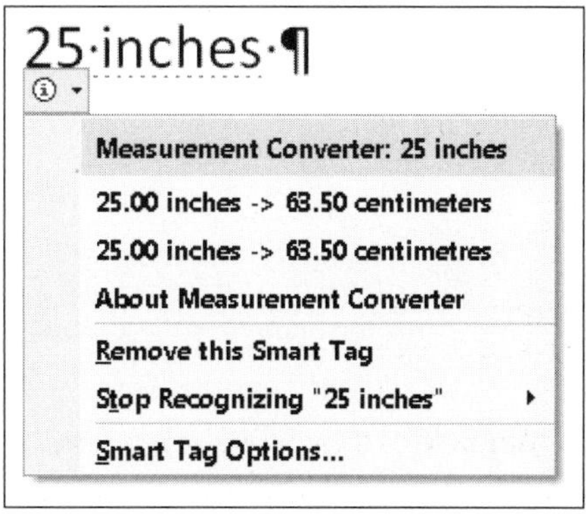

## Just the facts

**25·inches·¶**

Measurement Converter: 25 inches

25.00 inches -> 63.50 centimeters

25.00 inches -> 63.50 centimetres

About Measurement Converter

Remove this Smart Tag

Stop Recognizing "25 inches"  ▸

Smart Tag Options...

**Figure 23.13.** Using the Measurement Converter smart tag

■ You can manage macro security by disabling all but the macros that come from digitally signed trusted publishers or macros that you save in trusted locations.

- You can record macros to automate repetitive tasks.

- You can assign macros to key combinations or to buttons on the QAT for easy access.

- You can view and edit your recorded macros in Visual Basic.

- Smart tags provide an easy way to perform some typical tasks on recognizable types of data.

# Appendixes

PART VII

# Glossary

**.docm**   File extension for a Word 2007 macro-enabled document file.

**.docx**   File extension for a Word 2007 document file.

**.dotm**   File extension for a Word 2007 macro-enabled template file.

**.dotx**   File extension for a Word 2007 template file.

**aspect ratio**   The ratio of height to width in a picture or framed object. Preserving the original aspect ratio prevents visual distortion.

**AutoShape**   A built-in resizable shape that you can insert into your document.

**balloon**   A framed text element such as a comment or revision (in the sense of a word balloon in a cartoon).

**bibliography**   A list of documentary citations.

**bitmap graphics file**   A graphics file composed of a set of dots in a pattern, as opposed to a vector graphic file, which is composed of lines that can be manipulated.

**blog**   Short for weblog, an online journal Web site where you can post entries with text, links, and pictures, allowing comments from those who visit the site.

**blog entry**   A message by the blog's owner (as opposed to a comment).

**bookmark**   A link inserted into a document to mark a specific location in the document.

**borders**   The visible printing horizontal and vertical boundaries that you can elect to add to your table.

**caption**   Descriptive text that can be attached to a picture, equation, or table.

**cell**   In a table, an individual compartment within the table. In a datasheet, an individual data field at the intersection of a row and column.

**citation**   In a document using a bibliography, the reference point within the text that cites a source. A similar feature of the same name is used with tables of authorities.

**compatibility checker**   A feature that checks Word 2007 documents and templates to see whether they use any features not compatible with earlier versions of Word.

**content control**   A control added to a document to help automate data entry, such as a date picker or drop-down list.

**demote**   When using the Outline document view, lowering the level of heading (as in from Level 1 to Level 3, for example). *See also* promote.

**dialog box launcher**   A small button in the lower-right corner of a command group on the Ribbon that launches a dialog box with more extensive options, such the Font dialog box launcher on the Home tab.

**digital signature**   A digital-certificate–based method for secure electronic authorization.

**Document Workspace**   The area of the user interface in Word that shows the actual page.

**drop cap**   An initial capital that starts a chapter that is enlarged and often set in a different font, dropped into the paragraph or to the left of it.

**embed and link**   When you have a situation where you frequently create a report in a Word document format that includes data that you pull from a specific Excel spreadsheet, you can create your chart in Excel and then paste the chart into your Word document. The Word document is then *linked* to the Excel spreadsheet, and if you make changes to the data in the Excel spreadsheet the chart is updated in the Word document. You can also create a chart in Excel and paste it along with the values into Word with no link, if you don't need to update data from the Excel spreadsheet but want access to the data once in Word. This is called *embedding* the chart.

**endnote**   A note (usually in smaller type) that appears at the end of a document to indicate additional information that may be a digression or otherwise interrupt the flow of text if it were to occur in the body of the text.

**field**   A placeholder that can hold changeable data, as in a template or in a merge operation.

**field code**   The command syntax that determines the behavior of a field. When field codes are displayed, the field code appears within curly braces, such as { XE "index entry" }.

**footer**   A repeating line or lines at the foot of the page, usually containing information such as the page number, document author, and/or creation date.

**footnote**   A note (usually in smaller type) that appears at the foot of the page to indicate additional information that may be a digression or otherwise interrupt the flow of text if it were to occur in the body of the text.

**gridlines**   Nonprinting horizontal and vertical lines indicating the boundaries of each cell. These appear on the screen to help you while you are creating and working with your table (although they do not appear in Full Screen Reading view).

**group**   To group is to select several objects in a drawing and combine them so that they can be manipulated as one. Also, a collection of related commands on the Ribbon.

**gutter**   An additional outside margin that you can set when you intend to print and bind your document.

**header**   A repeating line or lines at the top of the page, usually containing information such as the title, page number, document author, and/or creation date.

**indent**   A paragraph margin or indentation.

**index**   A list of key terms found in a document, referenced by page number.

**index entry**   A key term marked for inclusion in the index, or that item's listing in the index.

**insert mode**   The typing mode in which characters typed on the keyboard are inserted between existing characters in the document rather than replace them.

**Inspect Document**   A command that allows you to check the document for hidden personal or sensitive data before sending it along to others.

**justify**   To align the text with the left and right margins.

**Live Preview**   A feature of Word 2007 that, when you move your mouse over text, shows you how a formatting feature or style will affect the text without having to actually apply the formatting change.

**macro**   A small custom program that helps you automate your work. A macro can be either recorded or programmed, and can run a command or set of commands.

**mail merge**   An operation that takes data from fields in one source and adds the data into corresponding fields in a Word document so that multiple versions of the document can be created automatically.

**malware**   Malicious software, such as a virus or worm.

**metadata**   Parts of the document that don't comprise the text of the document such as comments, revisions, and document properties.

**Microsoft Office menu**   The Word 2007 menu represented by the Microsoft Office logo that appears in the upper-left corner, replacing the File menu of earlier versions.

**orientation**   Vertical (portrait) or horizontal (landscape) presentation of the page.

**orphan**   The first line of a new paragraph when it occurs as the last line on a page.

**Overtype mode**   The typing mode in which characters typed on the keyboard replace existing characters in the document that appear to the right of the cursor.

**PDF**   An Adobe file format (PDF stands for Portable Document Format). When you save a file to this format, it "prints" the document into a PDF file.

**picture placeholder**   When editing documents with large graphic files, you can elect to show only picture placeholders (simple rectangular frames) so that you can scroll through your document more efficiently.

**promote**   When using the Outline document view, raising the level of a heading (as in from Level 3 to Level 1, for example). *See also* demote.

**Quick Access Toolbar (QAT)**   The customizable toolbar immediately to the right of the Microsoft Office button by default (or between the Ribbon and the Document Workspace optionally).

**Quick Parts**   Ready-made text elements that can be inserted into your document: document properties, fields, and building blocks.

**Quick Styles**   Ready-made built-in sets of formatted styles designed to go well together.

**record**   In mail merge operations, each instance of the set of data fields that corresponds to the recipient in the list is referred to as a record. A record corresponds to each row in a spreadsheet or to a record in a database. Also macros can be recorded, in that you can turn on macro recording and execute commands that you can then capture and replay to help automate repetitive command sequences.

**Ribbon**   The tabbed set of commands and controls at the top of the Document Workspace.

**Ribbon tab (or command tab)**   A set of related commands that runs across the Ribbon with a tab at the top, such as the Page Layout tab. Some Ribbon tabs appear only when needed, such as Picture Tools and Table Tools.

**Shape**   A vector graphics object that can be manipulated and resized to create a drawing.

**smart tag**   A tag applied by Word to identify certain text strings such as Outlook contact names, dates, addresses, and other data. Once a text string is identified with a smart tag, you can perform a short list of useful smart tag actions that pertain to that type of data.

**Status Bar**   The horizontal bar at the bottom of the Document Workspace that provides customizable status information, such as the current page number, word count, spelling and grammar check status, and so on.

**style**   A set of format settings assigned a name. Styles can apply to paragraphs, characters, lists, tables, or they can be linked (a combination of character and paragraph styles).

**style set**   A set of Quick Styles designed to work well together.

**table of authorities**   A list of citations in a legal document that can be generated automatically in word by tagging individual citations and then compiling a table of authorities.

**table of contents**   A list of headings in a document that can either be generated automatically by Word or created manually by the user.

**template**   A ready-made reusable document format that you create yourself or get from Microsoft or others.

**text box**   Shapes containing text that you can use to control the flow of text on the page. The boxes themselves can be invisible frames within which the text can flow, or they can be visible objects with borders and shading that you incorporate into the design of your document.

**theme**   Akin to themes in Windows, a theme coordinates overarching design values (coordinating fonts, colors, and effects for graphics) across an entire document or even across Office.

**trusted location**   A location on your computer for storing files containing macros from trusted sources.

**trusted publisher**   A macro creator added to your trusted publisher list (preferably digitally certified).

**vector graphics file**   A graphics file composed of lines that can be manipulated, as opposed to a bitmap graphics file, which is a set of dots in a pattern.

**watermark**   In Word, a text string or image printed underneath the document text, to be used either as a true watermark with stationery or as a printed message about the document, such as Confidential or Draft.

**widow**   The last line of a paragraph when it starts on a new page.

**wildcard**   A character or set of characters used in a search string to represent a type or set of characters rather than a literal one.

**wizard**   In Microsoft parlance, a set of instructions integrated with commands that walk you through some multistep procedure in the application.

**WordArt**   A Word feature that displays a graphically enhanced version of a string of text, designed for use in posters, advertising, banners, and so on.

**XML**   Extensible Markup Language, the Internet standard for marking up structured data, incorporated in Word 2007 document file format.

**XPS**   XML Paper Specification. The goal of this new file format is to create an XML-based PDF-like file format that also incorporates Microsoft Rights Management functionality.

# Resource Guide

This resource guide represents a list of additional resources for learning more about Microsoft Word, developing business solutions with it, seeing what Microsoft and third-party add-ins are available to add functionality to Word, and improving your writing.

## Resources from Microsoft

First of all, Microsoft Word itself has a resource guide built in: choose Microsoft Office ➪ Word Options ➪ Resources. It's a great place to start.

## Microsoft Office Online

In addition to the Resources screen in Word itself, be sure to check out Microsoft Office Online. Sure, a lot of this is trying to sell you something, but Microsoft knows that useful content needs to be added continually in order for people to come back to the Microsoft Office Online page. As a result, it is frequently adding useful tools, templates, and training to keep you going back there. As these sorts of pages go, it has a high useful stuff/marketing fluff ratio. To get to the main Microsoft Office Online Web page take your browser to `http://office.microsoft.com`. To focus just on Word, go to `http://office.microsoft.com/word`. This takes you to a list of Word-related feature articles, discussion groups, and so on.

- **Microsoft Office Resource Kit.** At times referred to by Office power users, IT professionals, and Microsoft staffers as the ORK (apologies to J. R. R. Tolkien), this began as a printed supplemental guide designed to assist IT staff and developers in deploying and creating solutions using Office products. If you click the

535

Office Resource Kit link from the Microsoft Office Online page, you are taken to a set of articles and links that are pertinent to IT professionals who support Microsoft Office users.

■ **Deployment Center.** If you click the Deployment Center link on the Microsoft Office Online page, you are directed to deployment information about all Microsoft Office system products to support deployment of Office in the enterprise.

## Microsoft TechNet

The TechNet program is a program designed to support IT professionals on all Microsoft products. To access Office-related TechNet resources, go to www.microsoft.com/technet/prodtechnol/office.

## Microsoft Office Developer Center

If you would like to know more about developing solutions using Microsoft Office, be sure to check out the Microsoft Office Developer Center. Microsoft is highly motivated to have developers take advantage of the XML-based Office system, and there is a rich amount of material here at http://msdn.microsoft.com/office. The Microsoft Developer Network (MSDN) runs this site, but you do not need to be an MSDN member to take advantage of the information presented here.

## Other Web sources

There are many online resources to help you learn about Word. Here are a few Web sites that I have found contain useful information. However, there are many more.

■ **The Word MVP Site.** (http://word.mvps.org/): This site is run independent of Microsoft but by those designated by Microsoft as Word MVPs (Most Valuable Professionals). The collective knowledge here is great, and this is a good resource when Microsoft's help fails you.

■ **Allen Wyatt's Word Tips.** (http://wordtips.vitalnews.com/): This site, created by Allen Wyatt, the author of several books on Word, covers lots of ground and has solutions listed by version of Word. You can also subscribe to a premium newsletter with more information.

■ **Making the most of Word in your business.** (`www.shaunakelly.com/word/`): Shauna Kelly, a Word MVP, gives useful tips on using Word.

# Recommended reading list

Here is a short list of books that I recommend for further information on writing. Some of the reference works I recommend also include much more exhaustive lists of pertinent resources.

## Writing style

Every writer has a list of favorite guides to style. Here are a few of my favorites.

Dupré, Lyn. *BUGS in Writing: A Guide to Debugging Your Prose.* Revised ed. Reading, MA: Addison-Wesley, 1998.

Strunk, William, Jr., and E. B. White. *The Elements of Style.* 4th ed. Boston: Allyn and Bacon, 2000.

Zinsser, William. *On Writing Well: An Informal Guide to Writing Nonfiction.* 5th ed. New York: Harper-Perennial, 1995.

## Usage guides

These books are geared to editors or those who write often or for a living. However, they are helpful tools for anyone who writes, and most are fairly accessible.

Bernstein, Theodore M. *The Careful Writer: A Modern Guide to English Usage.* New York: Atheneum, 1965.

Follett, Wilson. *Modern American Usage: A Guide.* 1st rev. ed. Revised by Erik Wensberg. New York: Hill and Wang, 1998.

Garner, Bryan A. *A Dictionary of Modern American Usage.* New York: Oxford University Press, 1998.

*The New Fowler's Modern English Usage.* Revised 3rd ed. Edited by R. W. Burchfield. New York: Oxford University Press, 2000.

Schwartz, Marilyn. *Guidelines for Bias-Free Writing.* Bloomington: Indiana University Press, 1995.

# Preparing for publication

These guides are helpful when you need to prepare your documents for a specific publication format.

*MLA Style Manual and Guide to Scholarly Publishing.* 2nd ed. Edited by Joseph Gibaldi. New York: Modern Language Association.

*The Chicago Manual of Style.* 15th ed. University of Chicago Press Staff. Chicago: University of Chicago Press, 2003.

*2006 AP Stylebook.* Edited by Norm Goldstein. New York: The Associated Press, 2006.

*Words into Type.* 3rd ed. Based on studies by Marjorie E. Skillin. Robert M. Gay and other authorities. Englewood Cliffs, NJ: Prentice Hall, 1974.

# Word 2003 to Word 2007 Roadmap

**W**ord 2007 brings the most significant changes to Word's user interface in many years. Many of the changes are welcome; some are not. I've divided this appendix into four main sections: one to tell you where to find help directly from Microsoft about what has changed from the previous version of Word, one to tell you about new features, one to tell you about features that have been removed or replaced, and one to summarize where you can find Word 2003 commands in Word 2007. I won't spend a lot of time discussing the new interface design here. Look at Part I, and in particular Chapter 1, to get a sense of how the Ribbon, Quick Access Toolbar, and other new user interface elements operate. I summarize the main changes here, directing you either to sections in the book or other sources for comprehensive information.

## Help from Microsoft on making the jump from Word 2003 to Word 2007

Fortunately, Microsoft seems to be fully aware that they need to help their customers get up to speed with the new and redesigned version of Office. Microsoft Office 2007 comes with a fair amount of information to guide you and introduce you to the new features. Also, Microsoft Office Online provides additional training and reference resources. I show you how to get to that material in this section. Please note, however, that some information will change over time, and Microsoft may elect to add or remove material, particularly from the online areas, between the time I write this and the time that you read it.

**Inside Scoop**

Documents cannot be freely swapped between Word versions with the new release. See Chapter 2 for more details on compatibility and use the Compatibility Checker (Microsoft Office ⇨ Prepare ⇨ Run Compatibility Checker) for more information.

## Help: What's new

To get to the Word Help information that pertains to new features, press F1 (or click the Help button, a white question mark in a blue circle in the upper-right corner of the Word window). Click What's new.

Click What's new in Microsoft Office Word 2007 to view a 2,000-word overview article. It's fine to give you a general idea of how things are organized, although it reads more like marketing, and there are few operational specifics.

Click Up to speed with Word 2007 to go to a Microsoft Office Online Web-based training course that lasts 30 to 40 minutes. You view screenshots of Word 2007 in your browser and can optionally listen to instructions in audio as you read along. The course includes practice, testing, and a quick reference card with some of the basic information you need to know with Word 2007.

Click Demo: Up to speed with Word 2007 to download and play an animated demo showing you how to use the Ribbon, Quick Access Toolbar, Quick Styles, and a few other things.

Click Reference: Locations of Word 2003 commands to get an overview of where commands are located in Word 2007. The overview doesn't get very specific, but click the New locations of familiar commands link and open the Word Ribbon mapping workbook link to get a comprehensive list of Word 2003 commands and where they are located in Word 2007. Strangely enough, this is an Excel workbook. Click the tabs at the bottom of the workbook that correspond to the pull-down menus and standard toolbar in Word 2003. Each tab represents a sheet in the workbook containing Word 2003 commands and their Word 2007 equivalents. For your convenience, I also include a similar reference section at the end of this appendix.

## If you are a developer...

If you are interested in learning more about Word 2007's XML functionality, click Automation and programmability in the top-level list of topics in Word Help.

To learn about programming in Visual Basic with Word, display the Developer tab by choosing Microsoft Office ⇨ Word Options ⇨ Popular ⇨ Show Developer tab in the Ribbon. Choose Developer ⇨ Visual Basic ⇨ Help to view Visual Basic help for Word to get a link to pertinent topics from MSDN (Microsoft Developer Network) on the Web.

For all developer topics related to Office, use your browser to go to the Microsoft Office Developer Center at `http://msdn.microsoft. com/office`.

# New features in Word 2007

Part I of this book focuses on the interface of Word 2007. However, I just touch on user interface changes here and also describe some additional functionality. The main improvements can be summarized as follows:

- Simplified Ribbon user interface designed around the document creation process
- Prefabricated document pieces
- Easily changeable, professional-looking ready-made designs with Themes and Quick Styles
- Slick and updated professional effects for drawings, text boxes, and diagrams, including prefabricated SmartArt
- Document preparation features to improve collaboration and security
- The ability to create PDF documents for distribution
- XML-based document file format for compact, secure file structures and potential for programming extensibility
- Miscellaneous: bibliography, contextual spell-checking, and blog entry features

## User interface changes

The *Ribbon* serves as a more friendly and flexible alternative to pull-down menus and dialog boxes. The Ribbon has tabs that adapt and size themselves according to the context of your work, as shown in Figure C.1. The command buttons have remained essentially the same; some new buttons and sliders have been added.

**Figure C.1.** A partial view of the Ribbon in Word 2007 that replaces the pull-down menu system

The tabs are like menus that are grouped for the most part by a phase in the document creation process. For example, all the commands related to reviewing a document, such as proofing tools, revision marks, comments, and document comparison are located on the Review tab. (Chapter 1 has a table that summarizes the function of each tab.) The

Ribbon takes up a fairly large amount of screen real estate, but you can minimize it to just the tabs by double-clicking any one of the tabs. The number of commands that display on the Ribbon varies depending on your screen resolution.

The File menu is gone, but it is essentially replaced by the Microsoft Office menu, which you access by clicking the big Microsoft Office logo button in the upper-left corner of the Word window, as shown in Figure C.2. Some additional features are added here as well, collected within the Prepare and Publish submenus. The Word Options button is also located here.

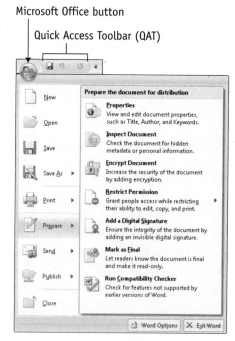

**Figure C.2.** The Microsoft Office menu in Word 2007 replaces the File menu.

The many movable toolbars have been removed from Word. Microsoft has eliminated all but the Quick Access Toolbar (QAT), which sits at the top of the document next to the Microsoft Office button, as shown in Figure C.2. Unfortunately, you cannot make this toolbar float around the page. You can move it to one other location: between the Ribbon and the Document Workspace. The QAT has only three commands on it by default: Save, Undo, and Repeat. It also has an arrow that you can click to customize it. Fortunately, if you want to have a toolbar with your most frequently used commands, you can add them very easily. You can either click the button on the QAT and select commands from a list, or you can simply right-click any command from a tab on the Ribbon and select Add to Quick Access Toolbar.

If you have created custom toolbars in an earlier version, you can still access them, providing the commands on them are available in Word 2007, but they now appear on a single Add-in tab on the Ribbon.

## Themes and Quick Styles

One of the key advantages of Word 2007 is that it includes many built-in and prefabricated document parts that you can use to create your document more quickly, spending less time on formatting and more on writing. One of these not entirely new features is themes (akin to themes in Windows) that coordinate overarching design values (coordinating fonts, colors, and effects for graphics) across an entire document, or even across Office. You can choose a theme or create your own, and have it apply not just to Word documents, but also Excel spreadsheets and PowerPoint presentations.

You can choose from built-in themes or create your own theme based on an existing one. Themes also work with Excel and PowerPoint, so that you can present spreadsheets, slide presentations, and documents, all with a unified look by using a set of two fonts (one for headings and one for body text), a small color palette of compatible colors, and a consistent way to treat graphical effects like SmartArt.

Quick Styles have also been added. Microsoft has taken the concept of character and paragraph styles one step further by introducing groups of preset Quick Styles that have been professionally designed for the most common types of text elements and that all complement each other within a set. For example, if you select a Heading Quick Style and a Body

Quick Style, you can change the style set for the document and both the Heading and Body styles change to new but complementary Quick Styles without having to create new paragraph styles for each text element.

## New ready-made document parts

Word 2007 still has templates, of course, but a new way to add prefabricated pieces to your document has been added: building blocks. You can select and insert them into your document by choosing Insert ⇨ Quick Parts ⇨ Building Blocks Organizer. Building blocks are ready-made document parts such as cover pages, headers, footers, tables, tables of contents, equations, watermarks, or custom document pieces of your own. The built-in building blocks are all stored in a file on your PC and can be added as needed to your document. The built-in building blocks are coordinated with Quick Styles and themes.

## Convey a concept with a drawing you select with SmartArt

The new SmartArt feature adds sophisticated diagram capabilities right into Word, allowing you to illustrate processes and show organizational charts by choosing from a large gallery of built-in diagrams, as shown in Figure C.3. You can add SmartArt by choosing Insert ⇨ SmartArt and selecting a diagram from the gallery.

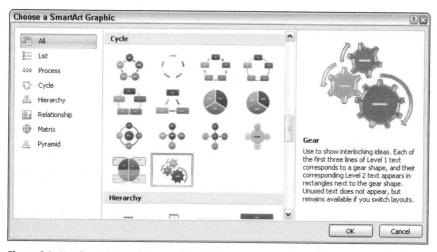

**Figure C.3.** Use SmartArt graphics to add a diagram to your document.

## Document preparation features to improve collaboration and security

Microsoft has brought together a set of new and existing document preparation commands. Choose Microsoft Office ⇨ Prepare (the submenu shown in Figure C.2) to access commands related to document preparation. New features include the Document Inspector (Office ⇨ Prepare ⇨ Inspect Document) that allows you to scan for and remove any sensitive hidden information from your document (such as comments, earlier versions, and hidden personal information) before distributing the document to a wider audience. Choose Office ⇨ Prepare ⇨ Encrypt Document to provide increased protection to your document. You also have increased control over just who can view and edit the document by choosing Office ⇨ Prepare ⇨ Restrict Permission. You can also add a digital signature to guarantee your document's authenticity and prevent tampering after the document leaves your hands, and you can mark it as final. Finally, because Word 2007 has many new and expanded features, you can run the compatibility checker if you need to distribute your document to someone who doesn't have the latest version of Word.

Choose Office ⇨ Publish to gain access to some additional distribution methods. You can create a blog post, post your document to a document management server, or create a Document Workspace and have the local copy synchronized with one stored on a shared site.

Word 2007 finally allows you to create PDF documents for distribution (although you must download and install this feature). Microsoft also provides the ability to create documents in XPS (XML Paper Specification) file format — an XML-based, PDF-like file format that also incorporates Microsoft Rights Management functionality.

## New XML-based file format

Microsoft Word 2007 has a new XML-based file format. You can still read older Word files and still save files in the old DOC format, but this is no longer the default. The XML format stores the structural data and the content of your document separately, making for more compact and robust document files. The XML structure also allows programmers to more readily develop applications that work directly with Word documents, so that Word can more readily be integrated into your organization's own network or Web applications.

## New bibliography feature

You can create citations and compile them into a bibliography, choosing from many different bibliography formats employed by different disciplines, such as MLA, CMS, and APA.

# Features removed, replaced, or hidden in Word 2007

I won't go into every feature that has been removed or replaced, but I will tell you about the most common ones. If you are not sure whether a feature is still in Word, consult Word Help, and specifically the Word Ribbon mapping workbook discussed earlier in this appendix.

## Where are the toolbars and File menu?

The File menu is actually just renamed. Most of the File menu commands from earlier versions are available from the Microsoft Office menu, as noted earlier. The tools have migrated to the Ribbon, but you can add any commands you want to the Quick Access Toolbar (QAT) for easy access. If you work with a custom toolbar, it will appear as an Add-in tab on the Ribbon. Unfortunately, toolbars no longer float.

## Changes in Help

Built-in help in Microsoft Word 2007 seems to have been "streamlined," if I may guess at what Microsoft might call it. The Office Assistant has gone away, and you can no longer type a question for help. Context-sensitive help appears greatly reduced. When you press F1 for more help as suggested when hovering over a command, you are not necessarily taken to the relevant section of the help screen, you are just taken to the generic Word Help screen. This is somewhat better with dialog boxes: if a dialog box has a Help button (a white question mark in a blue circle), you may well get specific information. The help content is definitely there, but at times, you have to work harder to get it. You may find that you need to use Word Help's Search feature much more than you did in the past, and that getting an answer when you are not connected to the Internet may be annoying — much of the extended reference and training information is at Microsoft Office Online.

## Text to speech and speech recognition

Unfortunately, these features, which were built into Word 2003 and Word 2002 (Speech under the Tools menu), have been removed from Word 2007. For information on how to add such functionality, go to `www.microsoft.com/enable`.

## Smart tags and AutoText are just hiding

Smart tags and AutoText have not been substantially changed. However, smart tags are turned off by default (refer to Chapter 23 for how to turn them on and work with them in Word 2007). AutoText is also still available, although it is not immediately apparent because it is buried in the Word Options. See Chapter 20 for how to use AutoText in Word 2007.

## Equations and diagrams

If you created equations using Microsoft Equation 3.0, you can still use them in Microsoft Word 2007, but they appear as editable equations that you can edit using Microsoft Equation Editor 3.1 by double-clicking the equations. However, you can't convert the equations to take advantage of the much more extensive equation tools found in Word 2007. The new tools are only available for Word 2007 document files.

Diagrams are still available in Word 2007; they have just moved and changed names. Choose Insert ⇨ SmartArt to see a great selection of ready-made diagrams of all types. Unlike equations, diagrams from Word 2002 and Word 2003 can be readily manipulated in Word 2007.

# Word 2003/2007 command conversion quick reference

Table C.1 gives a summary of menu commands and groups of commands in Word 2003 and their Word 2007 equivalents. I do not include keyboard

---

**Bright Idea**

If you don't find a command here, or if it says Not in Ribbon, click the arrow on the Quick Access Toolbar and then click More Commands. In the Choose commands from list, select Commands Not in the Ribbon. You may find your less commonly used command in this list. If you do, select it and click Add to add it to the QAT.

shortcuts here — most of them are the same and they are displayed next to the command in a ToolTip window when you hover over the command with the mouse. Press F1 and click What's new, then Reference: Locations of Word 2003 commands, then New locations of familiar commands and open the Word Ribbon mapping workbook link for an exhaustive list displayed in an Excel spreadsheet as described earlier.

### Table C.1 Word 2003 menu commands and Word 2007 counterparts

| Word 2003 Command | Word 2007 Command |
| --- | --- |
| File ⇨ New | Microsoft Office ⇨ New |
| File ⇨ Open | Microsoft Office ⇨ Open |
| File ⇨ Close | Microsoft Office ⇨ Close |
| File ⇨ Save | Microsoft Office ⇨ Save |
| File ⇨ Save as Web Page | Microsoft Office ⇨ Save As, Save as type Web Page |
| File ⇨ File Search | (Not in Word 2007: Use Windows Search) |
| File ⇨ Permission | Microsoft Office ⇨ Prepare ⇨ Restrict Permission or Review ⇨ Protect Document |
| File ⇨ Web Page Preview | (Not in Ribbon) |
| File ⇨ Page Setup | Page Layout ⇨ Page Setup |
| File ⇨ Print Preview | Microsoft Office ⇨ Print ⇨ Print Preview |
| File ⇨ Print | Microsoft Office ⇨ Print |
| File ⇨ Send To | Microsoft Office ⇨ Send |
| File ⇨ Properties | Microsoft Office ⇨ Prepare ⇨ Properties |
| File ⇨ Exit | Microsoft Office ⇨ Exit Word |
| Edit ⇨ Undo | Undo on QAT |
| Edit ⇨ Repeat | Repeat on QAT |
| Edit ⇨ Cut | Home ⇨ Cut |
| Edit ⇨ Copy | Home ⇨ Copy |
| Edit ⇨ Office Clipboard | Home ⇨ Clipboard |

| Word 2003 Command | Word 2007 Command |
|---|---|
| Edit ⇨ Paste | Home ⇨ Paste |
| Edit ⇨ Paste Special | Home ⇨ Paste ⇨ Paste Special |
| Edit ⇨ Paste as Hyperlink | Home ⇨ Paste ⇨ Paste as Hyperlink |
| Edit ⇨ Clear ⇨ Formats | Home ⇨ Clear Formatting |
| Edit ⇨ Clear ⇨ Contents | Delete key |
| Edit ⇨ Select All | Home ⇨ Editing ⇨ Select ⇨ Select All |
| Edit ⇨ Find | Home ⇨ Editing ⇨ Find |
| Edit ⇨ Replace | Home ⇨ Editing ⇨ Replace |
| Edit ⇨ Go To | Home ⇨ Editing ⇨ Find ⇨ Go To |
| Edit ⇨ Links | Microsoft Office ⇨ Prepare ⇨ Edit Links to Files |
| Edit ⇨ Object | Double-click object |
| View ⇨ Normal | View ⇨ Draft |
| View ⇨ Web Layout | View ⇨ Web Layout |
| View ⇨ Print Layout | View ⇨ Print Layout |
| View ⇨ Reading Layout | View ⇨ Full Screen Reading |
| View ⇨ Outline | View ⇨ Outline |
| View ⇨ Task Pane | (No equivalent) |
| View ⇨ Toolbars | (No equivalent) |
| View ⇨ Ruler | View ⇨ Ruler (checkbox) |
| View ⇨ Document Map | View ⇨ Ruler (checkbox) |
| View ⇨ Thumbnails | View ⇨ Ruler (checkbox) |
| View ⇨ Header and Footer | Insert ⇨ Header, Insert ⇨ Footer |
| View ⇨ Footnotes | References ⇨ Show Notes |
| View ⇨ Markup | Review ⇨ Show Markup |
| View ⇨ Full Screen | View ⇨ Full Screen Reading |

*continued*

## Table C.1 *continued*

| Word 2003 Command | Word 2007 Command |
|---|---|
| View ⇨ Zoom | View ⇨ Zoom (A zoom slider and buttons are also on the status bar) |
| Insert ⇨ Break | Page Layout ⇨ Breaks |
| Insert ⇨ Page Numbers | Insert ⇨ Page Number |
| Insert ⇨ Date and Time | Insert ⇨ Date & Time |
| Insert ⇨ AutoText | Insert ⇨ Quick Parts ⇨ Building Blocks Organizer, select AutoText and click Insert (or add AutoText button to QAT) |
| Insert ⇨ Field | Insert ⇨ Quick Parts ⇨ Field |
| Insert ⇨ Symbol | Insert ⇨ Symbol |
| Insert ⇨ Comment | Review ⇨ New Comment |
| Insert ⇨ Reference ⇨ Footnote | References ⇨ Insert Footnote |
| Insert ⇨ Reference ⇨ Caption | References ⇨ Insert Caption |
| Insert ⇨ Reference ⇨ Cross-reference | References ⇨ Insert Cross-reference |
| Insert ⇨ Reference ⇨ Index Tables | References ⇨ Insert Index (or References ⇨ and Table of Contents) |
| Insert ⇨ Web Component | (Not in Ribbon) |
| Insert ⇨ Picture ⇨ Clip Art | Insert ⇨ Clip Art |
| Insert ⇨ Picture ⇨ From File | Insert ⇨ Picture |
| Insert ⇨ Picture ⇨ From Scanner or Camera | (No equivalent) |
| Insert ⇨ Picture ⇨ New Drawing | Insert ⇨ Shapes ⇨ New Drawing Canvas |
| Insert ⇨ Picture ⇨ AutoShapes | Insert ⇨ Shapes |
| Insert ⇨ Picture ⇨ WordArt | Insert ⇨ WordArt |
| Insert ⇨ Picture ⇨ Organization | Insert ⇨ SmartArt ⇨ Hierarchy (for general equivalent) or add Organization Chart to QAT (available only in Compatibility Mode) |
| Insert ⇨ Picture ⇨ Chart | Insert ⇨ Chart |

| Word 2003 Command | Word 2007 Command |
|---|---|
| Insert ⇨ Diagram | Insert ⇨ SmartArt |
| Insert ⇨ Text Box | Insert ⇨ Text Box |
| Insert ⇨ File | Insert ⇨ Object ⇨ Text from File |
| Insert ⇨ Object | Insert ⇨ Object |
| Insert ⇨ Bookmark | Insert ⇨ Bookmark |
| Insert ⇨ Hyperlink | Insert ⇨ Hyperlink |
| Format ⇨ Font | Home ⇨ Font |
| Format ⇨ Paragraph | Home ⇨ Paragraph |
| Format ⇨ Bullets and Numbering | Home ⇨ Bullets or Home ⇨ Numbering |
| Format ⇨ Borders and Shading | Home ⇨ Borders or Home ⇨ Shading |
| Format ⇨ Columns | Page Layout ⇨ Columns |
| Format ⇨ Tabs | Page Layout ⇨ Paragraph ⇨ Tabs |
| Format ⇨ Drop Cap | Insert ⇨ Drop Cap |
| Format ⇨ Text Direction | Table Tools ⇨ Layout ⇨ Text Direction |
| Format ⇨ Change Case | Home ⇨ Change Case |
| Format ⇨ Background | Page Layout ⇨ Page Color |
| Format ⇨ Theme | Page Layout ⇨ Themes |
| Format ⇨ Frames | (Not in Ribbon) |
| Format ⇨ AutoFormat | (No equivalent; AutoFormat Options accessible by choosing Microsoft Office ⇨ Word Options ⇨ Proofing ⇨ AutoCorrect Options ⇨ AutoFormat or AutoFormat As You Type) |
| Format ⇨ Styles and Formatting | Home ⇨ Styles |
| Format ⇨ Reveal Formatting | Home ⇨ Styles ⇨ Style Inspector ⇨ Reveal Formatting |
| Format ⇨ Object | Right-click object and select Format Object from pop-up menu |

*continued*

## Table C.1 *continued*

| Word 2003 Command | Word 2007 Command |
| --- | --- |
| Tools ⇨ Spelling and Grammar | Review ⇨ Spelling and Grammar |
| Tools ⇨ Research | Review ⇨ Research |
| Tools ⇨ Language | Review ⇨ Set Language |
| Tools ⇨ Word Count | Review ⇨ Word Count |
| Tools ⇨ AutoSummarize | (Not in Ribbon) |
| Tools ⇨ Speech | (No equivalent) |
| Tools ⇨ Shared Workspace | Microsoft Office ⇨ Create Document Workspace |
| Tools ⇨ Track Changes | Review ⇨ Track Changes |
| Tools ⇨ Compare and Merge Documents | Review ⇨ Compare |
| Tools ⇨ Protect Document | Review ⇨ Protect Document |
| Tools ⇨ Online Collaboration | (No equivalent) |
| Tools ⇨ Letters and Mailings | Mailings |
| Tools ⇨ Macros | View ⇨ Macros (or Developer ⇨ Macros) |
| Tools ⇨ Templates and Add-Ins | Developer ⇨ Document Template |
| Tools ⇨ AutoCorrect Options | Microsoft Office ⇨ Word Options ⇨ Proofing ⇨ AutoCorrect Options |
| Tools ⇨ Customize | Microsoft Office ⇨ Word Options ⇨ Customize |
| Tools ⇨ Options | Microsoft Office ⇨ Word Options |
| Table ⇨ Draw Table | Insert ⇨ Table ⇨ Draw Table |
| Table ⇨ Insert ⇨ Table | Insert ⇨ Table ⇨ Insert Table |
| Table ⇨ Insert ⇨ Columns to the Left | Table Tools ⇨ Layout ⇨ Insert Left |
| Table ⇨ Insert ⇨ Columns to the Right | Table Tools ⇨ Layout ⇨ Insert Right |
| Table ⇨ Insert ⇨ Rows Above | Table Tools ⇨ Layout ⇨ Insert Above |
| Table ⇨ Insert ⇨ Rows Below | Table Tools ⇨ Layout ⇨ Insert Below |

| Word 2003 Command | Word 2007 Command |
|---|---|
| Table ⇨ Insert ⇨ Cells | Table Tools ⇨ Layout ⇨ Rows & Columns |
| Table ⇨ Delete ⇨ Table | Table Tools ⇨ Layout ⇨ Delete ⇨ Delete Table |
| Table ⇨ Delete ⇨ Columns | Table Tools ⇨ Layout ⇨ Delete ⇨ Delete Columns |
| Table ⇨ Delete ⇨ Rows | Table Tools ⇨ Layout ⇨ Delete ⇨ Delete Rows |
| Table ⇨ Delete ⇨ Cells | Table Tools ⇨ Layout ⇨ Delete ⇨ Delete Cells |
| Table ⇨ Select ⇨ Table | Table Tools ⇨ Layout ⇨ Select ⇨ Select Table |
| Table ⇨ Select ⇨ Column | Table Tools ⇨ Layout ⇨ Select ⇨ Select Column |
| Table ⇨ Select ⇨ Row | Table Tools ⇨ Layout ⇨ Select ⇨ Select Row |
| Table ⇨ Select ⇨ Cell | Table Tools ⇨ Layout ⇨ Select ⇨ Select Cell |
| Table ⇨ Merge Cells | Table Tools ⇨ Layout ⇨ Merge Cells |
| Table ⇨ Split Cells | Table Tools ⇨ Layout ⇨ Split Cells |
| Table ⇨ Split Table | Table Tools ⇨ Layout ⇨ Split Table |
| Table ⇨ Table AutoFormat | Table Tools ⇨ Design ⇨ Table Styles |
| Table ⇨ AutoFit | Table Tools ⇨ Layout ⇨ AutoFit |
| Table ⇨ Heading Rows Repeat | Table Tools ⇨ Layout ⇨ Repeat Header Rows |
| Table ⇨ Convert | Table Tools ⇨ Layout ⇨ Convert to Text |
| Table ⇨ Sort | Table Tools ⇨ Layout ⇨ Sort |
| Table ⇨ Formula | Table Tools ⇨ Layout ⇨ Formula |
| Table ⇨ Hide/Show Gridlines | Table Tools ⇨ Layout ⇨ View Gridlines |
| Table ⇨ Properties | Table Tools ⇨ Layout ⇨ Properties |
| Window ⇨ New Window | View ⇨ New Window |
| Window ⇨ Arrange All | View ⇨ Arrange All |
| Window ⇨ Compare Side by Side with | View ⇨ View Side by Side |
| Window ⇨ Split | View ⇨ Split |

*continued*

## Table C.1 *continued*

| Word 2003 Command | Word 2007 Command |
| --- | --- |
| Help ⇨ Microsoft Office Word Help | Click Help button or press F1 |
| Help ⇨ Hide/Show the Office Assistant | (No equivalent) |
| Help ⇨ Microsoft Office Online | Microsoft Office ⇨ Word Options ⇨ Resources ⇨ Go Online |
| Help ⇨ Contact Us | Microsoft Office ⇨ Word Options ⇨ Resources ⇨ Contact Us |
| Help ⇨ WordPerfect Help | (No equivalent) |
| Help ⇨ Check for Updates | Microsoft Office ⇨ Word Options ⇨ Resources ⇨ Check for Updates |
| Help ⇨ Detect and Repair | Microsoft Office ⇨ Word Options ⇨ Resources ⇨ Diagnose |
| Help ⇨ Activate Product | Microsoft Office ⇨ Word Options ⇨ Resources ⇨ Activate |
| Help ⇨ Customer Feedback Options | Microsoft Office ⇨ Word Options ⇨ Resources ⇨ Contact Us |
| Help ⇨ About Microsoft Word | Microsoft Office ⇨ Word Options ⇨ Resources ⇨ About |

# Symbols and Numerics

Beveled edge on pictures, 434
Bibliography
    converting to static text, 499
    creating, 495–499
    inserting, 498–499
    managing sources for, 497
    style selection, 498
    updating, 499
Black and white printing, 141, 142,
    192, 226
Black font color, 142
Blank headers and footers, 214
Blank lines on printed forms, 300
Blank Page option, 221
Blocks of text, selecting, 46
Blog entries, creating, 254–257
Bold text, 138–139
Book fold margins, 198
Bookmark, 96, 243
Borders
    page, 219–220
    paragraph, 164, 166–167
    picture, 432–433
    tables, 352
    text box, 455–456
Borders button, 154, 164, 166
Boxes. *See also* Text boxes
    on forms, 301–302
Brightness of pictures, 428–429
Browsers, Web options settings for, 251–252
Browsing by objects, 80, 93–94
Building Block Gallery control, 118
Building blocks, 443, 459–462
Bulleted lists, 177–179
Bullets button, 153, 177
Buttons
    adding to the Quick Access Toolbar, 13
    macros assigned to, 520–522

# C
Capital letter, dropped, 472
Captions. *See also* Labels
    automated, 501
    creating, 499–501
    inserting, 500
    options, 500–501
    for pictures, 435
Case, matching in a search, 61
Cells. *See also* Table cells
    chart, 416

Center button, 154, 155
Center tab button, 200
Changes group, 275–276
Changes to documents. *See also*
  Collaboration
    locating, accepting, and rejecting,
        275–276
    protecting against, 276–279
    reviewing, 272–276
Character(s)
    formatting, 133–149
    raising and lowering on the line, 145
    scaled in percentage, 144
Character spacing, 143–146
Character styles. *See also* Font(s)
    applying, 148
    new, creating, 146–148
Chart(s)
    axis, 416
    creating, 409–414
    creating using Excel, 411–412, 414,
        416–417
    creating using Microsoft Graph,
        413–414
    editing, 416
    formatting, 418–424
    layout, 418–421, 424
    selecting data range in, 414–415
    styles, 421–424
    templates for, 412–413
    types of, 410–412
    working with data in, 414–418
Check boxes, on forms, 301–302
Checklists, printed, 302
Citations
    creating, 495–498
    inserting, 495–497
    managing sources for, 497
    style selection, 498
    for table of authorities, 509
Clear Formatting button, 126–127,
    130, 175–176
Clip art
    and copyright, 425–426
    editing and formatting, 441
    finding, 437–440
    online, 440
Clip Organizer, 440
Clipboard, 46–47
Clipboard group, 12

# Q

Quick Access Toolbar (QAT)
  adding the Properties feature to, 33
  customizing, 86
  described, 12–13, 13–14
  Quick Print command, 226
  Save button, 34
Quick Launch toolbar, adding Word
  to, 6–7
Quick Print, 226
Quick Styles
  applying, 127–128
  applying character styles using, 148
  for charts, 421–424
  choosing, 124–125
  customizing, 125–126
  described, 105, 124–132
  removing styles from, 176
Quick Tables, 348
Quitting Word, 20–21

# R

Readability, 75–76
Reading Layout view, 79
Recipient list
  creating, 309–315
  filtering, 317–318
  finding data in, 319
  finding duplicates, 318–319
  managing, 315–319
  sorting, 316
  validating addresses in, 319
Recommend tab, 131
Record in Mail Merge, 306
Recovered documents, opening, 18–19
Red squiggles, 43, 67
Reference(s). *See* Bibliography; Citations;
  Cross-references
Reference aids, 485–511
Reference features in Compatibility
  Mode, 30
References tab, 11
Reflection effects in pictures, 434
Remove Space Before Paragraph, 161
Removing. *See* Deleting
Replace All, 59
Replacing
  formatting, 65–66
  with special characters, 67
  text, 57–59

Resizing
  shapes, 392
  tables, 349
  text boxes, 447–448
  windows, 98
Restrict tab, 132
Return address, storing, 328–329
Returns
  hard, 152
  soft, 152
Reveal Formatting pane, 130
Review tab, 11, 265–266, 275–276
Reviewing changes
  combining from multiple authors,
    282–283
  described, 272–276
  protecting document prior to,
    276–279
Reviewing Pane, 274–275
Ribbon. *See also* Developer tab
  Add-Ins tab, 111, 113
  described, 10–12
  groups, 12
  hiding, 86
  Paragraph dialog box, 159–160
  tabs, 11
  View tab, 79, 80, 81
Rich Text control, 117
Right Indent pointer, 158
Right page margins, 196–197
Right tab button, 200
Rights Management Services (RMS),
  476–478
Rows. *See also* Table rows
  chart, forming axis, 416
.rtf extension, 26
Ruler
  hiding, 86
  indenting using, 156–158
  positioning headers and footers, 213
  setting page margins, 196–197
  tab setting, 199–200
  viewing, 156, 157, 158, 196

# S

Saturation, 143
Save As command, 34–35
Save command, 34
Save Current Theme dialog box, 194–195
Save settings, customizing, 35–37

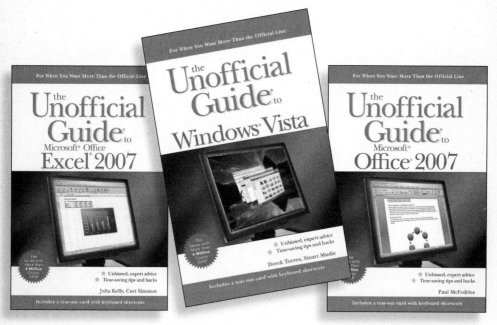